PRAISE FOR JAKE JACOBS

"Jake has offered an insider's look into professional gambling. Admittedly I am biased since he is my brother, and many of the stories involve me. But just look at this quote and tell me this isn't a book you want to read.

'Many of us also found that the gambler's life led to adventures we hadn't signed up for. Some of the things I have described in this book seem unreal to me now. Buried treasure, bags full of money, sailing through pirate infested waters, walking down dark alleys with a fortune in my pocket, looking for a black-market money changer, KGB and CIA agents!'"

~**Richard Munchkin, Author –** *Gambling Wizards*

"Jake's smarter than you. And me. And probably anyone else you've ever known. He took a ride on the gambling wagon that few, if any, other bona fide geniuses would have dared, and the ride is legendary. From a guy who wouldn't scare a bookkeeper, to a partner brave enough to slither down unlit alleys in suspect Asian neighborhoods and knock on slitted doors so he could hand off hundreds of thousands of dollars to complete strangers, to a man who ran foreign casinos, to being a member of the most exclusive team that attacked Atlantic City with precision technologies the joints couldn't imagine……Jake's not only done it, but he delightfully tells you how it was done. And he did it along with the absolute "who's who" of 1982-2000 Blackjack royalty. At 440 pages (it's hard to believe that it's only half), you'll read about things you never imagined. And you will want the sequel. You won't read a more human look at how smart guys play."

~**Max Rubin, Author –** *Comp City*

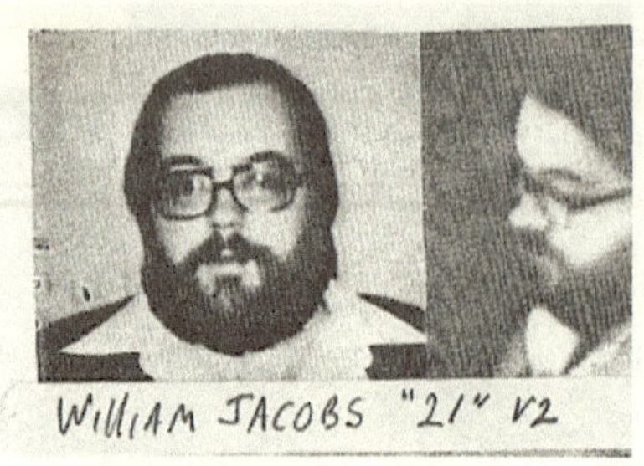

Late in the month of May,1982, surveillance personnel at the Las Vegas Hilton surreptitiously photographed the author. The camera they used was located in the eye-in-the-sky; it showed a view from above, of a lone figure sitting at a blackjack table. A caption described him as "white male, approximately thirty years old." The photo was used to create a flyer which was distributed to casinos around Las Vegas. It led several of them to bar him when he played. One, the Union Plaza, had security detain him. In the security office, the "back room," they took mug shots and copied his identification. The pictures and his name were entered in the notorious Griffin Book. Nevada casinos were now ready to turn him away, a heavyset man with glasses, long hair, and a long beard. Too bad for them that they never saw anyone like that again.

HAVE BETS, WILL TRAVEL

THE ADVENTURES OF A PROFESSIONAL GAMBLER

JAKE JACOBS

Cover art by Steven Novak

Cover design by Cheryl Ryan, www.cherylryan.com

Published by 3sides2 Author Services

P.O. Box 85161

Tucson, AZ 85745

Edition 2026

Printed in the USA

HAVE BETS, WILL TRAVEL

CONTENTS

PROLOGUE

The plane began its descent. Thick clouds surrounded it, cloaking the outside world. The shaking began – mild, increasing, then violent, a bull trying to batter the plane until its rivets fell out. It was the third time we'd tried to land. The previous two the plane had suddenly aborted the attempt, and pulled back up, out of the turbulence, flying above the clouds, circling. This time it committed itself. The pilot came on the intercom, but what he was saying was incomprehensible to me. I looked around, and could see the heads of the other passengers all nodding. They spoke the language. I hoped from their expressions I would have some clue as to what was happening. He might have been telling them anything from the time and temperature to the plot of *Star Wars*.

After his announcement, which had lasted more than a minute, he switched to heavily accented English. It was brief. "Ladies and gentle-man. This is pilot. Just now, we encounter heavy turbulence. And so, we crash."

As he said it, the plane tilted to the right, perpendicular to the ground. The nose dipped and the invisible wires that held this great crate of metal aloft were severed. A collective scream filled the cabin as we fell out of the sky ....

I snapped awake, sat up in the bed, which now felt like a plane ascending, while my body continued to fall. I looked around the strange hotel room, heart racing. Hell of a dream! The real plane, the evening before, made it that third time. It had twice aborted when it hit the layer of turbulence. It had taken a pounding the third time. But there was no announcement, and we did not fall out of the sky. The only damage was to my sleep the next day. Only four hours sleep on top of jet lag, after working the morning shift.

Now it was ten hours after the dream. It was four in the morning, and I had been working for five and a half hours. The stool I was sitting on, or maybe it was the floor of the casino beneath it, was rising and falling like a plane banking in the air. I could feel my body falling while the stool flew upward. It was making me nauseous. I was used to jet lag, but this after-dream was a killer.

The books will tell you not to play blackjack when you are tired. They will tell you to take a break every forty-five minutes. They will tell you not to play long sessions. The books are written for amateurs. I was a professional. I was betting one purple chip every hand, worth one hundred thousand won, or one hundred and forty dollars. What I bet hardly mattered. What Rocky was betting was paramount. His bets ranged from two hands with two purples, up to two hands with two golds. The gold chips were each worth a million won, so when he bet two hands of the table limit, we had fifty-six hundred dollars in action. Plus my paltry one-forty. I controlled, through subtle signals, every bet he made, and every play. I had to get it right, even if my stool was practicing loop the loops and Immelmann turns. Much as I wanted to stagger across the street and go to sleep, the team hadn't flown me halfway around the world and was not paying me one hundred dollars an hour, to take naps.

Years earlier a friend from another blackjack team joked that to test prospective players to see if they were ready, they should be made to tread water in the deep end of his pool. Two testers using power jets of water would spray the subject's face from both sides, while a third would stand on the diving board, peeling cards off a deck, and flipping them into the pool. If the guy kept the count, he made the team. At this moment I thought, "I could handle that."

When you are dizzy, your stomach turning over, you start to feel sorry for yourself. That's only human. I am playing blackjack, a tedious game. I have been playing this tedious game for going on six hours and still have an hour and a half to go. I'll catch a few hours' sleep, then be back here for another seven hours, because the casino is only busy on weekends, and we need to blend in.

Then I reflected on the bigger picture, beyond my momentary misery. I could be back in Chicago, working a five day a week job, one even more boring than blackjack. Here, outside the casino, was Hyundai Beach. There were hundreds of small tents, filled with people. They were eating live seafood. They were singing karaoke using portable sound systems. They were drinking, definitely drinking. Who knows? When I got off work at the crack of dawn, maybe the party would still be going on? Inside the casino I was at a table full of Japanese players. The guy next to me was wearing a red plaid sports coat that looked like it belonged in a comedy act, but probably cost two or three hundred thousand yen from a custom tailor in Ginza. Laugh at that! On his wrist was a Rolex, fashioned from a half pound of gold, and sprinkled with so many tiny diamonds it twinkled like the Milky Way. The hand it was perched above had an artificial pinkie. It was a really good fake finger; you'd need to look close to see it wasn't real. He'd cut off the original, and immigration officers frowned on men without pinkie fingers, hence the prosthetic. He, and all the other high rollers at my table, except Rocky, were ranking Yakuza. What was Mister Rolex doing? What were his friends doing? What were me and Rocky, all of us doing, that very moment in this posh casino? We were eating strawberry ice cream. That's not something you'd see in an American casino. Welcome to Korea!

I thought, not for the first time, and not for the last, that despite a little jet lag now and again, there were worse ways of making a living than being a gambler.

CHAPTER 1
THE NON-MAKING OF A GAMBLER

Tobaksa was nearly the title of this book. *Tobaksa* (toe-bock-sah) is the Korean pronunciation of 賭博士. Those are Chinese characters, and the Chinese or Japanese have their own pronunciations for them, but the meaning is "professional gambler." The first two characters represent the abstract concept "gamble," or "gambling." The third is a very old character which originally meant "knight." Now it appears in the words for "doctor" or "lawyer," and indicates the person is a professional. If you ask a Korean speaker the word for gambler, they're liable to say *"tobakggun,"* the last syllable, 꾼, pejorative, implying someone with a gambling habit. They might laugh if you used the word *tobaksa*, the concept of professional gambling being as strange to them as it is to Americans. There aren't many of us, and I know of no study of our characteristics. Generalizing is susceptible to error, but being a gambler, I'll risk it.

One way to grow up to be a professional gambler is to have a father who is a bookie. Like father, like son. There are women who gamble. I have women friends who were professionals. They are just very rare. I am not sure why. Sadly for my career prospects, my dad was a lawyer, and my mom an actress, though her dream was deferred for nearly forty years. She was fifty-seven when she earned her theatre degree, and then went out and earned her SAG, AFTRA, and Equity cards. Without their serving as role models, quoting betting lines, and laying odds, I grew up aspiring to more ordinary occupations. I wanted to become the youngest US president, because I turned thirty-five in an election year. I wanted to be a movie star. I wanted to be a billionaire. I wanted to be a bestselling author. Heck, I wanted to be all four! Then I discovered Juvenile Delinquent fiction, and read my way through *The Amboy Dukes*, *The Blackboard Jungle* and others. I watched *Dino*, *The Young Savages*, and *West Side Story*. By the time I was twelve, and our science teacher asked us what we wanted to be when we grew up, I said, "A sixteen-year-old dropout."

I got my wish. By that time I had changed my mind, and didn't see juvenile delinquency as a career path. I considered law, like my dad, but after clerking for him the summer after high school I decided there was too much paperwork, and not enough courtroom pyrotechnics. I thought about majoring in psychology, at Roosevelt University, where I matriculated after high school, but discovered that if I wanted to spend my days in the student lounge, smoking cigarettes, reading, and throwing quarters in a game called the Genius Quiz, no one was paying attention. After twelve weeks I was about eleven weeks behind, and dropping out seemed indicated.

I saw an ad asking if I wanted "employment in aviation" by Eastern Employment. Eastern was a major airline then, and I assumed Eastern Employment was the personnel department of the airline. It wasn't. It was an employment agency, whose come-on roped me in. My counselor sold me to prospective employers with enthusiasm. "I've got a sixteen-year-old college dropout, who scored forty-eight on the Wonderlic." I was ashamed of that score; I ran out of time before I got to answer the last two questions. His pitch wasn't selling them on me. I interviewed for the mailroom at R.H. Donnelly, whose personnel manager summed up the consensus. "You are going back to school." I insisted I wasn't, that I planned to start in the mailroom, and work my way up to president. "We can always hire a president from outside. We need someone who will stay in the mailroom for twenty years."

I admitted defeat, took a computer course, and operated computers for a few years. I went back to college, earned an AA degree, and took courses at the University of Illinois Circle Campus, before dropping out again. Then I went to work for a cab company while I pondered my next move.

Another route to becoming a gambler is to be obsessed with sports. Not me! I can tell you that Babe Ruth hit 714 homers, and Cy Young won 511 games. I can't name a single current baseball player. Ditto football. Who was the first man to rush for 1000 yards in a season? Why, it was Beattie Feathers, whose 1004 yards in 1934 was a record that stood for twelve years. Not only that, he averaged 9.9 yards per carry! The explanation for this prodigy was that he had Bronco Nagurski blocking for him. I know all that, but have no idea who rushes for the Bears these days. I was short, fat, and nearsighted. I was the kid picked last for teams. Not that I cared all that much. Contrary to the way it's shown in movies, I was a popular kid. I just sucked at sports, and hated gym classes with a passion.

Still another route is competitive gaming. Now we are getting somewhere. My dad's parents played bridge, and Grandpa Russell was described as a "very good card player." Of Grandma Doris' play, the less said the better. She also played gin, with my dad. When I was in my teens he taught me Hollywood scoring. I taught it to a buddy. I figured dad and grandma played for a penny a point and suggested we play for half a cent. I won six straight hands, blitzed him in all three lines, and won $8.75. He thought I'd hustled him. Then I learned from dad that he and grandma played for a quarter of a cent.

My other grandfather, Walter, played poker and pinochle. He won enough one year to buy a car and had plenty left over. He used to save his winnings and split them between the ten grandkids at the end of each year. By then he wasn't playing for as much, but it was still a nice little windfall. My younger brother Ric and I would play pinochle with dad and grandpa, for small stakes. We also played some nickel-dime-quarter poker with our friends, but after a year I didn't think my game was improving, while some of the others were getting better, so I quit a winner.

Ric was the one who seemed destined to be a gambler. By the time he started college he had taken up backgammon. He began playing in tournaments, and through contacts he made there, learned about a place in Chicago called the North Club. It was a bridge club, where the best in the city played for a dime a point, but it was also a spot for the best players of other games. He began playing backgammon for three dollars a point, and poker for two-four. He was making two or three hundred a week while he went to school. I got to be friends with some of the players, but the only games I liked were hearts and spades, for ten cents a point. Winning ten or twenty dollars was fun, but it was no way to make a living.

Time passed, and Ric moved to Las Vegas. By then he was called Munchkin. He went to dealer's school and got a job dealing twenty-one at the Golden Nugget. The family decided to see what his new life was like. Besides me and my folks, my youngest brother Bruce, and both sets of grandparents flew out there. As a former hippie, I was prepared to sneer at the decadence and rampant commercialism, but instead was entranced.

My dad left arranging the trip until the last minute. Four days before our flight we had no hotel reservations, and the town was booked up. Dad had some young partners who were Italian-American, and grew up with a guy named Jimmy, whose dad was Jackie Cerone. At the time he was only number three in the Outfit; he'd get to be boss some years later. This was the Lefty Rosenthal era, and magically we got four rooms at a "casino rate" at the Stardust. The Stardust was a great place to stay. Not because it was the best hotel in town by any stretch, but it might have been the most quintessentially Las Vegas Strip hotel in those days. For one thing, it had the most neon. The Stardust was not a high-rise hotel. It was broad, and sat close to the street. It had over a million light bulbs on its façade, an overwhelming sight.

Inside we had to stand in line to check in among a bank of slot machines. These were the old-style machines. You pulled a handle, and physical reels spun before your eyes. Payouts came in coin, spilling into a metal tray. One machine was loud, hundreds of them were cacophonous. Right where we were standing there was a Big Bertha, a gigantic slot machine. There wasn't anything special about it besides its size; the payout was ordinary. But it took two hands to yank the handle, and the reels rumbled when they spun.

After checking in, and eating, we went downtown to Glitter Gulch.

It was hard to out-neon the Stardust, but the corner of Fremont and Second had pride of place. There were casinos on each of the four corners, the Horseshoe, the Fremont, the 4 Queens, and the Golden Nugget. Each had neon wrapped around their fronts, and each one sat right on the corner, only a sidewalk's width away from the street. They used to say that you could stand on the corner at three in the morning, and read a book by the light. Read, hell! You could practically set the pages on fire.

The Golden Nugget, where Munch worked, was owned by Steve Wynn. Wynn had a classic gambler's background. His dad owned bingo parlors, and died leaving $350,000 in gambling debts. Wynn moved to Las Vegas in 1967, bought a piece of the Frontier, later shifted to the Golden Nugget, and by 1973 was the town's youngest casino owner. In 1977, right before my brother began working there, he built a tower for the hotel, and began turning the Golden Nugget into something resembling a Strip casino, despite its being downtown.

Dad managed to hit a jackpot on a nickel machine before we left the Stardust. The casinos gave out plastic cups to hold coins, and dad divvied up his score. Mom still had hers when we went downtown to see Munchkin at work. He was standing on a dead game when she dropped by his table, and after some chit chat showed him that she had "one hundred and forty-seven nickels," and wondered where she might play them. Munch told her there were some nickel machines at the far end of the casino, and she headed off to do what slot players do with one hundred and forty-seven nickels, lose them.

A few minutes later a boss sidled up, and started a conversation, since Munch's table was still dead. The boss leaned back against the table, arms folded, talking out of the side of his mouth. Meanwhile, mom appeared from behind the bank of slots, and made her way up the aisle. Just as she drew abreast of Munch's table, she swerved, shook her empty cup, and said, "Well, I lost my hundred and forty-seven nickels!" Then she walked off without waiting for a reaction. The boss's jaw dropped, and he said to Munch, "Boy, it takes all kinds!"

The next morning, my schedule completely out of whack (I'd worked nights for years) I was up early, and Bruce and I went down to the coffee shop. There were keno pads and crayons on every table, keno girls prowling the aisles, and boards showing the results of the drawings on every wall. Why waste time when you could gamble while having breakfast? Even crazier, the lounge was open for business, with a rock band playing. At eight in the morning.

I had three hundred dollars when I arrived, and three dollars when I left. I told people I had ninety-nine percent of a perfect time.

Over the next several years I returned once or twice a year. I even almost made an advantage play. Besides hearing about card counting from my brother, I had read Ian Anderson's bestselling *Turning the Tables On Las Vegas*. I looked over a basic strategy chart, and absorbed most of it. During one trip Munch introduced me to a friend of his named Roger. Roger had served in the Air Force as a member of the band. He organized a blackjack game on the bus, which he dealt, until he had won most of his bandmates' spare cash. Later they were stationed in the Philippines, and he found a book on card counting. He trained his buddies, and they visited Macau, where they counted down shoes, and called him in as the big player. Why not teach me, and we'd attack some of the Vegas casinos?

Roger's good friend was Howard Grossman. Howard had been a card counter, and years later would have an infomercial promoting a blackjack course he taught. "Most people think you should stand on twelve against a dealer's three. You should hit, and I'll tell you why!" Howard had switched teams and was working as a shift manager at the Nevada Palace, a smallish casino on Boulder Highway. He let us use the dealer break room, where there was a blackjack table, to practice. I think by the time we felt we were ready, Munchkin was getting off work, and we never did play. But it was fun practicing.

Besides the trips to Las Vegas, there was another thing nudging me in the direction of gambling. I started playing backgammon, played in some good-sized tournaments, and played for threes, or rarely, fives. I could win or lose over a hundred dollars at those stakes. A bigger deal than ten-cent hearts. Yet gambling still wasn't something toward which I inclined.

Then one day I got a phone call, which changed my life. I have received a number of them over the years. The call telling me there was an opening at the cab company was one such.

I started as a driver in January of 1974, when I was twenty, but by the winter of 1982 I had long been a full-time dispatcher. The show *Taxi* got a lot of things right, or so it seemed the few times I saw it. Picture Louie DePalma and you have a rough idea of me, only in the episodes I saw, Louie was nowhere near busy enough. People who saw me dispatch – and since my office was in a train station, I was on display – compared it to air traffic control. Apples and oranges. Air traffic controllers, if they goof, might kill a lot of people. If I goofed, they might be late for work. It's a different kind of stress. Otherwise, my job was much harder, and while the stress was different, it made up in quantity what it lacked in quality.

The business varied by season and by weather. The worse the weather, the busier it got. I did not know it when I took over full-time dispatching that fall, but the winter of 1976-1977 would be one of our coldest winters. Until it was overshadowed by the winter of 1977-1978. Then came 1978-1979, which holds the record for the coldest, and snowiest, winter in Chicago's history. After five solid months of extreme stress every nerve in my body was burnt out. I vowed that one more bad winter, just one, and I was out of there!

The fates heard me, and the next few years were gentle. I was stuck in a rut. I wanted to move on, but had no idea where to go, or what I wanted to do. It was looking as though instead of writing this book, someday I'd be writing *Forty Years a Cab Driver*. Then 1981-1982 reminded me of how much Chicago winters sucked.

It was the perfect time for the game-changing phone call. It came from Munchkin. "Are you interested in moving to Las Vegas, and learning to count cards? If so, I know someone putting together a team. He's taking new players." I asked a few questions, then told him to leave a light burning in the window, I was on the way. The next day I did three things. I stopped by the library and found one of the books he'd suggested I study, *How to Play Winning Blackjack*, by Julian Braun. I went to the travel agency, and bought a one-way ticket to Las Vegas. Then I went in to work and gave two-weeks' notice. On February 17, 1982, I flew to Las Vegas.

CHAPTER 2
HOW IT BEGAN

f a Vegas denizen from 1982 hopped in a Tardis and went back in time twenty-five years they might find themselves wondering why there were so few blackjack tables. In 1982 blackjack was by far the most popular table game, but in the fifties, craps was where the action was. What they might not notice, but what was true, was the odd fact that casinos had no idea what their edge was. They knew for the other games. Roulette was easy. American wheels have two zeros, thirty-eight slots in all, but pay as though there are thirty-six numbers. The house edge is 2/38, or 5.26%, or .0526. No matter how you express it, it's big. Craps is more complicated. It has more different sorts of bets, with different edges. The most important one is the pass line bet, which gives the house 1.414%. That's harder to calculate, but not that hard. You can work it out in your head. I did it once, just for fun. And so forth for the other games. Blackjack was different. The casinos knew the hold, and that reassured them. The hold is how much of your buy-in stays with them. Some customers win, and some customers lose, but let's suppose that on average out of every hundred dollars' worth of chips purchased, they only cash out eighty-eight. The casino holds twelve. How long a customer plays, how much they bet each hand, relative to their buy-in, and the house edge, all factor in. But the casinos don't need to know any of those things to figure the hold. All they need is the record of how much in, and how much out, over time.

If you didn't know the difference between the house edge, and the hold, don't be embarrassed. I met a high-ranking casino executive from Marina Bay Sands once, at a party, and *he* didn't know the difference. Because he was a high-ranking casino executive, he didn't want to listen my explanation. I hope you at least are paying attention.

Another difference between blackjack and the other games is that the player can make decisions which alter the odds. You can choose what to bet on a crap table, but you can't choose your roll. You can choose red, black, a number, or whatever your lucky system might be at roulette, but you can't affect where the ball lands. Even baccarat has fixed rules. Not blackjack. You may hit, you may stand, you may double down, split pairs, surrender your hand if they offer it, take insurance if the dealer is showing an ace. Those decisions change your odds, and change the house edge. You can calculate the theoretical edge if the player plays perfectly, every decision correct. The casinos couldn't. Not in 1957, because no one knew how to play correctly. There are rumors that a few players may have had a clue, who played near perfectly, but everyone else was just guessing, and many of their guesses were wrong.

In 1957 a team of mathematicians, Roger Baldwin, Wilbert Cantey, Herbert Maisel, and James McDermott got their hands on a souped-up piece of machinery, a computer. Did they try to solve Fermat's Last Theorem, the Reimann Hypothesis, or even how to split their dinner check? No, they decided to solve blackjack. Let's say they wanted to know if you should hit twelve against a dealer three, and Howard Grossman wasn't around to tell them. (He was only twelve then, after all.) They gave the player and dealer those cards, and had the computer deal from a deck containing the other forty-nine cards, thousands of times with the player standing, and thousands more with the player hitting. They could then compare how much the house won or lost either way, and see which was better. After doing that for all possible hands, choosing the best plays, multiplying the house edge by the frequency the hand occurred, and summing the whole mess, they had a perfect basic strategy. (Okay, not quite perfect. More powerful computers would refine it in later years, but they were damned close.) According to their calculations a player using correct basic strategy was breaking even with the house. The casino had no edge!

Luckily for the casinos, no one was playing correct basic strategy because no one was reading mathematical journals. No one, except other mathematicians. One of them was a young professor named Dr. Edward O. Thorp. Thorp realized something else unusual about blackjack, which set it apart from the other games. There is a saying that the dice have no memory; or the wheel has no memory. If black comes up nine times in a row, the odds that red will come up next time are still 9/19. It's true that black coming up ten times in a row is nearly six thousand to one against, but it has already come up nine times in a row, so it has gotten twenty-five hundred to one out of its system.

Blackjack is different. The game starts with a full deck of cards, four aces, four kings, etc. But let's suppose that you and the dealer get blackjacks on the very first hand. Half the aces are gone, and your chances of getting another blackjack have gone way down. That's bad. The extra money players are paid for their blackjacks is crucial in reducing the house edge to zero. On the other hand, if during the first few hands no tens and aces appear, your equity has gone up. Thorp, having realized this, and having done computer work to determine which cards were good for the player, and which for the dealer, assigned point values, and created the world's first counting system. This allowed him to modify his play of some hands. More importantly, it helped him decide when to bet more money, and when to bet less.

With backing from some New York gamblers, whom he called Mister X and Mister Y, he went to Nevada to test his system. You may read all about it in his book, *Beat the Dealer*. Using his system, he won money, and the enmity of the casinos. Who found various ways to discourage him, including cheating, and even (he believes) tampering with his car so that he found himself behind the wheel of a runaway machine careening down the side of a mountain.

Zowie! Johnny Rivers should have recorded "System Player Man," giving it his numbers, to take away their game. You never guessed mathematicians led such wild lives. They do, at least the statistics guys. Just stay away from the topologists; they are pretty twisted.

Thorp's book was a bestseller, and all over America people read it, and thought they'd found El Dorado. Would-be counters came to Las Vegas, and the casinos reacted by changing the rules. The players boycotted the tables, the casinos capitulated, and … Discovered that Las Vegas was El Dorado, for the casinos. Most of the card counters could count their own toes and have trouble coming up with ten. Blackjack became the most popular game.

Ah, but there were a few, a happy few, who really could count cards. One of them was a man named Alan Woods.

Woody was Australian. He had been an actuary. When Australia licensed its first casino, his firm got the account. They figured that to underwrite a casino, they would need to know about the games, and in the process discovered the existence of card counting. Woody learned to count, and by 1980 had quit his job, built up a bankroll, and was a successful player. He and some other Australians were in Las Vegas, and discovered the local backgammon club. It was in a bar in a prime location, at the corner of Spring Mountain and Las Vegas Boulevard. Over the years it changed names, from Dirty Sally's to Rumors, and changed formats, everything from disco to country and western, complete with mechanical bull, to a comedy club. What didn't change was the backgammon room, with boards built into the tables, and lamps with plastic covers for the bulbs in the shape of dice, at each table. It was a beautiful setup, and in those days had regulars who hung out every day, and tourists who heard there was action, and wanted a change of pace from the casinos.

Woody and the Australians were tourists; Munchkin, and his friends Timmy and Craig, backgammon players who had followed Munch from Chicago, were regulars. They told Alan and the others that if five dollars a point was too tame, fifty was more fun. Alan went to the president of the club, Michael "Max" Maxakuli, and asked whether playing Munchkin and his friends for fifties was a good idea, and Max said, "Not if you like money." They stuck with fives, and over time got to be friends.

One night Woody said, "Munchie, you and your friends are smart guys. There is more money in blackjack than backgammon. That's what you should be doing."

Munchkin already knew how to count cards, and had dabbled since even before he moved to Las Vegas. But he had a full-time job. He was still dealing, though he'd moved on from the Golden Nugget to the Castaways, on the Strip north of Caesar's. He would play, but whenever he got a few hundred ahead, he'd deposit it in a brokerage account, and buy stocks. "It takes a bankroll to make any money at blackjack."

"I'll stake you and your friends."

"Stake me? You barely know me!"

Woody reached in his bag, pulled out two ten-thousand-dollar wrappers, and dropped them on the board. "There. Go play."

The three began putting in hours playing. Craig won eleven thousand dollars. Timmy broke even. Munchkin lost sixteen thousand.

"You hear that, Alan?" said the other Australians. "That's a plane landing at McCarren with your next blackjack team!"

During his stay in Las Vegas, Alan had been playing with a team of young Americans. Through him they had gotten to know Munchkin and the others. When it was time for Woody to leave for Australia, he suggested they take on Craig in his place. Craig had, after all, won a goodly sum playing for him. Craig joined the team, Timmy went to dealer's school to learn craps, and Munchkin swore off blackjack forever!

Or at least until he was coaxed into joining another team, run by a guy named Arthur. This time Munchkin was the team's biggest winner. When the team broke its bankroll, Arthur announced he was going on vacation, so there would be a break before the next bankroll started. The team Craig played for was in continuous action, and they were interested in having Munch play for them. He wanted to make the move, but when he left Arthur's team, Arthur said he was always looking for new players, and Munch called me.

CHAPTER 3
CARD COUNTING FOR DUMMIES

had two weeks to turn myself into a card counter before I left home to seek my fame and fortune in Las Vegas. What did I have to learn?

I am assuming you know how to play blackjack, but that's a dangerous assumption. During a recent lecture I had barely gotten started when someone raised their hand, and asked how the game was played. In an early draft I wrote a detailed explanation, but realized the world is divided into two types of people, those that already know this stuff, and those who don't. Neither one wants to read about it. Instead, I have included a glossary of terms at the back of the book.

The first thing I had to learn was basic strategy. Before you learn to count, you should know how to play every hand. It sounds like a chore. There are three hundred and sixty hands to consider, everything from hard five against a dealer's two, to hard twenty against a dealer's ace. Every pair (and all ten value cards are pairs, e.g. jack and king are a pair) against every dealer upcard. All the soft hands, from ace-deuce to ace-nine, against all the dealer upcards. And there are four ways to play these hands, five if surrender is allowed, including standing, hitting, doubling down, or splitting pairs. But most plays are obvious, and most hands fall into groups. All hard hands worth seventeen to twenty (and not pairs), regardless of the dealer's upcard, are stands. There're forty hands right there! You can learn all of basic strategy in an hour or two. After that, practice until the plays are instantaneous.

On to the next step, counting. There are a lot of systems, some harder than others. The system in Braun's book is a very simple one, the Hi Lo. Most of the pros I know, even if they learned a more advanced count when they started out, use it. The advanced counts have the most to recommend them if you play a lot of single deck. Decent single deck games were already growing scarce by the eighties. The Hi Lo count is very accurate for betting, and because it is simple you are less likely to make mistakes, and will be less fatigued if playing long sessions.

The Hi Lo assigns a value of +1 to each small card, 2 through 6, a 0 to the 7s, 8s, and 9s, and a -1 for all ten value cards, and the aces. There are twenty cards which are counted +1, and twenty which are counted -1. The count starts at zero, and if you count all the way through the deck to the last card, you will finish at zero. There is a line in the movie *Rain Man* where a casino employee says, "No one can count a six-deck shoe." Nonsense. With six decks the highest possible count is +120, and the lowest is -120. I don't know about you, but I could count that high in first grade. In practice you would have to play a very long time to see counts much higher or lower than in the twenties. For instance, you are dealt a jack and a queen, and the dealer shows a six. The count is -1, because the six counts +1 and your two face cards count -2. You stand, the dealer turns over a five, hits with a four, and hits again with a three. The count is now +2. Learning to count is even easier than memorizing basic strategy. Though like basic strategy, you will need to drill.

Buoyed with confidence, you figure the rest will be as easy. Just when you figured that, it gets harder.

The count you have just mastered is a running count. It ought to be obvious that a count of +5 after half a single deck has been dealt, is much better than a count of +5 after the first half deck has been dealt from a six-deck shoe. You must do an adjustment to determine the "true count." There are two parts to this, and some players struggle with both. The first part is deck estimation. The cards which have been dealt are stacked in a discard tray. You must be able to eyeball the stack and make an accurate estimate of how many cards are in the tray. The idea is simple, but making accurate estimates takes practice. If you have a discard tray you can mark off half deck intervals, and practice eyeballing stacks of cards reaching each level. Otherwise, you may have to deal random stacks, guess, then count the number of cards to see how you did.

As you gain proficiency, you will work on the other part. Let's say you are dealing from a six-deck shoe, you have a running count of +11, and you estimate there are two and a half decks in the discard tray. What is your true count? To derive that you subtract 2.5 from 6. You have 3.5 decks remaining. To get the count per deck you divide 11 by 3.5, and round the result to +3. Your true count is +3. Try another. The dealer has dealt seventeen cards from a single deck, and your count it -4; what is your true count? Seventeen cards are about a third of a single deck, so there is two-thirds of a deck remaining. Dividing by 2/3 is the same as multiplying by 3/2, so your true count is -6.

I never had a problem doing simple math in my head, but some people really struggle with this. Once again, practice is your friend.

Now for the hardest part, index numbers. You have been counting cards for a reason. Knowing the count has two benefits. Based on the count you will change your betting, and your play. The betting is the more important change. I will talk about that later. Meanwhile, when to change how you play the hands is where index numbers come in. Here are five numbers: +3, +2, 0, -2, -1. Those are the index numbers for a total of 12, versus the dealer's 2 through 6. According to basic strategy you hit 12 against a 2 or 3, and stand against 4, 5, or 6. New rule, stand on 12 if your count is equal to or greater than the appropriate index number. If you have 12, and the dealer has 2, you hit unless your true count has reached +3, then you stand. If you have 12, and the dealer has 5, you stand unless the true count is under -2.

A chart of index numbers looks like a basic strategy chart except that each box has a number, instead of a letter code and a color code. When you learned basic strategy for 12, you had a block of two boxes where you hit, another with three boxes where you stood. Now you need to memorize five individual numbers. Lucky me, I have a good memory.

That's most of what you need to learn. Now you have to put it all together, and practice, practice, practice, until you can do it smoothly. By the end of the two weeks, I had practiced, and thought I was doing it smoothly. On February 17th, 1982, I boarded my one-way flight, and moved to Las Vegas.

CHAPTER 4
NEW KID IN TOWN

After picking me up at the airport, my brother took me to dinner, before we went to his condo. The venue was Khan's Mongolian Grill, on Maryland Parkway, where we were joined by Craig. "You've heard the streets are paved with gold!" He laughed.

We were finishing our meal when Craig spotted another diner, and said, "I know that guy." Evidently so, because he made his way over to our table, and began telling a story about something he had just seen at the Barbary Coast. It seems there was a card counter playing for very low stakes. The guy was betting reds, five-dollar chips, and was ahead fifty or sixty dollars. He sensed heat from the pit, gathered up his chips, and started walking.

"That's him!" said a boss. A gigantic security guard, six-eight our informant estimated, started chasing the counter. At the far end of the casino was an elevator to the parking garage. The counter dived into the elevator, the doors closed, but then … Bang! The guard hit the doors with a massive fist. They sprang open. Everyone in the casino could see the counter, cowering on the floor of the elevator, back against the wall, clutching his handful of red chips.

"And don't ever come back!" the guard boomed, pointing a giant finger at the kid. The doors shut, concealing his whimpering form, and the casino got back to business.

After Craig's acquaintance left, Munch explained that the Barbary Coast had a reputation. They wanted all of their bosses to know basic strategy, at the very least, because they had a zero-tolerance policy when it came to card counting. The scene just described was par for the course. He and Craig also discussed Rick, the guy who had told us the story. It seems Rick was a "spook." I didn't know what a spook was, but gathered it was a legal and ethical grey area.

Jesus, what was I getting into?

The next day Munch took me to meet my new boss. Arthur Peyser, or Arthur Goldberg as he was better known, lived across town on the northwest side. Originally an accountant in New Jersey, when Resorts, Atlantic City's first casino, opened in 1978, Arthur discovered card counting. The casino dealt a four-deck game with early surrender. Surrender as previously mentioned is a rule which lets the player give up his original hand without playing it, by conceding half a bet. It is done most often with bad starting hands like sixteen or fifteen, when the dealer has a ten or an ace up. The player surrenders after the dealer has checked their hole card to see if they have blackjack. With early surrender the player surrenders *before* the dealer checks. It's a much more favorable rule, and meant that players using correct basic strategy in Atlantic City started with a .3% advantage off the top. Coupled with the fact players were not barred when the casino first opened, at a time later described as the "free for all," and a later interlude known as "the experiment," it was easy to make money. Arthur made money. Enough that a stringer for Ripley's Believe It or Not wrote an item about him, "New Jersey man turns four thousand dollars into sixty-nine thousand playing blackjack, believe it or not!"

Arthur took his sixty-nine thousand, and moved to Las Vegas to count cards full time. In the next year and a half, he more than doubled it. Then the barrings began, and he was out of action. Meanwhile, he had a house and a pair of Pontiac Firebirds with the license plates "PLUS" for him, and "MINUS" for his girlfriend Monica. The hundred and forty thousand he had accumulated began to dwindle. That's when he decided to put his money and knowledge to work as a financier of blackjack teams.

Of course I didn't know this when Arthur opened his door. What I saw was a middle-aged man who looked like a two-hundred-and-fifty-pound baby. A baby badly in need of a bath and a shave. Arthur had a slack jaw, his mouth open like he was about to doze off and begin drooling at any moment. He had a glass eye which pointed towards Pluto, as though checking to see if there were any recent messages for him. This was his super power.

Arthur was an intelligent man who looked like a complete idiot. Casinos saw him and were convinced he was harmless. How could anyone who looked like that be a threat? Arthur's best casino was the Sahara. He would go in there and play single deck spreading quarter to double five hundreds. Card counters have to vary their bets, but the fewer decks, the smaller the spread needed to be effective. Bosses looked for people playing single deck, because it is a potentially better game, and because they thought, wrongly, that shoes were difficult or impossible to count. They knew card counters varied their bets. Someone playing single deck and spreading from one hundred to three hundred on one hand would trigger a red alert in most casinos. Arthur was going from one hand of twenty-five dollars to two hands of five hundred dollars, and he got away with that for months and months. It helped that he talked to himself while he played. Actually, he talked to himself even when he wasn't playing. And if he hit a bad run, he'd get up from the table and shamble over to the casino lounge. It had a piano, and Arthur was a decent player. He'd throw off the cover, and begin playing and singing. When he finished, he would return to the table, to the applause of the players and bosses. He'd take a bow, and resume play.

The Sahara finally tired of him; he was at its property in Lake Tahoe when the axe fell. The casino manager alerted his bosses that he wanted to be notified if Arthur was playing. He failed to tell them why, and that calling him at home was okay, so Arthur got in one last session in the evening, winning a few thousand dollars, and bringing his net win against the two Sahara properties to eighty-nine thousand dollars. He was on his way out the front door when the casino manager caught up with him, and said, "Mister Goldberg, the party's over."

Arthur's super power was also his kryptonite. He was disguise proof, and once a casino barred him, it never forgot him.

With Arthur that afternoon was a kid named Marko, who sneered at me and said he wanted to see who the new player was. Not that Marko had anything against me; sneering was just how he talked.

Arthur had a blackjack table in the corner of his living room. Of course he did. I sat down, while Arthur moved behind the table to deal me some hands. He gave me a betting scheme he wanted me to follow, I placed my first bet, and he began dealing. I was dealt a ten and a three, while Arthur was showing a seven.

As I was assimilating that, the count still zero, Arthur hit me with a two, hit me with a five, flipped over a four as his hole card, hit with a three, then hit with a ten. He scooped up the cards, paid me, and looked at me as if to say, "What are we waiting for?" While I thought, "Oh, shit!" Arthur was not a skilled dealer. His hands didn't move rapidly. But he was an experienced player, and the plays, my hand hitting thirteen and then fifteen against seven, and then standing on twenty, and the dealer hitting eleven, then thirteen, then scooping the cards and paying my bet after he busted, those were all automatic. He didn't wait for me to signal, and the whole thing was over in seconds. I felt like a kid whose pony had decided to gallop. I managed to reconstruct the sequence of cards dealt, realized the running count was plus three, and since it was a four-deck shoe it wasn't time to raise my bet. I shoved another chip out, and we continued. It was instantly clear that things were happening at the table much faster than in my practice sessions at home, and if Arthur was hard to keep up with, what might I run into in casinos?

I made it through the shoe with reasonable accuracy, if not outstanding speed. Arthur told me I was doing okay, but I should keep practicing. He was leaving town on a vacation, but there would be a team meeting to kick off the bankroll when he returned.

Leaving Arthur's, our next stop was a casino, for some live practice. There are many more casinos today than there were in 1982, but even then, there were a lot. The big ones were famous. What was surprising was all of the little ones. One of them was a hotel and casino near, but not on, the Strip called the Las Vegas Inn. It was on the south side of Sahara, next to the interstate. I don't know how many floors in its tower. Likely not enough to merit being called a tower. I do know how many blackjack tables in its casino, four. They were in a circle outside the coffee shop. Two were open.

Before we went inside, Munchkin handed me one hundred dollars, and gave me a betting scheme. The house edge on a shoe game with Strip rules was approximately half a percent. Each true count using Hi Lo is worth about half a percent. (For sticklers: the off the top disadvantage for the player on a four-deck shoe with Strip rules is -.48%, and the Hi Lo true counts average .56%.) In round numbers, you start with a disadvantage of half a percent, when the true count reaches +1 you are break even, at +2 you are half a percent to the good, and so forth. The betting scheme was simple enough: bet one dollar as long as the count was less than a true +2. When it reached +2, bet two hands of two dollars, at +3 two hands of four dollars, and increase the bet in double two-dollar increments until it reached +6. At +6 or above, bet two hands of ten dollars.

We sat down at a table, I bought in with my hundred dollars, got some of it changed to silver, and bet a dollar. Soon, the count increased, and I bet two hands of two dollars. It kept increasing, my bets went up, and in no time at all I was betting two hands of ten dollars. Even if we hadn't been the only customers in the joint, this was big action for the Las Vegas Inn. The table limit was only a hundred dollars, and I don't think they saw many bettors pushing out black chips. Or even green chips. This was all going almost the way it was supposed. Almost, except instead of raking in heaps of red chips as I won my twin ten-dollar bets, it was the casino taking away my chips as I lost them. In moments I was down ninety dollars!

I jumped up from the table.

"Where are you going" asked Munch.

"Can I talk to you?"

He got up from the table. The boss, the dealer, and the dealer from the other table all pretended not to be listening while they strained to hear what was up.

"I'm losing all of your money," I whispered out of the side of my mouth.

"Then you need more."

"Yeah, but I'm losing!"

"It happens." He handed me another hundred, and I sat back down. I managed to more or less break even for the rest of the session. Eventually my practice sessions would see me lose one hundred and eighty-nine of the two hundred dollars. Between the session with Arthur, and the sessions at the Las Vegas Inn, I knew I had work to do.

CHAPTER 5
HOMAGE

My family are readers. When my folks sold the house they'd lived in for nearly fifty years, there were thirty thousand books to deal with. Munchkin's condo had far fewer, but the bookcase was in my bedroom, and he had a lot of blackjack books. I read Thorp's *Beat the Dealer*, Lance Humble's *World's Greatest Blackjack Book*, and *Blackjack Super Gold*. Lawrence Revere's *Playing Blackjack As a Business* was at one time the book every self-respecting pro read. A California math professor named Peter Griffin had written the bible, *The Theory of Blackjack*. Everything you'd ever want to know was in there, if you could follow the math. Griffin was a friend of Munchkin's. He liked to play single deck blackjack betting one to four in silver. Which meant he had to find single deck games on the Strip with a one-dollar minimum. Munchkin had moved over from the Golden Nugget to a casino called the Castaways. They had dollar blackjack, and some of their tables had single deck. Griffin sat at Munch's table, they struck up a conversation, and thereafter when in town Griffin would seek out my brother's table. Griffin played a very complicated count, called a multi-parameter. He counted Gordon, which assigns +1 to 2s through 5s, and -1 to 10s. Then he kept separate side counts of the 7s, 8s, 9s, and aces, tracked the ratio of 5s to 6s, and counted the total number of cards dealt. It goes without saying this was hard to do. If Munch got to the end of a deck, and his hand busted, he would start rapidly hitting it again and again, his hand total quickly reaching the forties or fifties, as Griffin struggled to keep up, before realizing something was amiss. At other times he would reach the point where he was ready to shuffle, ten or twelve cards remaining, and Griffin would tell him what they were.

One day instead of dealing blackjack, Munchkin was assigned to roulette. Griffin came in, spotted him, and asked what Munch was trying to do to him? After a few minutes he said, "I might as well be handing you five-point-twenty-six percent of my bankroll!" Then he pulled out a five-dollar bill, got the smallest denomination chips possible (twenty-five cents apiece, I think), and bet one chip on red and another on black.

While they were talking there was a man betting the splits of the number twenty-seven. The roulette layout has its numbers in little boxes. A split bet is placed on the line separating a number from its neighbor. If either hits the bet pays seventeen to one. The player had chips surrounding twenty-seven on all of its borders, and twenty-seven finally won. Munchkin gathered the winning bets, and as they train dealers, stacked them up and then broke down the stack into even piles with a remainder. "Thirty-seven" he announced as the total number of chips.

"Six-twenty-nine," said Griffin, the payout at seventeen to one on a thirty-seven-chip bet.

Roulette players buy individual chips, and are assigned their own color, specifying how much they want those chips to be worth. For smaller payouts they are paid color for color, but for large payouts they must collect regular casino chips, which meant a boss had to be summoned.

"What's going on?"

Munch explained that the player had hit with thirty-seven chips on the splits. The boss looked baffled, and went to the podium to get a calculator. Munch said, "Joe, everyone knows it's six-twenty-nine."

Two more of the blackjack books were written by Ken Uston. Ken Uston was the world's most famous card counter. His first book, *The*

Big Player, told of how as a young vice president of the San Francisco stock exchange, he was recruited by a man he called Al Francesco, to play blackjack. Al was one of the game's great innovators. Casinos looked for players who seemed studious. They looked for players playing single deck. And especially they looked for players who spread their bets after observing a number of hands. Why not show them players who looked like wild men or drunks, who only played shoe games, and who didn't spread their bets? Players like that couldn't possibly be counting.

Al put together a team of skilled counters, who would sit at different tables, quietly counting while betting the table minimum, remaining unobtrusive. When the count rose at one of their tables, the counter would give a signal, and the Big Player would come over. The Big Player, or BP, would be signaled the count, and would make a show of splashing down large bets, a carefree high roller. The shoe would usually stay rich until the cut card, and the player would wander away from the table, ideally to another hot shoe at another counter's table.

Uston loved being the big player, loved assuming flamboyant personas, loved pretending to be drunk. (There were stories that it wasn't always faked.) Eventually the casinos caught on, and he began experiencing barrings. Some were "hard barrings," the security guards roughing him up, which led to lawsuits. The show 60 Minutes heard about him, and observed his play with a hidden camera, making him known to millions of viewers.

His second book was called *One-Third of a Shoe*. In 1978 New Jersey granted its first casino license to an Atlantic City property called Resorts. Because of the favorable rules and no-barring policy, it was a magnet for professional players. Uston put together a team, and joined up with another group of players headed by a man he calls Peter. He and Peter have many disagreements, one of which is Peter wanting his girlfriend to play. Ken reluctantly agrees if she can pass a test, difficult hands dealt by his "team tester," who Uston says is "one of the five best card counters in the world." He doesn't name the other four, but implies one might have the initials K.U. The girlfriend passes the test, but Uston remains dubious throughout their association.

In Atlantic City they have a friendly rivalry with another team, the Czechs. The Czechs win a lot more than Uston's team, which Uston puts down to their having a bigger bankroll. He is convinced, he says, that given time they would have passed up the Czechs because they used a superior count and were more skillful players. Ultimately, the casino begins barring people.

Uston would win money from his lawsuits in Nevada, from times where he was injured by security guards striking him. In New Jersey, though, his lawsuits led to the gaming commission ruling that casinos could not bar players. This was a mixed blessing, because the casinos retaliated by dealing games with rules and conditions much less favorable for the player.

Besides reading, I was networking. Not that I was trying to make connections with card counters, I simply fell into the milieu. Munch joined the other team, and besides Craig, I now met and became friends with his other teammates.

Among the advantages of team play is that teams usually have larger bankrolls than individual players. Let's say that you have ten thousand dollars; you can size your bets accordingly. Suppose I also have ten thousand dollars. If we team up we have twenty thousand, we can double the size of our bets, and each of us play on our twenty-thousand-dollar bankroll. Ten thousand was the share each member of Munchkin's team had to put up. There were six of them sharing a sixty-thousand-dollar bankroll. Instead of playing to double the bank, they would play to win twenty thousand. They would during the course of the year hit a lot of targets, get a lot of paydays.

Two of the other players lived in a rented house a mile northeast of Munch's condo. It had a swimming pool and jacuzzi, and became a hangout for players, not only those on their team.

One of the players, Ray Silverton, was slightly older than most counters. He was thirty-five, and a former house painter from California. His claim to fame was having been one of the kids on the series Spin & Marty, which aired on the original Mickey Mouse Club show. He had played in Europe on a team of Ken Uston's. He had been barred many times, and even without that discouragement, was not the most gung-ho individual. On a typical day he would rise in the evening, then boil himself in the hundred- and four-degree jacuzzi, broken up by cooling dips in the ninety-four-degree pool. Even though February nights in Las Vegas dipped into the thirties, you didn't notice it in the pool. Boy, did you notice it when you got out of the pool! Ray would eventually get out of the pool, and move to the living room sofa, where he would spend twenty minutes cleaning and rolling a large joint. Or two. Then it was only a question of whether to go out for a meal, then come back home and go to bed, or just go right to bed. Ray was known as "the Couch Iguana."

Another player was Bill Benter. Bill had been a physics student back in Pennsylvania. He looked like a former physics student, not ideal for a card counter. He'd had a further setback. A year or so earlier a casino called the Sundance opened on Fremont Street, east of the 4 Queens. It had high limits, and didn't bar anyone for the first month of operations. It was a trap. All the card counters in town played there, and all the while agents from the Griffin Detective Agency spied on them, and took notes. Ray had a friend named Mike Landers. He backed Mike. Mike was playing at the Sundance, and ran out of cash. He called Ray, and Ray asked Bill if he'd mind taking Mike some cash. Bill did, and when he handed it off to Mike, Griffin agents made note, describing Bill as a "card counting financier." Bill was pretty broke, so might have smiled at the "financier" description, but when he began getting barred all over town, he wasn't smiling.

The swimming pool at the house had a pair of water jets that snaked around, and kept it clean. They called them Oscars, and had "Oscar Wars" where they hosed each other with the high-powered streams. Bill told me of a brainstorm he had that, when they tested players they should make the candidate tread water in the deep end, while two guys sprayed him in the face from either side of the pool, and a third stood on the diving board pitching cards. If the candidate could keep the count, he was on the team.

Ray and Bill had a third roommate, Huey Hudson, a boyhood friend of Bill's. Huey wasn't on their team; he just lived there.

Another teammate, Miles Svoboda, lived with Marko, the sneering kid I'd met at Arthur's. Bill met Miles when they found themselves playing on the same table, raising and lowering their bets at the same time.

Finally, there was Frank DiCroce. Frank was a New Yorker who had learned to play in A.C. He was Italian, and when he played used a caricature of New York Italian as his disguise, shirt open to the third button, gold chains, Bronx accent. He would bring his girlfriend Linda along when he played, and she'd hang on him and do her own "New Yawk" dialogue with him.

There were two guys from another team who were friendly with everyone, Craig Brennan, and Darryl Purpose. They were hole card players. I will explain in more detail later, but it meant that they played games where they were able to see the dealer's hole card. Craig was a bit of a legend because he had gone into the Sundance to play a dealer. The dealer tightened up, and he couldn't see the card, but he had won money quickly, so he decided that rather than leave after only a few hands, he would wait until he lost two in a row. He sat there betting the table maximum, with no advantage, waiting until he lost two hands in a row. By the time he did, he cashed out up sixty-eight thousand dollars.

That drove Cathy crazy. Cathy Hulbert was Craig Chellstorp's girlfriend. She was a purist, and the thought of betting even fifty cents at a disadvantage gave her the willies. Craig Brennan just smiled when she brought it up.

Then there were the Australians, who were back in town. Besides Alan Woods there was John L, who would take his earnings back to Australia, and go into the tropical bird smuggling business. David Lang had trained in London as a race driver. Malcolm Sims was playing for New Zealand in the 1980 Bridge Olympiad, when he was recruited to play blackjack. He didn't believe you could beat a casino, so they offered to pay him ten bucks an hour, win or lose. He won fifty thousand dollars, and made a lot less than everyone getting normal splits. The next time he went for a normal split, and won sixty thousand dollars. Unfortunately, everyone else lost, so his hourly earnings weren't much better than the first time. He claimed that "Alan Woods has won one hundred thousand dollars in his blackjack career, and has a personal bankroll of one hundred and sixty thousand. I have won one hundred and sixty thousand, and I have a bankroll of … one hundred dollars."

Malcolm was recruited because Alan was also a bridge player, and knew Malcolm through bridge. Alan was playing for a team in Europe in 1980, near where the Olympiad was held, He suggested Malcolm to the man running the team, Paul Rylance. Paul was only half Australian, and had gone to high school in Liverpool with John Lennon. We were all at a party at Ray's and Bill's house, when I met the Australians. I was in the kitchen when introduced to Paul.

"I just finished reading *One-Third of a Shoe*. Ken Uston has pictures of himself in various get ups. In one he has long hair, and a full beard. You look just like him in that picture."

"Yes," said Paul, "Others have told me that."

"Did you grow the beard and hair as an homage to Uston?" It seemed a reasonable question. I figured every card counter wanted to be Ken Uston.

Paul's jaw dropped, and after a silent pause, he turned and stormed out of the kitchen. "How odd," I thought.

Two minutes later Cathy came running in. "Did you really ask Paul if he grew his beard as an homage to Uston?" I told her I did, and she whooped with laughter. "Didn't you know, Paul was Peter?" Not only was Paul in the book, but it turned out Cathy was "the girlfriend." She added that Uston made it sound like she was incompetent because he had no respect for women. In reality, "I was a better counter than Ken. Just ask Darryl, he was the team tester." Small world.

CHAPTER 6
THE TEAM IS LAUNCHED

There were eight of us in Arthur's living room. February had rolled over into March, and was somewhere between lion and lamb when Arthur returned from his vacation, and called the first team meeting. Two of the team members were old-timers, which meant they had played on at least one previous bankroll of Arthur's. You've met both. Marko, aka "the Dutchman," a university student from Holland, was one. The other was Mike, the player whose need for funds at the Sundance had made Bill Benter a marked man. Two were semi-experienced. One was my roommate, Timmy, who had played on the ill-fated bankroll with Munch and Craig. The other was a young guy named Jim McGinley. Jim had been playing on his own, but his bankroll was so small his living expenses exceeded his earnings. Two of us were new players. Besides me there was Huey, Bill Benter's buddy. Arthur was the seventh, and Munchkin, Timmy's and my ride, was the eighth.

Arthur explained how the bankroll worked. He was putting up forty thousand dollars. The unit size would be "half Kelly." John Kelly was a mathematician who came up with a formula designed to maximize earnings while minimizing risk. The actual formula is more complicated, but "bet your advantage" is an approximation. In other words, if your edge was two percent, you'd bet two percent of your bankroll. In the real world it was impossible to bet strict Kelly. What if your bet called for betting twelve dollars and thirty-seven and ninety-three hundredths' cents? What if you had negative expectation, as you would the first hand of a shoe? What if you had an edge, but were dealt a pair of eights and the dealer had ten, forcing you to split with a known disadvantage? In practice the betting would be "true minus one, in black." Translating once more, at a true +2, a .5% advantage, you would bet two minus one black chips, each worth one hundred dollars. Pure Kelly would call for one two-hundredth of your bankroll, and one two-hundredth of forty thousand was two hundred, so betting just one hundred was "half Kelly." Each true count was worth half a percent, so a true three called for three minus one, two black chips, a true four called to three black chips, and a true five called for four black chips.

Got all that? It gets slightly more complicated. Most of the time you would not have a true +2 or greater, and would have to bet the minimum. The minimum bet was a quarter, a green, twenty-five-dollar chip. The most you would bet was four hundred dollars, no matter how high the count went. In practice the maximum was usually going to be, not one hand of four hundred dollars, but two hands of three hundred dollars. That was because it was likely there would be other players at the table. The Cliff's Notes reason is that if you have, let's say, one deck's worth of extra high cards, and you are heads up against the dealer, playing two hands per round with you betting single four hundred, or three hands per round with you betting double threes, it ends up with you betting roughly the same total amount by the time the good cards are used up. If you have even one other player at the table, you are better off betting two hands, because you get more of the goodies. So instead of "one-hundred-dollar units," call it "double seventy-fives."

That bet scheme was what Mike and Marko would be betting. They were the old pros. Timmy and Jim were probationary, and would start by betting ten dollars off the top, then double quarters, maxing at double hundreds. Huey and I were on double secret probation, and would bet five bucks, then double tens, maxing at double fifties. We should also, Arthur said, Wong in and out. Wonging was a blackjack neologism named for author Stanford Wong, who advocated the method. You "Wonged in" to a game by standing near a table – back-counting – and when the deck was rich, sitting down and placing a large bet, without having bet a lot of minimums. In theory you would disguise your game by not showing them your bet spread, and earn more money by not betting into disadvantages. "Wonging out" was team policy; if the count became worse than true -1 you would leave that table and find another.

The team goal was to double the bankroll. When we won or exceeded forty thousand dollars, it would be time to "break the bank." As investor, Arthur would get half of the profits. The other half would be divided among us, forty percent based upon hours, and ten percent based on win. For instance, assuming we won exactly forty thousand after three hundred hours of play, and I had played seventy-two hours and won ten thousand of the forty thousand, my share would be twenty-four percent of sixteen thousand, and twenty-five percent of four thousand, or $4840. That's over $67 an hour, a lot more than I made driving cab. Though of course we'd have to win the money that quickly.

If you realized that this arrangement was unfair to Mike and Marko, because our hours were paid as much as theirs, even though we were betting less, you are sharper than we were.

There were more rules. Each player was to play a minimum of twelve hours a week. No tipping was allowed. Cover betting was only allowed to the extent of one to four. That is, if the count leaped you did not have to increase your bet all the way from minimum to maximum on one turn, you could quadruple it, then jump the rest of the way next time. Similarly, if you were betting the max at the end of a shoe you didn't have to drop all the way to the minimum for the first hand of the next shoe. Though moving to another table could solve that problem. Some other rules included not using bankroll money for rent, taxis, or what have you. Next meeting would be the following Friday.

Arthur distributed cash to each of us. I received a thousand dollars. Then Timmy, Munch, and I headed for a casino. Munch told us that while we might be tempted to hit the big casinos on the Strip, we should save them for when we were betting more money. Accordingly, we drove downtown, and went to the 4 Queens.

Las Vegas, especially in those days, was a surprisingly penny-ante town. The highest limits and highest rollers were at Caesar's Palace, where you could bet three thousand dollars. Some of the other major resorts had two-thousand-dollar limits, and a few had thousand-dollar limits, but of the six dozen casinos around town eighty percent had limits of five hundred or less. Some, like Foxy's Firehouse, with its twenty-five-dollar limits, a lot less. Players were described by the color of their action, black action denoting people who bet black, hundred-dollar chips, green for those using the twenty-five dollars chips, red for the fives, and silver for the dollar bettors. There were maybe three casinos in town, Caesar's, the Desert Inn, and possibly the Sands, where the dealers were not required to yell "checks play" if a player bet black chips. Some made the dealers call it out for green chips, and then if the player bet black, "Black action!" I am sure in a few toilets – we called them all toilets, e.g. "I was playing at Sands toilet" – I heard "checks play" when betting a couple of red chips. Caesar's had tables with three-dollar minimums allowed, though they weren't always open, red being the usual minimum. The others had one- or two-dollar minimums. You'd always see silver action, but in many casinos you could scour the tables and not see any black-chip players.

Downtown the highest limits were at the Horseshoe. When it opened the Sundance had offered higher limits, but I remember them as having a five-hundred-dollar limit by the time I moved to town. The Horseshoe boasted that it had the highest limits in Las Vegas. That was sort of true. There were famous cases where someone would through pre-arrangement with Benny Binion, come to town and make a huge wager. Once it was $777,000 on a pass-line bet on the crap table. There was also a policy that you could walk in off the street, and set your own limit with the first bet you made. But the posted limit was one thousand, and most of what you'd see on the layouts was red or silver. The Golden Nugget probably got the most action, most days. The 4 Queens was also a five-hundred-dollar club, and by Downtown standards high class.

It was a Friday evening, so it was busy. We spent a couple of hours

Wonging around. In the movies the young card counter goes to a casino for the first time, and right away starts betting hundreds or thousands of dollars, then walks out with wads of cash. I am not sure if I even managed to get a top bet, double fifties, out there. I finished stuck two hundred and forty-five dollars.

The next afternoon I returned to the 4 Queens vowing to punish them for that loss. It was slower in mid-afternoon, slow enough that I got a table to myself. I began playing and the very first shoe went hot. The count jumped, and it was time to make max bets. I had lost my buy-in, so I pulled out a one-hundred-dollar bill, got change, and bet two hands of fifty, stacks of red because that was the color I'd been betting, and the dealer didn't expect me to bet the whole thing. A second boss joined the first, and wrote something on a clipboard.

I lost both bets. I pulled out another bill, bought another stack of chips, and bet them all again. The boss with the clipboard made another note. Later, when I saw Munchkin, he explained that one of the jobs bosses do is record every hundred-dollar-bill dropped in the slots on the tables. Not knowing that, I had a strong sense of paranoia "Oh, no, they are onto me already," to go with the horror of losing consecutive max bets. Because I lost these next ones, and had to pull a third bill. This time, I got lucky, I only lost one bet, but I pushed the other, so I still lost fifty bucks.

The horror continued. Mercifully, because it was a four-deck shoe, it didn't last long. The cut card came out, and I staggered out into the sunlight, lightheaded. I had played ten minutes, and lost six hundred and fifty dollars. With last night's loss I was down eight-ninety-five. I had to find a payphone; to call Arthur and tell him I had lost almost all of the money he gave me. Including last night, I had only met the guy twice. What was he going to say? What was the penalty for someone on double secret probation losing all of their cash?

"Sounds like you've been fluctuating, the way you're supposed to. Come to the house, because you need more cash."

I went to his house, and he handed me three thousand dollars and told me I was obviously ready to bet more money. From now on I should bet the way Timmy and Jim were betting, ten-dollar minimum, double twenty-five-dollar units, maxing at double hundreds.

CHAPTER 7
GRINDING AWAY

Did I immediately rebound, start winning like the books implied I would? I did not. I did not lose every session, but I lost most sessions. I would book a winner, say eleven hundred, and think maybe I had turned a corner, only to lose five hundred, here, a thousand there, another three hundred somewhere else.

Twelve hours a week sounds like the life of Riley, but it was more of a grind than you'd imagine. I tried to find casinos that weren't completely packed. It seemed clear to me that I was responsible for playing in good games, and circling a packed pit, waiting for a seat at a crowded table to open up, didn't seem an honest way of earning money for the team. Though at least one of our guys saw things differently.

Malcolm was in the MGM one night. This was the original MGM, kitty-corner from Caesar's. It was then the largest casino in Las Vegas, with ninety blackjack tables, fifty percent bigger than the Mint downtown, whose sixty tables made it runner-up. The MGM dealt five-deck shoes. Yes, five. Single and double deck games were dealt by hand (though I once heard of a place that dealt double deck from a shoe). Las Vegas shoe games were mostly four-deck, though there were some six-deck games here and there. Eight decks had not yet come to town. Shoes with an odd number of decks were almost unknown. Almost, but not quite. The Orbit Inn, for instance, on Fremont Street at the eastern edge of downtown, dealt either a three- or a seven-deck shoe. I don't remember which, because they once barred Arthur for betting one to three in silver, so it was obviously a waste of time playing there. And whichever one they didn't deal, there was some other casino which did, thus, every possible number of decks from one to eight was tried somewhere.

Anyway, the MGM had five decks. It also, like Caesar's, offered double after splits, and surrender. Surrender we have talked about. Double after splits means that if you split, say, sevens against a three, and catch a four on one of your hands, you can then double down your eleven. Most casinos don't allow it, but it is good for the player. MGM was also a "good casino," in that it would take big action tolerably well. The downside was that the cut was two decks out of five. The deeper a casino deals, the better for the player, and generally speaking good penetration is much more important than good rules. MGM was still a playable game, but Marko was, according to Malcolm, who found it hilarious, "Backcounting a full table!" When this was brought up at a team meeting Marko was unabashed, "The count was really high! I was hoping a seat would open up." This style of play might not earn much money, but it kept Marko invisible to the casino, and free from heat.

Transportation was another reason it was hard to play. Munchkin worked full time, and used his car. Timmy had a car he would lend me when he wasn't using it. It was a 1968 Camaro convertible he called "the Red Rocket." It was a piece of shit. The plastic rear window was opaque, and the other windows didn't close properly, so it was filled with sand. It stalled at traffic lights.

One day I played at the Union Plaza. Rather than bother Munchkin I decided to walk home. Fremont angles, so I started walking southeast on it. Down near the Orbit Inn, and the cheap souvenir shops, I was hailed by a panhandling hustler. I was wearing a three-piece suit, and looked prosperous. I did have several thousand dollars in my pocket, but that was bankroll money. I told the guy I was very close to flat broke, which was very close to the truth. He sized me up, and as a hustler in Vegas had no doubt seen other sharply dressed people who were impecunious. He switched tacks, and asked if I had enough to afford blank press passes. They were just what they sound like; fill them out with your particulars, laminate them, and you were good to go. One was for Time, another for Playboy, a buck apiece. Who knows what secrets of life you might learn if you only stopped to smell the winos?

Home was further than I thought. Eleven miles it was, two hours and forty minutes, and major blisters on my feet. We were going to see a play that night featuring some friends, and I missed it. Last time I walked.

Losing also made it a grind. I asked Munchkin to come watch me play. I asked Arthur to come watch me play. I asked my teammates to come watch me play. I asked them all, "Am I doing something wrong?" To which they all told me I was playing just fine. Possibly betting slightly more conservatively than I should (constant losing was making me gun-shy), if they had to find a fault, but otherwise, the only thing they could tell me was that I was getting unlucky, "It will turn around."

But that was what it wasn't doing. I had been promoted to double fifties, with a double two hundred top bet, so was betting more, but enjoying it less. The windfall payday I envisioned was receding. It might have been a bit easier to bear if my teammates were raking it in, but collectively they were spinning their wheels.

CHAPTER 8
ODD WAYS OF MAKING ENDS MEET

had a couple of odd money-making opportunities come my way.

One afternoon Munchkin called me. He was at the Rainbow Club in Henderson. "When you see Timmy and Craig, tell them to get down here. They're paying three-for-two on sevens and elevens on the come-out roll."

Is that Greek to you? It meant nothing to me. I'd never played craps, and guessed whatever it was, was good, but that was all I got out of it. I was meeting Timmy and Craig for dinner, so when they came by the house, I repeated the message. They looked at each other, and said, "Naw, that can't be right. Where do you want to eat?"

We went to a place called Carlos Murphy's, where I had a Super Quesadilla. I don't care if they bring back Carlos Murphy's, but I wish someone would bring back the Super Quesadilla. Coming from Chicago I'd never heard of regular quesadillas. The Super Quesadilla covered a plate. Between two tortillas there was a heap of shredded beef, with onions, jalapenos, and plenty of cheese. On top of the quesadilla was a layer of salsa, more melted cheese, and more jalapenos. It was awesome.

"Want to see what's playing at Red Rock?" said Tim, after dinner. Red Rock was a multiplex on West Sahara.

"Maybe we should go to the Rainbow Club." I repeated Munch's message. Timmy and Craig once again agreed between them that I had gotten the message wrong, but what the heck, we could always go to the movies later.

Today the Las Vegas metro area sprawls south and east (and north and west) while Henderson has also grown significantly. Back then when you went south on Boulder Highway from Tropicana, there wasn't much to see. Eventually there was a road that cut due south from Boulder Highway, which you followed to get to downtown Henderson. Which looked like smalltown anywhere, except it had a few small casinos. One of them was the Rainbow Club, and it was celebrating its fifteenth birthday.

The Rainbow Club was small, and looked like the sort of casino you could find in downtown Las Vegas if you weren't afraid to venture off of Fremont Street after dark. Beyond the blackjack tables there was a crap table, and the crowd around it was thick. In the crowd were Munchkin and Ray.

Several hours earlier they'd been sitting at a blackjack table. As part of the fifteenth anniversary festivities the casino was paying two to one on blackjacks. That extra half bet was worth two and a half percent. You could flat bet, that is never vary your wager, and earn a net of two percent (don't forget that you started with a disadvantage of half a percent on the regular game) on your action. The table limit was fifty bucks, and if you bet two hands of the max, you were making two dollars every round. Even if the dealer only got through fifty rounds an hour, that was one hundred bucks. If you never varied your bet, who could say if you were a card counter?

Munchkin was looking around the casino, to see if other card counters were getting in on the action. He spotted David Sklansky. David wasn't a card counter. He could count cards, but that wasn't what he was known for. David was a poker expert. He had already written one book on poker, and contributed to another. Later that year he would pick up a couple of bracelets in events at the World Series of Poker. He knew what he was doing. The trouble was that what he was doing this day was not playing blackjack, he was playing craps. And so was another player who should have been on a blackjack table, a woman named Ann, who worked with Stanford Wong.

There was a mirror on the ceiling over the crap table, and Munchkin could see from his seat at the blackjack table what was on the craps layout. He heard a shout of approval, and saw that the roll was eleven, and the dealers were paying three to two. He did the math, and realized there was an edge, but it wasn't nearly as good as the one on the blackjack table. A few minutes later there was another shout, and this time the roll was seven, and once again the dealers were paying three to two.

"C'mon, Ray! We're going to play craps!"

There are many bets available to the craps player, but most players, even if they make side bets, make pass line bets. The come-out roll is the shooter's initial stab at making a pass. The two dice can total anywhere from two to twelve. If the shooter throws a two, three, or twelve, he loses. If he throws a seven or an eleven, he wins. Any other total is called a point. The shooter must hit his point again before throwing a seven; making the point wins, sevening out loses. Betting don't pass is the opposite of betting pass. Everything that wins for the pass bettor loses for the don't bettor, and everything that loses for the pass bettor wins for the don't pass bettor, except twelve (else the don't bettor would have an edge). For various reasons hardly anyone bets don't pass; it's even called "betting wrong," though the don't bettor is oh so slightly better off than the pass line bettor. The house, by paying three to two instead of even money on winning sevens and elevens, was offering the players a 9.7% edge. That's huge. There were fifteen sharp players betting fifty dollars each on the pass line, and one old man, obviously a local, betting two on the don't.

Craig jammed himself between two bettors, and dropped fifty on the pass line. It took Timmy awhile longer, but he eventually squeezed in. I was the last to get on. By the time I did the bonus had been operational for nearly six hours. The dice had been cold, and the table was breaking even, or even winning a bit. That changed just around the time we arrived. First Ann got the dice, and threw eleven straight passes. The next shooter threw two. Then Craig got the dice, and made seven passes.

While this was happening, the chip rack was emptied. There are procedures for doing what is called a fill. A set number of chips are brought to the table, and are carefully counted. The bosses sign off on the fill. It takes time. This time, though, the bosses panicked. The Rainbow Club had never seen so much action. They didn't understand what was happening, but they'd learned that in the long run the house won, so they were cracking the whip on the dealers, "get a roll!" Which meant, speed it up! Make the game go faster, so we can get into the long run. Them not understanding that right now, the faster the game, the faster they would lose. And when they ran out of chips, they used the same faulty logic, with extreme panic besides. I saw bosses run to blackjack tables (where there were also procedures for removing chips), grabbing armfuls of green, running them over to the crap table, and dumping them on the layout!

Some people, like Craig, got the idea it might be good to cash some chips. I wasn't on the game yet, so I went to the cage for him. A rack of green, one hundred quarter chips, is worth twenty-five hundred dollars, and unless you ask for smaller bills, you should get twenty-five crispy hundred-dollar bills. The cage ran out, and people were collecting twenties, and then collecting IOUs, because the till was empty.

But by then I was on the table, during Craig's run. He made his seventh pass, and they shut down the game. Craig, Munch, and Ray had won about fifteen hundred apiece. Timmy had won a thousand. I won two hundred and fifty.

There was an interesting question. Was the money I had won mine, or part of my team's? Since Munchkin and Ray had gone there specifically to play for their team, they treated their winnings as part of the team bankroll. I had to decide in advance what I was doing. Since my team's rules forbade playing other games, and I couldn't stop to call Arthur and see if this might be an exception, I decided that if I lost, I would have to eat the loss. That being the case, the win was mine. I did bring it up that week at the team meeting, explaining my logic. Arthur agreed, but said that if something like this happened again, call. I'm sure he would have been in his Firebird, foot to the floor, all the way to Henderson.

I should mention a time Arthur played craps, because it illustrates some things about professional gamblers. One day Arthur and another counter, an older player known as Uncle Will, were walking through Bob Stupak's Vegas World. That's the one known as the Stratosphere today. Stupak liked to offer exotic games to attract business. Many were concocted by Howard Grossman, who knew what he was doing. But anyone can make a mistake, and Art and Will hoped they might spot something they could take advantage of.

I don't know who was in the showroom, but it was an act they wanted to see. In those days every showroom had the same pricing scheme. They were laid out like nightclubs, even big rooms like the one at the Hilton which seated fifteen hundred. Whether you were seeing Cosby at the Hilton, Johnny Carson at the Sahara, or the Lido Show at the Stardust, for $17.95 you got two drinks and for $19.95 you got three.

They walked up to a dead crap game, and Art asked the boss, "If I bet a thousand on the pass line, will you comp us to the show?" A thousand was the table limit at Vegas World, and a glance around revealed no limit bettors in sight. The boss said, "Sure."

Arthur dropped ten hundreds on the pass line, established his point, threw a few more times, and sevened out. The dealer scooped up his bills, while Arthur reminded the boss, "My comp?" The boss wrote out a comp for two for the show, and that was that.

A pass line bet has an edge for the casino of 1.414%. Bet a thousand and your average loss is $14.14. Two show tickets cost $39.90, so Arthur made a profit of $25.76. True, he lost a thousand dollars, but he might have won a thousand. His possible results on the one-time bet, of being $1014.14 ahead, or $985.86 behind, are what the mathematicians call variance, or Arthur called fluctuation.

That story demonstrates three things about a professional gambler. First, Arthur knew the odds of a pass line bet. Knowing them was a tool in his tool kit. Professionals know what they need to know. Second, he did some math to conclude that by betting and getting comped, in the long run he would come out ahead. The math wasn't hard; the important thing is the mindset that looks for situations where a bit of math might reveal a profitable opportunity. Finally, Arthur was psychologically prepared to accept losing his thousand-dollar bet. Dealing with variance is among the hardest parts of professional gambling. Not everyone can do it. If you learn to do it, it lets you deal with losses. You won't like them, but you'll live with them. It also takes a lot of the fun out of winning. Some people can't stand that.

Another chance to make money on the side came from Arthur. He called one morning and said that if Timmy and I were interested in a few hours work, we should head over to the Desert Inn.

The room we were sent to was a suite. It was a two-story structure on the grounds behind the main tower. The first floor had a dining area, a living room, and a kitchenette. There was a stair leading to a loft bedroom above the living room. Inside the room was Chuck, leader of the Czech Team, and his girlfriend Sri.

You may remember the Czechs as rivals to the Uston Team in *One Third of a Shoe*? You might expect Chuck and Sri to be Czech, but they weren't. The only Czech was named Vladimir, who dropped by that afternoon, but Vladimir was so hot that they wouldn't risk him showing his face anywhere near the casino. He told a story about landing at an airport once – might have been in Sri Lanka – and they told him they knew who he was, and he wasn't wanted. "I've been barred from lots of casinos, but this was the first time I was barred from a whole country." Vladimir was Czech, but Chuck was an American from Burbank, Illinois. Even his ethnic background was Lithuanian, not Czech. Nor was Sri Czech; she was Thai.

Chuck was in no hurry to send us to the casino. We'd be paid ten dollars an hour for our time, and the clock was already running, but we would also get a free lunch. Chuck's comp was "full RFB and air." RFB stood for Room, Food, and Beverage. The suite was free, and while we weren't going to be ordering Champagne before working, we were urged to order surf and turf. In those days, steak and lobster was considered the top of the gourmet pyramid, and soon room service had sliced up a cow, boiled a bunch of lobsters, and iced up that Champagne of soft drinks, Coca Cola.

I didn't know about video players back then. They weren't common. Chuck's suite had one, and he showed movies while we dined. Later, on the way home, Timmy told me how appalled he was.

"How could he show pornography? While we were eating! And in front of a lady!"

"Timmy, Sri was the one who kept laughing, pointing, and saying, 'Look at that!'"

We finished our lunch just about when the big player showed up. That was the game we'd be playing, big player call-in, just like in Uston's first book. Our big player looked like a young Tom Selleck. He wore an expensive looking three-piece suit, as though he'd stepped out of the boardroom and was looking for action. Timmy, Sri, and I would be the counters. We would wait until we had at least a true three, and then light a cigarette – we all smoked in those days – to signal a hot shoe. The player would come to the table, and we would signal the count, the number of fingers scratching our arm, and where on the arm we scratched, would give him the running count. When he came to the table, we'd leave, and find another seat to start the process over.

Chuck was also in the casino. Chuck was probably hotter than Vlad, but he wanted to keep an eye on things, and direct traffic. He wore an untrimmed grey toupee, glasses with thick black frames that looked like they needed a fake nose and moustache to complete them, a light blue smock, and carried a plastic bucket for change. He looked like a Jerry Lewis character if Jerry had ever played a degenerate slots player. He lurked in the banks of machines, trying not to show too much of himself where the pit could see him. If you wandered close, he would suddenly pop out and say, "Try that table over there."

The first time the BP came to my table, I lingered long enough to see what he did. He dug in his pocket, and pulled out a fistful of purple chips, then stacked four each on two betting squares, double two-thousands!

Back in the suite a couple of hours later, he emptied out his pockets, producing a pile of five-hundred-dollar purple chips. Chuck counted them, "Sixty-five," i.e. thirty-two thousand five hundred dollars. "Yeah, I lost five hundred."

Chuck paid Timmy and me forty dollars apiece. Then he pulled me aside. "You've got a really good look. Are you interested in being a BP?" He told me that he made three hundred thousand dollars a year. One-third was the value he put on the RFB, one-third was blackjack winnings, and one-third was air fare. The big player was the one who received the comp, but Chuck was the one who used it. He had no fixed address, and only stayed in comped rooms. The BP also bought a round-trip, first-class air ticket from somewhere like New York City. In those days tickets were still paper, and were fully refundable. The BP would present the paper ticket to his casino host. They never asked for boarding passes. The casino would reimburse the price of the ticket, which would later be turned in for a refund, since no flights were taken. I knew a guy who used to come out from Washington D.C. and stayed in four or five casinos each trip, collecting air fares from all of them. Meanwhile, even though he'd purchased a first-class ticket, he flew on a second ticket, coach.

Chuck didn't tell me what I could make as his BP. I told him I would think about it, but I had already decided that his BPs had very short shelf lives. There were stories about Chuck. The time he was playing at Caesar's, betting three thousand a hand, when he spotted a familiar face. He got up and walked into the pit, where customers weren't supposed to be. He walked over to the podium, bent over, and examined the photo taped there. Yep, it was a wanted poster with his picture and name. Then he walked back to his stool and kept playing. There were other stories, about how instead of swiping an ashtray or towel, he went in the maid's closet and took a vacuum cleaner, which he disassembled and packed in his suitcase. This was while staying in a room under the big player's name. I thought I'd stick with Arthur.

CHAPTER 9
MY SIDELINE

Opportunities like playing for Chuck, or at the Rainbow Club, were too rare to count on. Luckily, I had a more regular source of income. I played backgammon.

When I left Chicago, I had been playing for two and a half years. In the pond that was Butch Maguire's, where we played every Sunday, I was a mighty big fish. My buddy John and I convinced the management to let us revive Sunday tournaments less than three months after I started playing. I quickly improved to where I was about as good as John. We started a points race based upon tournament results. In 1980 he was number one, and I was a close number two, with no one else particularly close to us in the standings. In 1981 it was the same, but this time I was number one, and he was number two. In the chouettes, a form of gambling on backgammon similar to King of the Hill, we started playing for fifty cents or a dollar a point. Two years later it was three dollars a point. The two of us were the big winners from the start, and remained so, even as the tournament began to draw better and more experienced players.

Butch's was a small pond. A club called Gammon's of Chicago opened in December of 1979. The best players in Chicago were out of action. Timmy, Craig, and Munch were in Las Vegas. Greg DeFotis and

Bobby Anderson got jobs as traders. What was left wasn't much. Chicago would become a backgammon power in the nineties, but it wasn't then. The players on the coasts would have laughed at the top players from Chicago. The top players did not include me. There were at least a half dozen players who were better, and plenty more who were roughly as good. I was a lot better than the casual home players, but among serious players I was nobody. That was about to change.

Living with Timmy and Munchkin helped, especially Timmy. Timmy Wisecarver was from Evanston, and was ten years older than me, almost to the day. He was very thin, with a pointed chin and pointed nose, thinning hair, and wire-rimmed glasses. One look and you'd guess that he'd been nicknamed "the professor" ever since kindergarten. He'd gotten a degree in Latin and classical Greek. Then he was drafted. In Vietnam, a junior lieutenant, he was riding in a jeep when it ran over an explosive device. I don't think his body received any permanent injuries, but I can't say the same for his psyche. Many times I walked up to him while he was deep in thought, stood right in front of him, and said, "Timmy?" And he would leap into the air, shudder like a kite in a gale, and scream, "Don't do that!"

When he got back from Vietnam he stopped in San Francisco, where he took up playing rubber bridge. That's money bridge, not tournament bridge, and he was good enough to support himself. When the backgammon craze hit, among the first places to take it up were bridge clubs. Timmy learned to play, and got very good very quickly. He moved back to Chicago around 1974, discovered the North Club, another bridge club where the backgammon players dwelt, and established himself as the best player in town. In 1976, convinced he was supposed to do something respectable; he took a job at a prep school in the east. He lasted one school year. By the time he came back he found to his dismay that a handful of players had passed him up.

He may not have been a world-class player, but he was a very good player. He was also a diligent student of the game. His name is immortalized in the Wisecarver Paradox, a discovery he made while poring over five hundred pages of computer printout, which he stored in one of our kitchen cabinets.

When I turned up, I became a project of his. On me he could

unleash pent up backgammon learning, and his instinct for teaching. He had a collection of recorded backgammon matches. We would play through them, deciding what we might have played, looking at what the expert player had done over the board, and discussing it if we differed.

One of the players who passed up Timmy while he was in the east was Craig Chellstorp. Craig was a former US Junior Chess Champion (succeeded the following year by another Chicago backgammon player, Greg DeFotis). Timmy took Craig under his wing when he moved to Chicago from San Francisco. By the time he returned from teaching in the east, his wings might still have been eagle-sized, but Craig was turning into a backgammon condor. By the time 1982 rolled around, though not well known (he preferred a low profile), Craig had become one of the best players in the world.

From 1978 to 1986 there was a tournament with the world's biggest prize, which was held in Las Vegas once or twice a year. There were three levels, a "world championship," open to anyone, a beginner's tournament open to people who had never won as much as two hundred and fifty dollars in a tournament, and the "world's amateur championship," also known as the Plimpton Cup, after George Plimpton, the author and non-professional athlete who wrote books about playing with professional sports teams. The Plimpton Cup was open to anyone who had never won one thousand dollars in a tournament, and did not make their living playing backgammon. The first prize was one hundred thousand dollars, second prize fifty thousand, and so on down to the final eight.

Craig had a proposal. He would teach a group of us; in return he'd receive ten percent of any money we won. Besides me and Cathy, three of the Australians, Alan, David, and Malcolm, were in town, and interested. Timmy and Munchkin were no longer eligible to play in the Plimpton, but they sat in on the sessions. We met twice a week, for a minimum of two hours per session, though they often went longer. Craig was not only a great player, but proved to be an excellent teacher, and the three months or so that we met were like a graduate course in backgammon theory.

Finally, there was Max. Michael Maxakuli had short limbs attached to a long, broad torso. He needed a solid frame to support his head. He had hair that would bend the teeth of a steel comb, a pirate's moustache, and eyebrows that threatened to sting if you got too close. He looked like a king of the Romani, but was "Albanian-Greek, like John Belushi." Max was so swarthy he made Belushi look like Brad Pitt. He was born in Albania around the time the war ended. His said his father was in the resistance, trying to do to the communists what he'd been recently doing to the Nazis. With less success, given the fate of Albania. Max and his mom went ahead to Canada when he was still an infant. Then when his father joined them, they continued migrating until they reached Milwaukee.

Around the time he turned thirty he was managing a hotel for his father, which went broke. Max sunk into a deep depression. He was living with a former Miss Milwaukee named Linda Kreugel, who urged him to move to Las Vegas where his best friend was living.

The friend was Ned Day, Jr., son of the famous bowler. Ned was a reporter for the Review-Journal, and the following story may be a digression, but is too good not to tell. Ned reported on crime and politics – in Vegas, usually the same thing. One day a man who worked for one of the wire services came to town. His name was Balls Barnes, and he was there to do a story on Tony Spilotro. Tony the Ant was in Vegas representing the Outfit's interests, though if you have seen the movie *Casino*, where the character played by Joe Pesci was based on him, you know how that worked out. Tony got his start collecting for Mad Sam DeStefano, a killer so crazy and vicious even his bosses were afraid of him. Once while collecting a debt for Mad Sam, Tony stuck the recalcitrant debtor's head in a vice, squeezed until his eyeballs popped out, then took a can of Ronson's lighter fluid, sprayed it over the man's face, and lit it.

When Balls Barnes said he wanted to know where Tony hung out, so that he could follow him, Ned told him he'd show Balls the outside of a certain bar, but he, Ned, was not going to follow Tony the Ant.

"The way he got the name Balls," Ned told me, "Was early in his career, when he was on the Africa beat. He got to sit down with Idi Amin. The first thing he said to him was, "Mister President, I've interviewed killers before, but you're the first one who ate his victims.""

Anyway, moving to Las Vegas and hanging out with Ned didn't help enough. Max spent his time lying on the sofa in his apartment. Linda discovered backgammon, brought home a board, and taught Max the game, thinking it might take his mind off his troubles. Max became obsessed. He went looking for someone to play besides Linda, and was outraged when he learned there was no backgammon club. "This is the gambling capital of the world! How could it not have a backgammon club?"

He started one, in a bar in the middle of the Strip. The bar was called Dirty Sally's, later Rumors. To promote the club, Max published a newsletter. Within a few years it had become a magazine, with an international circulation. Celebrities would call the club looking for lessons. Max figured he could teach and how would a Bill Cosby or Phyllis McGuire know whether or not he was qualified? Among the stars who appeared on the cover of the Las Vegas Backgammon Magazine were Jim Brown and Tina Turner.

I first met Max in Chicago. The annual Chicago Open drew players from around the country. Max had a backer, a Beverly Hills coin dealer named Joel, who shared his action in high stakes games. They strutted around in silk suits, and soon Max sat down to play another silk suit strutter, a local restauranteur named Freddie. The stakes were one hundred dollars a point, and at one point Max was up one hundred points. Then he lost it all back on a single game, ten thousand dollars gone just like that. These guys all carried rolls of money like the one sported by Cameron Mitchell at the end of *How to Marry a Millionaire*. I told myself that someday I would have a silk suit, and a roll of bills making a bulge in my pocket.

Max's name had come up one Christmas before I moved to Las Vegas. My brothers flew in every year, and Munch told us that the night before he'd lost fourteen thousand dollars playing backgammon. The money he lost belonged to a poker player known as CK, short for Crazy Kid.

One legendary adventure of CK's started when a friend spotted him watching a high stakes poker game. "Why aren't you playing? That looks like your meat."

"I'm tapped," his friend said. "Here," and handed him ten thousand dollars. An hour into the game CK said, "Hey, everyone, I will give you each a hundred dollars if we make the game one hundred-two hundred." Everyone likes free money, so they doubled the stakes. Another hour, and a similar offer, to make it two hundred-four hundred. At the twenty-four-hour mark the stakes were one thousand-two thousand, and CK was playing heads up with Major Riddle. After thirty-six hours the game broke up; he had won two hundred and ten thousand dollars, so after paying the backer he had one hundred and five thousand personal profits. Three days later he was broke.

CK enlisted my brother's services during the World Series of Poker. In those days the Horseshoe hosted the event. It would yank a few banks of slots, and put in poker tables. It had no regular poker room. The top poker players were treated like stars. One of the things they got away with was counting cards in the casino. CK didn't know how to count, so he asked Munchkin to sit at the table with him, and tell him how to play. While they played, there was a loud crash, someone yelled, "They are machine-gunning the casino!" Panic ensued.

It turned out that security had ejected a drunk, who threw a brick through the window in retaliation. The drunk was caught near the Sundance, a block or so from the Horseshoe, surrounded by Horseshoe security guards, and shot dead. Everyone knew that it was Teddy Binion who shot him, but officially the murder remains unsolved.

In December CK made another score, and had forty grand to play with. He went to the backgammon club, and played Max, losing over ten thousand dollars. The next night he lost again. The third night he told Munch he would back him. Munch told CK that it was a bad deal. He wasn't sure that he was a better player than Max, and whoever was better, half the win versus none of the loss was great for Munch, but would be terrible for CK. CK said he didn't care. Munch and Max played for four hundred a point, and when Munch lost thirty-five points, CK said, "I'm tapped."

By the time I moved to Las Vegas, the backgammon club had lost its longtime home at Rumors. The club met only on Sunday nights, at the Jockey Club in a condominium tower south of the Dunes. There was a tournament, run by Linda, with some of the grunt work, carrying boards and the like, done by a young friend of Max's named

Costa. One night after the tournament, Max and I were talking. Max liked to talk even more than I did, something my friends would have a hard time believing. When the Jockey Club was ready to lock up its lounge, Max wanted to keep talking, so he invited me over to his house.

Max's car was as flamboyant as the rest of him, a Citroen DS with the vanity plate GAMMON. He and Linda lived in Green Valley, a new development between Las Vegas and Henderson, a few miles southeast of Munch's condo. It was three in the morning when we got to his place, a sprawling ranch house. Linda was asleep, but threw on a robe and came to greet us. Half awake, she asked me if I wanted sandwiches. I demurred, but she ignored that, and returned a few minutes later with a plate of sandwiches. This turned out to be her standard greeting, no matter what time I came to the house.

Max was full of offbeat opinions. Among them, that *The Wanderers* was the greatest movie ever made. He collected movies, mostly midget movies. You wouldn't think there were all that many midget movies. There was *The Wizard of Oz*, and besides that? He was impressed that I had heard of *The Terror of Tiny Town*, a 1930s Western with an entire cast of little people. I think Max claimed to have one hundred titles, god knows why. He was prejudiced against Hawaiians. He said, "You can tell a lot about a culture by what they eat, and Hawaiians are the only ones who managed to fuck up pork!" And, "In a thousand years, the only thing Hawaiians invented was the nose flute."

I also got to hear the story about CK losing all that money. Max had forgotten Munchkin was part of the tale, but otherwise it was the same story. With a twist. After Max won the last of his money, CK told him, "I want to thank you." Max asked, "For what?" "Three days ago I had forty thousand dollars. I went out, bought an ounce of coke, got a couple of hookers. After that, I didn't know what to do with myself. I was sleeping all day, wandering around in a daze. But now? Now I am broke. Know what I'm gonna do? I am going to get a good night's sleep. Tomorrow I will get up early, go out and find a backer, get in a game, and make some money!"

Max knew a lot of poker players, and got to talking about cheating stories he'd heard from them. "Sometimes they would slip the mark some truth serum. Not sodium pentothal, another one."

"Scopolamine?"

"That's it! Oh my god, I can't believe you knew that. You're a genius! You have to edit my magazine."

That's how I became a magazine editor. There was no pay, other than all the sandwiches I could eat. Which was about what I was worth. My schedule was flexible, and the workload light. I dropped by once or twice a week and proofread something or other. Linda and one of her girlfriends had by now been putting the magazine together for years, and continued to do so. They'd hand me something to review, I'd find a quiet place, they find my quiet place, ask if I wanted sandwiches, and what I wanted on TV. Every room in the house had a television, and neither Max nor Linda could imagine someone occupying a room in which the television wasn't on. So after I said I wasn't hungry, and didn't want to watch anything on TV, the first thing they'd do is to grab the remote and tune in whatever they would watch, and then go make me some sandwiches.

One night I was in the living room, papers spread all over the sofa. The living room being too obvious a hiding place, neither Max nor Linda had found me. Whatever I was working on required more concentration than usual, though I was and am good at tuning out the sights and sounds of a TV. Then the doorbell rang. In trooped half a dozen people who announced that they had *The Texas Chainsaw Massacre*. They'd rented the movie, though at the time I didn't know renting movies was a thing people could do. The living room was where Max had his projection set up. Next thing I knew they had killed the lights and I was surrounded by people. As long as they didn't sit on my papers, I didn't mind too much, and when they started screaming, I would look up and see Leatherface was up to his tricks again.

One of the benefits of working for Max was that I got to read his backgammon library. He had what may have been the most complete collection then in existence. There were one hundred and three English-language books by then, and he had one hundred of them. He had copies of most of the magazines and newsletters. He also had drawers full of submissions, some unpublished. Two came in handy after I read my way through it all.

Max had fallen behind in preparing the next issue of LVBM, while he'd brainstormed an idea for a club. Among the benefits, let's say a member was playing in the World Championship in Monaco, and their next opponent was a German player, Herman Munster. The member could call for a scouting report on Herman. Another benefit would be a magazine for members. To publicize the club, and to make up for not having a new issue of the regular magazine ready, Max asked me to create the new magazine, and he'd mail that one out to all of the LVBM subscribers.

Magazines and newsletters then were long on social news, and short of technical material. You could get reports on where the latest tournaments were held, and who attended. But articles on how to improve your game were in short supply. Most of what there was featured elementary material. The Las Vegas Backgammon Magazine ran an irregular feature called "The Amazing Captain Cube." Most were written by a local player named David Eig, though Timmy, who hated being called Captain Cube, wrote an above average entry. The magazine I wanted to read would be all technical material, and I set out to create it.

Its name was The Backgammon Scholar. I found an article by Dr. Edward Thorp, and knew I had to publish it. It was actually simple stuff, explaining the math behind taking a double when the opponent has two checkers left, on his five and his two, and is only a 19 to 17 favorite. But it was Thorp! There was another article which was the sort of thing you'd expect Thorp to have written. It was by a pair of mathematicians named Keeler & Spencer, which solved proper cube action in an infinite game. It had no practical application, and was pure mathematics, but it was long, which helped fill the magazine, and boy, did it look scholarly! It had the integration and summation symbols, which weren't in Linda's toolkit when it came time to do the layout. She asked if she could use "f" for the integration, and I forget what for the capital sigma. I explained that wouldn't work, though it was creative thinking, so she drew them in.

For the rest I wrote an introduction, annotated a long game, and created a quiz, for which I did the analysis. This was my first backgammon writing. It would not be the last. Though it would be a long time until I did more writing. The first issue of the Backgammon Scholar was also the last, and was the last issue of anything published by Max. His fall comes a bit later.

Some other things Max did for me were much more remunerative. He got me my first student. The world of top poker players was much smaller then, and several of them played at the Jockey Club. Chip Reese was an extremely strong backgammon player. He was also considered by his peers to be possibly the best all-around poker player, even though some of them had won the big event at the World Series, while he'd only won side events. Two of the world champions were Stu Ungar and Puggy Pearson.

Stuey was a card-playing prodigy. He grew up in New York, where his dad was a bookie, watching his father and his father's friends play gin. Legend has it that when his father had to take a phone call one day they let Stuey play for him, and by the time the phone call ended it was already clear that Stuey was the better player. He was twelve. A mutual friend, years later, claimed that by the time Stu was fourteen he couldn't get a regular game, and so challenged the world's best player of some Persian variant – which Stuey had never played – to a game. He lost the first day or so, but by the end of day two was crushing the Iranian expert. Whether or not some of the stories about him were apocryphal, he was undeniably not only the best player of his era, but so much better that he had to give even the best players huge spots to get them to play him. With no gin action, he took up poker. Stuey was three months younger than I am, and by the time I moved to Las Vegas, he had already won the World Series of Poker twice. As a backgammon player, he wasn't as good as Chip, but he was much better than people thought, even coming in second in the professional championship held during the Plimpton.

Puggy Pearson was one of the Texas players, a group which included Amarillo Slim and Doyle Brunson. Max told me Puggy was a fourth-grade dropout, and it was possible he didn't actually know how to read. But "If you dropped him and Paul Magriel [Paul was a genius, and I do not use that term lightly] in the middle of a desert, who do you think would walk out alive?" Puggy had a flat nose, someone must have flattened it for him, and the eyes of a shark. He was not a good backgammon player.

Better than Puggy, though not more than an intermediate, was Nicky Vacchiano. Nick wasn't as good a poker player as any of them. He was second- or third-tier. But he claimed, and I believed him, to have been on the road with Minnesota Fats when he was sixteen. Of Fats he said the secret was that Fats was, "A card player with the pool players, and a pool player with the card players." He had no illusions about who he could beat and who he could not beat, and knew how to use others' egos to his advantage. So did Nicky. Nicky could beat most people at pool, and only played the ones he could beat. He could beat most people at "short cards," variants of gin, and only played the ones he could beat. In the poker room, he might not be in the $100-$200 game with Chip and the others. He'd be playing in the $50-$100 game with the rich fish. When it came to backgammon, he would not play backgammon with me or Munchkin, not even for five bucks a point. Unless we wanted to "play cards, an hour of cards for each hour of backgammon." He smiled, I smiled back, and we stayed friendly by staying out of each other's games.

Then there was Vartan. Vartan Sarkisian was in his fifties, and might have been called bearlike if his hair hadn't gone grey. I don't know if he played any poker – if he did, he would have been terrible at it – but he hung out with the poker players. I never asked what, if anything, he did. If I had to guess I would have figured he was a bookie. If you didn't know what someone did, that was a good guess. Even guys famous for other things, like Billy Incardona, another player at the club, who was a five-time nine ball champion, according to Nicky the best ever, was a bookie.

Max told me that the poker players, when they played backgammon with each other, used money spots. For instance, if Chip played Vartan he might spot him $1.50. That meant that for every dollar Chip lost, he had to pay $1.50. And it was cumulative. Here's the difference. Suppose the spot was figured only at the end. Then if Chip won 24 points, and lost 20, he'd collect 4 points. But a cumulative – "rolling," they called it – spot meant that if Chip won 24, but lost 20,

Vartan would win 30, and collect a net of 6 points. It's a huge spot. Chip gave Vartan, Nicky, and Puggy spots of anywhere from $1.40 to $1.50. Stuey was spotting them $1.30 to $1.40. I think Nicky played Puggy even up, and spotted Vartan $1.05. Somewhere along those lines. Max and Vartan planned that Vartan would secretly take lessons, and then with those spots would clean up. I was drafted to teach Vartan.

My game had already improved so much, so quickly, that I was ready for a student, and teaching is a great way to improve one's own knowledge of a subject. I was being paid ten dollars an hour, a bargain rate, but I wasn't as good a player, and nowhere near as good a teacher, as Paul Magriel, who when he wasn't teaching Saudi Arabian royalty for astronomical rates, was charging ordinary mortals a couple of hundred bucks an hour. (Though Paul was a born teacher, and a generous guy, who trained up the next generation of experts, gratis.) And considering how my blackjack was progressing, I was happy to earn ten bucks an hour.

Vartan was a nice guy, but a poor student. Week one I would teach him some basic things. Week two he would make the very same errors, and I'd say, "Vartan, remember ...." Week three I would say it with a note of asperity. Week four and I don't think I ever whacked him in the head and said, "Pay attention!" But from my raised voice I am sure he knew I was considering it.

One day Max was ranting about one of his pet peeves. There were cocky young players at the club, who would win money from those less blessed with backgammon knowledge and talent, and then rub it in by telling the fish how badly they played. Max had general complaints about their deportment, and specific ones about their lack of gratitude to him, for his backstage role in keeping them alive.

"A kid like David wins five hundred dollars. Who stops Frankie from taking it off him in the parking lot? Me, that's who!" Frankie was known as "Frankie the Fist," not only because he used to box. Frankie managed to earn a place in the Nevada Gaming Commission's Black Book, people who were barred for life from every casino in the state. Tony the Ant made it, and so did Frankie. Frankie showed up at the hearing in a rented tux, and when the reporters asked him why, he said he had "never received an honor before," and thought he should dress for the occasion. "Or what about Vartan?" continued Max. "You don't think the bartenders at the Jockey Club treat him with such deference just because he tips five bucks for a cup of coffee?"

"Vartan tips five bucks for a cup of coffee!?"

Max waved that off as irrelevant. "No, it's because before he stopped drinking he was known as 'Tom the Bomb.'"

"What?"

"You knew that back in Buffalo he was a capo for the Magaddino Family?"

I realized it was time to reconsider my pedagogy.

The most remunerative thing Max did for me was steer me to games at the club. He'd make the introductions, and in between tournament matches, I had lots of side action. It didn't all pan out. I played an older woman from Michigan named Rona Rose for forty dollars a point, splitting the action with Max. I received a personal check for five hundred dollars, for which I had to open a bank account so I could deposit it, before I could obtain cash. It bounced. Everyone else was good as gold. Especially Chris. Chris was in his forties, and must have loved Elvis when he was in high school, because he still had the haircut. I don't think Chris worked. Rumor had it that he had a rich girlfriend. He occupied his time playing a game called pan, and on Sunday nights played backgammon. The first time or two we played, for five dollars a point, I won around two hundred each time. After that he would only play me for two dollars a point, then still lose about two hundred dollars every time. It's hard to lose one hundred points! Managing it every week took special talent.

Having a winning night on Sunday meant the difference between TV dinners, and going out to Burger King the rest of the week. The need to win focused the mind, and really sharpened my game.

CHAPTER 10
THE WHOLE TRUTH

There came the day when Arthur told me that I had reached elite status; I was cleared to bet the maximum, double three-hundreds. I went to the Riviera, and soon the big moment arrived. I put out two bets of three hundred dollars. I was dealt a six-four on one hand, and a pair of fives on the other. The dealer had a ten showing. Basic strategy when you have a total of ten, and the dealer shows ten, is to hit. But the index number is plus four, and my count exceeded that. I doubled both hands, and caught a five on one and a four on the other. The dealer flipped over another ten, and scooped up my money, twelve hundred dollars. I lost three thousand dollars that session, which meant I was stuck fourteen thousand dollars since I started playing for Arthur.

"I have good news, and bad news. The good news is I got to bet double threes. I even got to double them! The bad news is I lost the hand, and three thousand altogether."

"You don't have to worry about betting double threes anymore; the bankroll can't afford it."

Arthur called a halt to play, while we regrouped. At the next team meeting he explained that he was refinancing. At the time it was rumored that just three players in blackjack history had accumulated a million or more from their play. One was Ian Anderson, the mysterious author of *Turning the Tables on Las Vegas*. Another was a man named John. The story was that John made his million, but by then was too well known by the casinos. He had plastic surgery to change his appearance, then decided to play single deck at Caesar's. The single deck game had Strip rules, plus double after splits, and surrender. It was worth +.2% off the top. John was taking up an entire table, betting seven hands of the limit, twenty-one thousand dollars a round. If he played perfectly, even without spreading his bets he stood to make forty-two dollars per round. The trouble was the enormous variance. He lost three hundred thousand dollars, got nervous, and went looking for teams to play for. He joined ours. I saw John at one of our team meetings but can't remember if I spoke with him. That was one of the problems with the team, players coming and going. There were dozens of players who made guest appearances, then vanished during that interminable bankroll.

The third millionaire was a multi-millionaire, if word of mouth was accurate. He was said to be worth two million dollars, my old friend Chuck, from the Czech Team. Chuck was refinancing us, but there was a condition or two. The immediate condition was that we all take polygraph tests.

Mine was scheduled for early one morning. I hadn't been on a day schedule in nearly a decade, but other than lack of sleep, I wasn't concerned. I had actually taken a previous polygraph. In 1970, the summer I turned seventeen, I was pulled over for a traffic violation – one corner of my license plate was turned up – and because we had pot in the car, my buddy tossed some lids out the window before I pulled over. My dad, who represented us, didn't believe our story, that it was a frame up, and sent us to John Reed & Associates, on Michigan Avenue. Reed had been a developer of the machine, and they were supposed to be the best in the business.

The examiner started the session by playing a card trick. I was to pick a card, then he would go through the deck twice, while I said "no" to each card. He would try to pick my card, and success would show that I was a good candidate for the lie detector. He picked my card, but while I lied to the five key questions, he said I had told the truth to all but two. I was surprised but didn't see anything ominous about that prior result. After all, I had nothing to hide, so nothing to worry about.

The examiner, a young man who looked like an off-duty cop, started out by asking background questions. Some would be used as controls, e.g. my name, my age, etc. Others would be key questions, and included whether I had stolen money from the team, whether I had made unauthorized borrowings, for instance for cab fare, or rent? Had I violated team policies? Had I tipped? I had, and he wanted to know how much. I couldn't say. "More than three hundred?" "Three hundred!? No, less than five dollars." A few times I had tipped the cocktail waitress when she brought me a Coke, using a fifty-cent piece I'd gotten when a blackjack was paid to an odd-dollar bet. I also confessed to having sometimes failed to jump or cut my bets as aggressively as team policy called for. He then did the same card trick I'd experienced twelve years before, and correctly guessed my card.

We went through the test twice, and then he told me he had to leave the room for a few minutes. I should use the time thinking about whether I wanted to change any answers. When he returned, he asked again if I wanted to change any answers. I said I didn't, and we went through it once more. "Are you *sure* you don't? Because I think you have lied to all of my questions. I will have to report that to Mister Goldberg, and tell him I think you stole the fourteen thousand."

"You tell him whatever you want, but I can't change any answers because I would be lying if I did!"

I stumbled out of there, blinking in the morning sunlight. My heart was pounding, my ears were ringing, and there were spots in front of my eyes. It is the one moment in my life that could without exaggeration be called Kafkaesque. I was accused of being a liar and a thief, cutting right at the core of my identity. I was innocent, but would anyone believe me?

I immediately called Arthur, and told him what had happened. Then I went home. Munchkin knew I was innocent, as did Tim, but I was a wreck. The team held a meeting without me, to discuss the result. It turned out that none of them believed it, and Arthur told the examiners I needed to be retested.

This time when I entered the office the person who greeted me was a balding, middle-aged man who said gleefully, "I knew you were fat!"

"Um, thanks?"

"The test doesn't work on us fat guys."

He showed me the sheets from my previous test. The polygraph machine they used had four pens recording my breathing rate, heart rate, blood pressure, and perspiration. The pens write on a scroll of paper, and in theory, when you answer truthfully the wavy lines are consistent and controlled, but when you lie the pens go wild and the lines jump. When I was tested two of the four pens were close to flatlining through the test, another was erratic, and only the one hooked up to my fingertip, measuring electrical impulses (perspiration), was producing something resembling a normal result.

He hooked me up, and had me hold my arm close to my body, which got my readings up from one and a half pens to two and a half. He redid the test and while it didn't show me as now acing the test, he claimed it showed me as mostly truthful.

Between that, and the feedback Arthur had gotten, we figured out that the first jerk, who turned out to be the son of the company boss, the second examiner, didn't understand his mission, because he didn't understand how blackjack playing worked. He took for granted that he was supposed to catch a thief. He knew the team was stuck a lot of money, and I personally was stuck nearly as much as our collective total loss. He hadn't caught a thief when I walked in – I think I was the last one examined – so it must be me who "stole" the money.

It was worse than that. It turned out that he had uncovered all sorts of other, genuine problems. Take tipping. The average amount my teammates tipped was three hundred dollars. Even Timmy, one of the most honest people I know, had tipped one hundred, the second least on the team behind my "less than five dollars." All of them had made cover bets. Some had been "borrowing" team money to pay for cabs, and one had "borrowed" his rent money. My minor sins looked way too good to be true.

I was back on the team, and changes were coming, which would help solve many of our problems, and might just help us win our way out of the hole we'd dug.

CHAPTER 11
PEEK-A-BOO

We were going to dig our way out of the hole by getting into "the hole." We were about to become a hole card team. It seemed like everyone was doing it. Darryl and Craig Brennan specialized in hole card play; Rick, who dropped by our table the first night I came to town, was a spook; on Munchkin's team, Craig Chellstorp was specializing in first-basing, and some of the others like Munchkin were dabbling. It was our turn.

Hole card play involved discovering the value of the dealer's hole card, and using that helpful information to win money. It had been around long before the discovery of card counting. There were many ways to learn a dealer's hole card. Most were illegal, such as marking or bending cards, or collaborating with the dealer. Some were legal but rare. For instance, dealer tells. Having a dealer deliberately tell you or show you their hole card was a form of cheating which could send both of you to jail. But some dealers did it unwittingly. Like poker players, dealers unconsciously showed that they "liked" or "disliked" their hand, after seeing their hole card. There were also dealer warps. The dealers would bend tens and aces when checking for blackjack. When you saw a hole card arcing up from the table, you could guess what it was.

If you started playing blackjack in the last thirty-five years, you might not understand what I am talking about. Today most casinos have a lens built into the table. If the dealer has an ace up, they slide their hole card in one way, a ten up a different way. The prism used will show if the dealer's hole card gives them a blackjack, but won't otherwise reveal what denomination the card is. Even the dealer has no idea whether their hand totals twelve, twenty, or something in between. Either a blackjack is revealed, or the total remains a mystery until the end. Before the readers were invented in the late eighties, whenever a blackjack was possible, the dealer's upcard being a ten value or an ace, the dealer had to peek at her hole card. Aside from the aforementioned methods for discovering the hole card value there were some common ones players were using.

Spooking was one method. If you have seen the movie *Casino*, you have seen spooking. In it, two guys who look as though they have taken time off from molesting children and chopping up people with chainsaws, are in Robert DeNiro's casino, and are up to no good. One is winning at a table, while his buddy sits across the pit, behind and to the dealer's left. From there he can see the dealer's hole card when the dealer peeks at it, and he relays the information to his partner. The method used to signal in the movie is a belt with buzzers worn under the pants. This is a method some teams used for signaling, but not for spooking. You don't need to send much information if you are a spook, stiff, pat, or "not sure" cover most cases, with a few more for things like "end of session" taking care of the rest. A couple of hand signals and you are in business.

In the movie, DeNiro and the security team take the two down in the basement and DeNiro smashes their hands with a hammer. The scene was probably based on a real incident at the Horseshoe, where the security guards beat the spooks with canes, nearly killing one. The casino paid three-quarters of a million dollars to settle it.

We were not sure if spooking was legal. Years later the courts decided it was, but meanwhile, we avoided it.

Another method was called first-basing. It was similar to spooking, but the reader sat at the table, on first base, the seat at dealer's left. When a dealer checks a hole card, they are supposed to protect the card, blocking it so no one but the dealer can see it. As they lift the left corner of the card with their right thumb, they form a tent over it with their left hand. A small percentage, roughly two percent, of the dealers developed a "lazy thumb." Their left thumb would separate from their index finger, creating a window in which the card's index might be viewed, if you sat at first base and positioned yourself to take advantage of the chance to peek. That this was legal was affirmed just a few years later when a former teammate of ours, arrested for cheating at the Imperial Palace, had his case wend its way to the Nevada Supreme Court. In their wisdom they ruled that if the dealer was sloppy enough to expose their card, the player was within his rights to take advantage of it.

If you knew the dealer's hole card every time they had a ten or an ace, you had a two percent edge if you played correct hole card strategy, as good as being paid two for one on blackjack. That's without varying your bet based on the count. Flat betting helped fool the bosses. Your plays also helped. Standing on twelve when the dealer was showing a ten made you look like a beginner. So did splitting threes, or a host of other strange-looking plays.

There was another type of hole card play, called front-loading. This was even better than first-basing, much better. It only worked on single and double deck games. Dealers are supposed to hold the deck angled down when they slide off their hole card. It slides forward onto the table, then they draw it back while it rests flat on the table surface, slipping it beneath their upcard. The most common types of front-loaders exposed their card to the seat in the middle. One way they did it was if they failed to tilt the deck sufficiently down, so that when they pulled the card off the deck it was tilted up, revealing itself to the player. Another mistake was to pull it up slightly when trying to slip it under the upcard. A different flaw, which led these dealers to sometimes be called "third-basers," would have the dealer pulling the card out to the right, angled up so the player at right could see it either when it came off the deck, or when they tried to tuck it. There was even a dealer at the Stardust known as "Old Baldy," who had a bonkers move. He pulled the card off to his left, brought it up as it passed by the middle of the table, then it was flourished to the right before it was tucked.

With this swooping move he showed everyone at the table if they made the slightest effort to look. The trouble with Old Baldy was that he was the house bust out man. If you were winning, and the bosses wanted to put a stop to it, they would sic Old Baldy on you. He was a skilled card mechanic, and bye bye winnings.

Knowing the dealer's hole card every hand, with perfect strategy, was worth nearly ten percent. That included doing things like hitting hard nineteen because the dealer had twenty. No one was that suicidal, but a less obvious strategy was worth seven percent, though it still took balls to double hard five into a ten.

Unlike first-basing, which favored tall players, to play a front-loader it helped to be short. For the average player the front-loader might be literally right under their nose. But the savvy reader would find ways to get low. One story was of the time that a boss in Caesar's saw a player across the aisle from the game he was supposed to be watching, suddenly stand, clutch his chest, and collapse on the table. The boss alertly hollered "security!"

There was a player in a wheelchair at the middle of the table the boss was monitoring. When the boss yelled for security, the player grabbed his chips, jumped up, and ran out the front door. This was thereafter known as the Miracle of Caesar's Palace.

We had a secret weapon when we decided to become a hole card team. His name was Roger. You've met him. He was the guy who was going to call me in as a big player, when I nearly made a dry run at advantage play several years before. Roger had joined our team, and Roger was a born hole card player. He could find dealers, and he could play dealers. Roger was very short, five-five when the tides came in, but if he needed to be tall, he could stand on the rungs of his stool at first base. And when he needed to be short for a front-loader, he had a head start. There was a player named David who sometimes came to the Jockey Club, who was Roger's size. David played front-loaders, and was very successful, but Roger sniffed at his technique. David would bend forward, place his forearms on the edge of the table, and rest his chin on his arms. That was the classic reader posture for seeing the dealer's hole card.

"Too obvious," said Roger. He did a drunk act, and would rest his hip on the seat, his elbow on the edge of the table, and slump horizontally. He was just as low, but it looked like he was inebriated, not intent.

When we moved into hole card play, Roger emerged as a leader.

While a reader could certainly also be the big player, which was what Craig and Munchkin did when they played hole cards, our method was to send out two-man teams. One would read, and one would act as big player. It helped camouflage the play, since the big player wasn't in a position to peek, and could act like he wasn't paying attention to what was happening at the table. It also helped keep players in line, since if you violated team policy, another pair of eyes was on you. While it might seem that two men were now doing the work of one, the time at the table was worth more than twice as much. That's before taking into account our new bets. I don't know how much Chuck put into the bankroll, but our new top bet would be double six-hundreds. And I would be betting them. Some players alternated as readers or big players, and some, like Roger, usually read, because they were so skillful. Me? My distance vision was good, but my eyes didn't change focus quickly enough. I couldn't see the cards when they flashed. No matter, I was a good big player, with the best look on the team. Everyone wanted to read for me.

There was a new job added to the mix, scouting. Maybe two percent of all dealers were first-baseable, but they didn't wear signs saying, "Make your withdrawal here." Front-loaders, because there were fewer handheld games, were even rarer. We had to methodically explore the casinos, looking for lazy thumbs, or decks held high. Even though I couldn't read dealers myself, I could spot the ones with potential. I often scouted with Roger, and could call him over to check out ones I'd found, to see if he could read them.

One night at around four in the morning we were walking through the Holiday Inn. For some reason they had one or two tables open at the far end of the casino, away from the rest. "Did you see that?" Roger asked me. "I think we've found a third baser!" The dealer had a weird move, and was flashing the card toward third base, not first, when he checked for blackjack.

Roger sat on the end, at third base, trying to get the card. The dealer made the odd move, but was now flashing it toward "third-and-a-half." Roger, leaned left, and the next time he nearly caught the card, but not quite. He leaned some more. The cat and mouse game continued. Roger was so subtle that I didn't realize how far he taken it until I noticed he had his feet hooked on one of the other seats for support. He was entirely horizontal, his upper body sticking way into the pit. It's a good thing no boss was paying attention, because even from one hundred feet away they'd have spotted him.

Roger was the ballsiest player on the team. One night he was reading a dealer at the Bingo Palace. Today it's the Palace Station, flagship of the chain of Station casinos, but back then it was a joint catering to locals. It was five-thirty in the morning, and the light over the table blew out.

"Hey, I can't see the cards!"

The boss apologized, but maintenance started at nine in the morning, so until then, maybe Roger could play at a different table?

"This is my lucky dealer!"

"I'm not sure what you want me to do?"

"Have you got a flashlight?"

The boss thought about it, went to the podium, found a flashlight in a drawer, and gave it to Roger. "Try this."

When the dealer next got a ten, Roger shined the beam right where he hoped to spot the card. The dealer was having trouble seeing the card in the dark, so turned it into the light to get a look. It was even better than before.

The boss came back a few minutes later, "How's that working out?"

"It's just perfect!"

When we did find a playable dealer, we each had a yellow notebook, into which we made notes. We'd write down the casino, the shift, the dealer's name and description. We'd describe the move, and if the dealer had been evaluated by Roger, or another player good at reading, there might be a percentage, how often the card was gettable. If we actually played the dealer, the date, time, and results would be added, as well as useful notes on how the pit reacted.

Some dealers were easy to find, because their reputations preceded them. Ronnie was a dealer at the D.I. He had a different move, not unknown, but less common than the lazy thumb. If a dealer was dealing handheld games, they held the deck in their left and dealt with their right. To protect the hole card when peeking they would use the deck in their left hand to block it from view. Some dealers used to dealing handheld games, when they switched to shoes, retained that move, only they no longer had a deck in hand. They slid their left under the hole card, karate chopping it, so to speak. This move looked like an oyster shell, which when open revealed the pearl that was the dealer's hole card.

Ronnie was an oyster, and because he'd been played by so many hole carders, he sensed when it was happening again. Unfortunately for Ronnie, the hole card technique he knew of was spooking. When he feared someone was looking at his card, he exaggerated his move in a way that made it easier for the reader on first base to see the card. One day he realized with a start that he was being read. Ronnie had lost most of his hair, and they say that the top of his head turned bright red.

"Joe!" He called over a boss. "This guy," he nodded at the big player, who was sitting between second and third," is getting my hole card!"

The player looked startled, as did the boss. "Don't believe me? Look! He has a fifteen, right? And I've got a ten. He should hit. But I have a six in the hole. You watch; he's going to stand!"

The boss's jaw dropped. He looked at the player, and said, "Are you going to stand?"

The player smiled and said, "I am now!"

The boss shook his head. "Ronnie, you're an idiot," and walked off.

Another famous dealer was Lillian. Lillian was a thin black woman with glasses, in her late twenties, who dealt at the Hilton on day shift. Rumor had it that teams from Japan and Iran had flown to Las Vegas just to play her. Roger and I couldn't pass her up. Her reputation was well earned. Roger got the card every time. Meanwhile, the count soared. A stratospheric count, knowing her hole card practically every hand, and a high limit casino, so I could bet double sixes – Life was good, no?

No! I was getting crushed. Someone at the table asked if I had my own printing press, I was pulling so many hundred-dollar bills from my pocket. There was an interesting bit of psychology at work. Players are conditioned by looking for hot shoes, where the count goes up. But while the count rises, it is bad for the player. It's when the count drops that you have an edge, because big cards are being dealt. At the same time, knowing the dealer's hole card is a good thing, so if you are seeing it a lot, it feels like that must be good. It isn't. If you are seeing the card by first-basing, it means the dealer is getting a lot of tens and aces. First-basing isn't so much giving you more winning hands, it is making you lose less on the bad ones. Some of the winningest sessions came from dealers who turned out to be no good. The play goes along, and you don't know the dealer isn't readable because they never get any tens. You win a lot of money, and then when they do start to get tens, you find out you can't see the card, call off the play, and walk away a winner. Lillian was giving us a double whammy: decks where small cards kept coming out, except for her upcards.

I was in nearly eleven thousand dollars. Besides the terrible result, we had a bigger problem. Lillian was a trap! The bosses had figured out that she was readable, but instead of showing her how to correct her technique, they used her to catch unwary hole card players. Three bosses had moved in on our game. One was standing behind Roger, one behind Lillian, and one behind me, where I sat on third base. I was dealt a twelve, Lillian had a ten showing, and Roger had signaled that she was stiff. I was supposed to stand on my twelve, against her ten. I hesitated. I could see the bosses behind Lillian and Roger looming, ready to pounce. I could sense the one behind me hanging over me like the Sword of Damocles. I swear, the bosses were growing, and were each at least seven feet tall. I couldn't stand it!

I couldn't look at Roger as I chickened out, and signaled for a hit.

She dealt me a nine, giving me twenty-one. She turned over a deuce, and busted with a ten.

It was as though the bosses deflated, shrinking to their normal heights. The temperature around the table dropped twenty degrees. The boss behind Lillian handed me his card, and told me that if there was anything he could do for me, room, meal, whatever, just let him know. I wish bosses were always so happy when I won a big hand.

Roger told me later that he had been willing me to hit. Hitting twelve against twelve isn't such a terrible mistake, and he, too, could see what was going to happen if I stood pat. We won back some of the money during the rest of the session. I think the net loss was sixty-six hundred, but don't quote me.

That was a bad result for a good game, but Jim had bragging rights. He was playing a loader at the Golden Gate. The Golden Gate had a two-hundred-dollar limit, and since our policy was to only play one session between dealer breaks, so it wouldn't look like we were chasing the dealer, he only got to play for forty minutes. He lost seven thousand dollars. In forty minutes. With a two-hundred-dollar limit. With a seven percent edge. Ouch!

The next day he and his roommate, Eric, were downtown, and hungry. Jim was as broke as the rest of us, and Eric was still hoping for his break, getting hired as a radio DJ somewhere. The Golden Gate had the cheapest bargain in town, fifty-cent shrimp cocktails. They served them at a counter in a corner of the casino just off the street. A very tall pit boss was able to see over the banks of slots, and came running over, just as Jim was about to pay.

Mindful of the seven thousand dollars Jim had lost the day before he cried, "No! No! Nothing is too good for a player of your caliber!" And he comped them to the pair of fifty-cent shrimp cocktails.

CHAPTER 12
ON THE RIGHT TRACK

Despite losses like those, we began digging our way out of the hole, albeit more slowly than we'd hoped. Meanwhile, we explored other techniques.

There was a legendary team operating then. I wouldn't get to know them until much later, but members included Rob Reitzen and Wally Simmons, both in the Blackjack Hall of Fame, and Mark Billings who I expect will be voted in some day. (Mark is the author of a couple of worthwhile books on gambling.) We heard that they were playing a game in Laughlin which sounded incredible. Supposedly the casino was dealing single deck, making the players cut using a cut card, and in the process, the bottom card was exposed to the player cutting.

Years later I would play a game with Darryl Purpose, where we tried to cut tens and aces from the bottom of a shoe, a technique known as ace steering, or "slicing and dicing." Aces and tens only appear five-thirteenths of the time, and a shoe takes a long time to deal. With a single deck we'd be cutting every few minutes, and not only tens and aces.

Imagine that Roger was sitting on first base playing two hands, I was in the middle of the table, playing three, and Jim was to my left, playing the last two spots. The deck is cut, a card is burned ("one"), our first cards are dealt ("two through eight"), the dealer gets a hole card ("nine), and the thirteenth card lands on the middle of my three hands. If the card was a nine through an ace, we'd cut thirteen cards, otherwise, we'd cut nine. Even if we missed, we had cushions. If the nine-card cut was off by one, we'd know it, because it would land on either Jim's second hand, or Roger's first, and was a poor card removed from landing on my hands, where the big money was bet. Otherwise, we'd know the dealer's hole card. If the thirteen-card cut was off by one, it would still land on one of my three hands.

We spent several days practicing, getting our cutting and signaling down, then drove to Laughlin. Unlike the current megacity, with its eight thousand people, Laughlin in those days had a population of 95. That's how I remember it, anyway. Of course it may have had thousands more, lurking behind cacti or under prairie dogs. Two of the citizens were old friends, Franklin Adams, head of the acting school I'd gone to as a kid, and his sister Jane. They lived in a trailer. I think all citizens of Laughlin lived in the same mobile home park. Google says that Bullhead City, Arizona wasn't incorporated until 1984, but there was something there calling itself Bullhead City. The people in Bullhead City crossed the river into Nevada to gamble in Lauglin. Meanwhile, any youngsters in Laughlin crossed the other way because in those days eighteen-year-olds could drink in Arizona.

Laughlin was founded in 1964 by a guy named Don Laughlin, who opened the Riverside Casino. I think there were five casinos in 1982, a weird little mini-Las Vegas in one of the hottest corners of the United States. Bullhead City hasn't reached the sublime heights achieved an hour away in Lake Havasu, where the temperature hit 128, but it's made it all the way up to 126 five times. Its residents go to Phoenix to cool off, in July. We weren't there to sunbathe, so the weather didn't bother us. As long as there was no heat from the pit bosses, we'd be fine.

Unfortunately, we couldn't see the hole card. Only one of the casinos offered the cut we sought, because we checked them all. And we spent time scouring the good one for a dealer we could read, but found none. If the other team played there, either they burned out the game, or Roger had spotted a front-loader on a previous trip, and imagined the dealers were all like that. It was a wasted trip. Could have been worse. I had friends who went to Australia and found that word they were coming had spread, and they were barred at all the casinos before playing a hand. Even though we didn't get to play, I had acquired a valuable skill I would use in the future.

About this time the team took up shuffle tracking. At least the team took it up in theory, though only a few of us took it up in practice. I got some instruction from Munchkin, who warned me that anything he taught I could not share with the team. This warning was echoed, more emphatically, by Craig. Because I am voluble, and because Arthur's team had gotten into hole card play, which other teams wished to believe they had sole rights to, Munch's team had come to the conclusion that I must have turned them onto what Craig and a few of them were doing. The player who started the rumor about us was Miles. In truth I could keep a secret, so didn't tell them that it was Marco, Miles' roommate, who was sneaking into Miles' room and reading his notebook.

Shuffle tracking was a recondite method, but not so abstruse that some of our players, such as Roger, weren't aware of the basics. I don't know that Munchkin imparted much more information than did Roger, but I know I was the only one who really mastered it.

What is shuffle tracking?

The classic shuffling method was called the Hilton. If you were lucky enough to be playing at a table in the Las Vegas Hilton in 1982, here is what you would find. The game is four decks, with Strip rules. The cut card is placed two-thirds of a deck from the end. Suppose that when the last hand has been dealt the running count is plus ten. The dealer removes the remaining cards from the shoe, and places them on top of the rest in the discard tray. She takes the stack out of the tray, and places it on the table. She lifts the top half of the stack off with her right hand, and places it next to the bottom half. Then she grabs one third of each stack, shuffles them together a few times, and sets the blended pile in front of her. She grabs another third, and when mixed, sets it on top of the first clump, then repeats with the last third, and stacks that on top. She picks up the pack, hands you a plastic cut card, and the next move is up to you.

If you have been paying attention, you may have realized that the very first group of cards she grabbed with her right hand was precisely what was left in the shoe after the final hand. The count was plus ten, so that clump had ten extra high cards. Since there were five times as many cards in the rest of the shoe, and she shuffled one-fifth of them into that ten-rich clump, the result would, on average, be a section one and one-third decks thick, with eight extra high cards, or a true plus six. That section is the back third of the shuffled shoe. If you cut one and one-third decks from the back, you can begin betting the new shoe, on the very first hand, as though the true count is plus six.

Congratulations! You have just figured out the most integral part of shuffle tracking. With some shoes that is about all you can do. You find a clump of cards rich in tens and aces; you watch how the dealer grabs them. Assuming she doesn't grab in the middle of them, and preserves the clump, you average it with the rest and have something to work with.

That's crude. We are in the Hilton, in 1982, so we can do better, much better. We'll rewind to the beginning of the previous shoe. You start, as always, with a zero count. At the two-thirds of a deck mark the running count is minus two. At the one and one-third deck mark it is plus four. At the two-deck mark, halfway through the shoe it is plus two. At the two and two-thirds mark it is zero. At the cut card it is, as we said, plus ten.

She shuffles as before. Aside from its other merits, the Hilton's dealers are very consistent, in the cut card placement, and in their deck grabs when shuffling. We have made note of the running counts for each one-sixth of the shoe. We number them one through six, from the beginning to the end. When the dealer first breaks the stack in half, sections one through three are on her left, four through six on her right. Her first grab is of sections three and six, next two and five, finally one and four. The count for section six is minus ten, we expect it to drop ten. The count for section three dropped from plus four to plus two, so a minus two is shuffled into a minus ten. That third of the shoe will drop twelve. The next two sections, two and five saw a rise of ten for section five, and a rise of six for section two, so they are plus sixteen when combined. Finally, the cards from one and four when combined will drop four. After we cut, we expect the first deck and one-third to drop twelve, so we treat it as a true plus nine. We expect the next third of the shoe to drop four more, so we start that section at a true three, and only when the running count is minus sixteen have we used up all the high cards.

Confused? Yes, it is hard, and it takes practice. Especially since while you are playing that shoe, you are also counting the six sections again, to prepare for the next shoe. Every shoe you will be keeping two counts, one comparing the movement you expect from your previous track, the other the movement you are seeing as you play it.

That's the Hilton. Other casinos, if they are trackable, are harder. There was one which was easier. It's long gone, taking its wonderful shuffle with it. It was called the Westward Ho, and was between the Slots of Fun and the Silver Slipper. The shuffle they had was called a Berlin. I assume because once upon a time casinos in Berlin shuffled this way. The Westward Ho also dealt four decks, and cut one. The dealer would take that last deck out of the shoe, stick it on top of the tray, bring out the stack, and break it in half. Then? They would grab the top half of the right-hand pile, and shuffle it into itself! Yes, whatever was behind the cut card was preserved. If the count was plus ten at the cut card, that stack, which would end up on the back of the pile, was going to drop ten. They would next shuffle the top half of the other pile, and place it on top. In the end, each deck was shuffled into itself, and when ready to cut the order was 1-3-2-4.

An example of how easily things could go wrong is illustrated by a practice session of my teammate, Mike. One of the easiest shuffles in town, nearly as simple as the one at the Hilton, was at the King 8. The King 8 was a casino favored by truckers, on Tropicana just west of the interstate. Its limits were only one hundred dollars, and the dealers hit soft seventeen, but it had a four-deck game with just a half a deck cut. They used a "four-part Hilton," that is, a shuffle very much like the Hilton's, but grabbing four half-deck sections instead of three one-third deck sections. Mike tracked a shoe and cut what he was sure was a very rich clump to the front. He bet double hundreds off the top of the new shoe. Instead of dropping, the count rose. Hmm, maybe the low cards in his clump all happened to be in that first smidgen? At any rate, if he was expecting a big drop, he expected an even bigger drop. It failed to come, and within the next few hands the count had risen some more. By now he reasoned that even if something had gone wrong, the running count was high enough to justify betting double hundreds on its own merit. The count never dropped, and at the cut card the shoe was still plus. He had evidently cut a half deck too early, and all the high cards he was looking for had ended up behind the cut card. Meanwhile, he had bet double hundreds, the casino limit, for an entire shoe.

"Thank god no one saw me!" he thought, then turned around, and there was Arthur, who had brought a new player, Tom Terrific, to test at the King 8. Arthur signaled for Mike to meet them in the coffee shop. Where, once they were all seated, he said, "Mike, the high cards can't be everywhere."

While it has nothing to do with shuffle tracking, since I brought him up, a word about Tom Terrific. I've mentioned that we had players come and go. Tom was one who happened along. He was in his early twenties, studying accounting. Lots of accounting students take up card counting. They tend to have an aptitude for the actual counting part of the game. Unfortunately, they also tend to look like accounting students. Tom was a lanky six-four, with thick glasses. He was clean-cut and earnest. As a new recruit he lacked many skills but he was able to keep the count, play proper strategy, and read signals. Which slotted him in as a big player for the hole card game. He was playing somewhere, betting double five hundreds. It's hard enough for older players to pass themselves off as prosperous enough to bet big money. Young players for the most part adopt a cover story known as "spoiled rich kid." Tom was a very ethical guy, and he "didn't believe in lying." When the dealer, impressed that this youngster could bet thousands of dollars, asked what he did for a living, he said, "I'm a dishwasher at Naugles." Luckily the dealer thought he was joking, but after the session it was explained that if he wasn't going to lie, avoiding answering was not dishonest.

CHAPTER 13

BUSTED, DISGUSTED, GRIFFIN AGENTS CAN'T BE TRUSTED

"Sir, could you show me some ID?" To this point I'd never interacted with casino security, and wasn't looking to break the streak. What to do if stopped was a topic of discussion. The consensus was that you should not give them your ID, and not accompany them to the back room. You were within your rights to refuse. If worse came to worst you could insist that if you were under arrest, they should summon real police, and if not, they had no right to detain you. They may not have had the right, but many of them didn't know that. Quite a few lawsuits arose because of security's failure to understand their limits.

In this case I decided to show my ID. I was on my way out of the Union Plaza. I'd been in it less than an hour. Conditions were crowded because it was early on a Friday evening. I had never gotten a count sufficient to raise my bet, so the only thing any boss would have seen, if they even noticed me, was a guy betting single green chips. Whatever the guard wanted, it had to be mistaken identity. I handed him my driver's license.

"Come with me!" And now it was too late. He had my license in hand, so I followed him. We went to the security office, the "back room." They took Polaroid mug shots of me, and then read me the

Trespass Act. That's a form of barring, a more extreme form than a simple backing off. Backing off is where you are told that you are welcome to play other games, but not blackjack. Sometimes they say you are not welcome in the casino, and you leave. When you are read the Trespass Act, it's a threat; they are telling you that if you return to the casino, merely set foot inside, you will be arrested for trespassing.

There are worse forms of barring. I mentioned the spooks who were beaten by guards at the Horseshoe. Early in his career Darryl Purpose was backroomed by a notorious guard at the Dunes, who put a gun to his head and demanded money or Darryl's body would be buried in the desert, never to be found. My friend Jon Ungar had a guard at the Imperial Palace threaten to castrate him with a bolt cutter. They robbed him of seven thousand dollars. (He made much more back in the lawsuit).

We had a member of the team who experienced a rough barring at the Dunes. His name was Danny, and when they asked for ID, he said his wife had it, and she was playing slots. He led them to a group of machines near the door, and bolted. He ran across the Strip to the MGM, and made it as far as the front steps. That was a couple of hundred yards of sprinting. He was nearly in the door when a Dunes security guard tackled him. The guards roughed him up, handcuffed him, and threw him in a Dunes security truck that had driven over.

Back at the Dunes they called in a Griffin agent. The Griffin Detective Agency was founded by a former cop named Bob Griffin. The agency published the Griffin Book, which was sometimes confused, but shouldn't have been, with the gaming commission's Black Book. The Griffin Book was much thicker, filled with names and photos of players considered undesirable by the casino. Many of the people in the book were cheats, who rigged slot machines, marked cards, and other illegal activities. But mixed in with them were people who had done nothing illegal. They had simply used their brains to count cards.

Not every casino used Griffin, but many did. Client casinos received copies of the Griffin Book, they received flyers of current active players, and they could call for an agent if they suspected a player of being up to something. There were three agents in the field each shift, one downtown, one working the north end of the Strip, and one the south end. They roved, but if needed, a pager sent them to the casino summoning them. By the time Danny was returned to the back room at the Dunes, a Griffin agent had joined the security guards. Followed soon after by a cop from Metro.

What most people don't realize is that the City of Las Vegas ends at Sahara. Glitter Gulch is in the heart of Las Vegas, but the Strip is outside of it. Most of it is in Paradise Township, part of the Las Vegas metropolitan area, which is part of Clark County. At one time Las Vegas had a police force, and Clark County had a sheriff. The agencies merged and became Metro, run by the sheriff. Metro, the metonym for the police agency, and its cops, had a foul reputation for thuggishness and corruption. Casino security guards had the reputation for being the knuckledraggers who failed to make the grade with Metro.

Once the gang was all there, security, Griffin, and Metro, they took mug shots of Danny, with and without his disguise. They counted his chips, twenty-six hundred dollars' worth, and said, "These are going back in the rack." After stealing his money in front of the cop, they handed him over, and he was arrested, though what they charged him with was a good question since he had committed no crime, unless it was assaulting a security guard's knuckles with his cheek bone or eye socket.

Danny made forty-five thousand dollars for his trouble. His was the only violent barring of a team member. Unless you count former team member Steve Einbinder, who was dragged from the crap table he was clinging to, by Imperial Palace guards, while screaming that someone should call the police, because he was being kidnapped. The I.P. didn't subscribe to Griffin, but had its own investigative arm. When I moved to Las Vegas Arnold Snyder had obtained a copy of a report the I.P. compiled in 1981, and circulated to casinos. Arnold published it in his Blackjack Forum. The report detailed surveillance of Tommy Hyland's team. Tommy, a legendary player, ran a large team out of Atlantic City. When they came to Las Vegas the I.P. got wind of it, and tailed them, tapped phones, even knew which hookers had been patronized by which player. It made for scary reading.

Though Danny was the only violent barring, some other players suffered from "Griffinitis." Arthur was barred one night at Sam's

Town. He refused to go in the back room, but did let them take a Polaroid while he stood next to the casino cage. They told him he should have known better, known that he was barred at Sam's Town. "I've never been barred here!" They told him that he had been barred at the California Club, Sam Boyd owned that casino, ergo Arthur was barred at Sam's Town. "Wait, if Sam buys the Dunes, does that mean I am now barred at the Dunes?" "That's right." "How would I know that?" "If he buys a casino, it will be in the papers." "Yeah? I don't read the papers, but you have my address, so send me a postcard to let me know." While he was playing, he'd been bothered by an inebriated female player who kept hustling him for chips. The casino's parting shot as they told him to leave, and never again darken Sam's door, was "take Monica with you." Which is disturbing, that they knew Art's girlfriend's name, and that she was known to tip a few.

Even more hectored than Arthur was Jim. Jim had managed despite being a silver chip player before he joined our team, to be Griffinized. Worse, he was "McNabbed." The most notorious agent was a guy named Mike McNab. McNab didn't have great insight into how people beat casinos, legally or illegally. He couldn't tell a spook from a dice slider. What he could do was recognize and remember faces. He was great at that. He knew Jim's face. Boy, did he know Jim's face! Jim was a young player, and must have had the sort of look that pit bosses worried about. It seemed like everywhere he played, the casino would put in a call to Griffin. McNab would show up, and say, "That's Jim!" They would haul him into the back room, and get a fresh set of mug shots.

One time it happened in the Golden Nugget, and when they made him empty his pockets, the first thing out was his playing cash. They counted it, seven thousand dollars. From his other pocket came an alarm clock. "Is that a bomb!?" "No, it's my alarm clock. I can't afford a watch." Another thing that happened was that Jim was barred from three different Denny's. This was an extension of the Sam Boyd principle explained to Arthur. Jim was barred by casinos who owned property with Denny's franchises, and when they trespassed him, they were comprehensive.

How did I end up barred by the Union Plaza? It was part of a run of barrings or backings off that started not long after I began shuffle tracking. Which should have made me safer, though not every place I had a problem with had a trackable shuffle.

The first was a gentle backing off. I was playing at the Sands, had played several days there, and the boss was very nice. "Play anything except blackjack." It wasn't the first time I had been backed off. I'd been backed off after playing a session of hole cards at the Marina. I don't think they had a clue what I was doing. They even comped me to a show. But they didn't like me betting the limit; it made them nervous. In the Sands I wasn't near the limit, but I think I'd won a few thousand, and they suspected I might know something.

Then I went to the Hilton. If you are going to play Hilton shuffles, why not play the original? If I had it all to do over again, I would have done things differently, but I was following team rules, which meant no cover, and if tracking, play alone. I went in on day shift, and opened up a dead game. The casino itself was dead, just me, my dealer, and a boss watching the game. The count went up, I won thirteen hundred dollars, I was all set to make my killer cut when ... some idiots, a young couple, where'd they come from? ... sat at my table and the dealer handed him the cut card.

Pissed, I moved to the next table, and started a new game. Once again the count went up, but this time I lost twelve-fifty. The boss stepped in, told me they did not want my action, and added "you haven't lost anything."

The boss was Mike Sterling.

The average boss in Las Vegas knows a lot less about the games he watches than he thinks he does. It was probably worse forty years ago. Most bosses and dealers were convinced they were expert players, and most didn't even know correct basic strategy. As for counting, they couldn't count past ten unless you let them take off their shoes. Bosses who were knowledgeable, and dangerous, were rare, and we knew their names.

John Scott, known as Scottie, was the swing shift manager at the Castaways, where my brother worked. The Castaways didn't believe in hard barrings, but Scottie could count and he'd back off anyone who knew what they were doing. At least if they knew what they were doing, and were a threat. Peter Griffin knew what he was doing, but only bet one to four in silver. Some casinos would take umbrage, but Scottie wasn't going to sweat the small stuff.

The MGM Grand had a boss named Vic Wakeman. Wakeman had a couple of nicknames. One was "the Midget." Casino surveillance, because the cameras and spy glasses were in the ceiling, was called the "Eye in the Sky." Wakeman was called "the Eye in the Rug."

Howard Grossman at the Nevada Palace had played with Ken Uston (and once got backed off by Scottie). He was another boss to avoid.

The Barbary Coast bosses actually knew basic strategy, and assumed any player who also knew it was to be eighty-sixed.

Caesar's had two bosses who were dangerous. The one most people worried about was known as the Weasel. He looked like a young button man sent out to Vegas by one of the Five Families. The other was an older boss named Jimmy Rogish. There were young bosses who knew something about card counting. There was another sort, the "old guy" from Steubenville, Hot Springs, Phenix City, or the like. They were the ones who had seen it all, and could smell a scam. Rogish was one of those, but he could also count.

And there was Mike Sterling, at the Hilton, a young boss who could count. Who I sat right in front of, playing with no cover. Oops! I didn't know how bad that was, not yet.

After the barring at the Union Plaza I grew paranoid. It seemed as though the next few places I played, I was getting heat even before I'd showed them any speed. I decided to play in a place I had never been, the Tropicana. I went in on day, but it didn't matter because I had never played a session there on any shift. The Trop had high limits, and my action shouldn't make them nervous. I sat down, pulled out a couple of hundred, and asked for green chips. I could swear the two bosses at the podium reacted to me. I knew that was impossible, because they had never seen me. I was just paranoid. But I'd swear they acted like they knew me.

Another player sat down, and asked for a thousand-dollar marker. An older boss came to the table to fill it. Suddenly, he turned to me and asked, "Are you a card counter?"

"What? No!"

"Are you sure? You look like a card counter."

"No, I don't count cards."

"You don't count cards?"

"I know basic strategy." I still don't know if that was a good answer, but it seemed to satisfy him.

Until he returned a few minutes later. "You're sure you don't count cards? You just know basic strategy?"

"That's right. Why would you think I count cards?"

"He said you did." He gestured at one of the two bosses standing near the podium, the ones who flinched when I first sat down.

"Why would he say that?"

"I don't know. But you say you aren't a card counter. Would you swear to it?"

"Swear to it? Um, sure."

"Okay, raise your right hand."

"Pardon me?" By now even people at nearby tables were watching, and the bosses were giggling.

"Raise your right hand." I did. "Say 'I solemnly swear that I do not count cards.'"

I solemnly swore it, and he said, "Okay, that's good enough for me."

I asked the dealer, "What the hell was that about?"

He seemed even more freaked out than I was. "I don't know. He's always goofing around."

Then the boss returned once again. "You swore you didn't count cards." I agreed I had done so. "But this sure looks like you! Doesn't this look like him?" He showed the picture to the dealer. "Isn't this you."

He showed me the picture, and I agreed it looked like me. Which made sense because it was me. It was a photocopy of a picture which must have been taken from an eye in the sky. It showed me sitting at a blackjack table, with a description, "White male, approximately thirty, heavyset ..." "Well, anyway, you swore an oath ..." He left yet again.

I didn't like my chances of winning any money from the Tropicana, and 'remembered' an appointment. I wanted to know about that picture, and asked where the boss had gone. One of the other bosses said that he was in a meeting, but I should speak to "them," and pointed to a couple of guys watching me from across the aisle. They must have been plainclothes security. I approached, told them that the boss had shown me a picture, and I wondered at its provenance. "Have you ever played at the Hilton?" One said, and it all became clear.

I figured no one would ever believe me when I said that I was made to swear an oath that I didn't count cards by the Tropicana shift manager. But I no sooner walked in the door than the phone rang. "That was unbelievable at the Trop?" It was Frank, from Munchkin's team.

"How did you hear about it?"

"I was playing right across the pit from you."

I got off the phone with Frank, and it rang again. "What did you do at the Trop?" It was Jim.

"You knew about it too?"

"I was standing behind you, watching you play when it happened. And Wayne," a teammate of Chuck's, "was at the next table."

I had witnesses from three different teams. It was obvious that I was burnt, that flyer from the Hilton, and soon the mug shot from the Union Plaza, dogging me. There was only one solution.

CHAPTER 14
A NEW MAN

When Hollywood makes movies about card counters, they love putting them in disguise. They dress them like Texas oil men, or put women in male drag; it's fun. Some of the books, like Uston's *The Big Player*, talk about it. Most players have found it isn't as easy as Hollywood makes it out to be.

Simple is often best. Craig Chellstorp, when he began drawing heat, had his hair permed, and grew a moustache. It breathed new life into his game. Roger tried something similar, permed hair being a style then. Roger had gotten burnt in an odd way. Chuck's team had won over thirty thousand dollars at the Barbary Coast, a feat so remarkable that as I tried to type this my fingers curled up, looked at me, and said, "Really?" Yes, really. The problem was that he had over thirty thousand dollars' worth of Barbary white chips, and had to leave the casino hastily, before they were cashed. Back then casinos honored each other's chips, and he was looking for people to cash them for him for a small fee. Roger took two over to Silver City. Had they been a smaller denomination, even black, there might have been no problem. White chips, worth five hundred dollars apiece, were not common currency, especially not Barbary Coast whites. Barbary Coast put out an alert, and when Roger tried to cash them, word went out that a very short fellow with glasses and neatly trimmed chestnut brown hair was wanted for questioning by Griffin.

Roger got contacts, and a perm. The trouble was he also got a dye job. He went blond, or tried to, but the result made him look like Harpo Marx. Shortly after his makeover he and Jim were playing in the Mint. There was an older boss, one of the ex-Steubenville types, who turned up on all shifts. Probably the casino manager. He was a dangerous boss, and when he showed up that day, Roger overheard enough to flash the "extreme heat, leave immediately" signal. Jim quickly picked up his chips, and disappeared through the slots and out onto Fremont Street.

The bosses fanned out, and when they couldn't find Jim returned to the pit. Roger continued to play first base, betting his five-dollar chips, as though he hadn't a care in the world.

"Dat guy is up to somep'n!" said the old boss. "I'll figure it out." Suddenly, it hit him. "Dat's it! He's grabbin' the hole card!" He whipped around, and scanned the opposite side of the pit for spooks, with no luck. He turned back to the other bosses. "Someone is grabbin' the hole card for him, and I'll get him if it's the last thing I do!" As he said this he looked right at Roger, and without a pause said, "Somebody sure fucked up the hair of that kid on first base."

Fake hair was even worse. When Danny was backroomed at the Dunes he was wearing a fake moustache and fake eyebrows. They weren't obviously fake, but they make him look like the villain from a silent movie. Once he was in the back room it was easy for security to spot that they were artificial.

Jim went all out, and wore a wig and fake beard. He was playing at the Silver Slipper when a boss came up, and asked, "Is that a fake beard?" Everyone at the table turned and stared. Jim gulped, and said, yes it was. "I knew it!" Said the boss. He went back to the podium and told another boss, "See, I told you that was a fake beard!" Neither of them stopped to wonder why Jim was wearing a fake beard, but he left before they did.

Tommy Hyland once donned a seasonally appropriate Santa Claus outfit. They may not have known it was Tommy, but they knew a bet spread when they saw it, which led to the immortal words, "Sorry Santa, you're barred!"

Halloween is a great time to put on a costume. In 1957 I dressed up like Wyatt Earp for the Fourth of July parade. I was four. Arthur was closer to forty when he tried it one Halloween. He walked into the Castaways in cowboy regalia, including a pair of six-shooter cap guns strapped to his hips. He looked like Arthur wearing a kid's cowboy outfit.

More successful was a pair who disguised themselves … Actually, they didn't disguise themselves. Their costume, if you could call it that, consisted of a toy dump truck and a toy rake. Whenever the count went up they loaded up the dump truck with chips. "We're sending it in!" They rolled the truck over to the betting square, and dumped the bet. If it won, "We're raking it in!" As they used the rake to do just that. Scottie let them play for a while, because the act was so entertaining. Style points count.

Bill Benter came up with one of the most legendary disguises: Neon Leon. Bill was one of the most clean-cut counters around. A former physics student, he had neatly trimmed brown hair, and wore dress pants and white shirts when he dressed down. He got a rooster cut, a punk rocker's Mohawk haircut dyed bright red. He bought purple velvet platform shoes, a purple jumpsuit that zipped down the front, and wraparound shades. He had a small bottle and tiny spoon on a chain worn around his neck.

When he played the Maxim he would pause on big hands, "Just a minute!" He'd duck under the table, and make snorting sounds. He'd sniff as he sat up, and say, "Okay," shoving out another five hundred, "double down."

It worked fine, until he cashed out. That's when security grabbed him, and dragged him in the back room. "When's it going down?"

"When's what going down?"

"C'mon, we know what you're here for. The deal. When's it going down?" They were convinced Bill was there to do a major coke deal.

"Look, it's empty! No cocaine." It took a while, but he convinced them that he was in disguise because otherwise the casino wouldn't let him play.

Security called the pit, "The guy claims he is a gambler 'with a system,' and you'd never let him play otherwise."

"We love him!" said the pit. "He can play any time!"

Despite that, Bill decided it was too much attention of the wrong sort, and hung up his shades and his coke bottle.

Munchkin had a similar experience when he became, the Mover from Vancouver. He had a pair of khaki overalls he wrinkled up, and work boots. He bought a baseball cap, and a large pair of sunglasses. He dirtied up his hands with grease from the wheel well of his car. As finishing touches, he stuck a fat cigar stub in his mouth, and talked around it with a Canadian accent he'd learned watching Bob and Doug McKenzie in the "Great White North" sketches on SCTV. His cover story was that he was bringing a truckload down from Canada to Texas.

Walking around downtown no one paid attention. He fit right in. On the Strip it was different. When he went into the Aladdin, security began following him. He set up on first base, standing to get a better angle, and began betting five hundred a hand. The boss naturally wanted to figure out who or what this weirdo was. When he sidled up next to Munchkin, it put him in position to possibly see what Munch was seeing, the dealer's hole card. That's when the cigar came in handy. From chewing it, there were large, disgusting globs ready to fall off. Munch would tease off a piece, and spit it out of the side of his mouth, at the boss. The casino version of the brush back pitch. He got one good play out of it, but like Bill, decided it drew too much of the wrong kind of attention.

Besides, a good act trumped a good disguise. One day Munch was walking through the Sands when he heard, "Hey! Hey you!" He recognized the New Zealand accent. Sure enough, there was Malcolm. "I saw your play. You were very good!" Munch had done 12 *Angry Men* at the Las Vegas Little Theatre. We'd all gone to see it. Malcolm decided for some reason that telling the boss he'd seen a local show helped whatever act he was putting on. Later, Munchkin told him he wasn't thrilled that Malcolm had outed him as a local. "Don't worry," said Malcolm. "When he asked if you were an actor, I told him you were, and probably *one of those*." He fluttered a limp wrist. The next time Munch played the Sands, the boss tried to pump him to confirm that he was local. The boss's mistake was doing it while he and Munch were at adjacent urinals. Munch ostentatiously tried to peer at what the boss had in his hand, causing the boss to change urinals midstream. And after that if Munch played on his shift he got very little attention from the pit.

Malcolm and David both liked flamboyance. Imagine if they teamed up! One fine night after dropping acid they dropped into Sam's Town. Cashing in on their accents, they told the awestruck pit they were English nobility, Lord Bolingbroke, and the Earl of Goodwood. A regular blackjack table? That was for peasants! They had a table moved into the pit, and there they played, while the staff basked in the privilege of serving them.

None of which solved my problem. There was a flyer out on me, and I was drawing heat everywhere I went. Luckily, I had looks which lent themselves to major modification.

Thanks to my lack of funds, I'd lost thirty pounds since moving to town. I wore glasses which meant that it was time for me to finally try contact lenses. Which I found I hated. After a few hours my eyes were on fire, and I couldn't wait to get home and claw them out. While I wore them, it changed a look I'd had since I was seven.

I learned something interesting while getting contacts. The doctor showed me a picture, a circle filled with smaller colored circles. Could I see the embedded picture? I could. He showed me another. I squinted and strained, but saw only colored dots. Ditto for the rest.

"You know what this means?" I didn't. "You are color blind. Profoundly!"

Ridiculous, I thought. I could see color just fine. There's red, that's green, I see you blue! What's the problem? It wasn't until the next year, when I bought a car, and told my roommate it was a "brown Chevy" that I realized maybe the doctor was right. My roommate said he couldn't find the car.

"What are you talking about? It's right at the end of the walk."

"You mean that bright green car?"

I went and looked. Yeah, it was bright green.

I had a full beard. It stopped growing after it reached my second button, but I'd worn it for half a dozen years by then. I had to trim it before I could shave it off, but away it went. If I had buttons on the back of my shirt, the second button is roughly where my hair stopped growing. For that I went across the street to a cosmetology school and asked for a perm. They did their best, but it didn't last long. My hair was too thin in both senses. I always wanted hair like a movie star, Elvis was the one I had in mind. I got hair like a movie star, only the star was Peter Lorre. When I went home at Christmas tricked out in my disguise for the family dinner, my cousin Glen saw me from behind, and his only comment was "you're losing your hair." He hadn't seen me in a few years, but for people who had seen me recently, the change floored them. Friends didn't recognize me until I spoke.

Casinos didn't recognize me even when I spoke. I was back in action!

CHAPTER 15
MOVING ON

Fall came around, and we were still working on that same bankroll. Having been the big loser, I felt an obligation to Arthur. At the same time, we'd had players come and go as they pleased. It was also, despite our branching out, not a well-run team. We had people playing who were not competent. Huey, for one, never got the knack. He would drill and test on the kitchen table. He'd be pronounced ready. Then he would walk into a casino and his game would fall apart. I gave notice. I had another offer by then. Craig and Munchkin would put up ten thousand dollars, to stake me and a player named Wylie Roberts. Winter was approaching by the time I left the team, and not long after, the bankroll finally broke. I received about fourteen hundred dollars. I think I had played four hundred hours by then, and still was a net loser, though almost even.

Wylie and I started winning right away. We were betting quite a bit less than what I'd been betting for Arthur, but winning is winning. Soon we were joined by a third player.

I'm not sure just how Craig found Dick Wolfsheim. Sure, he "knew him from backgammon." But Craig wasn't traveling to a lot of tournaments. The first I knew of Dick was when Craig told me he had found me a teammate. He was going to train him, and then Wylie and I would have a mate. Craig's "training" consisted of moving him into our condo. We had three bedrooms, all occupied, so Dick slept on the sofa the first few months. Like me, Dick had done his own studying of the basics. It was up to me to test him, to teach him how to shuffle track, and to take him out and test him in a casino. He learned fast, and soon was squared away.

Good thing because Wylie moved on. Wylie only played one or two bankrolls, but they were broken quickly, and as a replacement, Dick was a case of trading up. As a roommate, Dick was … interesting.

Munchkin told everyone that he was living in a "circus of eccentricity," and proposed a contest. He would poll our friends, and determine who was the King of Eccentricity. He excluded himself from consideration.

Me, eccentric? I have evaluated the evidence, and it is specious. Sure, I do "twiddle a twig." My twigs are dried maple leaf stems, which I twirl between my fingers. It's a nervous habit I have had since I was a kid. Seems normal to me. Yes, I did tell Munchkin a used vacuum cleaner I purchased was defective. (Speaking of eccentric, Munch had been living in the condo for four or five years by then, and didn't own a vacuum.) I was struggling to push it around the living room when he came home, and I told him it didn't work properly. How was I to know there was a lever you worked with your foot, that let the handle tilt? The thing didn't come with an instruction manual. As for the time I flooded the bathroom (and the hall) because I was reading in the shower and didn't notice the water had gone over the top of the bathtub, I think we can agree that it depends on the book?

Timmy won in a landslide. Darryl Purpose gave a good summary of evidence in Timmy's favor. He came over to the house one day, and when Timmy opened the door, books met his eye. Open books. They covered the living room table and the breakfast table. They covered the sofa, and the chairs. They covered the floor, and the kitchen counters.

"Doing a lot of reading?" he asked.

And Timmy answered in a manner that made it clear he thought his answer explained everything, "I'm airing out my bridge books."

Darryl nodded as if to say, "Of course you are." Then he asked if he could have a snack. Timmy invited him to help himself. Darryl looked in the refrigerator, which had what it always had, a gallon bottle of water, a box of Junior Mints, and six half empty bottles of Heineken. The cold water was for me and Munchkin; we like cold water. The Junior Mints were Timmy's. He liked them. So were the Heinekens. Timmy would open a bottle, drink half, then put it in the refrigerator. When he got thirsty again, he'd open a new bottle. With nothing in the fridge, Darryl turned to the kitchen cabinets, where he found more bridge books, and a five-hundred-page computer listing of backgammon bearoff equities. We ate out a lot.

Timmy also had a favorite pen. It was a nice pen, though no Montblanc. When he kept track of it, it was clipped to the neck of his sweater. When he lost track of it, which was frequently, he accused us of stealing it. When that happened Munchkin would say, "Timmy, have you looked in the refrigerator?" Timmy would insist he did not leave his pen in the fridge. Then he'd look, and there it would be next to the Junior Mints.

Years later Munch admitted to me that he was the one putting Timmy's pen in the fridge, whenever Timmy left it lying around. And that he had rigged the contest, because, "Of course Dick would have won!"

It's tough to explain why that was, because Dick didn't have many regular tics like Timmy's. He was just naturally strange. The only obvious eccentricity was his nudity. Since our dad walked around naked all the time, that wasn't so strange to us. It did bother Timmy, but he was still recovering from the morning dad went down to shower (the shower at our house was in the basement), found Munch and his friends in an all-night backgammon game, and walked over to watch for a few minutes. Timmy found our dad literally "hanging over his shoulder" disconcerting. Seeing Dick walk in the door and strip was also outside his comfort zone. As was seeing Dick, trying to be helpful, shouting "I'll get it" when the doorbell rang, and then doing so.

Dick seemed like he was only visiting the human race, though he was enjoying the visit. For instance, he bought a vibrator. Back in California he and his girlfriend had a rich and varied sex life. This was something he shared not only through stories, but through proximity, if you sat next to them in a movie, or even in Denny's. In Las Vegas he needed an outlet, so he bought a vibrator. It looked like a tool the Jolly Green Giant's dental hygienist used for polishing teeth. He was proud of his vibrator, bragged about it, and being generous, told me that I could borrow it if I wanted.

He had been living with us less than a month when he burned up his car. He went driving out to Red Rock with David Eig, and the car caught fire. By the time the fire truck arrived, it was a goner. He told me the firemen thought he was weird. It seems he had done some figuring. He owned half the car. All of his clothes were in it. There was the only documentation for a computer program he'd been working on to see if he could beat pai gow poker. He assigned dollar values, added them up, and came up with a total loss of about three thousand dollars. Then he started laughing because he'd had worse losses gambling.

Dick needed a car, and we found an outfit called Rent a Wreck that was up near Nellis AFB. Dick went up there, and called me with a problem. To rent the car they wanted a credit card. Failing that, they wanted a pay stub as proof of income. This is the sort of problem gamblers run into.

"Put her on the phone." I told her that I had a Nevada driver's license. She asked if I had a credit card? Um, no. A pay stub? What, who has that? Then I had an idea. "I can show you a magazine with my picture, which identifies me as the editor in chief. Would you like to see that?" "Sure!"

The trouble was that I couldn't find a copy around the house. I called Max's house. (And it bothers me, thinking back on this, because I remember Linda answering the phone, and later the door when I drove to Max's, but she should have been gone by then, a detail I'll get to.) There was a copy at Max's. We lived at Trop and Pecos. That was near the southeast end of town. Max was now living west of Rainbow and north of Flamingo, what was then the far west side, and more than nine miles away. Nellis Air Force Base was at the northeast end of town, about sixteen miles from Flamingo and Rainbow. It was four-twenty, and the place closed at five.

I wasn't an ex-cab driver for nothing. I walked into the office of Rent a Wreck with three minutes to spare!

I brandished my copy of the Backgammon Scholar. There was a picture of me in its front. It was taken when I still had hair below my shoulders, and a beard curling onto my chest. The photo was shot at an upward angle, revealing that even the inside of my nose was hairy. I looked like a werewolf.

"Wow!" she said.

"Now you'll rent him the car?"

"First I need a credit card or a pay stub."

"I thought you said you wanted to see this picture?"

"I wanted to see it, but I still can't rent a car without the other stuff."

"What if he leaves a deposit?"

She shook her head. "He'd have to leave the cost of the car."

I thought about that. The place was called Rent a Wreck for a reason. "How much is that?"

"Six hundred dollars."

"Jesus Christ Dick! Give her six hundred, and let's get out of here."

CHAPTER 16
WINNING WAY

That I could be so cavalier about leaving a six-hundred-dollar deposit shows how fortunes had changed. The previous year it seemed like everyone was winning but the team I played for. Chuck and the Czechs were doing fine. Tommy Hyland's team made a legendary score. They'd come to town for a weekend in June, the weekend of the Holmes-Cooney fight. Fights back then were held at Caesar's, an arena erected in the parking lot. Card counting teams descended on the town because there was so much action that the bosses were run ragged. Tommy and his group arrived in force. There were thirty or forty players. Rumor was they trained them to play a basic strategy calibrated for true three, so they didn't bother with index numbers, and when they got the count, they Wonged in for double four hundreds. They had a "massive positive fluctuation," and won two hundred and eighty thousand dollars. In one weekend, while we on Art's team struggled to get back to even.

Munchkin's team also set a standard for success. They were hitting their twenty-thousand-dollar targets and collecting pay every few weeks.

This year it was my team's turn. Wylie had won when he played, Dick was now winning steadily, and piling up the hours while he did.

We were reinvesting some of our winnings to grow the bankroll, and Dick was convincing friends and family to invest. Over the course of the year the bankroll grew from ten thousand dollars to ninety-nine thousand.

I was personally on a roll. I had losing sessions. Those come with the territory. But I won more than I lost, lots more. I was playing three different types of games.

One, which only worked in a few casinos, but was very effective, was playing double deck. The casinos in Las Vegas were not as nervous about double deck as they were with single deck. The Riviera was perfect for what I was doing. They had a long oval pit, and I would circle it. As I did, I would be looking ahead two or three tables. What I watched for was a dealer dealing the first hand to a table only half full. If I saw that, as I approached, I would look to see if it was covered with small cards. If I didn't see it, I kept walking without changing pace or showing my interest. But if I did see what I was hoping for, I would walk to the table without hesitation. I would have the table counted as I sat down, usually a true two or better. I'd plunk down an appropriate bet, and play to the shuffle. The bosses never saw me counting, nor saw me vary my bet by much.

I played a lot of single deck. Other than hole card plays, it was doubtful that any casino in Las Vegas would tolerate counting a single deck. Ah, but there was Reno! Up north almost all of the games were single deck. The Reno MGM Grand may have been the only place with shoes. They hit soft seventeen up north, but that was a minor matter. Most casinos dealt at least thirty cards, and one, the Sundowner, dealt forty or forty-five before shuffling. Not only did they deal these games, they tolerated my bet spread, which was one to five in black. I played in some casinos for hours without heat.

There were places that were suspicious. Caesars in Lake Tahoe had a single deck game which allowed players to double after splits, and surrender. They'd been hit, and they knew what card counting was. But now that I was on my own bankroll, I could take counter-counter-measures. When I sat down, I saw the boss make a call. For the next few minutes I played a strict parlay, doubling up my bets if I won, cutting back if I lost, regardless of the count. After five or ten minutes the phone in the pit rang, and when the boss finished listening, he came over, offered me his card, and comped me for dinner. I thanked him, and now that the coast was clear began betting according to the count. I won six thousand, and dinner tasted mighty good.

I was still shuffle tracking, and that was going very well. My two favorite casinos were Caesar's Palace and the Golden Gate. I never lost at the Golden Gate. One time I emptied the rack of green really quickly, and when they brought a fill, they brought black chips. They were wrapped in wax paper like Ritz crackers, and looked like they had never been out of their wrapper.

"I've never seen black chips in here," I said to the floor man.

"The only other time I've seen them was the last time you were here."

There was an older boss, I think he was the casino manager, because he showed up on different shifts. He never came to the table, but when I looked at the pit, he'd be at the podium glaring at me. One morning I won a few thousand, and went to the cage. I saw him out of the corner of my eye, heading my way. "Here it comes," I thought, the moment when he tells me I am barred.

"You're a pretty good player," he growled. I demurred, muttering that I was just lucky. "No, you're a good player. We ought to do some-thing about a good player like you!" Then he wrote me a comp for breakfast at the coffee shop.

Caesar's was also a great place to play. They had the aforemen-tioned double after split and surrender. They also got big action. At times it seemed like they didn't care if I was counting. I was over in the "kiddie pit," a remote section of the casino where they had lower limit tables. I saw a floorman tell the pit boss about me. The pit boss looked around, saw I was betting four hundred dollars, and waved dismis-sively, as though to say, "Not worth bothering about."

On the other hand, there was the Weasel. He came to check my game. He was the nemesis of so many of my friends, literally chasing some out the door. I was shuffle tracking, and when he saw me betting off the top, he came over, shook my hand, gave me his card, and asked if there was anything he could do for me? "How about dinner for two at the Palace Court?" The Palace Court was considered the fanciest gourmet room in Las Vegas. Shows how tastes change. Munchkin and I ate there and found the staff snooty, and the food unimpressive. On the other hand, the night before I had a comp to the Bacchanal Room. People laughed about the Bacchanal Room. It had a set menu, fifty bucks a head. Wine goddesses would come around, tuck your head in their bosoms, peel grapes and feed them to you. The vibe was entirely different. Everyone was having fun, and the food was good, better, we thought, than at the Palace Court.

I got heat a few times at Caesar's. Once I reached the last hand of the shoe, the count was high, I was betting five hundred, and I caught a pair of tens. Two tens add up to twenty, and ordinarily you would never split them. But when the count was high enough, if the dealer had a weak up card, a five, say, there was an index number, and splitting became a very profitable play. I split, caught another ten, split again, caught one more, and split again. I had two grand on the layout, caught more tens to make twenties, and the dealer busted. The bosses glared at me.

I had a good track, and left five hundred out. They were waiting to see me have a change of heart, but I left it out there. The dealer dealt me a twenty, and she had a low card as her upcard. The clump was very rich, and so I split, replit, and reresplit, once again ending up with four hands, two thousand dollars bet. But this was the first hand of the shoe, so now instead of a card counter, I looked like a wild man who didn't know how to play. I won the hand, and the bosses were happy.

I got heat from a Caesar's dealer once. We didn't tip, because it was hard to satisfy dealers' desire for tips commensurate with our betting, and our desire to leave the table with a profit. In later years I would find a happy medium, but at the time, I wasn't tipping, and this dealer wasn't happy. It was a silent and cordial mutual dislike until I was dealt an ace-seven. She had a ten. The ace-seven is a hand amateurs get wrong. It's a hand that you sometimes hit, sometimes stand, and sometimes double down. One of the plays that few get right is against a dealer ten; you are supposed to hit. Only pros hit. I scratched for a hit. The dealer was dealing rapidly; all the Caesar's dealers were fast. It being Caesar's, this dealer like many of her coworkers knew basic strategy. She started to deal the card, and then she jerked as though she'd been slapped.

"Hitting soft eighteen." She had figured out I was a card counter, and wanted to put heat on me. The floorman was a young man, standing over at the podium, trying to make time with a cute cocktail waitress. He ignored her.

"Hitting soft eighteen!" She called it out again, while I impatiently scratched for a card. The boss didn't turn around.

"Joe! Hitting soft eighteen!"

"All right already!" He turned around this time. "Hit the goddamned thing!" And went back to doing his own hitting, on the cocktail waitress.

The most startling was one morning on grave. I played a lot of graveyard. There was no one in the casinos. I could get heads up games, play nice and fast, and always get the cut card. I was in Caesar's at around 7:30 in the morning, nearing the end of a two- or three-hour session. I was doing an "up all night, and falling asleep at the table" act, pretending to nod off. There was an old boss I'd played in front of many times, and he was also sitting with his chin tucked on his chest.

A young couple came through, and decided to play a few hands on my table before heading to breakfast. They took note of my demeanor, and the woman said to her husband, "That poor man! Do you think we should wake him up and tell him to go to bed?"

The old boss's eyes popped open, he sat upright and said, "Don't worry about him! He ain't missin' a trick!"

CHAPTER 17
REVERSAL OF FORTUNE

We were a winning team, but Munchkin's team, after their great run the year before, was struggling. The seeds were sown during their success. An early sign was when they began rating games differently. They had a twelve-hour per week requirement, but they decided that shuffle tracking counted double. You only had to put in six hours, though the ones who weren't burnt out beavered up hours. If shuffle tracking was double, first basing must be triple! There were even theoretical games. Ray talked to me about his dream of playing the Sundowner in Reno. That was the one dealt so deep into the deck. I think Ray used a multi-level count, Uston APC, or Wong's Halves, which was better than the Hi Lo a lot of us used. Not *that* much better, but Ray also claimed that he could count faster than most people, "over three hundred hands an hour." Few pros worried about what count someone used, but counting fast made a huge difference. Using an advanced count was worth less than a game with better rules, and better rules were worth less than good penetration (the dealer going deep into the deck before shuffling). But speed? In a crowded casino you'd play fewer than a hundred hands an hour. At some tables as few as fifty. Heads up, playing over three hundred hands an hour? That really was worth six times as much as fifty hands an hour.

"The first hour I would only bet one hundred or two hundred. I would raise and lower my bet randomly. Only after they were convinced I was safe, then I would start really playing, and only spread one to three in black." As far as I know, he never got that game.

Some of the players decided that they were just better players than their teammates. It stood to reason that in the long run, getting paid based upon how much they won would favor them over the long haul. Others preferred the status quo. They came up with a compromise. The bankroll would be increased, to one hundred thousand. Instead of betting quarter to double fives, they would play one to eight in black. By staying in one color they looked more like regular high rollers, and with a larger unit and bigger top bet, they would win more money. This would also introduce more variance, which had the potential to create morale problems if they hit a bad patch. The real problem was the other decision they made.

They split the team into two groups. Each called themselves "the A team," the others the "B team." Munch, Craig, Frank, and Bill were on one team. Bill was inactive, invested, and would play when available, but he was doing an around-the-world trip with John Albright, Cathy's ex-husband. The other half of the team comprised Ray, Miles, and Jon Ungar. Jon had run a team of college mates, known as the Princeton Team. He had graduated, and was looking for someone to play with. It was agreed that the investors would receive thirty-five percent of the win from each group. Munch's group would apportion eighty percent of the remainder based on hours, and twenty percent on wins. Their target would remain twenty thousand, after expenses. There was talk of playing some games further afield than Las Vegas, so of course there would be expenses. The other team set a target of forty thousand after expenses, with thirty-five percent going to the investors, and one hundred percent of the rest going to the players based upon how much they each won. However, they would pay themselves a flat forty dollars an hour for time played, and that was considered an expense. Somehow, none of them foresaw any problem with this arrangement.

They each turned over a bank quickly, and it all seemed fine. Then Munch's group went on a tear.

Munch had some great wins during this period. One was at a casino called the Ambassador. It was located on East Flamingo, across from another small casino called the Continental. The Ambassador had a two-hundred-dollar limit. Munch found a first baser, and settled in to play. He was killing them, and decided that he would just keep playing until they threw him out, because they'd probably never let him back in.

He was sitting on first base. The shift manager was sitting on third base, to "keep the high roller company." That Munch was torturing them by winning so much, was more than he could bear, but at the same time he kept hoping that Munch would start losing. Every time Munch won a hand he'd say, "Nice!" through gritted teeth. And kick the table. Munch won eighty-eight hundred dollars, forty-four times the betting limit.

His biggest score was at the Las Vegas Club, which was at Main and Fremont, where the Circa is now. The Las Vegas Club claimed to have the best rules in town. It was a six-deck game with a bad cut, but it did have really good rules, all sorts of variations which made the game about even off the top if you knew the correct strategy. Because of the bad cut it was not a good game for a straight counter, but it had a trackable shuffle. Munch played there, doing a drunk act. The bosses roped off his table and had guards keep away the riffraff. He won over nineteen thousand dollars.

Craig and Frank were also winning. They quickly blew past twenty thousand, but the new arrangement required the other group to be at least even before the bank could break.

The other group was not at least even. Miles was losing. Miles was losing a lot. Eventually Miles was stuck one hundred and thirty thousand dollars. His new nickname was "the Dump Truck." Because he was losing, he needed cash to play. It reached a point where Munch and the others were up one hundred and six thousand dollars, and decided to stop playing until matters were settled. But despite their winning, they had hardly any of the team cash!

And there were disturbing reports coming from Atlantic City and the Bahamas, that Miles was playing craps for cover, that he was playing while drinking, that he was making twenty-five-hundred-dollar bets, triple the team limit. They brought him back and polygraphed him, and he admitted to everything, but insisted that he could justify all of it. The others didn't care whether there were reasons for considering some of the things he'd done; the team had policies, and he was violating them. His response was that he knew better, and he'd continue doing whatever he liked if he thought it justified.

Meanwhile, he and the others were holding the bank hostage. They not only wanted to play until even, they wanted to play until their side could break the bank. Months later, talking to Ray, he used the term "negative player equity," and it dawned on me what the problem was. Let's say that Ray's group got to even, and Munch and the others broke the bank up one hundred and six thousand, and pulled out. Ray's group would need to refinance. By this point the group had hundreds of hours, at forty an hour, and their group had racked up lots of travel expenses. The expenses including hours added up to about forty thousand dollars. New investors would not assume that debt. Hence "negative player equity." In effect, Munch's group, with its negligible expenses, were paying the investors thirty-five percent of the gross, but as investors in the other half were receiving thirty-five percent of the net.

There was arbitration, and everyone walked away unhappy. Craig in particular, because with his cash tied up, he had pulled his investment in my team early on, and when we raked in money, he made none from us.

CHAPTER 18
THE OTHER GAME

With Dick in the house, you might expect even more backgammon action, but by 1983 I was slowly being weaned from the game. There was no longer a backgammon club in Las Vegas. I mentioned earlier my surprise that Linda was at home in Max's new house on the west side of town. The reason for my surprise is that another memory has the two of them breaking up in the fall of 1982. Breaking up dramatically. Max went to Ireland to hang out with Chip Reese and the other poker players during a tournament. He returned to find his belongings waiting on the front walk. He didn't elaborate, but I heard from other sources about a long-time mistress who was a dancer in the Lido show. Linda heard about her, too.

I went to a party at his new house, where he asked me to write a flyer for a friend who had a beauty salon. While there, he said, "You don't do drugs." It was a question in the form of a statement, or a statement which was half question. He pulled out a cosmetics case filled with several grams of fluffy white powder. I sort of didn't do drugs. I was a proud child of the sixties, and had tried most substances that would take me up, down, or sideways.

Hallucinogens and I did not see eye to eye. I had had my flings with most uppers, including MDMA. We called it ecstasy back then, or "the love drug." I'd also had a few prescriptions for Dexedrine as a kid, and did plenty of bootleg white cross, Preludins, and black beauties. I did various downs, including ludes, Seconal, even junk. I had smoked enough grass that my nickname should have been Lawn. You know, typical kid stuff. All of that was a decade behind me.

But I would still toot if someone twisted my nose, and Max handed me the case with a straw stuck right in the pile. Lines were for wimps! Max had married one half of a set of twins, Denise Hemingway. She was a grandniece I think, cousin to the actresses. Denise also was fond of coke. Max would call me every few days, and wonder why it had been so long since I stopped by? I would come over, and we would go through an eight-ball between the three of us. I would finally manage to get out the door around eight in the morning, then would go home and blow my nose for an hour or two, so that I could breathe clearly enough to sleep. A couple days went by, my nose would be good as new, and then Max would call again.

Other than the stuffed sinuses, and a disrupted sleep schedule, coke didn't bother me, and I had no urge to seek more. What Max supplied – and it was free! – was more than I needed or wanted. Max wasn't so lucky.

He insisted one night that we go downtown. He wanted to show me the wedding chapel where he and Denise were married, and then see the show at Sinatra's. Sinatra's is a footnote to history, but at the time it was newsworthy because Sinatra's was being sued by Frank Sinatra. The club owner was fortunate enough to share the famous surname, and thought he had a perfect right to call his club Sinatra's. Old Blue Eyes thought otherwise. I figure a man has a right to use his own name, no matter who shares it, but after seeing the show, I could almost sympathize with Frank. It was a grab bag of cheesy acts in a grimy joint where you stuck to the carpets. I was talking to Max before the show about how chronic alkies sometimes used loaves of bread to filter alcohol.

"Squeeze!" Said a guy sitting at a nearby slot machine, who looked as though he'd used his shirt to filter some alcohol. "Great stuff!"

Between the wedding chapel, and Sinatra's, we were walking past a no-tel motel, when a wino emerged from the bushes, and staggered past us.

"Did you see his T-shirt?" Said Max. I confessed I had failed to notice. He told me it was some obscure airline. "You don't think that was a coincidence?" Did I think, or not think, that what was a coincidence? "C'mon! You know!" I didn't know. "That was the airline Martha Mitchell was on, when she crashed." Actually, I looked it up, and Dorothy Hunt, not Martha Mitchell was flying United, not the T-shirt's airline, but I didn't know that at the time. Nor did I see what he was driving at. "The CIA! They had him [the wino] wear that shirt to let me know they are watching me."

Some folks cannot handle their cocaine. Max would later be arrested for selling the stuff, and serve seven years in the state pen.

Despite the lack of regular backgammon, I was playing better than ever. Dick and I flew to Chicago for the Chicago Open, and so he could run up to see his brother and get a new car. Dick was from Green Bay, and his brother sold cars. I didn't win in the tournament, but played one of Chicago's top players for ten bucks a point, and won sixty points in about an hour.

In June I made two road trips to L.A. The first was to visit Munchkin. Munch was finally ready to make his move to Hollywood, and become a star. He got an apartment in Westwood which he shared with a college friend. While visiting, I stopped by the Cavendish Club, a bridge club which was also the home to the Los Angeles backgammon scene. I won eight hundred dollars from an obnoxious player, who lost twice that, the rest to two other players. One was a tall, skinny guy around my age, who the others weren't thrilled to have in the game because he was a hustler. His name was Mike Svobodny, and we'd get to be good friends in years to come. Two years later Mike would win the World Championship in Monte Carlo. By then he had cultivated a charming persona, and was welcomed by the rich pigeons of Europe, becoming one of the most successful hustlers of all time. He is the only person to have won both the World Champi-onship, and the World Cup. His adventures are chronicled in my brother's book *Gambling Wizards*. No surprise that he has been inducted into the Backgammon Hall of Fame.

After playing that night I drove back to Vegas, but three days later was on the way back to L.A. The 1st Cavendish Invitational was a good-sized regional tournament, with the top west coast players well represented. It became the first major in which I cashed. That Sunday I found myself in the finals against another player my age, Joe Russell. Somewhat disconcertingly, Don Adams, who was a regular at the Cavendish, was sitting at the table with us, watching the final match. When I missed a shot he'd turn to the other spectators, and say in Maxwell Smart's voice (actually, it seemed like that was his natural voice), "Would you believe, he missed it by *that* much?" I came in second to Joe, but second prize was nearly two thousand dollars. Joe would also win the World Championship, in 1989, and is also in the Hall of Fame.

Thanks to the win, I had about five thousand dollars in my pocket when we left that night. There were six of us in my car, me, Munch, Dick, Nack Ballard, Nack Ballard's girlfriend Lorien, and Steve Sax. The Plimpton Cup was starting Tuesday, and they were also going to play. Steve Sax was only around twenty-one, the son of a woman who managed the Cavendish. He is another Hall of Fame inductee. So is Nack. Nack was in the first class inducted. He'd already won a world championship, though not the one in Monte Carlo. His was what was also called the Professional Championship, the event held along with the Plimpton for people ineligible due to previous winnings. Nack had won it the year before. Besides being one of the best backgammon players of all time, Nack was one of the best Scrabble™ players of all time, one of the best Caucasian Go players, and master of several other games.

Nack and Dick each had about five thousand, I had five thousand, and Steve had several thousand. We had to stop by Munch's apartment because he had a lot of bankroll cash he needed to bring to Las Vegas, forty-two-thousand-dollars' worth. There was around sixty thousand dollars in our pockets when we stopped for dinner at a 24-hour Thai restaurant Steve knew. In Hollywood. Hollywood in those days was grim, a place for junkies and streetwalkers. Luckily, we were backgammon players and blended right in. We could walk around in a dangerous slum carrying sixty grand and no one bothered us.

Having cashed at the Cavendish, Joe Russell and I were lucky we'd sent our entries in advance. We were allowed to play because we entered early, but it would be our last year of eligibility. It would have been nice to win it, since it was my last chance, but the winner was a twenty-one-year-old from Michigan named Joe Sylvester, another player now in the Hall of Fame.

CHAPTER 19
THE SHOES ON
THE OTHER FEET

That spring Timmy was back in action. He'd drifted away from Arthur's team. He really wasn't cut out to be a blackjack player. He was lured back for a specialized role. Munchkin and Cathy had invested in a project of Darryl's, which would lead, as Munch's team dissolved, into Munch and Darryl teaming up, a partnership still in existence forty years later. In one of his books Ken Uston described a computer worn under the clothes which played perfectly.

Card counting systems have two jobs, to improve the accuracy of your betting, and the accuracy of your play. How well they do these things is described with the adjective "efficiency." A system has a betting efficiency, and a playing efficiency, each measured using either a percentage, or more usually a decimal representing it, e.g. 97% becomes .97. If you have no information on how much to bet, and either flat bet, or vary your bet randomly, functionally equivalent to flat betting, your betting efficiency is .00. If you have a computer, which can tell you with perfect accuracy how much to bet, because it has tracked every card, your betting efficiency is 1.00. When it comes to playing efficiency, even without counting, basic strategy is quite accurate. It is assumed you are at least familiar with basic strategy, so that is given a playing efficiency of .00, while perfectly accurate play is 1.00. Betting efficiency matters much more than playing efficiency, especially when playing against multiple decks. The Hi Lo is a 1-level count, its values ranging from -1 to +1. Its betting efficiency is an excellent .97, while its playing efficiency is only .51. There are multilevel counts, those with point values from -2 to +2 are 2-level counts, -3 to +3, 3-level counts, etc. Peter Griffin showed that a 4-level count could boost your playing efficiency to .67, while an infinite-level count could only get you to about .70. There is a gain from higher-level counts, but if you make mistakes, or need to play more slowly to avoid them, you end up worse off.

Griffin played a multi-parameter count, using a 1-level count, but with side counts of cards without assigned point values. He used the Gordon Count, and side counted sevens, eights, nines, and aces, plus the ratio of fives to sixes, and tracked the total number of cards dealt. Doing all that boosted his playing efficiency to 90%. Once again, the same caveats apply. Arthur backed a team, two or three players, who used a multi-parameter count, though they didn't try to match Griffin. Arthur called them "multi-parameter jerkoffs," which was apt. God knows why he backed them.

A computer, however, makes no mistakes, as long as the inputting is accurate, and is only as slow as its inputter. Uston boasted about his computer's perfect play. The downside was that all sorts of other problems manifested themselves. I have never met a counter who set their brain on fire by thinking too hard, but Uston's team had players set their pants on fire because something short-circuited. The books *The Eudaemonic Pie* and *Follow the Bouncing Ball* describe the difficulty of using concealed computers to try to beat roulette.

Undaunted, players worked on solving these problems. By 1983 magic shoes made their debut. Magic shoes had the computer built into the shoe, with wires running up the pants legs. The players used their toes to input card values. The computer would send signals to buzzers attached to sensitive parts of the thighs, indicating how to play. I never met the late Keith Taft, but he is in the Blackjack Hall of Fame. Taft was a gifted engineer. He was also evangelical, not someone you'd expect to devote himself to beating casinos, but devoted he was. Over the years many tales were told around the campfires of his exploits. For instance, there is a story that he once had his then fifteen-year-old-daughter hide inside a heating duct overlooking a casino floor. She was up there two days, with a stash of sandwiches, water bottles, and a fireman's friend. No one knows which casino, or what game they were attacking, but no one doubted that it happened. Keith created for Darryl magic shoes with a computer chip called Thor. Thor was more than a perfect player; Thor tracked shuffles.

Darryl, after years of play, was well-known to casinos. Even though playing with Thor didn't look much like card counting, Darryl betting the money would draw scrutiny. Hence, Timmy the big player. Darryl would sit at the table, betting the minimum, while wearing the shoes and operating the computer. He would relay the bets and plays to Timmy with hand signals.

Not that Timmy was around very long. That spring he began to grow restless. A midlife crisis overtook him. A benign one. He began dressing like the Waldo everyone searches for, with striped shirts, and suspenders, though his cap was sailor rather than stocking. He bought a Walkman, and wandered around singing out loud, whether at home, or out in public. Then he enrolled in school. Off he went to St. John's, in New Mexico. He earned a masters, married one of his professors, then moved east to teach at Georgetown Prep. He became head of the math department, and reveled in teaching geometry directly from Euclid.

Munch preceded him by moving to California. Some funny things happened after he moved. I got a call for him one day, and when I told the caller he was out of town, heard, "This is Howard Grossman. Tell him to call me when he gets back." Munch was due a few days later, and I relayed the message. He called Howard, who was the casino manager at the Nevada Palace. The call was short. Munch got off the phone, and with a bemused look said, "I just got barred. Over the phone!" A few days later he got another call. He said he had to go out to meet someone.

When he got back, he said he'd gone to have coffee with a guy who identified himself as the counter catcher at the Westward Ho. You may recall that the Westward Ho was the casino with the Berlin shuffle? Munch had been very lucky playing there. Unsurprising with that shuffle. He would go in, win a couple of thousand quickly, and cash out. It seems that because he was unpredictable, and often played graveyard, he was in and out before the bosses could summon the counter catcher. The counter catcher was a friend of Howard Grossman's, and asked Howard if he knew anyone fitting Munch's description. Howard did, and said, "Why don't you call him?"

It turned out that neither Howard nor this other guy knew about shuffle tracking. They wondered what Munchkin might be doing that he would make big bets off the top of a shoe? Around this time my ex-teammate, Roger, was exploring a technique which combined dealer warps with ace cutting. The idea was that the dealers bent the aces checking for blackjack, so you looked for a warped card and cut in front of it to give yourself an ace. Howard decided that's what Munchkin was doing.

"That doesn't work!" said Munchkin.

"I know, I tried. So did Howard. The only way it works is if you really bend the aces, and you have to do it yourself." In other words, card bending, which is illegal.

"Jesus! I don't bend cards!"

According to the counter catcher, Howard had decided Munchkin was a card bender, and had told the owner of the Nevada Palace that. He began frothing at the mouth, and saying he would have Munchkin whacked. Howard said, "Let me call him. I think I can persuade him to never show his face in here again." Which he never did.

"But why were you betting off the top?" The counter catcher wondered.

"Cover. I was betting big at the end of the shoe, so I threw out a few big bets at the beginning of the next one."

"I figured," he said.

When Munchkin left, Dick got his own bedroom, my old room, while I upgraded to the master bedroom. Then with Timmy leaving, we had a vacancy. We traded a Timmy for a Bobby.

Dick was a mathematician. He claimed that he'd taught himself calculus from the textbook his dad was using for a night school course.

Dad couldn't get a handle on calculus, but Dick taught himself. When he was seven. It's the sort of story you take with a grain of salt, but in Dick's case, people gave him the benefit of the doubt. People did, but not his dad. He and Dick did not get along. When Dick was ten, he announced that he did not believe in God. His dad grounded him "for life," or until he resumed belief, whichever came first. When Dick was fifteen, he ran away, to Madison, where he moved in with a girlfriend who was in the graduate department for mathematics. She helped him enroll, first as a probationary student, then full time once he proved himself.

A few years later he went to visit a different girlfriend in Santa Cruz. She wasn't home, no one was home, and in ringing the bell he broke a flower pot, then lay down and took a nap. That's where her roommate found him. "Who are you, and what happened to my flower pot?" The girlfriend was out of town, but Dick convinced the room-mate that "she would want me to stay here." By the time the first girl-friend returned, Dick was living with the roommate.

Santa Cruz is a university town, and Dick stayed and earned a couple of master's degrees in math and computer science. Like many grad students, he taught. His office door had a sign, "Institute for Applied Mathematics. Twenty Dollar Buy In." One of Dick's students was Bobby Turnbuckle.

We trained Bobby, and he joined the team. Just in time, because Dick left. Dick was recruited to learn to use the magic shoes. I am not sure if it was Darryl's idea, or Cathy's. At any rate, Dick left the team, and not long after moved out. So did Bobby. Cathy had broken up with Craig, and needed a place to stay. She poached my roommates. I asked about moving in with them. Munchkin had a three-bedroom condo, and we'd been making his mortgage payments as rent. But I was a smoker, and they were not. I also had custody of a pair of cats Munchkin left behind when he moved. I was on my own.

Before bidding Dick goodbye, I have a math story. The two of us often had dinner at the Castaways coffee shop, which had great specials after midnight. Some casinos, including the Castaways, had a new type of machine, a keno machine. Keno is a terrible game, putting the player at a twenty-five percent disadvantage, but Dick wondered if the machine programmers had gotten it right? Maybe there was an edge to be found. To work that out, he needed to see enough spins of the machine to figure out its structure. The machine took quarters, and there were several machines just outside the coffee shop.

Our check was $4.54, and I handed the cashier $5.04. "I'd like those quarters," said Dick. "How about flipping a coin, and if I win, I get those quarters, but if you win, I'll give you a dollar?"

I thought about that, and said, "Okay."

We flipped, I won, he handed me a buck and said, "Damn! I really wanted those quarters. Want to do it again?"

I thought even harder, and said "No."

We made it out to the parking lot when he stopped dead. "Wait a minute! Did I just give you two to one on a coin toss?" I said he had. "What was I thinking?"

"I don't know."

"And then I offered to do it again, and you said no! What were you thinking?"

"I don't know about you, but the first time, I did it because it was two to one on a coin flip. The second time I refused because now I was convinced you were up to something."

Of course what Dick wanted to do, was either collect the two quarters, or when losing give me the dollar, but still collect the quarters. But he didn't offer the bet that way.

The team, heading into the fall of 1983 now comprised me, Bobby, and John Albright, back from his round-the-world trip with Bill Benter. You might recall that John was Cathy's ex-husband. Blackjack is an incestuous business.

Indeed, who should come looking to recruit me, but Ray!

After the split the other team reconstituted itself with a merger. Ray, Bill, Miles, and Jon teamed up with Tommy Hyland. They were now playing mostly in Atlantic City, where Tommy had put together the most successful team in A.C. history. They also had magic shoes. Theirs were designed by another future Hall of Famer, Wally Simmons. Theirs also tracked shuffles. Each group claimed they had the best shuffle tracking computer. My recollection is that Thor may have played better, but theirs could handle a greater range of shuffles.

Ray claimed that the game they were playing was worth fifteen hundred dollars an hour. The split was fifty percent to the investors, and fifty percent to the players (based entirely on hours, I think, this time around). It seems there was an hours requirement for players, and most of the player investors like Ray, were now too well known to even attempt to play in A.C., which has far fewer casinos than Las Vegas. What Ray and the others were looking for, were players to play their hours. He'd pay fifty percent of his player share. If the expected hourly was fifteen hundred, and players got half, and sub-players got half that, it meant three-seventy-five an hour, on average.

I had enough interest to attend a meeting which included Ray, Bill, Jon, Miles, and Tommy. Being recruited were me, King, Tommy's older brother, Wylie, and probably a few others. Huey might have been one of them.

There were negatives. One came up in the meeting. Team policy included regular lie testing. I told them, "You all know what happened to me. I will never undergo something like that again." Miles said that they weren't using polygraphs. I think it was voice stress, though he may have mentioned sodium pentothal. It was a deal breaker for me, no matter what method they used, even tying us in bags, dropping us in Lake Mead, and seeing if we floated.

The other downsides were training, which was long, arduous, and unpaid. Once trained, we could not set our own hours. We could only play when and where our controller directed, for as long as directed. We might be burned out, or the game might become too hot to play, at any time, meaning time wasted, at our own expense, without remuneration. Meanwhile, the team I'd been playing on, my team, had a game I estimated as paying about two hundred and fifty dollars an hour. Maybe if they had offered to make me a full player, earning a possible seven-fifty an hour, and setting my own schedule, I would have gambled. As it was, turning them down was easy.

What happened with Wylie was a cautionary tale, though more for them than for me. Wylie went through training, and made some plays. One night he decided to play in a casino that the team shunned. He wore the shoes. He insisted afterward that he was planning to absorb the loss if he did lose, so it was only fair that he pocket the win. He won, thirty thousand dollars. The team felt that because he used the shoes, and team cash, it was a team win, even if an unauthorized play. I agree. But he told them where they could put their shoes, and took off with the whole win.

Meanwhile, I rejoined John and Bobby.

CHAPTER 20
THE BANKROLL FROM HELL

When you don't know that you might be discussing it years later, you may not make note of when things are happening. The latest bankroll had begun around the end of August or beginning of September. Lots of bankrolls began during that year, and there was no reason to mark the dates. Ray had already contacted me just before the play began on the new bank. I told John and Bobby I wasn't sure if I would be playing with them or not. By the time I turned down the offer from the other team, it may have been October. While I was waiting for the meeting with the computer team, my guys had not fared well. The bankroll was stuck, a lot, twenty or thirty thousand. Never fear, lads! Uncle Jake to the rescue.

I began playing, and won. They were still losing, but I was winning faster than they lost. Inexorably, we were gaining on breakeven. It took time, but eventually we were up around ten thousand dollars. Just ten thousand more and we'd be taking a payday. Then they began losing faster than I was winning. We wound up stuck about forty thousand.

During these months I made quite a few trips to Reno. Reno is four hundred and fifty miles northwest of Las Vegas. That's a lot of scenery, and all of it is boring. You do pass through some small towns along the way, towns like Tonopah. They are boring, too. They have some small casinos, like the Mizpah in Tonopah. If you were a real tourist, soaking up the historic aromas of Tonopah, and of the Mizpah, redolent of the Wild West and Nevada's mining history, I guess they'd be interesting. But if you were looking to win a fortune – and if you play blackjack for a living, what else would you be doing? – look elsewhere. There were interesting signs, if you are intrigued by warnings of danger you wouldn't expect to see in Evanston, Illinois. Watch out for cattle on the road, falling rocks, trucks loaded with explosives, trains loaded with explosives, low flying airplanes, and many more. Seventeen comes to mind as the number of different reasons you should drive carefully.

They left out rabbits. I made the drive at night, so that I could do eighty-five whenever I got the chance. It still took eight hours, what with Tonopah, Goldfield, and other slow patches. In the middle of Nevada there are jackrabbits. Lots of jackrabbits. They swarm the road, and unlike Bugs Bunny, they are not very bright. They run right out in front of your car. They don't care. They make a strange crunching sound when you run over packs of them at eighty-five miles an hour, in the dark. I have nothing against rabbits. I mourn the ones I killed. My goodwill was insufficient to save them, and I killed hundreds, even thousands of them that year.

I made the trip with Bobby at least once. Most of Reno's gambling is downtown, near that sign proclaiming Reno the "Biggest Little City in the World." The world was in bad shape judging by Reno. The economy in the early eighties was bad, and Nevada was suffering. Reno's downtown showed its age. There were a few casinos not right in downtown near Virginia Street. The MGM was one of them. Kirk Kerkorian had built it during one of the times he owned MGM. It was large, and it was lonely, and it was on its steps one night in mid-December that Bob turned to me, his lips blue, and asked "How do people live in this?" It was twenty-three degrees and Bob, who was born and raised in Phoenix, then lived in Santa Cruz, had never been exposed to twenty-three-degree weather.

I remember that because a week later, back in Chicago for Christmas, Munchkin and I left the backgammon club at four in the morning. I was driving mom's late seventies model Honda Civic. I'd warmed it up for forty minutes, and it hadn't helped. The windows were frosted;

howling winds had me fighting to keep the car in its lane. The radio announcer said that with the windchill it was minus seventy at O'Hare. Munchkin and I looked at each other, and wondered, "How do people live in this?"

Reno wasn't much warmer in January than it had been in December, but I was feeling the glow. A trio of guys up there had formed the Northern Nevada Backgammon Association, and were holding the first Nevada State Championships. The venue was the Peppermill, another casino not in downtown Reno. The turnout was respectable, more than respectable. The players came mostly from the West Coast, but both L.A. and San Francisco had active backgammon scenes, and the Open had a bracket of sixty-four.

I won. When I reached the final, I went to Nack, who was running a book, to see about possibly hedging. My opponent, a generation older than me, was named Aram Kouleyan. I'd seen him play, and knew I was much better. However, Aram had been around the L.A. scene for years, long enough to have won some tournaments. He was well known. Despite my second-place finish the previous June at the Cavendish, I was a former Chicagoan, and not well known. Nack's line was 11-10 pick'em. In English, you had to lay eleven dollars to win ten, to bet on either one of us. Nack was doing what bookies do, setting a line that would maximize, he hoped, his profit, attracting balanced action on both sides. I considered the line an insult. Instead of hedging, I pressed, betting $220 on myself to win $200. Nack then went to Aram, told him what I'd done, and Aram promptly bet $220 on himself. Nack couldn't lose.

Nor could I. I won 15-6 and collected over five thousand dollars prize money, five hundred from my buyback of a portion my Calcutta, and two hundred from Nack for the side bet. It came to six or seven thousand dollars. David Lang was at the tournament, and so was Jon Ungar. We went to David's suite at Harrah's, drank some of his room service Chateau du Pape Neuf, and played backgammon for five dollars a point. David would have been the big loser, were it not for one game where he won back one hundred and fourteen points. He finished dead even, Jon lost one hundred points (on that game), and I won a hundred points. Five hundred more dollars on top of the rest.

Good thing, because I needed it.

I had dug us out of the hole once again, gotten us back up to plus ten thousand, and then I started losing. Bobby and John began winning, but I was losing faster. Things turned around once more, and finally, perhaps a month after the Reno tournament, we were again plus ten thousand dollars.

I was in Las Vegas. Bob was in Reno. He'd been receiving tutelage from David Lang in the art of collecting room service comped wine. (I think Harrah's finally limited David before he asked them to build him his own wine cellar.) It was two a.m., and Bob called to tell me he was going out to win the rest of the bank that night. I don't know why I was going to bed so early, but that night I did. Bob called me again, at ten in the morning. He'd played all through grave, at the Cal-Neva, and he had lost thirty thousand dollars. We were stuck twenty. He was also out of funds.

I called Bill Benter, and asked if he had anyone up north. He told me Jon Ungar was in Tahoe, and we made arrangements for Jon and Bob to meet, and for Bob to get twenty thousand dollars.

I drove over to Bill's apartment with twenty thousand from our bankroll. While there he showed me that he had a personal computer. In the winter of 1984 that was a rarity. I'd only seen one other, the previous summer. A group of us had gone to Imperial Beach, near San Diego, to see a backgammon buddy, Todd Vander Pluym, win his third consecutive US Open Sand Castle Building Championship. While there we dropped in on Jason Vollmer. Jason was a former blackjack player. He'd been a teammate of Ron, the ex-husband of Craig's late ex-wife. Jason was married to a woman who was the sister of Frank's girlfriend Linda, who was friends with Cathy, soon to be Craig's ex-girlfriend. Cathy's ex-husband, John, was a teammate of mine. I could tease out more connections, but it shows you how incestuous professional blackjack is. Anyway, Jason and Craig were collaborating on a backgammon program for home computers (turned out well), and Jason had the first personal PC I'd seen.

Now here was Bill's, and he had an interesting question. What did I think about the possibility of beating horse racing? That was the project he was working on. Even if I hadn't been exposed to degenerate horse players, my old boss Dick at the cab company stealing five hundred and fifty thousand dollars from Western Union to feed his addiction, I had a practical answer. "Think about it, Bill. We try to overcome a half percent house edge at blackjack, and the best we do is a two percent edge if we get the hole card. The tracks rake seventeen percent on races. Don't waste your time!"

Money swapped; I got another two-a.m. call from Bobby. "I am going back to the Cal-Neva, and win it back." "Go get 'em," I told him. Eight hours later he called once more, "I lost the whole twenty." We were stuck forty thousand once again.

In retrospect, we should have broken the bank then. The three of us were completely demoralized. We played less and less, and made no headway. By summer we had more or less ground to a halt.

As for Bob's loss, I partly blame myself. There were two dots I failed to connect until much later. Bobby lost fifty thousand dollars in two nights playing graveyard shift at the Cal-Neva. I was cheated on graveyard shift at the Cal-Neva!

What happened to me was that I had gone in one night around three in the morning. The place was busy. I wanted a heads-up game, but they wouldn't give me a twenty-five-dollar-minimum game. Too many customers. I played at a table for a short while, but it filled up. While I was at the first table, the dealer went on break. The relief dealer was in her fifties, gray-haired, plump, grandmotherly. She'd only been on for a deck or two when the next table thinned out, and I moved over. Two minutes later the same relief dealer tapped the dealer on my new table.

"Huh?" I thought. She'd only been on the first table five minutes, and this wasn't how breaks worked. Depending upon the casino, breaks were fifteen or twenty minutes per hour. Either way, five minutes was too soon for her to move. What did I know? Maybe there was some glitch in their schedule.

This table filled up, and five minutes later I moved to a table across the pit. Within minutes, the dealer had moved to my table. This was no coincidence. I finished the hand, and got up. She smirked at me when I left.

Cheating casinos are not unknown. I've described Old Baldy, the house bust-out man at the Stardust. Munchkin knew a boss at the Castaways, one of the old-timers, who told him a story. That night Munch was acting as floor man. There was a high roller who was "George" (a good tipper), but the dealer was hot. Players usually tip dealers by placing an extra bet in front of their hand. If they win, the dealer wins the bet. If they lose, it goes in the rack. The dealer went on break, and as she passed Munch and the old-timer, she moaned about how unlucky she was in making tip money.

"Think she's unlucky? That ain't nothin'! I used to work at the Cal-Neva, back when Frank owned it." Sinatra owned a piece of it in the sixties. So did Dean Martin. So, unfortunately, did Sam Giancana, and that led to Sinatra's license being suspended. "There was a guy bettin' five hundred a hand, and a hunnert for the dealer, every hand! They sent me in to deal to him, and the bosses wouldn't let me lose a hand. Not one hand!"

There was also Tony, a backgammon player at Rumors, who had been shift manager at the Silver Saddle, and took the rap for his bosses when the Gaming Commission discovered they were dealing short shoes.

More recently both Munchkin and Dick ran into cheating dealers. The girl dealing to Munch was not an master mechanic. There is no point in dealing seconds unless you know what the first card is. There are moves which let the dealer surreptitiously peek, but she hadn't mastered them. She held the deck up to her face, pretending to scratch between her eyes, while she peeked at the card. Munch burst out laughing, "Nice move!" and took his action to another table. She was probably acting on her own, not at the casino's behest, else they needed to hire a better mechanic.

Which was probably also true of the dealer Dick spotted at the Bingo Palace. He was dealing from a shoe, which is usually safe because, while there are methods for peeking, which I will talk more about later, they often require prisms, which means evidence if the Gaming Commission raids the place. What this dealer was doing was sliding the cards out of the shoe, then over the edge of the chip rack. There was a reflection on the metal rim, and if the card was good for Dick, the dealer would burn it.

Despite all that, cheating really is rare. It has to be, or how would we ever have made our livings? I didn't think about "Grandma" and where Bob lost his money, until way too late. It is possible that he simply lost. Possible, but cheating was also possible. I'll never know.

I had no income, but plenty of outgo, especially with no roommates helping with the rent. I was borrowing against the bankroll, pending our recovery. If we didn't recover, I'd be owing money, and Dick, seeing opportunity, informed me that his "standard interest rate" was twenty-five percent.

In September I got a job. I'd been playing a lot of bridge. Teaching me bridge had been a project of Timmy's before he left town. He sent away for back issues of Bridge World, and the Bridge Bulletin. While Dick was visiting San Francisco he had him collect the bridge library Timmy had stored in a friend's garage. The very bridge books he so memorably "aired out." In 1983 and 1984 I read the collection, one hundred and fifty or two hundred books, and four hundred magazines. I worked all the problems. It whacked my reading speed. In January of 1984 I started playing at the local bridge clubs. I was the 1984 Rookie of the Year in Nevada, and got a letter from the governor to prove it.

A bridge player named Bill worked for an outfit called D.B. Enterprises. If you hear "boiler room" you probably think of *The Wolf of Wall Street*, and pumping penny stocks. In Nevada and California in those days, boiler rooms sold "advertising specialties." Those were pens, key chains, baseball caps, which advertised small businesses. Bill was making two thousand dollars a week in 1984 dollars, and was the apostle of boiler room selling. He loved doing it even more than playing bridge, and he and his wife Patty played bridge every chance they got. Making two grand a week sounded like an answered prayer, and with a recommendation from Bill, I was hired.

It was the most awful job I have ever had, and I have hauled steel and shoveled actual shit!

My shift began at six in the morning. That was nine o'clock on the East Coast, so we weren't even early birds when we called across the country. I had been on a late-night schedule for a decade by then. I was now rising around the time I would ordinarily be thinking about going to bed. During the time I worked at D.B.E. I never adapted. I spent most of my days walking around in a sickened daze. The first thing I would do on arrival was grab coffee. I was not, to that point, a regular coffee drinker, but now I needed coffee to wake up. The coffee was brewed in an industrial-sized machine, and it was potent. I would take two sips and a laxative effect kicked in; making a hurried trip to the bathroom was the second thing I would do.

In the movie, *Glengarry Glen Ross*, the sales team burglarized the office to try to get their hands on "the good leads." I could relate. The pitch we made was based on selling not our product, overpriced crap, but on our 15th anniversary drawing. If you bought, besides getting a box full of junk with your business' name printed on it, you received one entry into the drawing. The first prize was twenty-five hundred bucks, the second a string of "Aegean pearls" valued at fifteen hundred, and "altogether seven hundred and thirty-seven valuable prizes." Which were, if one trusted the company's valuation, and I wouldn't, collectively worth fifteen grand. If you did the math, and I may have been the only person not running the company who ever did that, it works out to not much more than twenty bucks a pop, and that is before you deduct out the three top prizes. (I don't remember what third prize was, but think it was valued at five hundred). That brought it down to fifteen bucks apiece if you were lucky. I don't know how long the drawing lasted, but it went on the entire ten weeks I worked there. Your equity in the drawing would be measured in single digit dollars, if not change for a buck. For this privilege you paid a couple of hundred dollars for the aforementioned crap. For instance, one hundred cheap plastic pens went for $219, or even more. There was a limit to how much you could charge, but I think the limit may have been as high as $269, if you sent them an immediate prize. Those prizes were valued at twenty bucks, worth a fraction of that, and came out of your commission if you sent one and failed to charge the customer a premium for their "prize."

You should understand that D.B. Enterprises was legitimate. Other boiler rooms were not. The two most infamous sales pitches were the "satellite dish" and the "Mexican vacation." The satellite dish scam promised customers five prizes, four of which may or may not have been awarded, and were decent prizes. Everyone else received for their "guaranteed prize" a satellite dish. Imagine yourself a happy customer. You've spent a couple of hundred bucks on junky pens. You get a call, "Herman! You've won! You've won!" "What did I win?" "You've won the satellite dish!" The salesman would now pitch you to buy another hundred pens to show your gratitude, and would hit you with an additional eighty-dollar shipping charge for your dish. Which, when it arrived, was plastic and a foot in diameter.

Bill had previously worked for one of those outfits, and when he called a "reload" in Wyoming, the customer was thrilled that he had won the dish. "You are? I mean, you are!" The customer said that where he lived, he needed a dish, and in anticipation had laid a slab of concrete alongside the house to receive it. "Oh … Well, I think you will get better reception if you put it on the roof. But don't tear up that slab just yet, because the grand prize in our next drawing is a helicopter!"

The Mexican vacation was similar. There were four terrific vacations, a Caribbean cruise, a trip to Paris, etc. Everyone else got the Mexican vacation. When they won, they learned it was a trip for two, winners to provide their own transportation to San Diego. Where they were loaded onto buses and driven down the Baja coast. There they were put up in trailers, and had to listen every day to a pitch for time sharing in the condos which were "going to be built" right where they were staying.

Which explains why, when I called one gas station owner in Texas, he told me that if I, or any salesman, called again, he would come to Las Vegas with his "AK," and spray our office. That's the sort of lead new salesmen got.

Bill and a handful of elite sales people, got leads to people who were still happy with us. The rest of us got the most burnt leads imaginable, to people who hated us. Bill, by the way, was not the most successful salesman. There was a guy there who went by the name Frank Burns when he made his calls. He was a New York Italian who was five foot six inches tall, and five foot six inches around. He was covered on every visible surface except his head, with black hair that jutted in wiry tangles. Every afternoon at quitting time, which was one o'clock, his secretary would gather leads the elite team had failed to sell. Then he would pitch them the next day.

"Herman! This is Joe Burns, from D.B. Enterprises. One of my people called you yesterday, and, you didn't buy!" The poor sucker on the other end didn't have a chance. The calls lasted about a half an hour on average, and they barely got a word in. Frank (his real name) was averaging eleven calls a day, and selling ten. He was making thirty-five hundred bucks a week, and he came in an hour late every day.

Meanwhile, instead of an office and a secretary, I toiled in a tiny booth, reading a canned pitch. I could hear the guy in the next booth. He had a mild speech impediment which caused him to slur his words. Words whose meaning he didn't know. He thought that Aegean pearls belonged to someone named Aggie. It was obvious that he was reading a pitch. He was making two hundred and fifty dollars a week. I also made two hundred and fifty dollars while there. That was the sum of my earnings during the entire ten weeks. I had theatre and voice training, what was described as a "radio announcer's voice." In my teens I had not only done a lot of stage work, I'd even done puppet voices on a television show for children. I think the reason I couldn't sell is that I was communicating too well. What I communicated is that deep down I didn't think people should buy the shit I sold.

At the end of ten weeks the manager, Conrad, called me into his office and said, "It's not like you didn't try."

After that it was a matter of organizing my exit. Of selling my car, my TV, my books (that hurt). On December 23rd, using a one-way ticket, I flew back to Chicago. Sitting in an airplane seat for four hours is uncomfortable when your tail is between your legs. I'd had plenty of good times in the not quite three years I lived in Las Vegas, but I was leaving a failure. A year before I had money saved, invested in the bankroll. I was making good money, living large. Now I was worse than broke, I was twenty-five thousand dollars in debt, about half to Dick at twenty-five percent interest. If there is one thing of which I was certain it's that when it came to blackjack, I would never play that fucking game again!

CHAPTER 21

AN OFFER I COULDN'T REFUSE

Did you ever look closely at the menu in a Korean restaurant? I did. The Chicago area was behind the coasts when it came to Asian food, but I was ahead of most Midwesterners. I was with some equally adventurous friends in a new Korean restaurant in Hoffman Estates. I ordered bulgogi, and saw that besides the English, there was the dish's name in hangul script: 불고기. Can you pick out the Gs? I got to wondering if I could decipher the Korean alphabet with a bit of effort.

I'd been back in Chicago for over two years, managing a video store my dad opened as an investment. It had been rough at first. I returned in winter, not a good time to move to Chicago. I was suffering from severe panic attacks those first months, and developed esophagitis, an inflammation which forced me to radically change my diet. By the time it cleared up I had a head start on losing one hundred and twenty pounds. I'd gone back to Las Vegas once, the following summer, to play in a bridge national tournament. I'd done no gambling. Back home I played some bridge, and some Scrabble™, but hardly any backgammon, and then only in local club tournaments.

Backgammon had seen some cheating scandals. When I lived in Las

Vegas there was a guy named Sal who sometimes came by the Jockey Club. Sal didn't play backgammon, but he was a famous dice cheat. He had a legendary move. He could lock up a six, and toss it down the table while the other die flew free.

There was also Stan Mack. Stan I knew from before I moved to Las Vegas. During one of the Plimpton tournaments, Stan was barred by director Henry Watson for being a known cheat. Stan was not what you'd picture as a dice mechanic. He was in his seventies, and claimed to have been a bare-knuckle fighter during the Depression. His hands were gnarly and arthritic. He was a very poor backgammon player, and his cheating move was hopeless. He would use one finger to manipulate a die while he shook his dice cup, letting the other rattle around. When he rolled he would bang his knuckle on the board like he was playing marbles, laying down the die he'd locked up.

Turns out Stan had more moves than that! He was a highly skilled cheat whose cover was that of inept cheat. Munchkin came to us goggle-eyed. "Do you know a guy named Stan Mack?" It seems that after Henry barred Stan, he rode downstairs on the elevator, stewing over being ejected. There, waiting to go up, was Munch, and Stan corralled him. "I want to show you something!" He took Munch up to his room, and showed him a case, inside which was his kit. With its contents he could duplicate any die, even transparent precision dice, and load them. It didn't matter what dice you owned; he could make loaded copies.

"How would you load dice for backgammon?"

Munch said, "I don't know. Sevens won't do anything special."

"Aces and deuces!" Stan's trick was to load them so they favored aces and deuces. Not obviously. They rolled other numbers, and seemed ordinary. But they were biased to roll aces and deuces. The harder you rolled them, the more chance the bias had to affect the result. If Stan needed aces or deuces – and he would try to set up positions where rolling those numbers would be good – he would let the dice roll across the board. If not, he'd kind of plunk them down.

Stan must not have been the only one using them. Danny Kleinman's books were increasingly filled with exposes of cheating. In one he quoted a conversation a player claimed to have overheard through the wall of his hotel room, another player telling Max, "These ace-deuce dice aren't working." Munch, meanwhile, had come to the conclusion that the night he lost fourteen thousand, Max had been using magnetized dice, the magnet hidden inside a cigar case he kept tucked in his boot.

Most of the notorious cheats were in Los Angeles, but Chicago had a few. The fear of cheating was a reason to avoid playing backgammon.

Instead of blackjack or backgammon, I worked. I had paid off my debts by now. I played some bridge and Scrabble™. And I exercised. Before work every morning I stopped by a dojang where I studied taekwondo, judo, and hapkido. The sonsaeng, Mr. Yang, was evangelical. I told him before I signed up that if converting to Christianity (I was raised Congregational, but had been an atheist since I was ten) was requisite, I wasn't interested. He assured me it was no problem, but he imagined he could convert me anyway. After the workouts, during our cool down period, he'd have us read Bible verses. When I came seeking some assistance with Korean letters I couldn't quite work out, he told me he'd be happy to help! His happy help turned out to be assigning passages from his Korean Bible for me to copy.

This wasn't the greatest method for learning Korean. I wasn't even sure I was interested in learning Korean; it was the alphabet which intrigued me. Around this time, in March of 1987, my youngest brother Bruce, the white sheep of the family, got married. The wedding was in Tucson, where he'd moved in 1977 to get his degree from the U of A, and never left. Dad and I made a point of visiting used bookstores when we travelled, and a stop at Bookman's was de rigueur for a Tucson trip. On one of its shelves, I spotted a small and worn hardcover called *Korean in a Hurry* by Samuel Martin. Written in 1954, its target audience was obvious from phrases such as "The war is over," and "My daughter will launder your shirts, lieutenant." It had no tips for reading the Korean alphabet, which didn't appear in the book. It used an outdated method of Romanizing Korean, and its grammar was stilted. I didn't know any of that; I picked it up thinking, "maybe it will be interesting."

If you know where I am going with all this, you're doing better than I was at the time. I wasn't expecting it when, less than two weeks later, Munchkin called and asked if I wanted to go to Korea. I'd go there to play blackjack for his team. They'd pay my travel expenses, and seventy-five dollars an hour for my time at the table, win or lose. I couldn't pass that up!

CHAPTER 22
PREPPING

Though I hadn't imagined I'd be going there, I knew the team had been playing Korea. Munchkin spent five weeks in the fall of eighty-six there, acquiring a girlfriend named Shin Jung and quite a few stories. In those days before the internet, blackjack players used to talk about "the secret game," the blackjack equivalent of Eldorado or Shangri-La. Somewhere there was a game so good that fortunes were there for the taking. Maybe it was in Asia? Stanford Wong wrote a book called *Blackjack in Asia*, but it cost two thousand dollars for a copy. Not every game in Asia was promising, but the game in Korea was. Alan Woods had visited Korea, played, and like most card counters, wore out his welcome. He told Munch's team about it, in return for the right to invest in their bankroll.

What made it good? There were casinos scattered around the country, but the largest was in the Sheraton Walker Hill, on the edge of Seoul. The high limit tables allowed players to bet two million won, around twenty-four-hundred dollars at the time. The game was four decks, cut one, which by then was better than the average game in Las Vegas, where six decks and mediocre penetration was becoming the standard game. The game had a trackable shuffle, a four-part Hilton. Best of all, it had a rule called "five-card surrender," or "five-card-automatic-half-win." There were some other nice rules; for instance, if the player made a total of twenty-one with either three sevens, or six-seven-eight suited, they were paid triple, and the table got a bottle of Champagne. Not worth a lot, but fun! The five-card rule was worth a lot. Imagine you are dealt ace-three, hit with an eight, hit with a two, and finally hit with another ace. You have fifteen, but if you wish you can ask to win half a bet. The dealers did not check their hole cards until after everyone finished playing their hands, so you could collect even if the dealer had an ace showing, and might later turn up a blackjack. A player who knew the correct strategy for the game had an edge of .6%. Counting, and shuffle tracking, with the spread we'd be using, was worth much more than a thousand dollars an hour.

As secret games go, this wasn't so secret. The Korean bosses didn't understand card counting, but they understood American players winning. Two of the players on the team had already been barred, Craig Brennan and Butch. The others figured it was just a matter of time. So, they regrouped.

Almost every player in the casino was Japanese. (Though we'd realize later many of those were ethnic Korean.) Japan, Inc. was still in ascendancy, the Japanese were rich, and the trip to Seoul from Tokyo was only two and a half hours flying time. The Japanese would fill the casino Friday evening, and keep it busy until Sunday night. The Koreans had a love-hate relationship with the Japanese. They envied their wealth, and coveted it. They disliked the Japanese, but were afraid of them. They also knew that the Japanese bet and played wildly, betting and losing, though naturally sometimes winning, lots of money. "They'll never bar a Japanese player!" said Munchkin.

They found a Japanese player, a young guy named Ray, who worked in a Japanese restaurant in L.A. Would Ray be interested in a trip to Korea? He would. And did he know other Japanese who might wish to visit Korea? He did.

I had two weeks to get ready. It had been well over two years since I'd played blackjack. Not only did I need to brush up on all I had memorized in the past, there were lots of new indices to learn. There were numbers for a pair of sevens, for six-seven, six-eight, and seven-eight suited. For the five-card rule there were numbers for three-, four-, and five-card totals. The former had numbers for hitting or standing, the latter for standing, or for collecting the half win. Besides all that, I had to practice shuffle tracking, and learn the signals. In the past I was the big player, and only had to watch for the signals; now I would be sending them. You might think every team had unique signals, but they tended to be standardized, which helped.

I also had to get ready for the trip itself. I had been to Europe when I was fifteen, nearly twenty years before. That passport was long expired. I had to get an expedited passport. I bought a Korean-English dictionary, and an instructional tape that featured an English-speaking man and a Korean-speaking woman. "The moon … *ddal.*" It's amazing how many words that seem common turn out not to be. I am not sure that I have ever used the Korean word for 'moon' in a sentence.

My air ticket had more legs than a Rockettes show. My international flight, to Seoul via Tokyo, departed from LAX, so I'd be stopping off to visit Munchkin on the way. First I had to fly to Las Vegas. Craig Brennan lived there, and wanted to test me. The test wasn't much different from the one Arthur administered years before. I had no trouble with it. After all the hours I'd played in the past, counting came right back to me.

As I was leaving, Craig said, "I'm so glad you're going to be there to look after things."

That seemed odd. "Darryl's going to be there." Darryl was, after all, a full-fledged member of the team, and Craig's partner for the past eight years.

"Exactly!" he said. And with that cryptic send off, I was on my way.

CHAPTER 23
I HAVE A FEELING WE'RE NOT IN KANSAS ANYMORE

The water was dark yellow. Almost like urine if the person pissing has health issues. But urine doesn't smoke, and my water was smoking. Korea, if you are trying to weird me out, you are succeeding.

Darryl and I were in the coffee shop of the Kaya Hotel. We'd flown out of L.A. on a Wednesday morning. The flight to Tokyo was twelve hours, and with a layover, and another two and a half hours to Seoul, adding on the time difference, it was Thursday night by the time we reached our hotel. We wanted a bite before trying to sleep. The Kaya coffee shop was in the basement, a dark, windowless room. The booths were pod shaped, and the waiters wore slippers. They would appear like wraiths, which was spooky enough. Now they were serving me yellow water that smoked.

It also tasted funny. Yes, I drank it. I learned later that during the winter months what I thought was water was called *boricha*, barley tea. Munchkin had taught me that "ice water" was *orum mul* (aurum mool). A Korean would later correct me, by telling me that I should ask for *naengsu*. The former is literally "ice water," the latter, the Chinese borrow word for "cold water." Should you find yourself in Korea, with a thirst, forget I told you about either of those. Ask for *chan mul*, which is native Korean for "cold water."

I had a lot to learn. For instance, hailing a cab. There were sixty thousand cabs in Seoul, if not more. More cabs than you could shake a stick at. Shaking a stick would not get you a cab, and neither would waving at them the way you would back home. That they'd interpret as waving them off. To summon one, you extend your hand palm down, making a raking motion toward yourself. I didn't know that, but luckily a cab stopped for me. Its passenger window was partially lowered. The driver wanted to know where I was going, which was good. There were people in the back seat, which was not so good.

When I told him where I was going, he indicated I should hop in. I wondered if I was being kidnapped, but the pair in the back seat looked like a couple on a date. The man asked, "Please, where are you from?" I told him. "Ah, you are American! I don't like American." Said in a very friendly way. Then, "Would you come have a drink with us?" I explained I had to be somewhere. He was disappointed. Given his limited English, and my more than limited Korean, I don't think our conversation would have gone far.

After grabbing dinner, I managed to flag down another cab, and headed for Walker Hill. Walker Hill was named for General Walton Walker, who died during the Korean War. Not many four-star generals die in war time, but Walker was in a jeep accident and "all of Korea was sorry to him" my friend Mia would later explain. The hill where he so valiantly crashed was a forty-minute cab ride away. The Sheraton Walker Hill was not like hotel casinos in Las Vegas. In Vegas, one entered the casino, and tried to figure out where they hid the hotel. At Walker Hill you entered a hotel and tried to figure out where they hid the casino.

The first thing I noticed on entering the casino was how quiet it was. Not that it was tomblike, but compared with Vegas the difference was immense. There were slots, but they were in a small room I passed on the way into the casino proper, and it was a closed room, blocking the noise. The casino itself was large, and packed, but the patrons comported themselves more formally than in Las Vegas. There was a crap table; Walker Hill had the only one in Korea. But there were no craps players. There was a dice game called sic bo. Those games were near the entrance. The rest of the casino was split between blackjack tables and mini-baccarat tables, blackjack in the near half, mini-bac in the far half. Beyond the mini-baccarat was big baccarat, a separate area with a full baccarat table and huge limits. The limit on the big baccarat table was twenty-five million won, roughly thirty grand, but that was misleading. As long as the spread between the sum of all of the player bets, and the sum of all the banker bets, was twenty-five million or less, the table limit wasn't exceeded. The million-won chips were worth at the time twelve-hundred dollars. A rack of chips held four rows of twenty-five chips, so a rack of gold was worth nearly an eighth of a million. Sometimes players would stack racks, and shove them in the betting square, as much as a million bucks wagered on a single hand.

Out on the main floor the action was less stupefying, but it still made Vegas seem like a place for mendicants. The mini-bac table limits were ten million won. There were some low-limit blackjack tables, with five-thousand won minimums and half-million maximums. I was looking for the high limits, which for blackjack were one hundred thousand minimum, two million maximum, or in dollars roughly one hundred and twenty to twenty-four hundred. I found a table with open seats, and joined the game. Or began to. The players pantomimed that I should wait until the end of the shoe. They didn't want me changing the order of the cards. Superstitious players were the norm.

Darryl and I would be alternating shifts throughout the weekend. We did not want bosses from more than one shift comparing notes, so I had timed my arrival to about ten-fifteen, which was enough time for the day shift to leave, and swing to settle in. Our big player was named Tosh, and he would find me and join my table at about ten-thirty. The shift ended at six in the morning. I'd send Tosh off the game around five, play another shoe or two, then split. Darryl would come in at six-fifteen. I'd come back a little after two in the afternoon, and then finish up playing graveyard Sunday morning. Darryl, would play our last shift Sunday afternoon. Tosh would get very little sleep.

The language barrier wasn't a problem. Hand signals are hand signals. Or it wasn't until I created an incident.

The Japanese players bet like samurai, but played like wimps. Every so often they would up their bet, and bang down a million or so, letting everyone at the table know that they weren't afraid to chunk it out there. But then when it came time to play the hand, the watchword was, don't do anything someone else might object to. Which meant they hardly ever hit a hand which might bust, split very few pairs, and never doubled soft hands.

I was minding my own business when I heard a strange sound. Was someone boiling a pot of tea at the table? I realized the hissing was coming from the guy next to me, and as I did, he boiled over, "Hit. Hit! Heet!! Heettt!!!!" He turned and began screaming at me, "No heet! No heettt!" I had hit my previous hand, and the players at the table, who loved to work out what might have happened had things gone a different way, decided that I had "taken the dealer's bust card."

The guy I'd pissed off looked like a Japanese John Carradine, if Carradine had been weaned with a lemon, leaving his face frozen in a perpetual pucker. He had eyebrows like venomous caterpillars, and a mad gleam in his eye. When describing him later I called him Mister Horrible.

Once he erupted, he grew increasingly volcanic. He stood up from the table, yelled at the other players, and they all stood and left the game. Almost all. Tosh wasn't going anywhere, and luckily there was another player who stayed. Another peculiarity of Korean casinos is that the players weren't drinking. They weren't drinking, though it was possible to order beverages; water, juice, and soft drinks were served. Unlike Vegas, they could order food. The menu was limited, fruit plates, noodles, or "omu rice," an omelet with rice. The third player had just ordered noodles, a huge bowl on a small table the waitress set up next to his chair. When the others angrily insisted he join their boycott, he waved them off. He wasn't leaving his noodles.

I had unwittingly created a scene, drawing attention to myself. It wasn't over. The group went out to the area between blackjack and mini-bac. There they harangued the bosses, hollering about what a terrible player I was. They wanted the bosses to open up a new table for them, while the bosses kept pointing and telling them that there were empty seats back at my table. I can't imagine it happening in Las

Vegas. The four who had left the table each bet on average a half million every hand. I was betting only a hundred thousand. I was expecting the tap at any moment. It never came.

The boycott lasted a shoe or two, and then they all came back. Mister Horrible eyed me through slits like a cobra's, and said, "Mister, no hit." I tried to say something conciliatory, but message delivered, he ignored me.

The rest of the night passed without incident. At five-thirty I was in a cab, heading home. Or thought I was. I was a bit vague on where exactly the Kaya Hotel could be found. I knew it was near a neighborhood called Itaewon, and figured if the cab could get me to Itaewon, I'd be fine. The trouble is that the street I knew as Itaewon was just one street in a neighborhood by that name. Somewhere along the way the cab took me into a maze of narrow alleys. Coming around a corner there was a bonfire, a sudden blaze. It looked like they were burning furniture to keep warm. Or planning to roast the first American they saw. One of those.

Somehow, we stumbled on the right street, I spotted the Kaya, and so passed my first day of gambling in Seoul.

CHAPTER 24
A DAY OFF

Monday morning, I felt reasonably rested. Darryl and I were on the same schedule for the first time in three days. He would now take me around and introduce me to the other things Korea had to offer. Our first stop was the Twilight Zone. The Twilight Zone was in Itaewon. The building had four floors above ground level, with bars or restaurants on each level. The Twilight Zone was up top, and claimed to be open "25 hours a day." There were some GIs sitting at the nearby bar who may have been in the twenty-fifth hour of their day. One youngster was "short," "four days to port call" he said. And was worried, "Do you think when I get back to the States I can still pick up a girl by saying, 'I buy you chicken?'"

The menus were upright cards in plexiglass holders on the tables, and one of the choices was "dog mandoo." I had heard about Koreans and dogs. Might Lassie be on the breakfast menu?

"Dog?" I asked the waitress, pointing.

"Dog."

"Woof! Woof! Dog?"

"*Aniyo!*" She was horrified.

When it came, it turned out to be a type of dumpling soup made with rice cakes. It wasn't the last fun I'd have with *ddok,* as it was more usually Romanized. I'd say "dog" and they'd say "duck." I'd say "duck" and they'd say "dog." The pronunciation is halfway in between.

After breakfast Darryl said he wanted to show me the money-changer, in case I needed to find him on my own. The Twilight Zone building was on a corner a block off Itaewon Road, at the intersection of Fire Station Street, and … Well, if I ever learned the formal name of the cross street, parallel to Itaewon Road, I have forgotten it. The road, or really alley, running uphill was called Hooker Hill. Like Walker Hill, it was named after a US general, albeit not one who served in Korea. Coming out of the Twilight Zone we'd made a right to the corner, Hooker Hill was to our left, but we turned right onto Fish Alley. Halfway down on the left was a smaller dead-end alley. Halfway down it, on the left, was a walkway back to a two-story apartment building. Our destination was upstairs, and all the way at the end.

We crowded into a vestibule where the occupants kept their shoes, and Darryl knocked at the apartment door. On the way upstairs he'd explained that we were looking for a Mr. Chang. He wasn't sure if we were in the right place, and the fact that "his sister is also a money-changer somewhere around here" was probably not helping pin it down.

An old lady answered the door. Because the apartment was a step up from the vestibule, she was nearly as tall as Darryl. "Mister Chang?" he said. She replied in Korean, waving her hand to make it clear we were barking up the wrong shoe tree.

Darryl was not so easily dissuaded. He reached in his shirt pocket, and showed her the roll of bills he was carrying. The largest Korean coin was a five-hundred-won piece, worth about sixty cents. There were bills worth one-, five-, and ten-thousand won. Then there were things which looked like checks. I would eventually come to understand they were checks, but because they functioned like currency, and for a long time I only saw them in two denominations, I thought they were currency. The smaller, purple ones, were worth one hundred thousand won, and the larger green ones a million. Darryl pulled out a wad of green worth ninety million. As soon as she saw that, the woman grabbed him, and tried to lift him into the apartment. At the time Darryl weighed three-ten, and his strength matched his size, but though he began waving a denial, and backpedaling, she nearly hoisted him.

I ducked out of the way, so he didn't back over me. Once he broke free, as we headed down the stairs, I asked what was going on.

"There was a girl in traditional Korean clothes sleeping on the floor. I think the lady figured I was looking for a girl, and she was trying to tell me her granddaughter didn't do that sort of thing. But then when I showed her the money, she changed her mind."

Our tour of Itaewon was off to a poor start, but it soon got better.

Imagine you are standing at the end of *Itaewonno* – Itaewon Road. Okay, you can't, so I'll have to do it for you. You are facing southwest, I think. Seoul is built around small mountains, and the roads are not laid out in grids. Southwest is about right. Follow the road to your left and you will pass the Crown Hotel on your way to the Han River. Turn right and within about fifty yards or so you will come to a Y. Keep right and a tunnel under Namsan – South Mountain – takes you downtown. Bear left and you'll find yourself passing between high brick walls topped with barbed wire. You are travelling through Yongsan army base, the Main Post on your right, South Post on your left.

Once upon a time Itaewon was the embassy district during the era when Korea's Yi Dynasty was under the shadow of China's Qing Dynasty. In the late 19th century, the waning power China, and the waxing power Japan, fought a proxy war over who would control the Korean court. The proxy war became a shooting war, the Sino-Japanese War of 1894. Japan won, and slowly extended its power over the Korean peninsula. In 1910 they made it formal, and Korea became a Japanese colony. By then the Imperial Army was headquartered at Yongsan ("Dragon Mountain"). After the Japanese surrender in 1945, when they moved out, we moved in. When the Korean War settled into an uneasy truce in 1953, Yongsan became the headquarters for our military, preeminent among the bases around the country. Imagine if Lafayette's French stuck around after they saved our bacon during the Revolutionary War, and had their most important base in New York's Central Park.

The Korean War was a UN project. The various nations who

contributed to the so-called police action maintained a rotating presence, but all forces, including Korea's, were part of a Joint Command, and the head of the Joint Command was the US Army four-star general in charge.

The road bisecting the base was four lanes wide. The most popular car in Korea then was the Hyundai Pony, a matchbox car grown large enough to fit five people, none comfortably. They were small enough that you could fit three abreast in two lanes, so there were always six lanes of traffic flowing between the walls. Halfway along there was a traffic light, which allowed cars to exit the base, and either turn onto the cross road, or to cross it and enter the opposite post.

None of which sounds interesting, but that depends upon your cab driver. The Ponies were surprisingly perky. I was in one once which briefly hit one-sixty. Kilometers per hour, not miles. They weren't that perky! "Briefly," because when we achieved that speed we were at the apex of a bridge across the Han River, and went airborne. A few seconds in space, a couple of dramatic bounces, and physics worked its magic, slowing us down. Picture six lanes of traffic, three lanes heading in each direction, all stopped, because the light at the base guard posts had changed. Your taxi could stop, several hundred yards back, behind a solid block of little cars. Where's the fun in that? At least three times I had one pull into the oncoming lanes, and try to pass. To do it they had to drive at forty-five miles per hour (or 75 KPH), hoping that no one pulled out of either post heading their way, and that they would reach the intersection at the very instant the light changed, because there was no way anyone heading in either direction would yield.

If you survived, when you reached the end of the base you came to Samgakchi Rotary. The first exit around a quarter of the circle led through an area called Namyeongdong. On your left was the USO and just past it the Kaya Hotel. Keep going and you'd come to landmarks like Seoul Station, and Namdaemun, the Great South Gate, better known these days for its shopping.

But we've wandered far afield. Now that you've looked left and right, turn around, and look at Itaewon. You will be looking at several hundred yards of shopping. The buildings are two- or three-stories, with shopping on every floor. Lining the sidewalks, probably illegally, are vendors selling T-shirts, socks, comic maps, belt buckles, "nine-dollar Reeboks" and "twenty-eight-dollar Rolexes." Inside there are shops selling eelskin bags. I found a cobbler and ordered a pair of slip-on shoes made of eelskin, which cost thirty-three dollars. They were beautiful! They were the sharpest looking shoes I ever owned. I wore them once. I don't know how the soles were constructed, but standing on them was torture, and walking on them worse. It's as though he put every ridge and every dip in the wrong place. What's worse is that even had he not done whatever the hell he did to the soles, they were unwearable. Eelskin is soft until it isn't. It stretches without resistance until it reaches its limit, then stops with a bang. It's like wearing a leash and suddenly being brought up short, over and over again. I gave them to the Salvation Army. Look for a wino with a pained grimace but great-looking shoes and you'll have found them.

I had much better luck with the tailor. Tailor shops abounded. Darryl took me to a guy other team members used. I was fitted for a silk two-piece, a pinstriped three-piece, five shirts, and three ties. The whole order cost just two hundred and twenty-nine dollars. Later I would buy Polo shirts, for four bucks apiece, and a "three-zipper bag." These had a hard bottom, with wheels, but soft sides, made from some sort of artificial fabric. When zipped they were about the size of a regular suitcase, and had a handle on top to carry them. The sides had three zippers, which when unzipped allowed the bag to accordion to your preferred height. When all three were open the bag was nearly as high as my chin. You could pack minimally before going to Korea, and return with a bag full of goodies.

A few hundred yards down on the left was the Hamilton Hotel. It was set back from the street, and up front was a Dunkin Donuts. (It was in the alley to the west of the donut shop that a crush of people a few Halloweens ago led to the death of one hundred and fifty-six people.) There was a traffic light at the Hamilton, and a street leading downhill towards the river. Continuing a block past the Hamilton you'd come to another light. To the right was Fire Station Street and the Twilight Zone. To the left a winding road leading up Namsan. On the way up you would pass the Chalet Swiss, where Koreans in Heidi outfits yodeled while you ate. At the top of the hill was the Hyatt, one of the fanciest hotels in town. Continuing straight on *Itaewonno* would take you into a district called Hannamdong, which at night was lined with nearly a hundred discos.

Backtracking, on the opposite side of the street from the Hamilton, during the first few hundred yards of shopping, there were several eating or drinking establishments catering to Western tastes. There was Papeye Chikin. I never tried it, for fear they cooked no better than they spelled. There was a Mexican place run by a Korean woman married to a retired Mexican-American army sergeant. Her knowledge of Mexican food was based on hearsay. There was the Nashville Club. It was a country and western bar, down in a basement. It was rumored to have black market food from the base (source of most black-market goods), and was open for lunch. It had a speaker above the door so shoppers were aware of its existence. The first time I heard "The Rodeo Song" was one noon. Nowadays songs with four-letter words playing in public don't raise anyone's eyebrows, but in 1987 it was a different story, "Did I just hear that?"

Then there was Wendy's. Wendy's had indoor and outdoor seating. The weather was warming, and sitting outside Wendy's was Tom Casey, who was known as the Mayor of Itaewon. Darryl knew him from a previous trip, and Tom knew my brother, so was happy to see us. Happy to see us, and happy to take us on a road trip.

Incheon is around an hour west of Seoul. After a stop near the waterfront, so Tom could show us seafood restaurants with live fish swimming in what looked like horse troughs, and where a female student yelled "Yankee go home!" at us, we went to the Olympus Casino. Darryl wanted to scout it. The place was empty on a Monday afternoon; the three of us were the only customers. We hadn't really planned how we were going to do this, so we decided we'd flat bet ten thousand won each. Tom didn't know a thing about gambling, but he knew we did, and we helped him play.

The rules weren't as good as Walker Hill's, but it was even off the top, four decks cut one, and … "Did you see that!?" Darryl asked me. Sure did! The dealer was doing a Berlin shuffle.

The boss came over, and sat on a stool to watch us play. He was young, university educated, and spoke passable English. I told him I studied taekwondo. So did he, and we spent the next two hours talking martial arts. I didn't bother to count. I could see from Darryl's bets when to raise or lower mine, and from the bet size could figure out how to play the hand ninety-nine percent of the time. The other one percent, after a very slight hesitation Darryl would say, "I'd double that," or whatever.

The staff found us fascinating. When we got up to cash out, we were up around a million won, over three hundred thousand each. Not bad considering we weren't trying for a big win. At the window they gave me, including my buy-in, a stack of crispy ten-thousand-won notes. I asked for a rubber band. Their English did not include that term, so I had to pantomime it. Easier said than done, but eventually they figured it out, and brought me a rubber band, then waited eagerly to see, what will the funny foreigner do with a rubber band?

The bills were really stiff! I folded them in half, and had to hold them that way, while I slipped the rubber band around them, twisted, and slipped it around once more. Nice and snug!

Sproing!! The rubber band shot my money all over the casino. Everyone in the cage and everyone in the pit watched the funny foreigner crawling around, picking up money.

Night had fallen by the time we left the casino. Tom took us on a tour through Incheon's Yellow House district. It comprised narrow, twisting alleys. The doors all had numbers on square signs sticking out above them, so you could see from a distance whether you were approaching "3" or "17." Next to the doors were windows, with women in nighties waving to us.

Back in Seoul we headed to Hannamdong, and the Sportsman's Club. Tom owned the Sportsman's Club. It was world famous in those days. When he opened it, back in 1979, it was the first disco in the neighborhood. Now there were ninety. But the others catered primarily to Koreans. The Sportsman's Club was for expats, a mix of business-men, and off-duty servicemen, mostly officers. Since I didn't go to discos back home, nor did I listen to disco music, much of what the DJ played was unfamiliar. A group in heavy rotation was Modern Talking. They were German, I think, but when I hear them, especially the song

"Brother Louie," I am transported to Asia. (There is a song of the same name by a group called Hot Chocolate, which was a hit in the US. This song is not the same.)

I said the Sportsman's Club catered to expat businessmen and US army officers. I didn't go to the disco to dance with them. Fortunately, it was also filled with many dance partners. I met one named Miss Kim. She told me she was a student. Back at the Kaya she followed up on that by asking for thirty thousand won tuition money.

Speaking of money, I had that wad of bills in my pocket! Not that I thought Miss Kim would rifle my pockets if I went to the bathroom or something, but it was team money, so locking it up seemed prudent. As I was no longer wearing anything with pockets, or anything without pockets, I had an excuse to dig in my pants for a pen. I had come up with a clever plan. My notebook was in my suitcase, which locked. I told Miss Kim that I had to record all of my expenses for my employers, including cab fare back to the Kaya, and the thirty thousand won I'd just given her.

There I stood, notebook in hand, pretending to write in it, before placing it back in the suitcase, and locking it away. When I had fished around for the pen, with a move a magician would have envied, I slipped the money out of my pants, and had it pinned behind the notebook. She looked a bit confused by all of this. Her English was good, but I doubt she'd seen many naked Americans practicing penmanship. Pretend writing finished, I opened the suitcase with one hand, and began with the other to drop in the notebook and the money hiding behind it. Jake, you are a smooth one!

Sproing!!

CHAPTER 25
ALLEY CAT

Thursday we were joined by more players. Jack was a new play caller, Richard a new BP. Jack's bags were delayed, so he had to stay at Gimpo, with instructions on how to find his way to the Kaya, while we brought Richard back with us. Richard was going to need funds, and we needed some converted from won to dollars and yen. He was, after all, coming from overseas, so buying in with lots of won would be a red flag. Darryl wanted to personally test Richard, so I was sent to Walker Hill to get money from Tosh, and then to see the moneychanger.

I took a cab to Walker Hill, and went as stealthily as possible to Tosh's room. Odds are I could have walked down the hall playing a tuba and the casino would have no awareness, but years of dealing with Vegas casinos made me cautious. Tosh handed off eighty-five million won, slightly over one hundred thousand dollars, and I took a cab back to Itaewon.

I was dropped at the mouth of Fish Alley. It was night, and I could see where it got its name. There were racks of dead fish lining the end of the alley closest to *Bokwangdongkil*. Further in, there were entrances to basement bars, with red neon signs, bars with names like Cherry Boy. Hmm, maybe they serve a lot of fruit juice?

I still had no idea where the moneychanger lurked. Alan Woods had called the day before, and mentioned that the guy spoke no English, and that he was "a friend of Marty." Marty was an American blackjack player who lived in Korea, lived at the Kaya Hotel. I had never met him, but had caught a glimpse of someone getting off the elevator who might have been him. He wore a raincoat and looked like a cross between a leg breaker, and a flasher. He sized me up, could see I wasn't a candidate for flashing, and he probably didn't need to break my leg.

I had a secret weapon, a Korean-English dictionary. When I reached the spot where the dead-end alley branched off from Fish Alley, and spotted a fiftyish woman standing sentinel, I approached her, and said, "*Chang-sonsaeng odi ee-yay-yo?*"

"What!?"

There were many things wrong with what I'd said. Starting with the fact that "Chang" has a vowel sound closer to "palm," than "chain." Also, that string of syllables that sound like I was singing "Old McDonald," the "ee-yay-yo," were the wrong verb. What I tried to ask was "Where is Mister Chang?" The word "*odi*" means "where?" The verb, at the end, mangled pronunciation notwithstanding, means "is." Korean has two different words for "is," one for existence, the other for identification. It's the difference between "Mister Chang is at the theatre," and "Mister Chang is a theatre."

I tried again.

"I don't know any Mister Chang!"

I began babbling, "I heard his sister lived around here, maybe over there," I pointed down the dark alley.

"You want moneychanger?"

I looked around. I wasn't crazy about the denizens of Fish Alley knowing my business. "Yes," I whispered.

"Five thousand!"

"Two thousand."

"Five thousand! And after, you come see my girl."

I paid the five, and said I'd think about seeing her girl. It isn't a lie if your fingers are crossed. Then she led me into the dead-end alley. There were no lights, and it was pitch black. I was walking into darkness with a pimp, with a hundred grand in my pocket. This was not a happy moment. Especially since I am a born coward. Fortunately, I compensate by being foolish, else I'd never have any adventures.

We went partway down the alley, then she led me to the same apartment building, up the same stairs, and to the same apartment Darryl and I visited on Monday.

"This isn't right!" I said.

"After, you come see my girl!" she said, and left me alone in the dark vestibule. In which I could dimly make out a lot more shoes than previously – men's shoes.

The door flew open. The man standing there, with the advantage of being a step up, towered over me. "Yai!!" he yelled, though whether that was a greeting, a question, or a cry for reinforcements, I had no idea.

"Me ..." I patted my chest " ... Marty *chingu*." ("I am a friend of Marty's.")

"Ah!" His eyes lit up. "Mistah Mah-tee, pofeshiona gambla!"

Inside the apartment we took seats at a table, and he wrote on a piece of paper. There were two rows, marked "$20" and "$100," and two columns marked "Buy" and "Sell." In the $20 row he wrote the numbers 820 and 836, and under them in the $100 row 832 and 837. He then pointed at the appropriate spots and said in a high-pitched half scream, "Twenty dollah bill, I buy, I sell. Hunnet dollah bill, I buy, I sell."

I whipped out my dictionary, and showed him the entries for "volume" and "discount." He loved it. And moved the line, once I explained I was interested in hundreds, to 832-836. A half-percent spread is pretty good for changing money. I told him I wanted to buy twenty-five thousand, and also a million yen. The yen he couldn't do, and the dollars he couldn't do tonight, but told me I should come back in the morning. He also explained that when we turned up on Monday, he was doing military reserve. The old lady was his mom, and that's what she'd tried to explain to Darryl. When she saw how much he wanted to change, she tried to get him to come in and wait. Oh, and the young woman on the floor? Mr. Chang had just gotten married, and that was his new bride. It took over an hour to communicate all of this, since as Alan had warned me, he spoke no English. We used the dictionary to figure all this out.

I got back to the Kaya just before Jack turned up. "I either paid three dollars for that cab, or three hundred!" He was white with fear that he'd paid three hundred. He'd paid three thousand won, which was actually about three dollars and sixty cents, so he was fine. Exchange rates weren't his forte.

The game plan for the weekend was that Darryl and I would take the first shift on Friday night. I would call plays for Tosh, and he for Richard because he wanted to be sure the new guy worked out.

As it turned out, Darryl and I, though we'd have preferred to sit further apart, wound up on adjacent tables, me on first base, him on third, so we were facing each other. Not long after I sat down, I sensed a presence, and there was Richard standing behind third base at my table, his back to Darryl. Richard was in his forties, and worked as a translator. He wore glasses, and a cheap tweed jacket. He looked like a junior accountant, and not a high roller. His body language said, "I don't belong here," and his staring at me was not subtle. I coughed to signal that he was doing something wrong. He kept staring. I coughed again. I heard Darryl cough from the next table.

Richard kept standing and staring. I coughed a bit louder. The Darryl coughed; an eruption so powerful I saw the dealer at his table drop the cards she was shuffling. So powerful it practically blew Richard into the wrong seat, at my table. Oh, well, I guess I had him. Tosh, meanwhile, wandered by, scratched his head, and sat at Darryl's table. Not every play goes as planned.

CHAPTER 26
GASTRONOMY

The rest of the weekend passed uneventfully. Darryl and Tosh left on Monday; Jack and I would call plays for Richard one more weekend. Jack was around forty, and owned a pool hall in New Jersey. He had a great look for a blackjack player; he looked and sounded like a mobster. He told me that when dealers or bosses asked what he did for a living, he'd glare at them long enough to make them nervous, then growl; "Vending machines."

He already looked like he was ready to fit people for concrete over-shoes. A recent event had him looking meaner than usual. He told me that he'd bet everything he could lay hands on, laying eight to one I think, that Marvin Hagler would beat Sugar Ray. It was a bet he "couldn't lose." He lost.

Jack was not built for overseas travel. He discovered that the Kaya's coffee shop served eggs, and that's what he ate, every meal.

Meanwhile, Tom Casey took me to the newest Itaewon sensation. Across from the Hamilton Hotel was a building with a Burger King a short flight up from the street. Above the Burger King was a brand-new Denny's, the first in Korea. Tom thought this was terribly exciting!

Inside we met the manager, a Chinese guy from Hong Kong brought in to train the staff. He was drilling them when we walked in,

"Welcome to Denny's! Smoking or non-smoking?" He was only in town for thirty days, and it took about three after he left before the potted plants were moved around to block aisles, and the whole restaurant was smoking. But for the moment, it was like any American Denny's. Which meant nothing to me. I'd just come from America, and back home Denny's was low on my list. Tom was enthralled, and could recite all the items in a Grand Slam Breakfast. I told Jack about it, but after one trip to Itaewon, he decided to stay in his room, subsist on room service, and count the days until he was back in the USA.

Perhaps I should have stuck with Grand Slam Breakfasts. One of the team had met a girl named Mia while in Seoul, and it was suggested I look her up, as she could perhaps show me around. Munchkin had mentioned his girlfriend, Shin Jung, and said Mia might know where I could find her. Mia was happy to meet me. On my free nights she said I should come around and she'd help me look for Munch's friend.

So I did. One of those nights, I dropped by the A+ Café, which was downstairs from the Sportsman's Club. Mia, a waitress there, suggested I wait next door after I finished eating, in her friend's dress shop. The women were snacking on fish cooked, or at least heated, on top of a space heater. Pro tip to travelers: never eat fish strips cooked on top of a space heater!

Once Mia was off work, we went out "looking for Shin Jung." Besides me and Mia there were several of her girlfriends. One, Min Won, was someone she was trying to fix me up with. I wasn't particularly interested once I realized that Min Won really wasn't interested in me, but it was an ongoing project of Mia's. Also joining us was a customer Mia had waited on, a half-Japanese, half-Korean woman who told me she taught school in Japan.

Mia decided the best place to look for Shin Jung was in the fanciest discos in town, ones inside the top hotels, the Lotte, the Shilla, the Chosun. Each had a cover charge, and paying for half a dozen cover charges at each stop, plus drinks, was draining my wallet. After some grumbling, we went to a cheaper disco, the Sportsman's Club.

By now it was after midnight, and I was not feeling well. Mia went down to a drug store, and returned with a bottle of medicine. I drank whatever it was, and felt even worse. "That means it's working," she assured me.

Mia and her friends wanted me to dance with them. The teacher wanted me to dance only with her. She whispered that we should ditch "that waitress," and begged me to take her back to my hotel. I might have overlooked her ingratitude toward Mia, if I were feeling better. She was pretty cute. But I was by now feeling awful. I told Mia I had to go home, and they dropped me at the Kaya.

I made it to the room in the nick of time, stripped off my clothes, ran to the bathroom, and had to make a decision as to which end of me to aim at the toilet. I chose the right order, somehow. Things came out one end, came out the other, came out the first again. Then came one of the lowest points of my life. I was on the bathroom floor, in a hotel halfway around the world from home. I was certain I would die there, alone. It was three in the morning. Perhaps a maid would find me in nine or ten hours. They'd inform Jack, someone who barely knew me. It was a grim way to go.

An hour went by, and I was able to crawl to bed. It was a day and a half before I could venture out, to Denny's for bland American food. Not the Grand Slam Breakfast. I hate eggs.

I was recovered in time for the last weekend of work. Two interesting things happened, one in the casino, and one at the hotel.

It was late, near the end of swing. Call it five in the morning. Mister Horrible showed up at my table. He looked like he was having a bad night. There was a young player to my left, who I noticed actually knew something close to basic strategy. When Mister Horrible showed up, though I couldn't understand exactly what was said, I gathered that the kid commiserated with the older man, and told him that I knew what I was doing. It is permitted, and not uncommon, for players to bet on each other's squares. Mister Horrible extended a chip across the young guy, toward my square, and asked if I'd mind.

"Great!" I thought. A bit of public relations with one of the high rollers. I indicated that it was okay, and he placed his bet next to mine. I was dealt a twelve against a six, but the count was below minus one, so it was a hit. Talking about it later with others on the team they agreed that I should have stood. That using my discretion, giving up a small bit of EV to possibly gain longevity in a valuable game, was fine. But at the moment, I did what was expected, and hit. I caught a ten, busting, everyone else stood, and the dealer, who would have busted had he hit with my ten, caught a card and the whole table lost.

Mister Horrible looked at me in disgust, shook his head, and wearily headed upstairs.

The other occurrence was the following night. I'd played day shift, and was sleeping, having to rise early to play the morning shift. I woke about one, went to the toilet, then tried to go back to sleep. There was a knock at the door.

"Who is it?" A female voice answered.

I opened the door, and found one of the most beautiful women I'd ever meet, standing there. She spoke no English, but wanted to come in. I let her. Being a good host, I asked if she wanted to take a shower. She did. I managed to learn that her name was Miss Pak, and that she knew the word "doughnut," which she used after blowing a smoke ring. I'd heard a story from Tom Casey. When Stanford Wong was in Korea gathering data for his book, Marty and Tom had taken him around. One night, for a joke, they sent a hooker to his room. He sent her away. Maybe I'd be a famous blackjack author today if I'd sent Miss Pak away. At any rate, I didn't. That Tom (I had still never met Marty) might have sent her seemed the only explanation. When I asked if she knew Tom she nodded in agreement, but as near as I could tell, she nodded in agreement no matter what I said.

In the morning, I tried to leave without waking her, and when she woke anyway, indicated she could stay as long as she liked. She came downstairs with me. In the lobby, she seemed to know some of the staff, at least well enough to bum a cigarette. The last I saw of her she was chatting with one of the older women who cleaned rooms, and during the night slept behind the front desk.

When I saw Tom Casey that night, and asked if he had sent her, he asked if I was kidding. I can guess who paid for Wong's hooker, and it wasn't Tom.

After the last play Richard checked out of Walker Hill, and moved over to the Kaya. In the morning, I was in charge of settling whatever cumulative bills we'd racked up during our nearly three-week stay. A thought occurred to me. "Mister Lee," I said to the manager, "the other night there was a girl, Miss Pak, who seemed to know some of your staff …"

He looked around, whispered I should come outside. Once out of earshot he said, "You know …mamasan?" I agreed I knew the term. "Sometimes guest … talk to bell captain. Bell captain talk to mamasan. The other night, guest talk to bell captain, want girl come stay all night." The guest was staying in Room 305. I was in room 503.

CHAPTER 27
PORTS OF CALL

Richard and I flew to Tokyo. He was staying one night; I was staying two. He'd arranged to meet a friend named Rikki, who, he bragged, was the biggest dealer of black pearls in Japan. Rikki's first comment on seeing his "old friend" was, "Ah, Korean tailor." He let us know he could take us to a much better tailor who could whip up a much better suit for only a few thousand dollars. This was the tail end of Japan, Inc. The Japanese were rich, on their way to conquering the world, or at least its economy. There were stories in later years, after things went bad, that at peak value Japanese real estate was so expensive that visitors to Ginza were invited to take a hundred-dollar bill and fold it into the smallest possible square. They would be led outside, where they were told to place the bill on the sidewalk. "That bill wouldn't buy the piece of ground it's resting on."

I don't know about average Japanese, but the ones playing at Walker Hill exuded arrogance, and Rikki would have fit right in. He was friendly enough, but there was condescension in his comments.

He took us out to dinner, at a knockoff of Denny's. He took us down to the waterfront, where a model home was on display. It was a two-story, two-bedroom house, on a lazy Susan. It rotated so that the sun was always where you'd want it at any time of day, at least in theory. He told me it cost about two hundred and ninety-seven thousand. As for where to put it, a young couple buying it as a starter home could not afford land. They'd have to find a place a two-hour commute from the city, and take a long-term lease.

I told them my brother had asked me if I could drop by the Raksa Theatre in Asakusa. Munchkin and two partners were sending dance shows to Japan. Their client, Sato-san, was a very rich man whose mother had been a stripper at the Raksa eons before. When he got rich, he bought the place. At the theatre I offered to buy the tickets, which shocked and pleased them. Tickets were three thousand apiece, which if it were won, would have been around eleven dollars. I'd momentarily forgotten that won and yen had different exchange rates. The yen had been soaring just then, and I'd changed money at one twenty-five to the dollar, so those tickets cost seventy-two dollars.

Munchkin's show was only half the evening's entertainment, and he and his partners had created only half their show. That half was an R-rated version of a Las Vegas dance show. One of his partners, Minnie Madden, was an up-and-coming choreographer, who would later do major shows, including Disney on Ice. The dancing was terrific, sexy, slightly kinky, but truly artistic. The other half of their portion was supplied by strippers they hired in Vancouver. Then came the other half of the show, the Japanese half. We didn't stay for that, because I wanted to say hello to the dancers in Munch's behalf. I gathered, though, that the Japanese half was a hardcore sex show, possibly with audience participation.

On the stairs, I greeted dancers. Mind you, I didn't know them, and hated to bother them as they seemed eager to go to parties or clubs. "Introduce us to some dancers!" Richard said. I did, though the next dancers down the stairs were male dancers from the artistic half.

The following day Richard took me to a place he was eager to visit, Soapland. He called it Yoshiwara. Yoshiwara was a famous red-light district during the Edo period. Was this Soapland in that district? Beats me. During the day it looked dead. The clubs all had signboards out front, showing "membership" fees ranging from ¥5000 to ¥25,000. We passed most before Richard found one he said would take *gaijin*. They would, but wanted me to hurry inside before anyone saw me. It was believed that AIDS was a disease of Westerners, and if Japanese customers knew a club entertained *gaijin*, they would shun it.

Richard explained that the club had only two girls who went with Westerners, so if I didn't like the first one, I should speak up and they'd bring out the other. Meanwhile, after I went with my girl, they would take him elsewhere for a greater selection. He was catching his plane after that, so we wouldn't see each other again until next time we were both in Korea. The price was ¥24,500, but that was all-inclusive for "seventy minutes." There was a ninety-minute option, but seventy sounded fine.

When I was a freshman in high school I wrote a paper on 19th century China. Among the *casus belli* for the first Opium War was a Chinese demand that British emissaries kowtow. I knew that a true kowtow required touching the floor with nine points, feet, knees, hands, elbows, and head. The woman who came downstairs demonstrated proper technique. She was homely, with a pocked face, but how could I refuse someone who'd just done that to me? Her name was Itsumi, and she spoke passable English.

She led me upstairs, to a room with a small bed, a bathtub, and a tiled floor next to the tub with a drain in it. She ran a bath, had me get in, and scrubbed me. Then, while I soaked, she blew up an air mattress, and lathered it.

She had me get out of the tub, and lie face down on the air mattress. Remember Slip-N-Slides? They were a toy when I was young, a plastic runway you'd wet, and then slide along. Itsumi lay on top of me, and used me as a Slip-n-Slide. She also proved that her body was a Swiss Army Knife of cleaning instruments. For instance, to scrub my legs she had a Brillo pad growing between her legs. For those hard-to-reach places, like the inside of my anus, her nipples were surprisingly effective. Then she had me turn over. A traffic cone had sprung up on that side, but it proved no impediment to her progress, as she slid over, under, around and through it.

She dried me off, and had me wait on the bed while she policed the area. Once the tub was drained and scrubbed, the floor nearly dry, and the mattress put away, she joined me.

We were going along just fine, when I heard a noise. "Ah! Ah!"

Evidently a fake orgasm preceded by fake arousal was part of the package. "Aah! Aah!" She was getting louder. "Aaahh!! Aaahh!!" A lot louder. "Yaaahh!!! Yaaahh!!!" It dawned on me that as long as I kept going, she felt obliged to increase her passion. I wasn't ready, but now began to worry about where this was going. Surely there were human limits. "Yaaaaiiihhh!!!! Yaaaaiiihhh!!!!" I tried to hurry, but working under pressure wasn't helping matters. "Yaaaaaaiiiiihhhh!!!!! Yaaaaaaiiiiihhhh!!!!!" Good grief, the woman might die. Hurry, Jake! Hurry!

Finally, the moment of truth. "AIIYAAAAAAAAAAIIIIIIYEEEEEEEEE!!!!!!!!!!   Thaaaaaaaaaaaaaaannnnnnnnnkkk Yooooooooooooooo!!!!!! Faann-taasss-tikk!" I almost fell off the bed laughing. Almost, but that would have been rude. Instead, I said the only sensible thing, "You're welcome."

From Tokyo, I had one more stop before flying to L.A., in the wrong direction. Years later, after they built the new airport at Chek Lap Kok I read anecdotes by pilots talking about how scary landing at Kai Tak was. Good thing I didn't know that, because I always told myself it must be a piece of cake, since pilots landed here all the time. Hong Kong is a very dense place, which means people live in high rise buildings. Kai Tak was right in the middle of the city, on the Kowloon (mainland) side. As we headed in for our landing, I swear I could see what was on the television screens of people in the apartment buildings we passed. It is also right on the water, so moments after we touched down, I glanced out the window and spotted a Chinese junk floating by, practically under the wing.

April in Seoul and Tokyo was still brisk. Not in Hong Kong. By the time I walked out of the terminal, and spotted Woody waiting for me in the crowd, my shirt was sticking to me.

Alan's apartment was in Tai Koo Shing, a neighborhood on Hong Kong Island, east of the action. He shared a three-bedroom apartment with a doctor named John Simon. The rent was seventeen hundred a month – seventeen hundred USD dollars, or its equivalent. In early 1987 it seemed flabbergasting that someone I knew was paying seventeen hundred dollars a month rent. Only a few years previously, in Las Vegas, Cathy and my former roommates were paying nine hundred for a four-bedroom house with a pool. How was seventeen hundred possible?

Alan explained. It seems Bill Benter failed to heed my good advice about not betting on horses. Less than a year later he and Woody set up shop in Hong Kong. Then proceeded to lose almost the entire bankroll over the next year or so. Bill went back to the States to make some money playing blackjack before returning. Meanwhile, Woody refinanced, and began winning. His bankroll, he bragged, was now two hundred and fifty thousand dollars. Wowsers! Unfortunately, he explained to Bill, thanks to the refinancing, Bill's share was but a piece of a piece. A pittance. Bill was not taking the news well.

After an elaborate Chinese dinner the next night, it was time to head home, via L.A. and Las Vegas. Back to reality.

CHAPTER 28
BIG NUMBERS

"*Ship-man-man.*"

"What you say?"

I drew it for her, "1,000,000,000."

We were sitting in the Buckingham, a café across the street and up a flight from Wendy's. Yes, I was back in Korea. I had hardly unpacked when the phone rang, Munch calling to see if I was ready to go back, this time for four weekends. I'd been running a video store for the past two years, an investment of my dad's. As owner, dad had some ideas about our inventory. One was that since Betamax was the superior technology, we should stock lots of Beta. Another was that instead of buying three or four copies of the newest release, buying a dozen used older films, "classics," was the way to go. There were other problems, such as our location. It seemed a good idea at the time, but wasn't. I convinced dad that he already couldn't afford the place, and if he had to hire people to run it while I was gone (I worked cheap) he'd lose all his money that much faster. I managed to sell the tapes, pay the bills, and wrap everything up in record time, and soon was back in Seoul.

After the first weekend, working the usual three shifts on top of jet lag, I did the sensible thing and went to the Sportsman's Club. By midnight I was beat, and Tom Casey offered to drive me to the Kaya.

To the Kaya, with a stop at the Buckingham. Tom was meeting a girl. Tom had a live-in girlfriend named Jina, but that didn't slow him down. The girl he was meeting spoke no English, so she brought a translator. Her friend's name was A Rha, Kim A Rha. Whose translation skills weren't required. Tom and the girl sat on one side of the booth, Tom tickling her, she giggling. A Rha sat with me, while I tried to work out how to say "one billion" in Korean.

Munchkin, besides teaching me how to order ice water, had also taught me the Korean numbers, all before my first trip. Or one set of numbers. I would learn there are two sets, and as you learn Korean you will need to master both, and know when each type is used. For the moment, I knew the Chinese-derived numbers, which are more useful. The vocabulary I'd learned comprised thirteen nouns, one through ten, hundred, thousand, and ten thousand. With them I could count to 99,999,999. To say that you would say the Korean equivalent of "nine thousand, nine hundred, and ninety-nine ten-thousands, nine thousand, nine hundred, and ninety-nine." But how to say "a billion?" Ten thousand was *man*, and ten was *ship*, so I tried "ten ten-thousand ten-thousands."

I'd had a similar conversation last trip, with Mia and her friends. The result after a short conference was, "You can't say that." Years before I'd read George Gamow's *One, Two, Three, Infinity,* in which he claimed the Hottentots could only count "one, two, three, many." I figured maybe Koreans were like that. They could only count but so high. Almost one hundred million was pretty good, but after that, they were stuck.

A Rha looked at what I'd written. She rewrote it this way, "10,0000,0000," and said, "*Ship ok.*"

I studied it a second, wrote "1,0000,0000," and asked, "Is this *ok?*"

"Of course!"

Now I got it. Where we used ten to the third power as a base, thousand, million, billion, they were using ten to the fourth, *man, ok.* "Are there more?"

"Of course! *Man, ok, jo, kyong* ..." She rattled off eleven of them! Later she would write them for me on a napkin. The Korean, not the Chinese. I am convinced she knew what she was talking about, but have yet to meet anyone who knows them beyond *kyong*. And "anyone" includes a Chinese teacher who used to teach math and physics. A bit of trivia about *kyong*; though one of the meanings for the character used to write it is ten quadrillion, it has a more common meaning, capitol. It's pronounced "kyo" in Japanese, "jing" in Chinese. In Japan Eastern capitol is Tokyo, while in China the Northern and Southern capitols are Beijing and Nanjing. Knowing *Kyong* I could now count to ten to the twentieth minus one, while A Rha could count to ten to the forty-eighth minus one.

I had found the woman of my dreams!

It didn't hurt that she was gorgeous, a former actress and model. Meanwhile, I was exhausted, and I had to get up early in the morning and fly to Japan. "I will be back Tuesday night. I have to see you again!" She said she'd like that.

Korea had strict rules about taking money out of the country. You could bring in more than five thousand only if you declared it, and you could only bring out more than five if you had previously declared it, and not in won. Though if you did leave with won, good luck changing it. There was an exception. If you were Japanese, and you won at Walker Hill, you could get a note from the casino authorizing you to leave with your winnings. Ray, the first BP used by the team, who helped recruit many of our subsequent BPs, had been BP over the weekend, and would be carrying cash out of the country. I would fly to Japan in the morning, meet him at Narita Airport (we were on different airlines), wire the money to Alan Woods in Hong Kong, then return to Seoul.

There was no way to accomplish all of that the same day, so I would be staying overnight in Tokyo. I saw no reason to pack a bag. I could wear my clothes two days, and make things easy on myself. (I didn't use carryon bags at the time.) All I brought with me was two books, tucked in the inner pockets of my sports coat.

At Narita I found a desk with ads for hotels, and booked an overnight stay at one which, I was told, was near a bus stop. It turned out Ray's flight was delayed by four hours, so I bought two more books, and used my two outer pockets for those. I was slightly concerned about one detail. I have a better than average memory, but I am terrible with names, and not great at faces. I had just met Ray over the weekend, so didn't really know him. Then again, he was a young Japanese guy. How hard could it be to spot one at Narita Airport?

He spotted me first, once his plane arrived. We went over to some nearby seats, and he dug into his bag, and began pulling out bundles of yen, each wrapped brick containing one hundred ten-thousand-yen notes, a million yen in each. A million two in one, I learned only after I had removed my books, stuffed bricks in my inner pockets, my outer pockets, and my pants pockets. I may have mentioned that I'd lost one hundred and twenty pounds, so I arrived at Narita trim and lean, but with all that yen bulging in my pockets I was back to looking like a young Santa Claus.

"Which bundle had the two hundred thousand?" I asked Ray, after he told me he was supposed to receive it on arrival. He didn't know, so I wound up pulling out all the yen, stacking it on a couple of seats, so we could find the slightly larger bundle.

Ray looked around, bemused. "You Americans are so interesting."

"How's that?"

"You pull out all that money, with so many yakuza around."

"What? Where?"

"All over." He waved a hand. I don't want to be the one to say that all Japanese look alike, but when it came to sorting yakuza from non-yakuza, I couldn't. I found the bundle, gave him his cash, and bulked back up. I had to carry my four books by hand, as I went to the ticket counter, and bought one for the bus to my hotel.

The ride took nearly two hours. Unlike Kai Tak, Narita is not in the middle of town. By the time I reached my stop it was around ten thirty at night. The driver pointed down a very dark street, and I walked two blocks to find my hotel, hoping no yakuza were following me.

At the hotel I showed them my reservation, and asked the desk clerk if she had a shopping bag. She did. From the look on her face I could tell she was dying to know why this foreigner wanted a shopping bag. She is still wondering.

In the room I tried to count the money. Ordinarily if someone hands me cash, I count it right away, but wasn't going to do it at Narita, even if all the yakuza were busy elsewhere, getting tattoos or fighting rival gangs. I was, after little sleep the night before, and a very long day, even more exhausted than the previous night. I spent forty minutes counting the same set of bills over and over, then thought, "screw it!" I put the bundle back together, put all of the bundles in the shopping bag, went into the bathroom and covered the bundles with a triple layer of toilet paper, put three of my four books on top of the pile, then put the bag in the bathtub and drew the shower curtain. Let a hotel sneak thief penetrate that defense!

You'd have known me in the morning if you had breakfast at my hotel (included in the room charge); I was the only guest who brought his own shopping bag. I went to the desk to check out, and asked if they knew of a bank where I could wire, and change, money.

"Here."

"Here?"

"Here" she assured me. I wrote down my desired transaction, and her eyes bulged, "Not here!" I think she was confused in any case. I imagine she was talking about changing money. Walker Hill might have been able to make wire transfers for guests, but I don't think a budget hotel in Tokyo was set up for it.

The bank she directed me to was providentially right near my bus stop. I walked in, and a very young Japanese man, maybe twenty-three, and an even younger assistant, greeted me. I told him I wanted to wire fifteen and a half million yen to Hong Kong, and then buy ten thousand US dollars (which I would carry in and declare when I returned to Seoul). Could they do that for me?

He practically yawned in my face, letting me know that it was no big deal for a hotshot banker like him. Then he asked the key question, "How you do?"

"What do you mean?"

"You have account?"

"No, cash."

"Cashee?"

"Yes, cash."

"Cashee? Where cashee?" He was befuddled.

"Here cashee." They watched with interest as I placed my shopping bag on the counter. They were fascinated as I pulled out my books, and placed them next to the bag. They were even more entertained when I pulled out wads of toilet paper and tried to tuck it as neatly as possible. They were still okay when I pulled out the first brick, maybe even the second. By the third brick they had begun to hyperventilate, and it grew louder the more I extracted. Itsumi could have taken lessons.

"That's a lot of money! That's a lot of money!" My banker was panicking. "Just a minute!"

He and his assistant ran off, and returned with a pair of plastic baskets, the small ones restaurants use to hand back change. They didn't just return; they returned and began running in a circle crying, "Just a minute!" The leader suddenly changed directions, turned, and bumped into his assistant. The assistant wheeled around, and now led the way, the leader chasing him clockwise instead of counterclockwise. By now I had all the money out, stacked in piles on the counter. They stopped, the leader took a deep breath, told me one more time "Just a minute!" then pointed at a chair near the wall and added, "You wait."

"Sure, I brought a book. Four of them."

I sat down and read *From Banzai to Levis*, a classic accounting of marketing in Japan in the 1960s. A chapter later the banker appeared with a clipboard, and asked me, "Why do you send money?"

"Why do you want to know?"

He sucked air through his teeth, then said, "For emperor."

"Ah," I said, "debt."

"Dettu?"

"Yes, 'debt,' dee ee bee tee. I owe, so I" I put my hand over my heart, to show it was serious, "must pay!"

"So desu!" He nodded his understanding. And just like that, fifteen and a half million yen was sent to Woody. He couldn't, unfortunately, change the money to dollars. They didn't have enough. But that wasn't a big problem. I left the bank, caught a bus to the airport, and flew back to Seoul.

CHAPTER 29

WHY THE WINDOWS FACED A BLANK WALL

"Why did you play that card?" Back in Korea, A Rha and I were now dating. We were sitting on the floor in the living room of her apartment, where she and her landlady were playing cards. The game was called Go-Stop, "because you go, and stop," and I was trying to learn it. "Why that card, and not that one?" I pointed.

"Tobaksa!" The landlady grumbled.

A Rha laughed, and I asked her what it meant. "It means 'professional gambler.'" The landlady was basically saying that kibitzers were not appreciated. "Professional gambler," I liked the sound of that!

·Later, we were at the Kaya, me, A Rha, and her cousin, Lee Misuk. I asked if she could teach me Go-Stop. She said we needed a *hwatu*. "A what oh?" The deck used for the game, itself an object which intrigued me, was called a *hwatu*, though if you are in Japan call it *"hana huda,"* which means "flower cards." She told me the bellman could get a deck at a nearby store, and called down to the desk.

She looked puzzled by the response, hung up, and told me they couldn't do it now, because of a "demo." I asked what she was talking about, and she said there was a riot going on in the alley downstairs. I decided to open the window, and check.

A couple of odd things about the rooms at the Kaya. One was the emergency kit which hung on the wall next to the window. It was made of red plastic, and contained a mask to cover one's nose and mouth, and a rope, I guess so that you could rappel down the side of the building if there was a fire. Or if you were me, you could throw the rope out the window, and then fall five stories when trying to rappel. Only, you couldn't, unless you were built like a reptile, because the window was two or three feet high, but only about five inches wide. Also, instead of facing out, it faced sideways, towards a blank wall less than six inches away.

I cranked it open, and could hear shouting. Suddenly A Rha and her cousin began coughing, and begging me to close the window.

"What's wrong?" She borrowed my dictionary to find the translation for *nunmul gasu*. I decoded it: *nun* means 'eye,' *mul* means 'water,' and *gasu* means 'gas.' Hmm, eye water gas … Tear gas!? By now my eyes and throat were catching up. It would be months before I would find out why they were rioting behind the Kaya. Turns out that Korean intelligence was headquartered across the alley. Students had been staging demonstrations – demos – opposing Chun Du Hwan's regime. A student leader had been brought to the building across the way, and interrogated, or perhaps just tortured for the heck of it. At the time the way it was explained I thought they were holding his head under water. Now I suspect they were probably waterboarding him. He had asthma, and he died.

A few days later I would be caught outside of my bank, while a procession passed by. I'd swear they glared at me when they spotted me. The US forces were seen as aiding and abetting the regime, so Americans were not the students' favorite foreigner.

I just mentioned "my bank." It was the team's bank, but I had been entrusted with a change purse containing a safety box key and a chop. One of the guys had taken me downtown, to the *Sangop Unhaeng*, the Commercial Bank. The box was in the name of Butch, a team member I hadn't met, and the chop, if you looked closely, had his name, in Hangul script. I was now the team's bank guy. When I walked into the bank, the entire staff stood, and then bowed. There was a small meeting room, where I would go to confer with Mr. Lee, my personal banker. Mr. Lee was in charge of foreign accounts because he had majored in English. He couldn't actually speak it; Korean English classes didn't teach conversation, which created a market for native speakers who did teach it at language schools.

Nor could either Miss Lee speak English. One Miss Lee was some sort of assistant, the other was the tea girl, whose job was to make and serve tea to Mr. Lee and important customers like me. The first Miss Lee was the real brains facilitating transactions. I'd write down the numbers, she'd grasp them instantly, and take care of matters. Then she and I would wait patiently, though we sometimes glanced sideways at each other, to see how we were holding up, while Mister Lee, who looked like he'd prefer being waterboarded, tried to explain what had been done, for me, in English. Once he survived his own translation, he always looked pleased, "Thank god this bank has me taking care of things!"

Meanwhile, back at the *hwatu* … A Rha did her best to teach me the game. I also picked the brains of other Koreans whenever I could. The trouble was that none of them knew how to teach the game. Eventually I worked out that there were four suits and twelve ranks. You'd think that would be a good place to start, but it never occurred to any of them to mention it. There were lots of names for things, but again, I guess it didn't dawn on them that because I was learning the game, I didn't already know them. There were many oddities, for instance there were five kings, not four, and they were of different ranks. And some rules seemed like they were created just to fuck with me.

For instance, who goes first the first hand? We draw, and low card goes first. I had to figure that out on my own, which is especially hard when you haven't figured out what the ranks are, so how do you know which card is lower than which?

But finally I did. And one day we were in the Buckingham, and because it was slow, the waiter was going to play with me and A Rha. We drew cards, and she said he would go first. I said wait a minute, low card goes first, and my card was so and so, yours was such and such, and his was the highest, naming all three ranks. A Rha looked startled, and she and the waiter conferred, and then she told me I was very smart, obviously amazed I knew as much as I did, but then told me that the waiter was going first because while I was right, the rule was reversed, "Before six o'clock. All of Korea knows this!"

I was sure I was being conned, that A Rha was humoring the waiter because he was an older male. So next time I saw Mia and her friends, I waited until a opportune moment, then said that she would go first because of blah, blah. "But, if it were before six o'clock, I would go first because …" etc. I was expecting her to ask what the hell I was talking about, but instead she said, "Of course. All of Korea knows this."

CHAPTER 30
HOUSEKEEPING

The loudspeaker woke me. The sound was coming from the lane beneath my bedroom window. Whatever the speaker was saying, it sounded urgent, though I suppose anything coming at you from a public address system at close range sounds urgent.

"The North had invaded!" That was my thought. What else could it be? The DMZ is only twenty-five or thirty miles from Seoul, and on its other side are a million soldiers, fanatically loyal to an aging dictator they worship like a living god. Missiles might rain down on us at any minute. Civil defense drills were a weekly affair, compliance mandatory. This was the no-foolin version of the duck and cover maneuvers we used to practice in grade school.

I shook A Rha awake. "What's he saying! What is it?"

She blinked, trying to focus, then asked me, "You want to buy some garlic?"

Down below the blue truck with its load of garlic and its window rattling broadcast system continued down the narrow road, sharing its joyful news, that fresh produce could be yours at reasonable rates. I tried to go back to sleep. I'd arrived the night before, and forced myself to stay awake until A Rha finally showed up, at four in the morning. I thought she'd be there to greet me; she thought I'd be tired and go right to sleep. I'd been asleep three hours when the garlic truck woke me. Tired I was, and ....

What the hell? I could hear someone practicing the piano, playing scales. Over, and over. That's how I learned that the new apartment was across the street from a storefront where piano lessons were given.

We had an apartment. After I returned from my second trip I had told Munchkin about my new girlfriend, while he told me about his now ex-girlfriend. Shin Jong had called him, and told him she wanted to get married. Munch said that it was premature, that he liked her but barely knew her. She said she really wanted to move to the US, and if not Munch, she had two other boyfriends who might be able to arrange it. When he heard that Munch told her he thought she ought to ask one of them. "But I like you best!" Anyway, I gave Munch A Rha's number, and when he made his next trip, he got in touch with her. A Rha helped find the team an apartment.

It was downhill from Itaewon. The road across from the Hamilton Hotel went down towards the Han River. About three hundred yards down an alley on the left led in, then turned right to run parallel to the main road. Right after the turn was where our building was. I was sharing the apartment with a team member I hadn't previously met, Butch, and his wife, Ashley. They'd also got on like gangbusters with A Rha.

It was funny, after starting out playing for a team where even taxi fares were too extravagant an expense, to now be playing for a team with its own apartment on foreign soil, its own travel agent back in Los Angeles who handled the many overseas flights, its own makeup artist.

Yes, makeup artist. Munchkin produced movies when not playing blackjack. The production company's makeup artist, Judy, had been enlisted to help Craig and Butch, the two team members who had been barred at Walker Hill. Butch was a body builder, whose nickname was No Neck. Dark body makeup for all visible skin surfaces, a bushy black wig, some nose plugs to flare the nostrils, and clips attached to his temples, connected by an elastic band hidden under the wig, which pulled the corners of his eyes back, to give them an Asian look, and Butch became Samoan. Or something.

Craig, who was tall and slender, got the dark makeup, the eye puller, and a dark wig under a turban; he was Indian. The first session he played at Walker Hill with his new look, who sat down at his table but a real Indian. It was the first and may have been the last sighting of an Indian in Walker Hill. Now there were two at one table.

"Where in India do you come from?" The newcomer asked Craig.

Craig froze, as the names of cities in India hid from his consciousness in embarrassment. "Uh … Los Angeles?" Somehow, he got away with it.

Those two were not the first team members to change skin color for a play. Darryl had made a play in Atlantic City wearing the magic shoes. He darkened his skin, and dyed his hair black, cutting it into a short, curly perm, a modified Afro. He borrowed an ankle length fur coat, and a genuine Rolex. I don't think he borrowed the girlfriend, but was actually dating the companion he brought with him. She was professional model caliber, wearing the sort of dress that had bosses watching something besides the cards. He won one hundred and twenty-five thousand dollars, then had her tell the bosses they had "had a fight." He had gone back to New York City, and she would go fetch him back. They never saw him again.

Butch and I were calling plays for Richard, who was back as a BP. Richard was more comfortable at the table. Perhaps a little too comfortable. He was failing to stack his chips in a way that facilitated my counting them. When I checked his results after our session, the number didn't match what I thought it should be. I told Butch, and Butch saw him going south with chips during their session. He went to his room to talk to him, and Richard refused to open the door, then grabbed an early flight out. He was the only big player we had a problem with. Most players are honest, but there are exceptions. On the plus side, it was around this same time the team acquired Rocky. Rocky was a manager at the restaurant where Ray worked. He was in his mid-forties, and would prove to be our best BP. Indeed, he became known as "Rocky, the World's Greatest BP." Though it took time for him to earn the name.

Butch and Ashley left for the States. I wanted to stick around for another couple of weeks, and having an apartment made that reasonable. Munch suggested I play the Olympus while I was in country. The limit was only five hundred thousand, but with its shuffle it was a good game. I went there three days in a row, nearly the only business in the casino. I lost four million the first day. I lost five more then next day. That day, the same boss I'd had the long conversation with was working. He seemed really concerned, and told me I ought not to come back. I came back the next day, and had won about half of it back, when the shift manager barred me. The young boss, as I was cashing out, said, "I told you, you should have stayed away."

While I stayed, the team had a meeting. Alan Woods was in the US, and was an investor, so it was a good time to break some bankrolls. Bankrolls plural. They hadn't settled up in a while, another good reason for doing accounting. The meeting was at Butch's place in Lake Tahoe. They called me, a forty-five-minute international call being another expense Arthur never would have authorized. Their first pass at balancing the books found them off "a bit." The bit being eighty-nine thousand dollars. Nearly an entire bankroll. The call to me was a Hail Mary of sorts. My own records were impeccable, every dollar or yen or won accounted for, whether playing results, or expenses. I wrote everything down, if not the moment it happened, certainly before bed. No, what they were hoping was that I had some idea of what other people had done. I have that sort of memory, and could supply a lot of information – "Then Darryl won eight million, seven hundred thousand …" – but I didn't know everything everyone had done.

Fifteen hours went by, and the eighty-nine thousand was whittled down to fourteen. Of which, they thought, half was attributable to currency exchange fluctuations. That left seven thousand that they could not reconcile. The seven thousand seemed to have been owed to Alan, and the question was whether or not he had been paid. No one was sure. They would ultimately settle it with arbitration. A panel of other advantage players was convened to hear evidence. Alan's evidence was that he had never recorded receiving the money, and he always recorded things. Phil, another team member, also had evidence, to whit, a Caesar's Tahoe cocktail napkin. On it he'd written "Alan

$7000." That must mean he'd paid him because, "what else could it mean?"

Malcolm, who was on the panel, asked to interrogate a witness. Doing his best impression of Perry Mason, he paced back and forth, hands clasped behind his back, as he asked, "Mister Woods, isn't it true that when you have a big win, you are sometimes sexually aroused, and when you return to your room you masturbate to relieve tension."

"Yes, that's true."

"And isn't it also true that on one occasion, you were so inflamed, that you thrust your Johnson into the ice bucket, to cool yourself down?"

"Malcolm, you know that's true, but what does it have to do with the seven thousand?"

"Nothing, but, *I love that story*!"

The panel retired to deliberate, and when they returned rendered the Solomonic judgment that the parties should split the difference, the team paying Alan thirty-five hundred. (Months later neither party was sure if they had.) Alan said that he was withdrawing as an investor. That it was the most profitable blackjack team he'd ever been involved with, but the bookkeeping might endanger his sanity.

Meanwhile, back in Seoul, I was hearing revelations from A Rha. One was that she had a job, and had been kidnapped because of it. There was a flourishing black market in Korea, most of it goods acquired from the military bases. I'd been told my very first trip to buy a bottle of Chivas duty free on the way in. There was a black marketeer south of the Twilight Zone who paid a premium for them. I made the mistake once of buying Martell cognac, thinking the more expensive booze would fetch a greater profit. It turned out it didn't work that way, and the buyer only reluctantly took it off my hands.

Another item in demand was tobacco. I'd heard stories of guys who gave their girlfriends a pack of American cigarettes, only to have the police confiscate them as soon as the boyfriend was out of sight. This had just changed. A trade deal was struck, and Korea was now willing to import American cigarettes. A Rha had gotten a job working for R.J. Reynolds, going to nightclubs in Itaewon and Hannamdong, selling its products. Coming out of a disco she was forced into a car, and threatened by representatives of Philip Morris. The bosses at R.J. Reynolds assigned her protection, in the form of a motorcycle driver named Mr. Go, who would transport her from place to place.

Another revelation was personal, and strange. She and her cousin sat down with me. They told me A Rha had something to confess. They were clearly nervous, and making me nervous. Was this the prelude to something I did not want to hear?

"My cousin, I told you her name Lee Misuk? This is not true. She is really ... My sister! Her name Kim Jiyoung."

"Okay ..." To this day I have no idea why they thought it mattered either way.

Korea had a revelation, since things were being revealed. A bit of background is in order. Back in 1981 Seoul was awarded the right to host the 1988 Olympics. The Koreans were well aware that when Tokyo hosted the 1964 Olympics it was a coming out party for the new Japan. Korea saw the 1988 Olympics as its coming out party, and began planning and anticipating with a fervor those who didn't visit Korea in those years cannot imagine. There was a big clock downtown, like the Doomsday clock, but this one counted down the days to the Olympics. The count was under five hundred, and the country was practically blacking out from holding its breath in quivering excitement.

The problem was the demos. Ever since the death of the student they'd gotten more frequent. Might the Olympic Committee decide the disruptions threatened the safety of visitors? Might they look for a last-minute change of venue? That couldn't be allowed to happen! The president, Chun Doo Hwan, a dictator who had been in power for seven years, and showed no sign of stepping down, stepped down. He announced he was handing the job to his right-hand man, Roh Tae Woo. This was stunning news, but more was to come. Roh said he'd do it only if elections were held in December. Free and fair elections. December was still months away, and could Roh and Chun be trusted? We'd have to wait and see.

Still another sort of revelation came my way. I learned about karaoke. The way that happened was that Tom Casey asked if I wanted to go for a drive one night, to see a room salon. He was going to Gangnam. Seoul is divided into districts called "ku" (or "gu"), and those are further divided into smaller areas called "dong." For instance, Itaewondong and Namyeongdong are part of Yongsangu. Gangnamgu was across the river. The Korean word for river is *gang*, the Han River being *Hangang* in Korean, and *nam* means "south," so Gangnam is "river south." Even then, years before Psy had his hit song, it was trendy and expensive.

Kisaeng are Korea's answer to geisha. They were entertainers whose connection to prostitution varied with the era. Like geisha, there are still kisaeng, though some calling themselves that are part of a different noble tradition than "skilled dancer and musician," the noble tradition of "high class hooker." There are also room salons, which are similar to the clubs found in Japan. They are hardly inexpensive. We were heading for one of the better ones.

The owner, Mr. Lee, Tom told me on the drive, was a famous gangster. He killed someone, and spent years in prison. "They made a movie about it!" Now he was worth a hundred million dollars, Tom claimed, and he owned the place we were going to. Why we were going there I never learned; perhaps just to say "hi." Tom knew a lot of people.

At the room salon we were escorted to a room in the basement with enough seating on a horseshoe shaped sofa for a dozen people. A low table had a bottle of Chivas, ice, glasses, shrimp, ginseng, honey, Coke, and water. I asked if I could have beer, and some bottles were brought in.

Mr. Lee was about fifty. He looked as though, despite adding pounds over the years, he was still very healthy. He had two women with him. One he identified as his niece. Maybe she was. I don't think he'd have a reason to hide it from us, if she was his girlfriend. There was also one of his hostesses, who was there to pour drinks for us. Tom told me that customers usually paid one hundred thousand won apiece for a visit to this particular room salon, and that was probably a minimum.

We were joined by a musician. Karaoke is etymologically related to karate. When Funakoshi Gichin coined the word karate a century ago, he combined *kara*, or empty, with *te*, which means "hand." Karaoke means "empty orchestra." Most of you have probably been to a place offering karaoke, and expect a sound system, and a screen which shows the lyrics. This man was a one-man band, who played music, to accompany the singers.

A microphone was produced, and the niece sang a popular song called "Jae." They urged Tom to get up and sing. Tom said no. Mister Lee got up, and demonstrated that he could kill a song as well as a rival, by which I mean he was pretty good. They asked Tom to sing. He said no. The hostess did a number. They asked Tom. You know what he said. It was getting embarrassing. Someone had to take one for the team!

I got up to sing. I always liked the song "Sounds of Silence," so thought that would be a good choice. I often tell people that I am tone deaf. It isn't true. I am just "tone hard of hearing." I am also rhythmi-cally challenged. Instead of "shave and a haircut, four bits," I am about forty-nine cents, or maybe fifty-one. When I was young, I went to an acting school, and played Harold Hill, King Mongkut, Billy Bigelow, and Captain Von Trapp, so figured I could get through "Sounds of Silence." The difference is that for those roles I had rehearsal, and I had memorized the lyrics. Do you know all of the words to "Sounds of Silence?" Turns out I didn't. Nor was it clear which of us was setting the tempo, me, or the guy with the keyboard strapped to his chest.

I will say that when I finally ground to a halt, and my listeners knew I would sing no more, they applauded. Maybe it was because I got up and sang, or maybe it was because I stopped.

Later I asked A Rha if she knew about Mr. Lee, famous gangster. She didn't, at least not from my description. She had other things on her mind. One was moving.

She had found a place of her own, and we needed to move her furniture. The mover was not what I expected. He was a skinny old man, with a white beard down to his chest, and a cart. By the time A Rha's belongings were loaded, he had to tie them down because they were heaped several feet above the top of the cart. There were poles on either side; he picked them up, and set off, pulling the cart.

The new place was nearly a mile away. Maybe it only seemed that far, because of all the hills, and the twists and turns through narrow alleys. The new place was also up a flight of stairs that were closer to ladder than stairs. By the time he had the last of her things up them, he was gasping for breath, so I gave him a cigarette. In the long run smoking wasn't good for his lungs, but in the short run it helped stop them from seizing up.

"How much should I give him?"

"I told him ten thousand, but he is very good man. Give him twelve."

A few days later I learned there was something else on her mind. She took me to see Jiyoung, who did not look so hot. "Let me die!" Didn't sound so good, either. I asked what was wrong, and A Rha told me it was rectal cancer. She offered to show me, and Jiyoung was past caring, but I said I'd take her word for it.

We got Jiyoung loaded into a cab, though easier said than done since she couldn't sit. We took her to a hospital, and given the length of her stay, a matter of days, I think the English A Rha groped for was not "rectal cancer" but "abscess."

I learned a few things during her hospital stay. One was that ramyeon was very cheap, only a few hundred won in a vending machine, though Jiyoung warned me that students who ate nothing but ramyeon died. "Scientist give to mouse, only ramyeon, and mouse die!"

I learned that something I doubted was actually true. A movie from a few years earlier, *Choose Me*, had a character who said all sorts of things no one believed, because they were too unlikely to be true. Near the end the audience learns that they are all true. I was getting the feeling that things A Rha told me were not always true. Her cousin turning out to be her sister was a case where she had lied. But some things which seemed like stretches turned out to be quite true. One of the things she told me was that her uncle was a major general. In the Korean army back then, that was a very high rank indeed. One day their aunt came to visit. A Rha had warned me that she and her aunt didn't get along very well because they were both alpha females. The aunt did present as a take-charge sort. She spoke English quite well, and somewhere in the flow of conversation mentioned, "My husband, the major general."

The final revelation was that Korean hospitals won't let you out until you settle the bill, and if you can't pay, and stay, the meter keeps running. I paid around a thousand dollars to ransom Jiyoung.

With no big players lined up for the immediate future, it was time to head back home. I told A Rha I'd be back soon, though it turned out not as soon as I hoped.

CHAPTER 31
MEMORIES CAN BE BEAUTIFUL

"Do you have trouble sleeping?" I thought that was an odd question for Bill Benter to be asking me. We were sitting in an Italian restaurant on Atlantic Avenue, rumored to be a front for a mobster from Philadelphia. It had a reputation for good Italian food, though the only thing I found notable about it was that the Budweiser they served me, in a can, cost six bucks. Good thing Bill was buying. He and Huey, my old teammate, picked me up at the airport in Atlantic City. I'd arrived in a tiny plane, after transferring in New York, tiny planes being all the local airport could handle. I told Bill I slept just fine, and he said, "If you have trouble sleeping, let me know."

Bill had been talking to Munchkin, and asked if he knew any card counters with good memories. Munch said, "What about Jake?"

That's how I came to be in Atlantic City, brought there to try to play the Memory Game.

Here's how the game came about. In the high roller's room at Harrah's, when a game was dead, the cards were fanned on the table, face up. The dealers had to follow a set procedure for dealing, so the cards which would be on the bottom of the deck at the beginning of the shuffle were always in the same place. Some dealers, often experienced ones, developed a glitch. When they riffled the cards instead of both hands working in synch, one was consistently behind the other. If the faster hand was the one releasing the cards at the bottom of the deck, it turned out that they would make it through the entire shuffle without ever being mixed. One of the regular dealers in the pit, a guy named Scott, had the glitch. Boy, did he have the glitch! Some dealers "clumped," as we called it, five or ten cards. Scott clumped fifteen or twenty.

Bill would find Scott on a dead game, and memorize the first few cards. He'd go to the toilet, and write them down. He'd come back, chat with Scott a bit more, memorizing more cards. When he had a dozen or so he would try to work out the best way to play if he were three, four, five cards in. He would memorize the suit and rank of the first two cards. Then he would go back to the table, sit down, cut the clump to where he wanted, watch for the key cards, and then possibly have a lock winner or two.

I was in Atlantic City to play Scott.

In the more than sixty years since *Beat the Dealer* came out, there haven't been many legendary teams. Then again, there haven't been all that many real, professional players, which cuts down the number of teams. The two books Ben Mezrich wrote about the M.I.T. Team feature very different casts of characters, with little overlap, but the team is usually counted as one. Some other teams who are legendary, Al Francesco's team, which included Bill Erb, Blair Hull, and Ken Uston; Ken Uston's subsequent team; the Czech Team; Rob Reitzen's team; the Greek Team; and the Holy Rollers are seven. I was fortunate enough in the late eighties to freelance for two more. The Korea team had been in existence in some form since at least 1979, though its Korea years were during the late eighties and early nineties. I guess it was still the same team when I played in Biloxi in 2004, because Darryl, Munchkin, and Phil were part of that group, though by then so were James Grosjean, Max Rubin, and others. The other team might be the most legendary of all. The Tommy Hyland team formed when Atlantic City got its first casino. I haven't talked to Tommy in a couple of years, but he may still have people out there playing, forty-five years later. Some of its greatest years had to be during the late eighties, when it was a computer team, concentrating on playing Atlantic City.

This was the same group that had tried to recruit me in 1983, after the team Munchkin was on split, and some of its members merged with Tommy. Tommy, Bill, Jon Ungar, and Miles, were all active in 1988. I am not sure about Ray. He told me a story about playing with the group. Did he tell it to me in 1983, or did he make a cameo appearance in 1988? Either way, it's a good time to talk about losing money.

As Jane Austen once should have said, "It is a truth universally acknowledged that a man in possession of a good fortune, can lose it if he gambles." Everyone loses, and all it takes to lose a lot of money is a lot of money. It's the way these people lost it in the following stories that is unique. Losing it, or almost losing it, the way they did takes a real professional.

Ray's story was that he was going back to Vegas from A.C., and took a cab to the airport in Philly. That's a long trip, and the driver invited him to sit up front with her. Ray had a briefcase with a lot of cash, which he tucked under the seat. Guess what Ray forgot, when he paid the driver and got out of the taxi? He was almost in the terminal, when it dawned on him. He turned, ran to the drive lanes, and yelled "come back!" She didn't.

He called the cops. It took time to convince them that he didn't just lose a little money, he lost a lot of money. They sent an alert to the toll booth. Unfortunately, the cab had already passed Go, or at least passed the toll booth, and was on track to collect Ray's two hundred dollars, several hundred times over.

He took a cab back to Atlantic City, and was put in touch with a police detective, who freelanced as a private detective. Ray claimed it was Dave Toma himself, who helped track down the missing cab. The cab was posted when he caught up with it. The driver was not the one who had driven Ray; it was her boyfriend. The briefcase was gone. The detective brought him in, and sweated him in an interrogation room. At one point he picked up a phone on the table, spoke with the District Attorney, and agreed they could go for a ten-year sentence if the cabbie didn't cooperate. The cabbie broke down, and agreed to take the cop to the cash. He might have hung tough if he'd noticed the telephone wasn't plugged in.

The money was buried at a cabin belonging to his mother. They recovered thirty-five thousand dollars. Ray had a Dirty Harry moment: did I lose forty-five thousand, or only thirty-five? He couldn't be sure until he got back to Las Vegas, and checked his records. He paid the cabbie a thousand-dollar tip, the carrot he and the detective had agreed would go with the stick. He paid the detective three thousand as a finder's fee. And when he got back to Vegas, he learned the girlfriend must not have told her boyfriend the whole truth, because it had been forty-five after all.

Laurie Chang was cleaning John's apartment (back before they were married). She found eight-thousand-dollars' worth of chips in a drawer. Then she found twenty thousand in traveler's checks in an envelope. She decided maybe a thorough cleaning was in order. More chips here, more checks there, and when the dust settled, she found one-hundred-and-sixty-five-thousand-dollars' worth of forgotten funds. "I thought I was a little light," was Johnny's reaction.

Darryl has multiple "losing money" stories. For instance, the time he left eighty thousand dollars he was carrying around in a brown paper bag, in the waiting room of his allergist. Or the night he stopped in Barstow.

Barstow, California is a famous restaurant town. No, really. It is famous for a McDonald's which is in a railroad car, and was for many years the only restaurant not conforming to McDonald's architectural norms. (There also used to be a pair of restaurants the other side of the interstate, one called Bun Boy, and directly behind it, the Mad Greek. Make of that what you will.) What drew people was that Barstow is halfway between L.A. and Vegas, and so was the perfect stopping point, just about when you'd like to stretch your legs and grab a Coke.

One night Darryl and one of the other guys stopped there. It was three in the morning, and when Darryl came out of the restaurant, he made a lucky find, a one-hundred-dollar bill. Finders Keepers! Then he spotted another nearby. "Wow," he thought, "someone is losing ... Oh, shit!" He ran to the car, and sure enough, the back window was open, the bag with all the money on the back seat was agape, and it was a very windy night in the high desert. He claimed they crawled around in the dark on their hands and knees, covering a radius of one hundred yards, but found every bill.

There was also the time he was smuggling seventy thousand dollars out of Poland, in his socks, as one does. He boarded the plane and promptly fell asleep. Gravity is a wonderful thing. First his sock went down, then as the plane climbed, so did all the money. Hundred-dollar bills flowed like a river down the aisle. Stories like these may be why Craig told me how glad he was that I was going to Korea to look after things.

Perhaps the most remarkable story concerned Miles and Tommy. Miles was in the Bahamas, and thanks to a win had one hundred thousand dollars. He did not want to declare it, and since he knew other team members would be playing there, he came up with a brilliant plan. He rented a car and bought a shovel. He drove to the countryside, dug a hole, buried the money, and then drew a treasure map, "Turn left at the old oak tree, then walk sixty paces ...."

Miles was not a guy you'd want drawing treasure maps, but you could do worse. You could send Tommy to find the money. But lo and behold, Tommy rented a car, bought a shovel, followed the map, dug where X marked the spot, and found the money. The trouble was that money-eating bacteria live in the dirt, and the cash was covered with black mold which stank.

He put it in a safety box at the casino cage, which had everyone wondering about the smell. When he bought in at the table, they wondered about the mold. Still, this might have been a happy story, except for a guy named Stanley Sludikoff. Sludikoff published a magazine called Gambling Times. He and Tommy had some sort of beef, and Sludikoff tipped the Bahamian authorities that Tommy was down there playing with a computer. Tommy was locked up while they decided what to do with him. There was no law on the books saying you couldn't use a computer in the casino. If there had been, they wouldn't have played there. The authorities decided that if there wasn't a law, there ought to be one, and the fine was, let's see, how much have you got kid? Hmm, one hundred thousand? That's the fine for using a computer, one hundred thousand! Just to rub it in, Sludikoff ran a photo of Tommy in handcuffs being deported by the Bahamian police, with the sanctimonious advice that if only Thomas John Hyland had subscribed to Gambling Times, this would never have happened to him.

The apartment Bill and Huey took me to was in the Ritz. The Ritz was an old building, dating to the 1920s. Atlantic City! The city was run for ninety years by three successive bosses. In the middle, from 1911 to 1941, was Nucky Johnson, inspiration for the main character in the series Boardwalk Empire. Nucky had an apartment in the Ritz, and used the building to host the legendary gangland conference of 1929. That was in 1929. In 1988 it had seen better days.

The team had a two-bedroom apartment on the fifteenth floor. Living in one bedroom on a full-time basis were Richard Dougherty and Girl George. The other bedroom, on the opposite side of the common living area, had bunk beds, so that up to a dozen people could crash there if needed. The living room had a lot of batteries, spare parts, soldering irons, and belts with wires and buzzers attached. It also had a microfiche machine; no one was quite sure why. It was known as the Sweat Lodge.

The view from the fifteenth floor looked down the Boardwalk towards most of the casinos. Only the Tropworld Casino was on the other side of the building. It was a grim view, especially in winter. It did boast a good view of a payphone on the Boardwalk. The advantage of that was they could enjoy Bill's favorite prank, phone gobbing. Other than a sight line to a pay phone, all you needed to phone gob was a jar of Vaseline and a pair of binoculars.

Bill would send Richard down, as Richard handled the odd jobs, and he would coat the ear piece of the phone with a big gob of petroleum jelly. The hard part was hanging up the phone with the receiver balanced on the edge of the hanger, so as not to lose jelly.

Ideal targets were gangs of youth, boys or girls, didn't matter. Each was fun. When a target was sighted Bill would call the number. The leader would invariably be the one to saunter over to the payphone, grab it, and jam it up against their ear, "Yeah?" Then they jerked the phone away from their ear, and begin feeling, to see what had just given them an earful. Which drove the jelly deeper into the ear, and with the girls, into their hairdo. The guys would sometimes, after looking around and failing to spot anyone doubled over with laughter, finding a hiding spot, hoping to catch the prankster. The hiding spots were under the gaze of anyone in a nearby building who happened to have binoculars.

What was it like down on the beach? Put it this way, if the Knight and Death from *The Seventh Seal* met on the Atlantic City beach, instead of chess they'd play Russian Roulette. If you turned your back on the grey and desolate seascape, you'd be looking at the Boardwalk. When the game Monopoly was invented the first players probably thought, "Gee, they named the properties after ones in Atlantic City." Growing up in the Midwest, and playing Monopoly long before I even knew there was a town called Atlantic City, my reaction – even though I knew the truth by then – was, "Gee, they named the streets here after Monopoly!"

Back in the 1880s, a hotelier got tired of guests tracking sand into the lobby. He built a wooden sidewalk outside his place, a board walk. Most of the sand shook off before patrons entered. Others copied him, and the Boardwalk reached four miles in length. It was a wide promenade, with rolling chairs, pushed at high speed by some of the healthiest young people on earth, wheeling people between hotels. Fast as they were they were routinely passed by Girl George, who power walked up and back. A feat all the more impressive because she wore headphones and also read a book while walking, yet managed to avoid collisions.

There was a time when eager visitors gazed in wonder at the splendors of the resort. That time passed into a flashier era, around the time Nucky Johnson ran the town. The Depression hit, and what was flashy became gaudy, then sleazy. It never got better. By the time I arrived the Boardwalk was lined with shops selling salt water taffy, dollar stores, fortune tellers, and vacancies. Interspersed were the casinos. If the depressed aura of the small shops was a warning of the failures of capitalism, the casinos were a warning of its success. They were supposed to be elegant, and classy, as imagined by such classy guys as Steve Wynn and Donald Trump. There is a stereotype that New Yorkers are loud, rude, brash, and obnoxious. You should see them in a casino! The ones with money, anyway. There were also plenty of senior citizens. They were bused in, lured with the promise of a free meal and redeemable coupons. Half of them ended up losing their social security money playing slots. The other half, to help make ends meet, would eat the lunch, redeem the coupons, then sit on the beach wondering why they weren't dead already.

Now that we've talked about the attractive parts, let's talk about the rest. The casinos had doors opening onto the Boardwalk, and into parking areas under the buildings, accessible from side streets. None had doors opening onto Pacific Avenue. That's where the crack whores and the cheap motels they used for their dates were found. Another block in was Atlantic Avenue, worse than Pacific, the urban decay interrupted by mob front Italian restaurants. Arctic Avenue was another block. Even the Mafia knew better than to stick a restaurant on Arctic. Beyond that, the projects; abandon all hope, ye who enter there.

You didn't have to go that far to find horrific slums. We drank at a bar on Tennessee Avenue, half a block off the Boardwalk. The street's windows were boarded up, the glass that used to fill those windows was in shards all over the pavement. The bar was in a basement. You'd never know it was there unless you knew it was there. It was an Irish bar. Not a festive faux Irish pub. It just had a lot of Irish drinkers. That and Irish bartenders rumored to be IRA killers on the lam.

We went to such places because there was nowhere else to go, and nothing else to do, besides drink. God knows the place drove you to it. The casinos closed at four on weeknights and five-thirty weekends, but many bars stayed open all night. Were we crazy walking around the dark streets, sometimes with thousands of dollars in our pockets? Not to worry, the muggers had more sense than to walk around there.

There was a movie theatre. It was a half hour away by bus. I went there with Girl George and Boy George, to see *Rain Man*. Boy George wasn't part of the team. He was a kid from New Zealand who was in town playing for Zeljko, a Tasmanian player of legend. He tried to convince me to go to Egypt with him to play for Zeljko. Instead, I convinced him to go see *Rain Man*. There's a scene where Dustin Hoffman and Tom Cruise are in Caesar's Palace in Las Vegas, playing blackjack. Raymond, Hoffman's character, says, "Queens coming!"

Tom Cruise then asks if he is sure, and says to the dealer, "Wait a minute. We are going to double down." Like this is the most amazing play anyone has ever made. As I remember it, the hand was ten against a six, so even your granny doubles down, but anyway it starts raining queens, and suddenly they are rich. Shift to inside the eye in the sky. Security is trying to figure out the play, "They aren't using a computer. They aren't getting the hole card. And they can't be counting cards, because *no one can count a six-deck shoe*." At which point Boy George stood up and screamed, "Oh my god, I've been wasting my entire life!"

Some of the younger team members hung around to drink and crash at the Sweat Lodge. Besides Richard and Girl George, the permanent residents, and me, permanent when in town, there were area residents who either had their own apartments, or stayed in town after nights where the team played. These included Huey, Miles' brother Fred and his girlfriend Marsha, and a guy named Dewey who went to high school with Miles. It was a hard-drinking crew. One night, before I arrived, they'd come in at dawn, and went on a mini-rampage. You know those scenes in movies where someone knocks over a bookcase, and they start falling like dominos? Someone thought it would be funny to try it with the bunk beds. Funny to everyone except Malcolm, who was in town and sleeping in one of the bunks.

He rose in fury, an enraged Gulliver among the Lilliputians. Who just laughed. But the next day he gave Bill an earful, Bill gave the others a talking to, and later warned me that if I "had trouble sleeping," to let him know right away.

Rehearsing for my upcoming play was on my schedule, which consisted of going next door to the Trop, and flat-betting hundreds in the high-rollers pit, while memorizing random pages sent to a pager I wore. When not practicing, I had the time and inclination to make myself useful.

One job available any time was scouting. Not all dealers clumped, so like the old days when I scouted for hole cards, this time around I looked for clumping dealers. My best afternoon, I managed to scout every dealer on day shift at Trump Plaza, regular and relief. There were more than eighty blackjack tables, so seeing all in one shift took concentration and dedication. As there was a master book of dealers, and I scouted dealers who'd been scouted before, I found that some of my predecessors were either not diligent, or overly optimistic. My ratings were consistently lower than those I found in the book.

Another job, less often available, but another for which an hourly rate had been assigned, was chip cashing. There were eleven casinos in town, and we played most of them. By then the CTR had been invented. The Cash Transaction Report was designed to prevent money laundering. Any transaction exceeding ten grand had to be reported. Any set of transactions exceeding ten grand in a twenty-four-hour period had to be reported, whether buying in, or cashing in. I suppose this was a laudable regulation. Without it we'd have never had the show *Orange Is the New Black*. Still, it was an annoyance for card counters. Not only because the authorities who might be alerted didn't understand card counting, many assuming that since they didn't understand what we were doing it must be illegal, but also because we took pains to conceal who we were from the casinos. It could get awkward if John Doe had to sign a form under his real name, Richard Roe, just because he bought in for more than 10K.

Hence, the briefcase. Whoever managed a play, usually Bill, Miles, Tommy, or Jon, they had charge of a briefcase filled with cash and chips. There were five-hundred-dollar chips from every casino we were playing. If it looked like more would be needed for an upcoming play, someone would be sent to buy in for ten thousand on a crap table at the target casino. They'd make a few line bets, then bring the chips home to add to the briefcase. After plays were finished the big player, and many of the support personnel had smaller chips. These were collected in plastic bags. The chip casher would make a casino run, from casino to casino, cashing them in.

Then there were the plays themselves. The team was busily playing the Computer Clump Game, so a clumping I would go. A play might have as many as fifteen people involved. The manager upstairs in a room. All four managers were by then far too well known to show their faces in the casino, which would set off alarms. Three or four players would lock up a table, taking over seats and playing multiple hands, as vacancies occurred, until no civilians remained.

Getting rid of civilians sometimes took special measures. Even in the old days when we played hole cards it was an issue, since the first base seat was a requisite. Roger once, playing drunk, introduced himself to the guy on first, "Hey, buddy, I'm Joe Blow, who're you?" Learning the man's name, he told the dealer, "Gotta pee! Save my seat," and left his drink and chips. He went and paged the other guy to a house phone, then stole his seat. Munchkin once solved the problem by barring the player. It was another hole card player, so he walked up, tapped his shoulder, and whispered, "Sir, we don't want your action anymore." The kid turned white, and skedaddled.

The table lockers included specialists known as the Cigar Boys. They would surround civilians slow to get the hint it was time to move to another table, light up, and use poison gas to drive them away. Once, Dewey found himself outnumbered, three ladies, all together, versus him and his cigar. So he offered to take them all to lunch, hinting that he'd be willing to show all three of them a "good time." They were all as old as his mother, and just laughed at him.

Let's say that the table lockers have locked up a table. Time for the first inputter to move in. By then all of the casinos knew about magic shoes. In any case magic shoes wouldn't work for this game. The shoes the team had formerly used only needed to input the count values for Hi-Lo during the dealing. During the shuffle it was more complicated because the program needed to know things like how many grabs, how accurate the dealer was, and other variables relating to the shuffle. But it could still be input with fast toes. The shoes had been built by Keith Taft, but the programming was done initially by Bill, or Bill and Wally Simmons. Then to fit it into a microcomputer Wally would rewrite it in assembler language, and it would be burned onto a chip using EPROM, Erasable Programmable Read-Only Memory. The chip was inserted in the shoe, different chips for different casinos depending upon the shuffle.

For the Clump Game the actual card values, suit and rank, had to be input. Too much for toes. Our inputters wore keypads under their shirts. They could cross their arms, and input on a keypad under one arm. They also wore jackets, with a hole cut in a pocket, so they could stick their hand through the hole, and input data. Two or three would take turns. Inputter one would input a shoe, and output the next one, while inputter two input that shoe, to output shoe three. Sometimes a third inputter would handle shoes three and four. Though it was seldom a play lasted that long.

The inputters stood behind the table, and to hide the fact that they kept one hand in a pocket, there were team members who acted as "gallery," blocking the pit's view of the inputter, while letting the inputter view the table.

That there was a big player goes without saying. The big player wore an elastic belt under his clothes, with buzzers that attached in back of the knees or lower thighs. Under ordinary circumstances you wouldn't actually hear the buzzing; only the big player could feel it. Though one night a player, Randy, was in the Atlantis near closing time. The casino was dead, and unusually quiet. BZZT!-BZZT!, BZZT!-BZZT! Everyone at the table heard it, but no one thought to check Randy's pants.

There were also spotters. Spotters hung back, observing the play from a distance, watching for unusual pit activity. If they saw bosses converging, they could shut the play down. A special sort of spotter was used in Bally's Park Place. That casino had a security guy called the Meter Man. If you took a radio, tuned it to an area between stations, and held it near a computer when it was transmitting, it would squawk. The Meter Man would, if a computer play was suspected, try to sneak up behind the inputter and hold his "meter" close to her back. The Meter Man Spotter would watch for the Meter Man.

I described the inputter as "her." We had at least one male inputter, Huey, but he was not among the best at the job. Debby Hyland, Tommy's wife, was good, but our top two were Sue, Tommy's sister, and Girl George.

One of the hardest plays I ever made was a clump play, though it started as routine.

Richard Dougherty was a legend. He was believed to be the second most arrested player in Atlantic City history, after Tommy. After the no-barring policy of the early days, the casinos threw out players right and left. The barrings came in three stages. First there was a simple "we don't want your action." The second time around, they would read the player the Trespass Act. Third time's the charm, go directly to jail without passing Go! Tommy, Richard, and others on the team reached stage three at all the casinos, then kept going back. Richard was arrested so often that after the cops busted him at Bally's, and took him to the station for processing, they'd ask, "Where can we drop you, Richard?" And he'd say, "How about the Trop, and I'll see you in half an hour."

Richard got his family involved. Besides me, one of the other table lockers one afternoon at Trump Castle, was Jimmy Dougherty, Richard's younger brother. The big player was Dick Dougherty, Senior. Dick was a very good big player, because he was a degenerate gambler. Richard's cousin, Linda Fiorentino (yes, that Linda Fiorentino), was a math prodigy. Dick Senior used to take her to bars, when she was five, and win bets that his niece could multiply numbers faster than anyone in the bar. When he walked into a casino, the bosses were thrilled, because they expected him to lose a lot of money. (Dick loved being a big player, betting more than he ever had before. Unfortunately, once the casinos realized he was winning, and his career was over, he was permanently out of action.)

Anyway, four of us locked up the table, me on third base, and unlike the others, who were playing green, Bill told me to play black just to show the bosses variety. We got the table locked up, we'd gotten the minimum raised to quarters, and then we waited, and waited. I don't know what the hold up was, but we were in the game a long time.

Senses lulled, no one saw Dick arrive at the table. I was the first to spot him, when he said, "Jimmy, stand up." I glanced over, and saw him standing directly behind his son. He was wearing a porkpie hat, and holding a bandana over his mouth, to disguise the fact that he was speaking. It looked like he'd come to rob us.

I figured it would look weird of we all stood simultaneously, so I got a jump on the others, and literally jumped off my stool. The pit boss happened to be standing right next to me, and said, "Oh, are you going, sir?" I was, after all, the black chip bettor. As he was saying this, I heard Dick, voice muffled under the bandana, say, "Jake, stay there."

I said, "No! I am not going anywhere. It's my … sciatica! Got to stretch my legs."

Before the boss could process that, several more things happened. All three of the other players – keep in mind, we were not supposed to know each other – stood up at the same time, grabbed their chips, and walked away. Though first they had to block access to the table in case a random civilian got the mistaken notion that one of the newly opened seats called to them. Dick sat down at centerfield, and said, "Can I get a hundred-dollar-minimum game?" And I quickly said, "A hundred dollar minimum is fine with me!" The boss's head was spinning.

We got it sorted. Then at some point Dick whispered I should "take a break." I had another attack of sciatica. I left my chips at the table, and walked swinging one leg, to the end of the pits, where there was a house phone. I called upstairs and asked Bill what the Sam Hill was going on. He explained they wanted me to eat cards for part of each shoe. "You do know this looks weird?"

I limped back, and saw it wasn't time yet to rejoin Dick, so I goosestepped back and forth in the aisle until it was time to play. Then after playing I had another attack of sciatica, went to the house phone, and so on. The playing itself wasn't all that hard. I was flat-betting after all. It was trying to sell my bizarre behavior that was taxing. Especially since our table was a center of attention. Dick was betting double twenty-five-hundreds, the limit on the casino floor. We probably won a solid five figure sum, before Dick departed, I played one more shoe to make it look good, and finally got to walk my poor sciatica out of there.

The hardest play without question, was when I finally played the Memory Game.

You may have guessed that this would not be as simple as walking into the baccarat pit at Harrah's one fine night, and starting to play. To lay the groundwork I went there several days ahead of time, and played baccarat. This would help establish me as a high-rolling, non-threatening gambler. It would also help explain my having thousand-dollar orange chips when I did play.

Bill told me to play for an hour, betting one or two thousand dollars a hand. He also suggested an extra special move, to try to mess with their minds. Baccarat is a very simple game. There is no strategy to it. Every play follows fixed rules. There are three possible bets, and one, the tie, has a huge house edge, so we may ignore it. Players bet either Banker or Player. The deal passes around the table, the designated dealer being the Banker. The cards are actually dealt by a house dealer; the moving deal being a mere formality. Any player may bet on Banker or Player, regardless of who is designated as Banker. The Player has a small disadvantage. To compensate the house collects a commission on winning Bank bets. The Banker has a slightly smaller disadvantage than the Player, but to avoid dealing with change, I bet Player.

Then came my turn as Banker.

"Whose two-thousand-dollar bet is that?" The dealer pointed to a Bank bet.

"It's mine. I'm the Banker."

"Well whose thousand-dollar-bet is that!?" The dealer pointed to a Player bet.

"It's mine."

"They are both yours!!?"

"Sure. I bet two thousand on Bank, because I am the Banker. But you know I always bet on Player, so I bet a thousand on Player. For insurance."

"Oh …" Said the dealer. "Well, which should I root for?"

"The big one, of course!" Like it was the most obvious thing in the world.

If I wanted to convince them I was an idiot, I think I succeeded. The action I gave them also drew a host, which was part of the plan. I had a business card printed, identifying me as Dave Rothstein, owner of a plastics company in Glenview, Illinois. Rothstein was in honor of Arnold Rothstein, the legendary gambler whose fictional alter egos include "The Brain" in various Damon Runyan stories, and Meyer Wolfsheim, the "Man who fixed the World Series" in *The Great Gatsby*. Dave, I chose because it sounds a bit like Jake. And Glenview, Illinois because it is right near my hometown, Des Plaines, so I knew the area well. Even knew a couple of brothers with a plastics company who lived in Glenview. I told him I was in New York City on business, and had come down to check out Atlantic City. I was interested in coming back in a few days. I gave him the date, and he set up a comp to a suite.

In those days you could get away with a lot that you couldn't now. For instance, I had no credit cards, and I had no form of identification other than my fake business card proving I was Dave Rothstein. But by coming in before the host's shift, I was able to bluff my way into the room; they called the host who assured them I was a swell fellow. They didn't want to lose a juicy high roller like me.

The plan was complicated by the fact that Scott wasn't working that night! I did a short appearance, playing some blackjack and baccarat, and then asked to extend my stay. Which they did only reluctantly. We'd chosen one of the busiest holiday weekends of the year, Washington's Birthday. They did agree to another night, and fortunately, Scott was on the next night.

Unfortunately, he was on relief. Remember, we needed him shuffling. Though we didn't actually need him dealing the first hand.

Who dealt the first hand of the shoe was not important, but how many cards we got to see was important. Enter Anita. Anita was part of the team. Tommy recruited a lot of people from his country club, and I think that's where he found Irv and Anita. They were a married couple who Tommy had used over the years. Anita would sit with me, and at the beginning of the shoe would play several hands, betting purple five-hundred-dollar chips while I bet orange. We'd bet five spots until I told her I wanted to "play alone for a while." I'd do this when a clump was expected, and would play only one hand a round, so that when the clump arrived, I wouldn't overshoot. That was the general idea.

Here is how things were supposed to work. We get on the table where Scott will shuffle, asking for a five-hundred-dollar minimum to keep away the riff-raff. We play five hands on the first hand of the shoe. As we play, a team member who has been trained in the Harry Lorayne memory technique wanders by, and stops to watch the high rollers for a minute. We have a rotating cast of characters for this, so none turned up two shoes in a row. They memorize the entire hand, in order, a task simplified because for them suits don't matter, only ranks. I memorize the first two cards only, suits and ranks.

When the shoe ends, while Scott shuffles, I glance at my watch. I don't wear watches, so mine was provided by Bill. It was a very cheap watch, obviously cheap. More psychological gaming by Bill, who reasoned that big players wearing fake Rolexes was something the casinos had seen. Only eccentric millionaires wear three-dollar plastic watches. Why the watch? I was wearing my Korean silk suit, and one of my tailored shirts. In my left breast pocket was padding on the bottom, and cardboard lining around the edges. The padding boosted the pager I had placed in the pocket so that it wasn't too deep to read. The lining kept the pocket from closing over the pager, blocking my view. The suit covered the pocket. We assumed the eye in the sky would be watching me closely, and didn't want to give them the opportunity to zero in on my pager and begin speculating. Part of what I'd practiced was the move with the watch. I would place my left arm across my stomach, about halfway between my navel and my solar plexus, then draw in close and slightly back. This would pull the left side of my suit jacket to the left, exposing the pocket. Now as I looked down at my watch, I was actually focusing on the pager, reading the ten-digit number on its display. I would try to spend no more than two or three seconds.

The average person can retain seven items in short-term memory. When I was six I was tested by a psychologist named Dr. Stavrianos. One of the tests had her reciting strings of numbers to me, then asking me to recite them either forwards, or backwards. She probably started with a short string, maybe four digits, and worked her way up. I don't know what the average six-year-old retains, but after she determined that I could do nine digits forward, and eight backward, she stopped that part of the test. What I was doing was rare enough that establishing my actual limits wasn't necessary. As a thirty-four-year-old, ten digits was easy.

Where did the ten digits come from? The person who had memorized the layout earlier, immediately hied themselves to a house phone, and called up to the suite. Bill transcribed the information, and called a computer operator, who input the data. The computer produced the string, which was relayed to a pager company in New York City. By the time of the shuffle, it had been sent to my pager.

When the new shoe began, I was retaining the two key cards, and the ten-digit number. To that I would add two more key cards, from the new shoe. I had cut the clump to show up about a deck and a half in. At about the one deck point, I would have Anita sit out. I would watch for the key cards, figure out which digit applied, play the indicated number of hands and strategy. Each digit was a code telling me to play one to three hands of a particular strategy, so I had nine options when things were good, and the zero when there was no good option available. Then I would try to forget those key cards and the ten-digit string, remember the other key cards, and wait for the shuffle.

That was how it was supposed to work.

Because Scott was on relief, I had to guess where he might shuffle next. At least he was relieving a four-table pit, and not bopping all over the casino. Knowing where he'd next shuffle didn't solve the problem. To get a useful clump I would have to lock up a table and play the first hand of a shoe in anticipation of him coming to shuffle. It takes a while to play an eight-deck shoe, so Scott was often on for one end, but not the other. His dealing the first hand wasn't necessary, but my being there for it was. Coordinating this was very hard.

It was made worse because Bill wanted me to report upstairs every time I played a clump, or every time we nearly got one, but missed. Which meant any chance of developing a rhythm, or getting some advance notion of where Scott was heading, went out the window. When I say report upstairs, I mean he wanted us to leave the pit and go upstairs to report in person, not by house phone.

Anita also comes into this. She was the three-dollar plastic watch of "girlfriends." Just as the casinos had seen fake Rolexes, they'd seen card counters with "trophy girlfriends" who would distract bosses with wayward winks and daring decolletage. Anita was the distracting alternative. I allow for the possibility that in her day Anita may have been attractive, but her day was VE-Day. The acronym MILF hadn't been invented, but if it had, it would not have applied to Anita. Bill hoped that Anita would have them wondering, since she was literally twice my age. When we went upstairs, would the bosses imagine I was up there banging the bejeezus out of her? Given how often we went upstairs for a quickie, they most have figured we were part rabbit.

Whether the bosses spent a single second thinking about my watch, my girlfriend, or our frequent absences, it didn't diminish the heat. They pretended to be cordial. I was a high roller, and they did not know what I was up to. They did know something was up, and they didn't like it. Another peculiarity from their point of view was that I kept hopping around the pit, and asking for a five-hundred-dollar minimum game every time I did. Some even noticed I seemed to be chasing Scott. Aside from being weird, there were other red flags. It became evident that they had tried to check my fake address and phone, those didn't check out, and they wanted to wangle a peek at an ID. I continued the "left my ID in New York" stall, but they weren't happy. Also, they never asked, and so never got to hear the "won them in a poker game in New York" explanation, but I simply had too many orange chips in my pocket. I don't remember exactly how much ammunition I brought to the table, but it was in the forty- to fifty-thou-sand-dollar range. Where did that come from? The minimum number of bosses standing directly on the game, watching me play, was two. Whenever I gave them a lot of action, four more would materialize. The six bosses would form a solid wall, all glaring at me.

I was betting one to three chips per betting square most of the time. When a lock winner came, I was betting five chips on as many squares as called for. Triple five-thousands was enough to raise their hackles. Though the biggest shoe of the night was not one with a lock winner. I won forty-seven thousand dollars. I went into the shoe stuck twenty-three-five, and ended it up twenty-three-five. That was just a random fluctuation. But they didn't know that, and seeing me win almost fifty thousand in one shoe did not make them happy.

I said before that memorizing ten-digits numbers was easy. I learned that there was more to it. As the night wore on, the numbers and the key cards began to pile up. I was still remembering earlier combinations, and had to work on not mixing them up. The strain of selling my act to the pit was also draining. By two or three in the morning, when we went upstairs, I would collapse. My room was filled with people, like the stateroom scene in *A Night at the Opera*. They were having a great time. The play was exciting. I would give Bill a report, then lie on the floor (there wasn't room on the bed). I was aware of people milling around, and stepping over me. I closed my eyes and tried to recharge my battery, until they nudged me, and said it was time to go back down. It was around four by the time I went upstairs for the last time, thoroughly whipped.

Bill told me there were five or six of us that tried to play the Memory Game. Only Miles and I succeeded. Miles ended up generating sixty-thousand-dollars' worth of lock winners. He had Scott on one table all night. (I don't know if he had to keep running upstairs.) Despite the handicaps, I managed thirty-eight thousand, five hundred. Don't ask me why it wasn't forty thousand. I know there was a reason, but I forget what it was. There were other differences. After calculating how much theoretical expected value the practice sessions, the baccarat, the action Anita and I gave other than the lock winners, and the meager play by the spotters, from the thirty-eight five we subtracted eighteen-five. My play netted a theoretical twenty thousand dollars profit, for which I received fifteen percent, or three grand. That was theoretical profit. The actual overall results of everyone's play came to minus seventeen thousand. I was thirty-seven thousand dollars unlucky.

Miles, meanwhile, though generating sixty thousand in theory, won one hundred and fifty thousand in practice. That's at the blackjack table. He also played a bit of baccarat that night, winning another twenty thousand. And he, too, played a session of baccarat the night before his play. He won fifty thousand. Harrah's was more concerned by his baccarat win than they were his blackjack. A flag was placed next to his name as a suspected baccarat cheat. If he was spotted in any Harrah's property, anywhere in the world, at any hour of the day or night, the world manager for Harrah's casino operations was to be notified immediately. Nice to know they are on top of things.

Besides the three thousand I earned for the Memory Game, I'd made another fifteen hundred for miscellaneous activities. Forty-five hundred for a three-week trip was good money. I knew I'd be back.

CHAPTER 32
PRETTY AS A PICTURE

When we walked into the new apartment, the first thing Phil did was flip on a light. The second thing was break out laughing. To explain why, you need to hear about two businesses along the main drag in Itaewon. One dealt in paintings, and the other in photos. The former, next to Korea's worst Mexican restaurant, was a commercial artist who painted to order. The other was on a corner of the intersection of *Itaewonno* and *Bogwongdonggil*, the intersection shared by the Hamilton Hotel, and Burger King. There was an arresting photo in the window. The two most important birthdays for Korean males were the 60th birthday, and the one hundredth day. The former signified completing five twelve-year cycles, the Chinese zodiac five times over. In olden days it meant you had lived a long time. The hundredth day was a milestone because it meant you were likely to survive. Modern tradition dictated a portrait photo of the lucky lad be taken. The baby was posed sitting in a chair, a miniature throne. The photo on display in the shop window was around sixteen by twenty. The baby was very chubby, with rolls of fat, and had a wizened face. It was an arresting picture, made not just arresting but SWAT Team take-down, because as was also traditional, the baby was stark naked, and it's *kochu* on display. That's the Korean word for 'pepper,' though his looked more like a little brown carrot. Team members used to crack up every time they passed it.

On his most recent visit to Seoul, Craig bought a copy of the baby picture, and had brought a photo of Phil. He took both to the commercial artist, who painted a hybrid, a naked baby with Phil's head. That's what was now hanging just inside our door.

Phil retaliated. He had pictures of Craig and Butch, and had a new version done, still him as the throned baby, but with his hands placed on the heads of his teammates in benediction. That went next to the first painting. Come summer there would be one more addition, a bit different from the others. In Carson City there was an old restaurant with a painting as arresting as the baby picture, albeit for a different reason. It was of three African-American boys, sitting on or near a rail fence. They wore overalls and straw hats, and were eating watermelon, big grins on their faces. In the nineteen-thirties people probably thought it was cute, but fifty years later it was, "I can't believe this is still hanging!" Someone on the team commissioned a version with the faces of Craig, Munchkin, and Phil. That one was hung in the kitchen. I had to explain every time I brought someone new to the apartment. I don't think any of the Koreans got American humor.

The apartment was our new apartment. The landlady in the old apartment turned off the water heater every night at eleven. Craig and Butch would come home at odd hours, wearing their disguises, which required a lot of washing. They had to wake the landlady in the middle of the night. Neither side was happy. A Rha helped once again, finding a new place for us.

If you headed away from the Hamilton on *Bogwangdonggil,* waving at the picture of the baby as you passed the photographer, the street ended at a road which ran parallel to the river. One hundred feet before you reached the end, on the left, was a small street and a bus staging area. We'd tell cab drivers to take us to the *Bogwangdong cheongcham.* Past the buses the road split in a Y. Turn left and head uphill, and a short distance up on the right you'd be at A Rha's apartment. Turn right and on the left would be ours. We were more or less back-to-back. It was more spacious than the other apartment, and quieter.

Having A Rha nearby was handy, but not as much as you'd think. There were tensions in our relationship. Munchkin warned me before I left that on his previous trip, he had heard rumors that A Rha was seeing other people.

One was a guy named Jay Bang, the black sheep of a powerful family. Jay had lived in the States, and had a US green card. With it he was able to enter Walker Hill. Where he allegedly lost a million dollars. The Korean economy is dominated by chaebol, family-owned conglomerates like Samsung, LG, or Hyundai. One of them owned, among other properties, the biggest newspaper, the Chosun Ilbo. Jay's older brother ran the family business. He called Slim Chun, who owned the casino at Walker Hill, and laid down the law, Jay would no longer be allowed to play.

Jay hung out at the Sportsman's Club, and he had been telling everyone A Rha was his girlfriend. I was sitting with him when the head waitress, Miss Lee, asked him, "Where's your girlfriend, A Rha?" She didn't know A Rha was my girlfriend, and he nearly fainted. I guess he thought I'd kill him. He quickly denied to her that he had anything to do with A Rha. Just as A Rha denied it to me, her anger sounding legitimate at the thought anyone would link her with Jay.

Another supposed lover was Captain Frank. I was never in the military, but I saw a lot of it in those years. It was by now fifteen years since the end of the Vietnam War, so it was a peacetime army. (Though up north on the DMZ the troops bragged that they were the only ones anywhere in the world who were issued live ammunition every day.) From what I could see it was a bureaucracy, and the soldiers played office politics, albeit while wearing uniforms to work. Frank was slick. He was a good-looking guy who wore a real Rolex, because he'd married a Korean from a rich family, and she kept him in baubles. He also may have had some sort of first aid training. As you may recall, Jiyoung, A Rha's sister, had a rectal abscess. He offered to help A Rha repack and redress it.

Frank once told me a story. He was on his first tour in Korea. He had his car shipped over. He had to pick it up in Busan, and was driving north when he picked up a girl who was hitchhiking. This was prior to 1982, and the countrywide curfew was still in effect. At midnight everyone had to be inside. It was getting late, so Frank headed to a base, possibly Camp Humphreys in Pyongtaek. He had the girl hide in the trunk of his car, and the gate guards waved him in, and directed him to the Bachelor Officers Quarters, or BOQ. Which luckily were deserted. He and the girl did what he was hoping to do. But then he remembered all the lectures about "native women" and the diabolical diseases they carry. Terrified that he might contract Pusan Penis, he ran to the bathroom. The BOQ was not Marriott Suites, no toiletries provided. All he could find was a can of Comet, and so he scrubbed his nether regions with that.

Doesn't sound like someone I would seek out for medical assistance, but A Rha did. Abscess makes the heart grow fonder, so after attending to Jiyoung in her bed, he attended to A Rha in hers. Or so he boasted. Another claim A Rha denied, though with more bemusement than anger. I gave her the benefit of the doubt, but seeds were planted. It didn't help that I expected we'd spend our free time together, but she was often mysteriously away, and never thought to pick up a phone.

Despite my suspicions I consoled myself in knowing that it could be a lot worse. I was with Tom at Wendy's one day, when a guy who lived in Pyongtaek dropped by our table. He was the principal of a middle school on the base at Camp Humphreys. He was probably in his late thirties, tall, handsome, a very "eligible" bachelor by Korean standards. He'd recently given his girlfriend a diamond engagement ring, and a million won to pay rent and expenses, while he spent a month stateside. When he returned, he found the rent unpaid, the ring sold, and his fiancée back dancing at the Golden Gate Club, where he'd met her. When he asked, "How could you?" she just laughed.

I felt very sorry for him, though my sympathy was tempered when he mentioned the same thing had happened twice before.

A funny thing happened at the bank this trip. For some reason the team decided that we needed to wire fifteen thousand dollars to Alan in Hong Kong. Though he wasn't invested in the bankroll, Woody still helped us move money around, and may have had investments in other projects.

I went to the bank. After the usual bowing me in, I went to the conference room, soon to be joined by Mr. Lee. While Miss Lee the tea girl served us, I explained that I wanted to send fifteen thousand US dollars to an account in Hong Kong. Mr. Lee sucked in air through his teeth, a sign that something was wrong, but he preferred not to tell me. "Wait a bit," he said.

The "bit" turned out to last more than two hours. I read both the Korea Times and the Korea Herald, then started on a book. Finally, he returned.

It seems there were three problems with my request. First, because I was not Korean, I wasn't allowed to wire money. Second, even Koreans were only allowed to wire five thousand dollars, not fifteen. Finally, the Commercial Bank was not authorized to wire money, so even if I were a Korean wanting to wire five thousand, they could not help me. The reason it took over two hours was that was how long it took to solve the problem.

Mr. Lee had a cousin who worked in a bank which did wire money. So, he withdrew funds from my account equivalent to fifteen thousand, and sent Miss Lee, the tea girl, to his cousin's bank with the money. Then his cousin wired five thousand in her own name, five thousand in his name, and five thousand in the tea girl's name. Problem solved.

One week later the team decided they needed the money back in Korea. Phil had to fly there, and his trip was so rushed that, racing from bank to cab to Kai Tak, he was nearly run over in the street. He seemed to think that was the interesting part of the story. I thought that if it happened in Seoul, the cabbie wouldn't have missed him.

CHAPTER 33
NEXT PHASE, NEW WAVE

My next trip to Atlantic City was pushed back three weeks. I learned the hard way that extreme weight loss – my one-hundred-and-twenty-pound loss qualified – often precipitates gall stones. I was admitted to Northwest Community Hospital early in the morning, through the emergency room, and given a comic book called "You and Your Gall Bladder." It, and the doctor, and the nurses, all agreed that there were only two courses of action. One was to have surgery right now. The other was to go home, have more agonizing attacks, and then have surgery. After I was allowed to call Korea and tell A Rha that while I sure hoped I'd see her again, there was a slight possibility I might not, I agree to the operation.

I needed a few weeks to recover. Even when I did fly to New Jersey I had to have assistance with my bags. One benefit was that I decided before going under the ether that I would use the hospital stay to quit smoking. If I had nicotine cravings post-surgery, I would tell myself they were side effects of painkillers. I only had one, and it was shortly after my return to A.C. I was part of a play at the Trop. As I was walking into the casino it hit me, I would be sitting at a blackjack table, and not smoking. If I was on my own, I might have gone off somewhere, and had a smoke while I pondered what to do. Instead, I reminded myself the others were waiting for me, and my legs did the rest. I made it through the session without a nicotine fit, and have never had the urge since. I had been smoking a pack a day since I was eleven, and now was a non-smoker.

The game we were playing had changed. Gone was the Clump Game; now we were playing New Wave. That was Miles' brainwave. Miles had told his brother and Marsha, and perhaps a few other credulous souls, that his function was to be the team's resident genius. He would sit naked in an empty bathtub eating raw cookie dough, at least when not doing whippets, small canisters of nitrous oxide he bought by the pallet load, and dream up new ways for the team to make money. Miles was certainly a smart guy, but so were Tommy, Jon, and Bill. Of the four, if I had to pick a "genius," I'd have picked Bill. If I had to make a second choice, I'd still have picked Bill.

Regardless, Mike had dreamed up New Wave, and it was a winner. Mike was vague about its nature. I asked him what I should look for when scouting, and he said that maybe clumps were important, or maybe big grabs. Whether it was because he didn't really know, or didn't want me to figure out how it worked, I am not sure. My educated guess was that the program's algorithms looked for strings of cards either unmixed, like clumps, or not very well mixed. Either way it would have a general idea of what cards, on average, to expect in the immediate future. It was a bit like counting and shuffle tracking, but instead of tracking the shuffle, it was, "Oh, here's this card and that card," and maybe "they are mixed with those cards." It would predict what was coming, sending the following signals to the player. There were four signals. One was a soft tch-tch-tch. That meant small cards were coming. There was a neutral dit-dat, dit-dat. If big cards were expected a louder Bzzt-Bzzt-Bzzt was sent. Finally, "super big," which meant aces or a whole mess of high cards were coming, was BZZT!-BZZT!, BZZT!-BZZT!, BZZT!-BZZT!

The program analyzed the player's results. After the session it would tell us how we did, in theory. Results ranged from one and a half to two and a half percent. (If less, we were playing a bad dealer.) The big player would sit on first base, and play two hands, betting up to double thousands. It was a lower profile game all the way around.

There were only three players needed to play it, two in a pinch. While it might be done with just an inputter and a big player, the game was stronger if there was a "third-baser." The third-baser would wear the belt receiving the signals, and give the big player hand signals on how much to bet. The big player would play basic strategy. The third-baser, though, might make some crazy plays. If big cards were coming, the third-baser would take as few cards as possible, standing on all hands of twelve or more, no matter what the dealer was showing, and not splitting pairs. If small cards were coming, the player would hit every-thing, and split almost everything.

One day I was playing with Rocky, and Sue. Yes, Rocky, the World's Greatest Big Player, was on loan from the Korea team! I was the third-baser. The dealer was a Korean guy, the floor man Indian. The dealer was an asshole, who sucked up to Rocky, flirted with Sue, gave me a hard time, and called the floor man Gumby. He was constantly haranguing me for the way I played. Finally, a hand came up, where I had fifteen, and the dealer had six. I had the option of not hitting if it seemed prudent, and given the noise he'd been making, I thought I'd sit this one out. I waved my hand, to show I was going to stand.

"What, you aren't going to hit?"

I waved again.

"But you always hit those!"

Fuck it! I scratched for a hit.

"You're going to hit fifteen when I have a six?"

I scratched again.

"How can you make a play like that?"

I scratched harder.

The floor man finally intervened. "Give him a card."

"But he is hitting fifteen against a six!"

"If he wants a card, give him a card."

I scratched again, he hit me with a five, giving me twenty, turned over a ten in the hole, and instead of making twenty-one, and scooping the table, he busted. He was furious. The boss laughed at him and said, "You probably think he did that because he's counting cards."

Another time also at Trump Castle, the inputter was again Sue, but the big player was an old guy named Frank Fittipaldi. Frank was closer to eighty than seventy, which made him a useful big player. Bosses never worried about Frank. Two interesting things happened during the session. One was the arrival of Wendell. Unlike Las Vegas, where the path to boss ran through experience as a dealer, A.C. hired some people directly to work the floor, and took them as young as eighteen. Wendell was one of them. By now he was twenty, and was no longer a mere floorman. He came to the table to talk to the floorman. He was very tall, and lean, with really long fingers. He carried a clipboard, and made notes while he talked with her. Twice the dealer started to make a procedural error, picking cards with the wrong hand, or paying from the wrong pile, or something.

Started, but didn't finish, because the dealer's hand hadn't moved more than a few inches in the wrong direction when Wendell caught it. Something like, "We'll be rotating the tables in the south pit with – Don't use your left hand – the four tables closest to the door." The dealer each time, was brought up short, as though a leash had been jerked. Wendell didn't even look up from his clipboard.

It was terrifying. Because someone that sharp might pick off our play at any moment. After the session the first thing Sue and I said to each other was, "Did you see that!?" I guess we were so smooth he didn't pick us off, but I would never want him around while playing.

Though you wouldn't say we were smooth if you saw what Frank did, luckily not while Wendell was around. Most big players for the New Wave game played a modified basic, to make it easier for them. One where they would stand on twelve against a two or three. Frank had been playing a long time, so he knew regular basic strategy, though his grip was shaky. When he was dealt twelve against a three, he stared at it, then asked the dealer, while watching me out of the corner of his eye, "Twelve against a three, isn't that a double down?"

I coughed to indicate he was making a mistake, i.e. "Don't do it."

"I seem to remember it's a double down." I coughed a bit louder.

"What do you think, dealer? Isn't it a double down?" To which besides my cough, there was added Sue's.

"I really can't say, sir."

"Gee, I really think it's a double down."

At this point Sue and I both, in unison, began swinging our heads from side to side and hacking away: left "cough," right "cough," left "cough," right "cough." I'm surprised bosses from the other end of the casino didn't come by to tell Frank, "These two who are with you do not want you to double down!"

Frank finally decided he knew for sure what was going on. "It is a double!" he said gleefully, and shoved out another eight hundred dollars. He caught a seven and made nineteen. The dealer turned over a ten, and caught a five. I guess it was a double down, after all.

Frank was one of the stars of the counterfeit chip fiasco. Remember how we stockpiled five-hundred-dollar chips? Counterfeiters had picked the casino where Frank was playing to duplicate the purples. Frank had a couple of the bogus chips, and was backroomed. Tommy was running the play that day, and was worried about how Frank would hold up. Richard was the team's odd job man, and this was an odd job. One Richard was perfectly suited for. If getting backroomed, or even arrested, was required, who was more qualified than Richard?

Meanwhile Frank was holding up just fine. "I know nothing about nothing. I got these chips playing here. If you gave me counterfeits, you owe me money." They looked at Frank, sweet old Frank; of course he wasn't a counterfeiter. They were just about to let him go, when Richard arrived and said, "Guys, you have an old man in the back room. He's with me!"

Soon Richard and Frank arrived back at the Sweat Lodge, in the custody of the New Jersey State Police. They tore the place apart, even the ceiling panels. They looked at the microfiche machine, and said to Tommy, "Show us what's in there." Tommy looked at it in horror, and said, "I wouldn't even know how to turn that thing on!"

After examining the other chips in the briefcase, and finding a couple more fake chips, they confiscated the four bogus ones, but otherwise cleared the team of involvement in their manufacture. They did, however, later share most of what they'd learned, including the location of the Sweat Lodge, with the casino.

Not long after this, the microfiche machine no one knew what to do with, was done with. Richard came home drunk one night and said, "I'm sick of looking at that!" He threw it out the window. There was no foot traffic alongside the building at that hour, but the sound of a microfiche machine hitting pavement after falling fifteen floors nearly gave heart failure to a couple of crack whores on Pacific Avenue.

I was along for another Richard adventure. The equipment ran through a lot of D-batteries. We took a walk down the Boardwalk one evening, stopping in a dollar store. The cashier was a big-haired woman who cracked her bubble gum. The owner was a fat cigar chomper.

"Got any D-batteries?"

"Yeah, we got 'em," the owner said around his cigar butt. He led us down an aisle, pointed to a box on a bottom shelf. In it were around thirty or forty D-batteries.

"I'll take 'em," said Richard.

"All of them?"

"Yup."

The owner eyed Richard suspiciously. Could the kid be a mad bomber? "Whacha gonna do with all them batteries?"

"Oh!" Richard's eyes widened. "I got my wife one of those vibrator thingies. She told me if I brought home batteries, tonight's the night!"

The guy almost swallowed his cigar. What sort of cosmic orgasm could forty D-batteries unleash? "Ya hear that, Mona?"

Snap! "I hoid."

"Guy bought his wife one of those vibrator thingies."

"I said, I hoid!"

While we played all over town, it's funny how many memories are of just two casinos. One was Tropworld. It was next door to the Ritz, and if you were doing it old school, just trying to count cards, it was the best game in town. They were the only place still offering six deck games with a not too terrible cut. It was even trackable. I didn't want to draw attention, and queer my chances for playing the team games, but figured I could do some counting in my spare time, with a two-hundred-dollar top bet, and stay under the radar.

I was doing it when I became aware of a substratum of counters, the weekend warriors who thought they knew what they were doing, but shouldn't quit their day jobs. I met one when he bumped into me. I was backcounting, another thing the Trop hadn't cracked down on – most places had a "no mid-shoe entry rule" – and got a count. As I stepped forward a guy banged into me on his way to the table. I started watching the people around the pit, and realized there were four guys lurking who might as well have been wearing signs saying "backcounter at work." I got the one who collided with me off to the side, and asked what he thought he was doing. Unsurprisingly, he hadn't spotted me, and was nervous, but when he realized I wasn't working for the casino, and planning to throw him out, he admitted he drove down in his spare time to seek fame and fortune. I told him that waiting for a true four, then betting fifty bucks, was probably not as many dollars per hour as he thought it was. He said he had a secret weapon, he used Uston APC.

Another guy was simply nuts. I saw him being dragged out of another casino, the Golden Nugget, arguing with security. The first time I saw him in the Trop he was on the same table as I was, when the cut card came out. The procedure was to deal it to the player whose turn it was to receive a regular card, so it was sitting in front of me. This guy was sitting on my left, talking to himself, when he turned to me, out of the blue, and said, "You'd better let me cut." I told him I felt lucky, thanks. "Do you know where to cut?" He asked me. I said, "Well, I know where I'm going to cut."

The dealer laughed, held out the deck, and I cut the clump I wanted. The other guy frowned, started grumbling to himself, and then pointedly sat out the first deck. During which my clump came out just as I expected, the running count dropping to minus ten. Now, as I prepared to leave the table, the guy started making big bets (for him). Then he split sevens … against a nine.

Why did I leave the table if I had a likely clump that first deck I could play the next deck? One of the things I was doing was combining backcounting with shuffle tracking. I would see where the clump was going, and where it was cut to, then wander away, and show up when it was time to sit down. I would walk up to the table without having been around to count the shoe, sit down, and bet into the clump. The pit hardly ever saw me not betting two hundred a hand. One night the same nutty player was on my table, arguing with the dealer and floorman because he wanted to bet two hands of fifty.

The floorman told him he was limited to one hand. "Check it," he insisted.

She went to the other end of the pit. There was one of Atlantic City's most feared bosses, Mickey. Mickey and a couple of other bosses were using ceiling mirrors over the pit to count the shoe, and monitor the play. She spoke with Mickey, came back, and said, "You're right. Mickey says *you* can do anything you want." The guy thanked her, while I could see Mickey and the other bosses laughing. The kid didn't know he had just been insulted.

The other casino which features in so many memories is Trump Castle. I've mentioned playing the Clump Game there, and acting as a third-baser. I also was a big player there. To check in I had to ride a tall escalator up a floor. At the top, greeting me, was a life-sized cardboard cutout of the man himself, and a sign telling me that I should head right to the gift shop because it was selling *Trump: The Art of the Deal*. I visited the gift shop, and not only was I greeted by a display with copies of the book, but there was another display of *Trump: The Art of the Deal, the Board Game*. There was also a rack of magazines, all of them back issues, selected because they had articles about one Donald J. Trump. Up in my room, there was a magazine, about the wonders to be found around town. Every article was either about Trump properties, or about the recent activities of Donald or Ivana. I'd heard of Trump and his book. I was in his hotel and casino so naturally I had heard of him. What I hadn't realized was that any human could be that egotistical. It was going to be a pleasure taking his money!

It was made even more pleasurable when I celebrated in the gourmet room, fully comped. Eating a two-hundred-dollar meal, the wine alone ninety dollars for the bottle, was extravagant in 1988. The next night I spent two-thirty, including a one-hundred-and-twenty-dollar bottle of wine, at Ivana's (of course it was called Ivana's), the gourmet room at his other property, Trump Plaza. The snooty Maître d insisted I had to wear a jacket – something Vegas had stopped insisting on many years before – so I wanted to really punish them. If they let me have a shot of Louis XIII it would have been punishment they deserved, but my comp didn't extend to one-hundred-and-twenty-five-dollar shots. (My waiter, a cute old fellow who reminded me of forties' character actor Cuddles Zakall, was apologetic, and brought me something which, now that I have tried Louis XIII, I liked much better. I wish I had paid attention to the name.)

Another team member stormed the Castle, and gave it the sacking it deserved. There was a certain dealer who was probably the greatest clumper who ever failed to shuffle the cards. He dropped clumps twice as big as Scott's, thirty or forty card monsters. I never got to play him, but Girl George spotted him one day, dealing Big 6, and pointed him out. You couldn't miss him. He was six-three, over three-fifty, with skin tags, and vitiligo. When he was nervous, he sweated so much that puddles formed on the layout.

Calvin made him nervous. Calvin had a brief but spectacular career as a big player. Before Anita was my arm candy, she was Calvin's. Actually, Bill's idea was that Calvin was her boy toy, that the bosses would think she was keeping him. Calvin was in his twenties. He was in medical school, at Harvard, and was preppy as hell. He was also black, so the bosses didn't think that he was her boy toy. Young, black, betting big money: he was a drug dealer! That was as far as their imagination ran. Whatever. He won one hundred and twenty-five thousand dollars in one sitting.

The dealer was rotated to Outer Mongolia or some other hidden outpost, but a few months later he returned to the blackjack pit. It was time for: Return of Calvin. Who still bore no resemblance to Super Fly, except in the bosses' minds. This time around Calvin won one hundred and thirty-five thousand dollars, while the dealer sweated so much a lake formed on the layout.

I haven't talked about the most interesting thing about the New Wave plays, the inputters. I mentioned that they sat at the table during the play. To hide what they were up to, their keypads went under their skirts, strapped to their thighs. When they sat down, they would scooch in close to the table, put a coat or sweater on their lap, and their purse on top of that. Their left elbow would rest on the table's rail, while their right hand rested in their lap under the coat. This worked well for a while, but eventually bosses began to ask themselves why so many women were masturbating while they played. The word went out to be on the lookout for women at centerfield when there was big action on first, who kept one hand in their laps.

Introducing, fake arms! The inputters were sent to specialists in prosthetic limbs. These specialists made artificial limbs for amputees, so they were experts in creating realistic substitutes. They would measure and photograph the inputters' actual hands, and create extremely lifelike duplicates.

When the inputter went to the table things were as before. But now the real arm was hidden under their shirt and coat. The fake arm was in the coat's sleeve, the fake hand at the jacket's pocket, thumb hooked inside, but the rest of the hand clearly visible. Two hands, count 'em, two! No way they could be inputting unless they had three arms.

This worked for a long time, until an inputter glanced down, and found a boss eying her hand from a distance of about four inches. Fortunately, not all casinos worked it out at the same time, and the game lasted for many months.

While we were paying using the fake arms, we discovered an even better game, the Skylight Game. Caesar's had two floors of mall above the casino floor. There was a skylight above one of the quarter pits, and a skylight on the floor above, and finally a skylight in the roof. The inputter could stand on the floor above the casino. There was a low wall around the skylight. They could lean over the railing and look straight down at the tables. The table was twenty-five or thirty feet below, and the glass created a slight distortion. The only inputters who were good at the Skylight Game were Girl George and Sue, but they were our two-woman army in the war against Caesar.

Now the BP played alone. No magic shoes, no third-baser, no inputters anywhere in sight. The pit wondered why they were being hit by so many players, sitting on first, playing two hands up to double thousands, and regularly winning. But since they could not see an angle, they took no action.

Then one day Sue was inputting away. She saw one of the bosses leaning against the podium below. He was watching the player, slightly bored, his gaze wandering. He happened to look up. Then he looked back down. Then a few seconds later his head snapped up. He turned around, grabbed a phone, and made an urgent call.

Sue powered off her computer, and drifted over to the door of a shop some distance away. A few minutes later the boss, and a security team, came thundering up to the skylight. They looked down, looked around, looked around some more.

The team waited a few days, then sent a player in with instructions to sit on first and play two hands, making random bets. Within minutes there was security up at the skylight, looking for an inputter. Goodbye Caesar. It seems you are finished rendering unto us.

I did suggest a possible variation. Bally's Park Place had this enormous escalator, at the bottom of which was a quarter pit. There was a sightline to the tables, but the distance was around one hundred feet. What if we had glasses that worked like binoculars, I wondered? I think it was at U Penn that I found a College of Optometry, and a professor named Dr. Brain. Girl George was sent to pick Brain's brain. The bad news for us was that the glasses weren't practical. They'd stick out three or four inches, binoculars on a frame. The inputters would be too conspicuous. The good news for Girl George was that she dated him for a while.

One night Bill asked me to get up early the next morning, to drive with him to Trenton. There was a state senate subcommittee holding a hearing on whether to pass a law barring the use of electronic devices in casinos. He said he wanted me to testify. "You want what?" Bill explained that Tommy was scheduled to testify, advocating against any such law. "But Tommy's not a good talker. You're a good talker!"

I actually had experience testifying before state senate subcommittees. The summer I turned thirteen I played a ten-year-old genius a man wanted to buy for his company, "in the interests of national defense." The entire play took place in the hearing room. Then, I had a Pulitzer Prize winner's dialogue to recite, and weeks to memorize it. What on earth was I going to say in the morning?

Three of us drove to Trenton, me, Bill, and Phyllis. Phyllis was a woman Bill was dating. She was from Hong Kong, where he was preparing to move. His story of the falling out with Alan was similar to Woody's, but with some details Woody skipped. Three of them had gone to Hong Kong to bet on the races, Bill, Alan, and Wally Simmons. They had a one-hundred-and fifty-thousand-dollar bankroll, sixty percent Alan's, a third Bill's, the rest Wally's. Wally and Bill worked sixteen-hours days programming, while Alan did accounting, because he wasn't a programmer, and he liked accounting. It did not take sixteen hours a day to do the accounting. The office was in the apartment, and so was paid for from the bankroll. It was also Alan's residence, which meant he was being subsidized by their dwindling bank. Wally didn't like living in Hong Kong, and left after a month. Bill and Alan worked together for two seasons before the bank grew so small Alan felt compelled to refinance it, after which he informed Bill his percentage was now in single digits. When Bill pointed out he was doing most of the work, Alan offered to pay him ten bucks an hour.

Bill left, furious, and was getting ready to return and launch his own operation by the beginning of next fall, when the new racing season began.

Luckily for silver-tongued me, Tommy was already on the stand when we arrived, and took seats in the back. They must have heard from the casino interests earlier. There was a ranking boss from Harrah's (not one I recognized) who had brought a pair of magic shoes as evidence. Your technology is out of date, sir.

Tommy was telling the senators about methods the casinos used to harass card counters. After the early days, when everyone could play without being barred, came the time when everyone was being arrested. Ken Uston put a stop to that. Uston had filed lawsuits, in Nevada, and in Atlantic City, against many of the casinos for barring him. At least once, very violently. A security guard at the Mapes in Reno broke bones in Uston's face. For that, Uston received monetary compensation, but the courts upheld the right of casinos to bar unwanted customers. In New Jersey, the courts ended that right.

The casinos, unable to eject the likes of Tommy, found ways to harass him, and other counters. One method was to break the shoe, and reshuffle the cards, every time he raised his bet. I'm not sure they believed that they could break the casino of the habit through persistence, but Richard was sent to the high roller's pit at the Trop. He played at a hundred-dollar minimum table, and would throw out a larger bet after half a deck, making the dealer spend most of his time shuffling cards.

There was a player at the opposite end of the table, a toadlike figure, who was displeased. He ordered Richard to beat it. Richard refused. He warned him that the next time they broke the shoe, he would "call Philly" and order a hit on Richard. Richard shrugged, bet, the shoe was broken, and the guy called for a house phone!

Then he decided that waiting for someone to drive down from Philly would take too long. "Do it again, and I will kill ya myself!"

Richard said, "Do what ya gotta do."

He raised his bet, the boss told the dealer to shuffle, and with a roar the other player launched himself. He was not aerodynamic, but managed to belly flop onto the layout far enough to grab Richard by the throat. "Call the cops!" Richard yelled, as they rolled around on the floor.

They did, and the casino said they wanted to press charges against Richard for disturbing the peace. He said that was fine, but they would need to provide the name of the high roller, because Richard would press charges for assault and battery. It ended in a standoff, no one pressing charges.

They found less dramatic ways of dealing with Tommy. For instance, they lowered the limit. He was on a table whose normal limit was one hundred to twenty-five hundred. They lowered the limit to one hundred, one hundred minimum and one hundred maximum. As they did a boss informed the players at the table, "Sir, you have the manager's permission to bet over the posted maximum. Ma'am, you have the manager's permission to bet over the posted maximum." Everyone at the table, except Tommy.

His stories were making an impression. Then he made what was the most effective argument against the law. What was it? That the law was entirely unnecessary, the casinos calling upon the power of the state, to do their job. If the casino personnel are competent, no law, and no law enforcement, are needed. Take the Clump Game as an example.

Competent Pit Boss, "Scott, there is a problem with the way you shuffle. Let me show you."

Scott, "Thanks! I will work on fixing it."

Memory Player, "Hey, where'd my Clump Game go?"

Unfortunately, Tommy used the wrong word. What he said was something like, "If it was my house, I'd know how to protect it."

In context "house" clearly refers to a casino. It would be understood that way by professionals on both sides of the table. It was not understood that way by the senators. By one in particular. He had already established himself in my mind as representing the District of Cosa Nostra. It was also clear that he and the Harrah's boss had a psychic connection. When Tommy said "my house," Senator Mafia said, "If someone brought a computer into *my* house, we'd know how to deal with him!" Said deal involving blowtorches, cattle prods, and cement shoes. The senator pictured Tommy wearing a concealed computer, trying to sit in his home poker game, down in his knotty pine basement. He went on, "Mister Chairman, we don't need to hear any more! Let's just recommend the bill be passed, and be done with it."

The Chairman said. "I agree. I can't see any reason anyone should be allowed to use a computer in a casino." The mob guy and the Harrah's boss smiled. However, the Chairman was a decent man. "But the things this young man told us are really troubling! I think we need to add a player's bill of rights, to prevent casinos from continuing these abusive tactics."

Two heads snapped around, two sets of eyes began flashing messages back and forth, the mob guy plainly asking, "What do I do?" and the Harrah's boss replying, "Abort! Abort!" Then the senator said, "On the other hand, Mister Chairman, there is no need to be hasty. Perhaps we should table it for further discussion?"

Tommy had saved the day. And so, the use of computers in New Jersey was saved for another few years.

CHAPTER 34
BEACH BLACKJACK BINGO

The plane began its descent. Thick clouds surrounded it, cloaking the outside world. The shaking began – mild, growing, then violent, a bull trying to batter the plane until its rivets fell out. It was the third time we'd tried to land. The previous two the plane had suddenly aborted the attempt, and pulled back up, out of the turbulence, flying above the clouds, circling. This time it committed itself. The pilot came on the intercom, but of course what he was saying was incomprehensible to me. I looked around, and could see the heads of the other passengers all nodding. They spoke the language. I hoped from their expressions I would have some clue as to what was happening. He might have been telling them anything from the time and temperature to the plot of *Star Wars*.

After his announcement, which had lasted more than a minute, he switched to heavily accented English. It was brief. "Ladies and gentleman. This is pilot. Just now, we encounter heavy turbulence. And so, we crash."

As he said it, the plane tilted to the right, perpendicular to the ground. The nose dipped and the invisible wires that held this great crate of metal aloft were severed. A collective scream filled the cabin as we fell out of the sky ….

I snapped awake, sat up in the bed, which now felt like a plane ascending, while my body continued to fall. I looked around the strange hotel room, heart racing. Hell of a dream! The real plane, the evening before, made it that third time. It had twice aborted when it hit the layer of turbulence. It had taken a pounding the third time. But there was no announcement, and we did not fall out of the sky. The only damage was to my sleep the next day. Only four hours sleep onto top of jet lag, after working the morning shift.

This weekend featured a couple of firsts. One was that this was the first time Munchkin and I had been in Korea at the same time. Another was that it was my first trip to Busan. We'd finally worn out our welcome at Walker Hill. Rocky had personally won over five hundred thousand dollars, and that got their attention. He was told that he could continue to play, but would be limited to a bet spread of between three hundred thousand and one million. His having his bet restricted was preceded by my being barred at Walker Hill. It was Butch's fault. Butch didn't like the hassle of putting on and taking off his makeup. He went without it. I arrived at Walker Hill for my shift, and found him lurking near the taxi stand, to warn me he had gotten barred. I found out later that I had chosen the same table and very same seat he'd just been ejected from. It drew a bulls-eye around me. Walker Hill had one boss, Mr. Kim (of course), who knew something about card counting. Along about two in the morning he sidled up to me, tapped my shoulder, and asked me to come chat in his office.

I made preparations to go back by shaving my beard, getting my hair cropped, and getting fitted for contact lenses. I even went looking for a toupee. Not many Korean men wore toupees then. The only shop which encouraged me to come in was a barbershop that offered "extras" with the haircut.

I wouldn't learn whether my disguise was effective for several years, when I faced down Mr. Kim. The other casino with a two-million-won limit was the Paradise Beach Hotel in Busan, and it was our new target. We'd arrived in Seoul on a Thursday, as usual, spending one night at the Kaya, and then had flown to the other end of the country Friday afternoon.

We were staying at the Green Beach Hotel. It was not as nice as the

Kaya, which was itself known for its character more than its charm. The Green Beach had two things going for it, it was cheap, and it was across the street from the Paradise Beach.

The Paradise Beach was considerably smaller than Walker Hill. Its game was not as good; no five-card rule, not a trackable shuffle. Even so, its rules were good enough that it was even off the top, it was also four decks, cut one, and it had a two-million-won limit. It had potential. By the end of that first Saturday, it had demonstrated that. The bankroll was already off to a good start, up thirty or forty thousand before we arrived, with not many hours played. By Saturday night we'd broken the bank, Munchkin winning most of the money. He received the lion's share of the profits. Then, things turned around, and by the end of the two weekends we played, we were stuck one hundred thousand on the new bankroll.

"You guys lost an entire bankroll!" Butch moaned, the next time I saw him. He couldn't quite work out that we still had the equivalent of four more bankrolls in the bank in Seoul. The one hundred thousand was just a number. Though when you are losing it, it feels pretty salty.

I gave you a bit of a feel for the place in the prologue. Paradise Beach had more character than Walker Hill. The beach outside, Hyundai Beach, was lined with tents. In Korean they are called *pojang macha*. In Itaewon they appear at night along the main drag, and serve food and drink. In Busan there was a huge concentration, hundreds of yards of tents. The food was better, or at least, was of a type you wouldn't see much of in Seoul. Busan is a port; its name means harbor and mountain. The tents served fresh octopus, crab, lobster, fish. Most had sound systems, so that either the venue provided musical entertainment, or customers could sing karaoke. The party lasted until dawn.

Inside the casino the crowd was similar, albeit smaller, than at Walker Hill. They were a bit more ostentatious than up north. I saw a man strutting around in a gorgeous black kimono. Rocky told me that it probably cost twenty thousand dollars. He also said that the kimonos sold to American tourists had been stripped from dead bodies, worn during their final viewing. Japanese wouldn't buy them, but it was taken for granted Americans wouldn't know the difference.

The yakuza connection was more obvious. I've described Mister Rolex. He had a slave. The man must have been in his seventies, with a long white beard. There was a lounge overlooking the casino. The old man was one of the only people I ever saw sitting there, like a spectator at the world's most poorly attended sporting event. Mister Rolex, when short of cash, would holler, and the old man would come racing to our table, bowing repeatedly. Rolex would hand him a key to his safety box, to fetch more funds.

One time, around three in the morning, Rolex suddenly began exercising. He flapped his arms as though trying to elbow enemies approaching from his rear. I was sitting nearly in the line of fire, his left elbow whizzing past my ear. Then he leapt backwards off his stool, and began doing rapid deep knee bends. By the time he finished he had worked up a sweat.

"Towel, ya, towel!" he barked at the dealers. They brought him a couple of towels, while he waved over the servant. He stripped off his coat of many colors (mostly red), bent forward, and pulled up his shirt. The old man toweled him down. Then he took the towels from the oldster, wadded them up, and tossed them on the table to the horror of the dealers. He sat back down, glanced at me, and threw me a straight arm salute, "Ho! Mister American!"

To which I replied, "Hello Mister Japanese." He found that very funny. It was good we were hitting it off, because we'd be seeing a lot of each other.

After two weekends, Munchkin left for the States. Not me. We had an apartment, and it looked like we'd be playing in Busan a lot that summer. I stayed.

While back in Seoul, I broke up with A Rha. She had been vanishing without calling, this latest time for several days. When she finally answered her phone, I stormed over to her apartment. She was in bed. "Where have you been?"

She told me she had been sick.

I went into a tirade about not calling. I believe I mentioned that just when you thought she was telling a whopper, it would turn out to be true? Like the time she told me that a friend of hers was a "famous television comedian." When I tested that by asking Mia if so and so was "a famous comedian?" Mia said "No," then added, "She's not that famous." While I was chewing out A Rha for her obviously phony story about being sick, I noticed something next to her bed. A stand with an IV. "What's that?" "I told you I was sick. I didn't want to worry you, darling!" I thought about it. "Nevertheless ….

Later, I would have both the cleaning woman she had helped me retain for our apartment, and her own sister, Jiyoung, drop unsubtle hints that A Rha had been cheating on me. I don't know whether that included Jay or Frank, but she was in a relationship with Mr. Go, the guy driving her around to clubs on his motorcycle. Typical of A Rha, even several years after we'd broken up, and her relationship with Go was obvious, she pretended that he was just a friend.

I wasn't single for long.

Munchkin had stumbled on the Angel Shop. He always was more of a shopper than me. The larger buildings along the shopping street in Itaewon were filled with many small shops. The Angel Shop sold clothing, and was staffed by Miss Lee. It was across the hall from a shop selling Gore-Tex ski outfits, staffed by Miss Lee's friend Miss Kim. Miss Kim was better looking than Miss Lee. Lee was only four-eleven, with a large head and dreamy eyes. But she was teaching herself German by reading *Steppenwolf*, aided by a Korean-German dictionary. She was the more interesting of the two. Though it was apparent that Miss Kim was also very sharp. Women like those two, or the Miss Lee who assisted Mr. Lee at my bank, when it should have been the other way around, were Korea's wasted resource.

After a few visits and chats, I cagily brought a newspaper with an ad for the movie *Dracula Mimangin*, starring Sylvia Kristel. The English title is *Dracula's Widow*. I had sounded out the hangul script for "Dracula," but the rest was three Chinese characters. "What is this?" I asked. Lee explained that the characters *"mi-mang-in"* meant "not-dead-person," i.e. "widow." I had already discovered that she liked horror movies, and invited her to go see the movie on an evening when she was off work.

The movie was awful. The title vampire had a cult of devil worshippers, and some were played by African-American actors. Lee asked me afterward if black people in America were more inclined than whites to be devil worshippers. It was the first time I realized that we exported our racism in subtle ways.

The theatre was in Namyeongdong, near the Kaya Hotel, and after the movie we went to a nearby restaurant. It paired well with the movie; it was creepy. The seating was up a ladder, in an attic room. In those days the norm was to holler for service. Otherwise, you were left alone. By the time we arrived the place had emptied, but the dirty dishes from previous diners were still on the tables. I heard a noise, looked over, and spotted a rat standing on a nearby table, chattering at us while it picked at the leftovers. After we finished eating, we shared our first kiss. It was a lingering one, and one thing led to another. It was fortunate that the manager didn't decide to climb the ladder. We would never have gotten dressed in time. While we were occupied, I could still hear the rat, chiding us for being naughty. A real Donald Segretti moment.

One day it was Lee's turn to show me something in a newspaper. The top three universities in Korea were SNU (Seoul National University), Korea University, and Yonsei University. However, there was an all-women's uni, the Radcliffe or Vassar to their Harvard-Yale-Princeton, called Ewha. It was originally a missionary school, founded in 1886. That summer it decided to offer Korean language classes for foreigners. "Why don't you see about it?"

I went to the school for an interview. They were offering a beginner class and an advanced class; the interview would sort applicants. By now I had been studying on my own for over a year. I hadn't gotten far, but I did have some skills to show for my efforts. I could read hangul script, for starters. Hangul was created over five hundred years ago. The country's most famous king, Sejong the Great, had commissioned a group of scholars to devise an alphabet. Till then literate Koreans learned Chinese, which led to many borrowed terms, such as *mimangin*. There was also a method of using Chinese characters to write native Korean speech, as cumbersome as it sounds. Naturally literacy was restricted to the aristocrats, and scholars. King Sejong wanted to promote universal literacy, and a phonetic alphabet was a good start. Though centuries would pass before his dreams came to fruition. The holiday Hangul Day, celebrating its introduction October

9, 1446, was part of a covert nationalist movement during Japanese occupation.

At any rate, hangul is phonetic, and simple. I learned it in two hours. I demonstrated to Teacher Han that I could read. The problem is that there is reading, and there is reading. You can learn well enough in an evening to read 광화문, sounding it out: Kwang-wha-mun. Knowing that it means "heaven(ly) change gate" is another matter. Being able to spot it on the front of a bus when it pulls up, and instantly know it will take you to a place downtown where the "changes" are to other buses, is when you are truly reading.

Reading hangul script was not the only test. I had mastered very elementary conversation, and could greet people, give my name, and say other simple things. Then there was aural comprehension. Teacher Han rattled off a sentence. I have always been good at tests. I had no idea what she said, but it seemed as though a "yes," or rather a *"nae,"* would work. That's how I answered. She smiled, then shifted her body a bit, and in a different tone spoke a different sentence. I tried *"aniyo,"* and having successfully answered "yes" and "no" convinced her I could follow a conversation. She put me in the advanced class.

It would be a few weeks before the class met. Meanwhile, I met a prospective fellow student, George. Most expat residents could be lumped into groups. There were businessmen who were not affiliated with the US military. There were businessmen who were affiliated with the US military. There were military and civilians who were with government organizations. And there were the English teachers. If you are a native speaker of English, you have a marketable skill overseas. George was an English teacher. He was also, like a character out of Graham Greene, a remittance man. He came from Philadelphia's mainline. His grandma might have palled around with Tracy Lord. George was a black sheep; someone the family paid a stipend to stay away. He had first gone to South America. It was one of those countries with death squads. George missed the memo at first, but once clued in he marched down to the police station and said, "Do you know what's going on around here?" Naturally, they did as they were the ones doing the killing. His friends got him out of there before he could learn at firsthand all about death squads.

George was a nice guy, and not stupid. He was just … simple. Take the time he asked me "can you cum, and not know it?" I asked what he meant, and he said he had been persuaded by some of his fellow English teachers to go with a girl on Hooker Hill. It was taking more time than she had allocated, so she told him he had "cum already." I started giving him the talk his father should have given him twenty-five years before, about the release of fluid prior to … He stopped me. "But I was wearing a condom, so how could she feel that?" "Let me get this straight; you were wearing a condom, and she said you had cum already?" He nodded. "Well, George, these women are trained professionals, so they know these things."

George was the one who came up to me, at Wendy's. and said that he would be taking Korean with me, as would "Doctor Black." Like the mysterious "Mister Marty," Black was a raincoat wearer I'd seen but never spoken with. As the day approached George let me know that while Black and I would be going to Ewha, he wouldn't. He'd decided to take a taekwondo class instead. "Good thinking, George! You don't need to talk to them if you can beat the shit out of them."

The class would be meeting for eight weeks, with a one-week break in the middle, on Mondays through Thursdays, which was good, because Friday was the day we flew to Busan, when a new play caller and big player showed up. The new play caller joining me was Frank, Munch's old teammate from the early days. He'd also been in Atlantic City, originally to try to play the Memory Game, though he never managed it. He did play as a big player, driving us nuts because he spent a lot of time getting dressed for the part. How long does it take to put on a gold chain and unbutton a few buttons?

His first Friday in town, we went to Gimpo to catch the shuttle. The shuttle flights ran all day, until around 7:30, and cost twenty-five thousand, nine hundred won, around thirty-six dollars. A typhoon was blowing through Seoul, and when we reached Gimpo I learned all flights were grounded. Our big player was already there, so we needed to find a way to Busan. I turned us around and was heading for the taxi stand when a tout waylaid us. "Where are you going?" When I told him, he pointed out that with the planes grounded, my chance of getting a seat on the Busan train on a Friday night was nil. He said he'd take us for sixty thousand each.

"C'mon, Frank. We're taking a cab to Busan!"

"I thought it was all the way across the country?"

"It is."

Like the time I was fifteen, and took a cab across the Alps, it was dark, I slept, and I missed all the sights along the way. It was dawn by the time we reached Busan, but we only missed one shift.

I got to use a move I had learned years before, but hadn't gotten the chance to employ. Paradise Beach Casino used a second cut card on the back of the shoe, which concealed the value of the bottom card. This time, when the dealer offered me the cut, the card slipped a bit and I saw an ace peeping at me. I made a quick calculation. After the cut the dealer would burn a card, deal to seven players, then herself, then me on first base, then Rocky who was seated next to me. That meant he would receive the tenth card. I sliced it thin, and then gave the signal for a maximum bet.

Rocky knew that unlike Walker Hill, where I could shuffle track, and we might bet off the top, in Busan we never bet big off the top. But Rocky wasn't the World's Greatest Big Player for nothing! When I signaled, he caught it, and casually changed his bet from one hundred thousand to two million. The player on third base you have met before. It was the same kid who convinced Mister Horrible to bet on my square, way back on my first trip to Korea. When he saw Rocky up his bet, he jumped his bet. Which did not make me happy. Having anyone recognizing that Rocky was making smart plays was not good. Mimicking his bets was worse, because it might make the dealers or bosses take note.

Meanwhile, the cards came out, and Rocky's first card was a ten. Around she went, and on the next round – Boom! – the ace landed right where I wanted it. The dealer paid Rocky three million, dealt the rest of the round, caught a twenty, and scooped up everyone's bet including the wiseguy's. Take that, interloper!

Speaking of Mister Horrible, he was also in Busan. The next day he was on the table with me and Rocky, on the late shift. He'd been having a terrible weekend, losing tens of millions of won. He came to our table, and harangued Rocky in Japanese about the way he was playing. Even without knowing Japanese, I could follow the gist of it. It would have been great if we were dealt happy hands, the sort of hands he would have no objection to. It wasn't to be. It seemed like both Rocky and I were catching hands calculated to drive him bonkers, twelves we had to hit, on hands he would never hit, soft doubles he would never double, you name it, we got it. Naturally, none of our plays worked. We kept busting, and in his mind, taking the dealer's bust card. All three of us were losing, but he was getting hammered.

Finally, he began screaming at Rocky. Once again, it was clear what he was telling him. That I was a moron, so my bad plays were to be expected, but Rocky was playing "like an American!"

There was a woman who was playing in Busan that summer. I heard that she had a nightclub, maybe more than one, in Ginza. All the yakuza called her "Mama." Mister Horrible, it was safe to assume, was also one of the tattooed legions. Probably a ranking member. Whoever Mama was, she pulled rank. She was playing baccarat, but Mister Horrible's screaming was distracting everyone. She told him to shut up and go to bed, and he shut up and went to bed. That was the last time I saw him. Just as well. If he ever saw me in Japan, he might have had me whacked.

Outside, the party went on. Sunday night was my night to join it. It was on Paradise Beach that I had some run ins with octopi. Once I spotted one walking across the sidewalk, heading the wrong way, inland. I pointed him out to a passerby, who tracked down the owner of the tent he'd escaped from. Another night I was sitting in a tent, having a beer. There was a red plastic bucket on the table, filled with them. One intrepid fellow climbed to the rim of the bucket, adjusted his goggles, and threw his scarf back over his shoulder. He saluted his fellows, "I'm off lads, wish me luck!" Then he jumped to the table.

I pointed at him, "Look, he's escaping." The proprietor didn't speak English, and when I pointed, he misinterpreted my meaning. He grabbed the fugitive, threw him in a pot of boiling water for a short bath, then pulled him out and chopped him into a plateful of pieces. I wasn't hungry, but I was too embarrassed to try to explain, so I took some chopsticks, picked up a nearby octopus shin, and brought it toward my mouth.

It was writhing. I could feel it struggling when I touched it to my lips. It was trying to slither free from the chopsticks. But when I bit into it, it stopped struggling. See me for more tips on dealing with foods that fight back.

This weekend it was not an octopus I had to deal with. Strolling along the sidewalk alongside the tents, I was greeted by a girl, who asked if I wanted to visit her restaurant. I was amenable. Once there, I was fobbed off on "her friend," who was "hungry." I bought her a crab. There were some university students in the tent, and they asked me where I was from. The girl whispered I shouldn't talk to them, but I didn't think much of it, until I got the bill. Their food was tacked onto my tab. Suddenly, while I tried to sort out the bill, everyone disappeared. The tab came to around sixty-five thousand won, roughly ninety dollars. That include six or seven lobsters, a dozen crabs, and a lot of beer. If I weren't so pissed, I might have been impressed by how cheap it was.

I told the owner that I was making a citizen's arrest. We were going to the police station. I took him by the wrist, and led him away. His name was Mister Oh, and he kept saying, "Why do you want to arrest Mister Oh? I'm just a poor boy." He wasn't denying that he ripped me off; he seemed to think he was entitled because "he was just a poor boy," while I was "a rich American."

Once we got to the street, I realized there was a slight problem, I had no idea where to find the police station. I took him inside the Green Beach Hotel, and asked the night clerk to call the police.

The clerk wanted to know what the problem was. I explained, and he wanted to know why I was "picking on" Mister Oh, since "he is a poor boy, and you are a rich American." He did call the police.

While we were waiting, who should walk in but the wiseguy from the casino. Who was also a busybody, wanting to know what was going on? Once he found out, he said, "Why are you doing this? He's just a poor boy, and you are a rich American." Yeah, what would you do if he ripped you off?

Things can always be worse. Who should walk in but Rocky. Rocky was staying at the Paradise Beach, as we had our big players do. But after the last play of the weekend, we wanted them to come by our rooms for some last-minute accounting. Rocky quickly sized things up, and summoned an elevator, pretending he didn't know me. It didn't help, because as soon as he saw Rocky, the busybody looked from him to me and said, "You two are together?"

At last, the police showed up. I explained what had happened, how I certainly did not eat seven lobsters and a dozen crabs, and had been ripped off. Mister Oh didn't deny it, but the police simply said, "He's a poor boy, and you are a rich American," and left. In other words, Mister Oh was a little fish, and I had to throw him back.

CHAPTER 35
PLAYING CUPID

"Hello!" The speaker was a girl named Sabi. Frank and I were having breakfast in the Twilight Zone. It seemed empty, until a tousled head materialized over the top of the seat behind me. We'd woken her up. Sabi was a street kid. She'd been a teenage runaway, who'd arrived in Itaewon a few years before, and lived by her wits since then. Everyone who hung around Itaewon knew Sabi. That she singlehandedly downed seven Latina G.I.s was probably exaggerated. That she had singlehandedly downed seven bottles of soju probably wasn't. I introduced her to Frank, and thought little of it.

That night Frank and I were hanging out at the Sportsman's Club. Lee worked late, and she would meet me there when she finished work. Sabi turned up, and complained, not for the first time, that I never introduced her to my friends. I said, "Don't you remember Frank? Sabi, meet Frank. Frank, meet Sabi."

When Lee showed up, we left for home. It was a schlepp from the Sportsman's to the apartment, but I liked walking. Lee and I walked at one pace, while Frank pulled ahead. Sabi was following him home. We had turned onto Bokwangdonggil and started downhill when he dropped back the first time.

"She's following me!"

"I can see that."

"She can't come home with us."

"Tell her that."

A short while later, he dropped back again. "Okay, she can sleep in the living room tonight, but that's it!"

Further on, "I'll sleep in the living room, and let her sleep in my room. Just for tonight."

Obviously, Frank had no chance. Sleeping with Frank did not entirely solve Sabi's housing problem. The team policy was that girls were not allowed to stay in the apartment if we weren't there; they could not move in. Sabi found the damnedest room I've ever seen. It was in the courtyard of a house. It was built into an exterior wall. There was a wooden door, or wooden lid, with a padlock. When open, it revealed a space about three feet off the ground, eight feet long, four feet deep, and three feet high. That was her new abode. There was an outside toilet, with a tap for washing. All the comforts of home!

CHAPTER 36
SCHOOL DAYS

Classes were in the late afternoon, Monday through Thursday. I arrived the first day eager to learn. There were ten of us. The three most fluent students, who would soon vanish because they were too fluent for the class, were businessmen, one American, one Italian, and one British. They had all lived in Korea for ten or more years, and picked up a lot of Korean. There were four young women, all ethnic Korean, none Korean citizens. Three were American, and one German. Their parents sent them to Korea during school break to learn Korean. They all knew some, but none was fluent. In eighth place was Doctor Black. (The American businessman was named White, which was mildly amusing.) Black was "an English teacher," but unlike the majority of that tribe, he taught at a university, there at Ewha, in fact, and he taught psychology, not English. He'd been in Korea for two or three years, and knew a smattering, though not as much as the women. Less fluent than Black was Pearl. She was a Filipina whose boyfriend was a high-ranking executive with Pepsi. She'd been living in Korea for eighteen months. Her Korean wasn't very good.

It was still better than mine. I sat there baffled the first day. The entire class was conducted in Korean. No English at all. After class I went to Teacher Han, and told her I was in the wrong class. "I didn't understand ninety percent of what was said." While explaining this, I realized one reason the class was entirely in Korean was because she didn't speak English. She understood a bit, and could manage a few short sentences, but she was far from bilingual. She told me that I was very smart, and I would try hard, so she was sure I would be okay. Much later it dawned on me that letting me drop down to the beginner class would have reflected on her. So, I struggled with Korean II.

The bus to take me back to Itaewon was out the back gate of Ewha's campus. Across the street was Yonsei University, the Berkley of Korea. There were demonstrations every day, and the smell of tear gas was always present.

Tear gas, by the way, at least the sort the Korean police used, wasn't a gas. It was a powder. It hung in the air in a mist. There was a bus stop in front of Wendy's, and when buses from downtown pulled up, the people getting off carried it on their clothes. We'd be sitting there drinking coffee, a bus would unload, and suddenly we were all choking.

The previous year Chun Doo Hwan stepped down to stop all the demos. Roh had agreed to become acting president, if there was a free election. In December, 1987 what was the first truly legitimate election in Korean history was held. There were four candidates. Besides Roh, the incumbent, there were the Three Kims: Kim Daejung, Kim Youngsam, and Kim Jongpil.

Kim Daejung had lost the election in 1971 to Park Chunghee. It was believed that he actually won, but Park stole it. During the election season Kim was hit by a truck, an accident which was no accident. He would be plagued by hip trouble ever after. He went to Japan, but was kidnapped by the KCIA. They had him in a boat, in the sea between Japan and Korea. Kim later wrote that he was sure the plan was to dump him in the water, but a US military helicopter turned up, and hovered over the boat.

Back in Korea he spent years under house arrest. He was released when Park was killed, but was back under house arrest when the

Kwangju Massacre happened. Kwangju was his hometown, so Chun claimed Kim had fomented rebellion, and sentenced him to death. The Carter administration, working with the incoming Reagan administration cut a deal. Kim was exiled to the US for "medical treatment," and Chun became the first foreign head of state to visit the Reagan White House.

You can't keep a good man down. Kim returned to Korea around the same time Ninoy Aquino returned to Manila. He fared better. Aquino was killed; Kim was subject to house arrest once again.

Meanwhile, with Kim spending so much time under arrest or in exile, Kim Youngsam, his old friend, took over as head of the opposition party. Each man was convinced that it was his turn to run, and by running against each other, were now bitter enemies.

The final Kim, Jongpil, was the former head of the KCIA. He was an archconservative, and a hawk's hawk. He had no chance. In the election he received ten percent of the vote. The liberal opposition received fifty-five percent of the vote, twenty-eight percent to Kim Daejung, twenty-seven to Kim Youngsam. Which gave Roh thirty-five percent, and the presidency. I read that even if one of the Kims had dropped out, the result would have been the same, the Kim Daejung loyalists would never have voted for Kim Youngsam, while those who supported KYS would never have supported KDJ. There was a regional rivalry dating to the Three Kingdoms Period. The eastern half of South Korea, roughly corresponded to the former Shilla Kingdom, the one that had consolidated the peninsula. The western provinces, collectively Chollado, were the former Paekche. Park, who was from Kyongsang, the east, had deliberately snubbed Chollado. Roh and KYS were also from Kyongsang. I asked Miss Kim one day, when she was not busy selling Gore-Tex, about this. She was from Daegu, part of Kyongsang. Was it true that supporters of Kim Youngsam would not have voted for Kim Daejung if Kim Youngsam wasn't running? She assured me that was true, because people from Chollado "were wicked!"

Lee, meanwhile, preferred Roh. Preferred put it too mildly. She loved Roh! She was gaga over him. One day when she was off work, I took her to the Blue House. I'd heard they were allowing people to tour the grounds. We entered at one end, and found ourselves on a road with high walls on either side. It was a bit like walking past Yongsan. I figured the entrance must be somewhere, and hurried Lee up. Ahead of us was a pack of oldsters, up from the country on a tour. Soon they were behind us. Where was the damned entrance, so we could see something besides bricks?

Next thing we knew, we were out on a main road. That was it? I was annoyed. Lee was disappointed that we hadn't taken more time, to stop and smell the bricks. We were about a hundred yards away from the gate, when here came a motorcade.

"It's him!" Lee practically peed in her pants. It was him, Roh Taewoo himself, heading the way we came. He turned in as we ran back to the gate. Where the guards would not let us in, even though we had just come from there. The pedestrian entrance was at the other end, and that was that. As Lee begged, we could see the motorcade stop. Roh got out, and shook hands with all of the old folks. If I hadn't hurried her, she could have shaken hands with him.

She made us wait, so we could get pictures of her with the people who shook the hand of the president. That she forgave me for making her miss meeting him, proves it was true love.

But what about the riots? Didn't the election resolve matters? It resolved a matter; the country now had a democratic government. But one reason ordinary Koreans joined the students was economic dissatisfaction. Korea's growth during the previous quarter of a century had been remarkable, but ordinary Koreans didn't share in its new wealth. The riots continued. At Yonsei, and downtown. Lee and I nearly got caught in one of those. We were wandering around a shopping district, when a group of students, fleeing cops with their Darth Vader helmets, their metal shields, and their clubs, came around a corner, heading our way. I grabbed Lee and we ducked into the nearest shop.

We nearly started a riot one night. We had gone to the Kimchi Museum near Yongin. Yes, there is a museum devoted to kimchi. On the train heading back to Seoul I saw an ad for a movie I thought she might like. She was enthusiastic, so we headed for Myongdong when we got off the train, to the only theatre showing the movie. When we got there, Lee asked someone if we were in the right place, and was told that it was at a different theatre.

"No, this is it." I could see it on the marquee.

"That man told me it wasn't here."

"He's wrong. See, it says *Fatal Attraction*."

Lee squinted. She wore glasses but never in public. Without them she was nearly blind. "That says *'uihom ae sarang*."

Which was what it said in Korean. I recalled something I read. "Oh, yeah, the Korean name is 'Dangerous Love.' This is it!" The box office was at the other end of the building. She grabbed my hand and dragged me there. Dragged me through a thick crowd of people sitting on the ground, while I hipped, and hopped trying to avoid stepping on anyone, and they grumbled as we passed. I remembered why I had read about the movie. There had been a trade agreement liberalizing the rules for importing American movies. *Fatal Attraction* was the first movie brought in under the new agreement. It was feared that American movies might kill the domestic market. These people were staging a sit-in, led by a film director. The theatre had received bomb threats, and snakes let loose during screenings.

As we bought our tickets, I could hear the buzz of the crowd growing louder and more menacing. The manager was terrified, and kept urging us to hurry, get our tickets, and get upstairs and out of sight.

We were near the top of the stairs when Lee stopped. "That's odd."

"What's odd?" I asked as I came close to lifting her bodily up the last few stairs.

"Those people are saying that we are un-Korean."

"Imagine that."

Inside, she went straight to the washroom, and when she returned told me breathlessly that a woman in the john had explained there were protests about this movie. She had come close to trampling half the protestors, and never noticed, because she wasn't wearing her glasses.

Luckily, there were no bombs, and no snakes. The only damage to us was emotional. Lee had never seen a movie that intense. They weren't making movies like that in Korea in the eighties. When the lights came up she was sobbing on the floor. A couple asked me if she'd be alright, and if I needed help with her. I thanked them, and said she'd be fine. After five minutes or so she was able to leave. Even *Hellraiser* hadn't shaken her that much.

CHAPTER 37
THE LUNCH CROWD

There was a saying when I was growing up, that if you stood at the corner of State and Madison, sooner or later everyone in the world would pass by. The Wendy's in Itaewon was like that, especially if you were sitting at Tom Casey's table. One of those somebodies was a businessman in his late forties, who was telling Tom all about his ex-girlfriend, who Tom seemed to know. He'd thrown her out in the hallway of his hotel, and tossed her clothes after her. I missed the first part of his story, where he explained why. She pounded on his door, but he wouldn't let her back in. "She was going out with two other guys at the same time as me." I don't think that was the reason for the breakup, just color commentary. "One of them was a junior high school principal. He gave her an engagement ring, and money for rent. She kept the money and sold the ring. The other guy was supposed to be a gambler from the States. Anyway, Shin Jung is back dancing at the Golden Gate in Pyongtaek."

Another guy had an impact on my life. Bill was a warrant officer, newly arrived, to teach math on the base. He'd done a Korean tour or two before, when he was an enlisted man, the most recent five years ago. He mentioned he had a language course he and a buddy had picked up during that earlier stint. He said they bought two copies of the texts, and he made copies of the tapes. The course cost around four-fifty, but he'd sell me his materials for a hundred bucks.

The course was created by the Foreign Service Institute circa 1960. They had courses for most major languages. These days they are publicly available for downloading online. From what I was told FSI rated the difficulty of a language based on the number of hours it took to teach American speakers of English enough for a certain level of proficiency. Spanish took six hundred hours, and (these are approximations, from memory) French and Italian eight hundred, German twelve hundred, and Russian fifteen hundred. The most difficult languages, for American English speakers, based on instruction time, all took about twenty-four or twenty-five hundred hours. They included: Mandarin, Japanese, Thai, Arabic, and Korean.

The course I purchased came with two volumes, and enough tapes to match the lessons. Book one had eighteen chapters, book two another twenty-nine, forty-seven weeks altogether. The foreign service officers in the course would number six at a time, with two teachers, one a native speaker of Korean, the other a fluent Korean speaker whose native tongue was English, who would help explain grammar. It was expected that students would spend fifty hours a week studying.

If you have learned a foreign language, you may already know what I am about to say, but at the time, the course was a revelation! I had been fumbling along for more than a year, and this course was a quantum leap! Why? It was organized. And unlike the silly tape which was all vocabulary, these tapes were structured to really teach. The first few lessons were very simple. (And I wonder how the FSI students dealt with fifty hours of lesson one, which taught little more than "Hello, my name is?") But they built on each other. After listening to, and repeating the practice dialogue, there were exercises which used and expanded on the vocabulary in the lesson, and drilled the student in the grammar introduced to date.

Suppose you wanted to say, "Sabi drank seven bottles of soju." The Korean for that is, *"Sabi-shi-ga soju ilgop-byong-ul massyeossda."* That's "Sabi-a person-subject marker soju seven, using the number system for counting this particular item-bottle-object marker drank." A drill might have you swapping beer-four-glasses, or changing drank to drinks. You have probably noted the subject and object markers, and the unfamiliar word order. Aside from always appearing at the end of a sentence, Korean verbs have many, many forms. It all sounds complicated, and it is, for us. Just as English is complicated for Koreans. We all learn our grammars automatically, almost literally with our mother's milk. But as we age various parts of our language learning apparatus go from programmable to hard-wired.

I was trying to learn the language at age thirty-five, and I did not, and do not, have an aptitude for picking up languages. Yet the difference the course and those tapes made was incredible. I spent four years taking Spanish in elementary school, and two years taking Latin in high school. None of those years was language taught to me like this. What a waste of time!

By the time I reached lesson four I could already see a marked difference. I could even begin comparing myself with others. I am not sure the state of things today, but in the late eighties there were hardly any university courses in the US teaching Korean. Most of the Americans tackling the language did so because they were living in Korea. A rough ranking would find G.I.s or others spending a year or so in the country, at the bottom. They had a vocabulary of possibly a few dozen words, a pidgin not much better than baby talk. Those were the fluent ones. Not only the short timers. Tom Casey had been in Korea for twenty years, except for eighteen months at Fort Dix in the mid-seventies, had been married to a Korean, and had a live-in Korean girlfriend. He didn't know much more than the average G.I., though I think he understood more than he could speak. Next up the ladder were English teachers, the ones who had been in the country three, four, five years, and had made some effort. They might know a few hundred words. A big step up were the Mormon missionaries. The Mormons had their own program for teaching youngsters, and those kids were pretty good. Then there were the graduates of the Defense Institute's language school in Monterey, California. I got to know several former intelligence officers, who were now working in Korea as civilians. Even they seemed somewhat less than fluent. One, an oddball who sat with us at Wendy's one day when I was there with A Rha and her aunt, told them he used to debrief North Korean defectors, and began shouting what sounded to me like a canned pitch. I don't know what A Rha and her aunt thought of it. I could see from their eyes they were non-plussed. I assume he was using North Korean dialect, which might well have gotten a southerner arrested if they used it in public.

There were exceptions. I knew a couple of German businessmen who had been in the country a long time, and were very fluent. One, especially. He was a Moonie. He also had an export business, and taught German on television. A bit of this, and a bit of that. He became a Korean citizen. He would baffle security at Kimpo, as they tried to nudge him into the immigration line for foreigners, and he'd tell them, in nearly perfect Korean, that he was Korean. Look, here was his Korean passport (he had taken a Korean name), with his photo.

But there were also guys who had a reputation for fluency, who turned out to be not so adept. One was Colonel Fred. He was an older guy, with stained false teeth and a bad salt-and-pepper toupee. I assume he was a retired colonel; else why would they call him that? If he made colonel, anyone could do it. Colonel Fred sat around Wendy's like a spider, the young women his flies. He would wow, then try to woo, them with his remarkable command of Korean. When I met him, I was impressed. Now that I had my tapes, I realized that when he ordered a Coke he would say, "*Cola chuseyo*," but when he ordered a beer he would say "*Maekchu chusipsio*." The verb in both is functionally the same, the former polite informal, the latter polite formal. They are interchangeable, but he never interchanged them. He must have learned the one when he learned how to ask for a Coke, the other when he asked for a beer, and didn't understand that he could swap.

Then I listened to a conversation he had with Steve. They were talking about the term *"budongsan."* The colonel said, "It means 'real estate broker.'" Steve explained that it was a broader term which meant real estate itself. "Look," he drew three Chinese characters, "that's *budongsan*, and they mean "non-moveable asset," in other words, real estate." Fred couldn't grasp it.

Steve was one of the exceptions. Steve and his brother Darryl came to Korea in 1979, when their father, an air force colonel, was posted to Osan AFB. Steve was in college, Darryl in high school. They both dropped out, and when their dad was transferred out, they stayed. They boarded with Korean families for a while, picking up a lot of practical language along the way. They were pals with Tim, who'd been a sergeant in the air police. Now all three taught English, and after nine years in Korean, and real effort, they were extremely fluent. Tim liked to show off his fluency; the brothers were more reserved, especially Darryl. As far as I could tell, at the time, Steve was the furthest along of the three.

There was the time he took me and Bill to eat dog. Dog restaurants had been common in Seoul, but with the Olympics approaching they'd been ordered out of town. Bad PR. Steve knew of one in the countryside, and we split the cab fare. There are a couple of names for dog stew, the most common being *boshintang*. It's considered a health food, especially if by health you mean "erect penis." Middle-aged men are its target audience. The restaurant was in a Quonset hut, and served only two dishes, *boshintang*, and *samgaetang*, which is a ginseng and chicken soup, another health food. The dogs to be consumed are a particular breed, and are farmed for that purpose. There were kennels outside the hut.

While we were waiting, Steve got into a conversation with the owner about food preparation. It was one of several times I heard him in an off-the-wall conversation: food preparation, religion (with a missionary), etc. These are not topics you pick up in any standard course, and require a very large vocabulary and verbal agility.

While waiting, he also showed me something else he'd picked up. Koreans eat with chopsticks and a long-handled spoon. The chopsticks are shorter than Chinese or Japanese chopsticks, rounded, and made of metal. They are harder to grip with than their counterparts. The spoon is also metal, and comes in a set with the chopsticks. Steve warned me that what he was about to show me was considered impolite, but when at home or among friends, common. Chopsticks are used to pick up small items, such as the side dishes served with a meal, or for noodles, while the spoon is used for the stews, or possibly dishes like bibimbap. Normally you set one down while using the other. What Steve did was keep them both in his hand at all times. If using the chopsticks, the spoon was reversed, pointing back toward the elbow, when in use, the chopsticks were reversed. I never practiced enough to master the magic.

Speaking of chopsticks, have you ever seen one of those cartoons where pins are stuck in a voodoo doll, while the victim flinches in surprise, clutching the spots where the pins go in? I am sure it was coincidence, but every time I stuck my chopsticks in the stew, a dog outside the window yelped. Perhaps I – all of us – should be vegetarians. I am not, and am not sentimental. I have eaten life forms most Americans wouldn't. But having tried dog, I am not tempted to try it again.

CHAPTER 38
SECRET AGENT MAN

As the Olympics approached, strangers were drawn to Korea. Most of the ones seeking information worked for news agencies. The eighty-eight Olympics promised to be a big story. Korea itself was convinced of that, and did what it could to spread the word. Even the taxi company got into the act. The Ponies were vanishing, replaced by "Pal Pal" taxis, *pal-pal* being Korean for "eight-eight." These were larger Hyundais, with higher prices. Some of the reporters had embedded early. The Korea Herald had a sportswriter who was significantly better than the rest of its staff. He could have found work with most US papers, but he was angling for the big time. By becoming "the man" when it came to English-language coverage of Korean sports, he figured he'd springboard up to a plum job after the Olympics. He didn't, but nice try, thanks for playing.

Reporters were not the only ones seeking information. There were spies coming out of the woodwork. Korea in those years was already on high alert. I had friends who lived in an apartment building on the slope of Namsan, which had a view, from a distance, of the Blue House. There were signs all over the building warning that photography was not permitted. I am not sure if they would really know that you snapped a Polaroid from your apartment window, but I don't think anyone wanted to test it. There had been border incidents ever since the War. Fighting nearly erupted over the chopping down of a tree. North Korean commandos had invaded in 1968, and made it to within a thousand yards of the Blue House. In 1983 a bombing in Burma missed Chun, but took out quite a few visiting Korean officials. In 1987 a pair of spies planted a bomb on a plane, the male spy biting a cyanide capsule when they were apprehended, the woman trying to do the same, but failing. North Korea was boycotting the Olympics, and North Korea was only twenty-five miles from Seoul. Might they hurl missiles while the athletes hurled javelins? Could saboteurs be in place, ready to act when the games began?

"Someone is trying to take your picture!" I was seated out front of Wendy's, with Tom, Bill, and Roger, when one of the street vendors came over to warn us. We looked to where he indicated, and spotted an Asian male hiding behind a rack of socks fifty feet away. We all found ways of ruining the shot; Tom turned around to look inside Wendy's, Roger and I held our beverages in front of our faces, as though drinking, and Bill turned slightly so his back was to the photographer. He saw what we were doing, and walked off.

"He must have my picture already," said Roger. Roger was a non-com at Yongsan. He was in army intelligence. I don't know what he did for army intelligence, but knowing Roger, I doubt it was doing much to win the Cold War. Still, he was undoubtedly right, anyone in army intelligence in Korea was surely on file with the KCIA. If the photographer was KCIA. Tom agreed and was sure there was also a file on him. That was a safe bet. Which meant the snoop wanted a shot of me, or Bill.

An hour later Bill and Roger had left. Our tipster returned, "He's back." Sure enough, the snoop had crept back to his hiding spot to try again. But when he saw it was me and Tom, he turned and walked away. Which meant he'd been after a picture of Bill, who was newly arrived in Korea. Which also meant that, since he didn't take my picture, whoever he worked for had a file on me.

Whoever *he* worked for. There were other agencies. There was a dim-witted guy who hung around the Sportsman's Club. I think he was a police informant. He tried to follow me home one night, chatting with me as we walked. But when he realized it was a long way, he gave up. There was the man in the blue suit. He was a nerdy looking man of about thirty; he looked like a slightly overaged university student, though students didn't dress like he did. He would sit around Wendy's, drinking Cokes, and eying the customers. Eight o'clock was quitting time for him. One night he followed Miss Kim to the traffic light across from the Hamilton. The Gore-Tex shop closed earlier than the Angel Shop. She'd dropped by Wendy's to chat on her way home. He'd seen her talking to me, and since she left right at eight, to go catch her bus, it was convenient for him to follow her, and pump her for information about me.

There was a KGB agent. At least, he was from the USSR, and didn't seem to do much besides hang around. I know he accomplished something under cover, because one night he came running into the Sportsman's Club. There was a broad staircase running up to Hooker Hill from Hannamdong, next to the Sportsman's. KGB rented an apartment near the top of the stairs. He burst into the club, wearing rubber sandals, with a towel wrapped around his waist. Tom and I were sitting at the bar near the door when he ran in, and he said, "Quick, where can I get some condoms!?" I don't think it was the sort of under-cover work his bosses sent him to do, but he'd thrown himself into it.

The most serious encounter was also at Wendy's. His name was Gabe. Gabe seemed a testament to the idea that mediocre people could become modest successes in spite of themselves. He had both too much and too little hair. He was losing it on top, but had caterpillar eyebrows, a moustache, and lots of body hair, all jet black. He looked like the kind of guy, who, if a woman found herself seated next to him, she would change her seat. Miss Kim, his interpreter, didn't seem to mind him. I think most of us mentally put quotes around "interpreter," though perhaps that was all she did for or with him.

Gabe and Miss Kim turned up at Wendy's, inevitably. He told everyone he was in Korea on behalf of a group interested in building golf courses in North Carolina, and were looking for investors. Then he and Miss Kim took off on a trip around the peninsula, because, having met the Wendy's crowd, they needed a vacation. Though I can't say I blame them. I'd recently come back from a trip myself. There was a one-week break between halves of the Korean language course. Lee got time off, and we went by bus to Busan and back, with a stop in Kyongju, former capitol of the Shilla Kingdom. I was amazed by how well preserved an 8th century complex was, until I learned it had been destroyed during the war, and rebuilt.

One afternoon at Wendy's Gabe was at our table when Fast Eddie joined us. Eddie was an English teacher, with a slightly more exotic background than most. He was half-Italian, half-English, and grew up in Kenya. Eddie was a wheeler dealer, who told me how he, and other English teachers, supplemented their modest incomes. Lacking work passes, they had to make visa runs. The nearest port was Fukuoka. They would go there, buy an expensive watch, an expensive camera, or both, at the duty-free shop, then sell them on the black market when they returned. Which explained why, when I had to make a visa run after nearly ninety days in the country, the immigration officer noticed that I had left and returned the same day, and asked to see my wrist. (I had no watch or camera.)

Eddie was eating a burger and drinking a milkshake when Gabe introduced himself, and asked what Eddie did for a living. Eddie said he taught English.

"Is that all you do?"

"I do some importing."

"What do you import?"

Eddie pulled the shake away from his mouth, looked Gabe in the eye, and said, "You know, you're an awfully inquisitive motherfucker."

Everyone at the table sat up straighter. Everyone except Gabe, who didn't even blink, "So what is it you import?"

A few weeks later, Gabe, Tom, and I were at the usual table, and Gabe turned to me. "I know some guys here who are interested in opening a hotel in Las Vegas. They'd like to talk to you." That I was in Korea to gamble was common knowledge. I told him that I doubted I would be much help, and said the first thing they would need to do was see if they could even get a gaming license. "Oh, no, they don't want to open a casino, just a hotel." I still didn't see how I could help, but when Gabe asked what my number was, so they could call, I began to rattle it off without thinking. I had barely started when Tom kicked me under the table, and I inverted two of the digits.

A week or two later he saw me again, and said that his friends were trying to reach me, without success. I told him my friends were also complaining, "You know the Korean phone system." I suggested he give me his friends' number, and I could call them. He didn't look pleased, but gave me a phone number. "That's the US Embassy; ask for Mr. Kim."

The US Embassy? Sure enough, when I called it was the US Embassy, and when I asked for Mr. Kim, they put me right through. Which was also strange. Our Korean Embassy was one of our biggest. I have no idea how many Koreans worked there, but Kim is the most common surname; twenty percent of the population is named Kim. There had to be dozens of Mr. Kims working there, but they knew immediately where to connect me.

Mr. Kim was very happy to hear from me. "I have been trying to call! What is your number?" I gave him the same number with the switched digits. "That's the number I have been calling, but it doesn't work!" I told him the same thing I told Gabe, "Damned Korean phones!" He said, "When can we get together?" I told him that I hadn't lived in Vegas for years, and knew nothing about the hotel business, so I couldn't be of any help, sorry, then got off the phone.

The only way that Gabe was not CIA, was if he worked for some other US intelligence agency out of the Embassy. Why me? Well, if everyone else you meet is either in the military, working with the military, or teaching English, then you find someone who claims he is in Korea because he is a professional gambler, who would you investigate? I recently filed a freedom of information request, and after a month or so received a cryptic response that either they had no information, or it was still classified.

CHAPTER 39
TROUBLE IN PARADISE

Rocky and I were in the middle of a session when the bosses at the Paradise Beach informed both of us that our bet spreads were henceforth limited to "one hundred thousand, three hundred thousand." The casino realized how much Rocky was winning, and must have called Walker Hill. Not even three hundred thousand to a million, like Walker Hill, a measly three hundred thousand maximum. Not that we'd play either way, but still. The fact that they tagged me, too, was even worse. It wasn't only the big player; it was the nature of our play they had figured out. Presumably so had Walker Hill, if they recommended limiting us both. Unless the Paradise Beach decided just to limit me on principle.

I was dubious, but the team must have thought that was the case. It was only a week or two later that they told me they would be sending Darryl and a BP, and I would be the other play caller. "Do you think it's a good idea? Sending me?" They told me to relax, that the big player had never played, anywhere, ever. And Darryl hadn't yet been to Busan. It would be fine.

We flew down on a Friday, as usual. The only change up we made was having me test the waters on a couple of shifts, alone. I went in a little after ten that night, and sat down. The casino was very quiet, and

I was at a dead game. They told me I had to bet three hands if I was alone. I bet three hands of the minimum, one hundred thousand each. Within a minute the shift manager charged up, and waved a finger in my face, "You! One hundred! Three hundred!" I pointed to the table, "Only one hundred." He shook his head, "One hundred! Three hundred!" Then he retreated a distance, to stand by the podium and glare at me, while I wondered why they didn't tell me to play one hand. Soon every boss, and every dealer who was free, had been brought by the table to stare at me, memorizing everyone pore of my face.

This would have been a very good time to take a loss. Instead, I have never been dealt so many blackjacks in so short a time! I was only going to play for around forty-five minutes to an hour, then clear out so Darryl could come in. In that time, flat betting, I won sixty-five units! Six and a half million won worked out to about nine thousand dollars. While it wouldn't rate as an especially good win for a big player betting double two millions, even for them it wasn't a bad result. The bosses were not happy.

In the morning, I came in at the tail end of grave, to play another short session, and let those bosses see me. Once again the shift manager had to remind me that my bets were limited. Not that I had ever bet more than one hundred thousand, even before they were limited. This time during the half hour I played, I was not as lucky as the previous night. I *only* won three and a half million. It was faintly ridiculous.

I took a break just before shift change, and then returned for day shift shortly after. They must have gotten the scouting report, because no one warned me about my bet limit. Soon the big player joined me. His name was Steve, and aside from playing with Darryl the night before, he had never set foot in a casino. He did fine. He was a bit nervous, but he didn't make mistakes.

I won another million and a half during the six and a half hours we played. Steve won forty and a half million. The combined win was the equivalent of fifty-seven thousand dollars, my best session to date. The other players at the table were convinced Steve was lucky, and when his bets went up, so did theirs. We won because the dealer busted a lot, which meant the whole table won, collectively seventy million won, or about one hundred thousand dollars. When I sent Steve off the table, the others all quit. I was alone for the next shoe. Three bosses came to count, and recount the rack, and assess the damage. They were pale, they were sweating, and they looked to me for sympathy and under-standing. "Too much! He win too much!" I agreed. "Luckiest player I ever saw!" They just shook their heads. "Mister, he win too much."

After that, I cooled off, only breaking even for my next session. Darryl had a twenty million win on Sunday.

A funny thing happened leaving Gimpo Airport Sunday night. Darryl and Steve climbed into the back seat, while I hopped up front. As we were driving to town, the driver said to me, "I bet I can guess where you are coming from." I told him to go ahead, and he said we were coming from Busan. That was an amazing guess since an international flight was more likely. Then he said, "And while you were there, you stayed at the Green Beach Hotel." It was the same driver who had taken me and Frank down there the night of the typhoon.

The next weekend Darryl started off with another twenty million won win. Saturday afternoon Steve and I were playing, when he got the tap. A boss asked him to accompany him to his office. Ten minutes later they were back, Steve looking frightened, while he collected his chips. He was looking sideways at me the whole time, trying not to make it obvious, but letting me know it was trouble. Which I had already figured out, but Steve was new to all this.

Now I got the tap. A boss was at my side, asking me to come with him. I played dumb. "In a minute, I am in the middle of a shoe." He was persistent, and I sighed elaborately, and went with him to the office. There he told me that he was the casino manager, and he didn't want my action anymore. I acted outraged, "What's the problem? First you tell me I can only bet one hundred, three hundred. I have only been betting one hundred, like you asked." He kept shaking his head and repeating he didn't want my action. I went back to the table, got my chips, cashed out, then went across the street to give Darryl the bad news.

Back in Seoul I paid a visit to Mr. Chang. He'd moved the money changing operation out of his home, and into a business across the street, the *Yesu-Nim Chaekbang*, or "Honorable Jesus Bookstore." Mr. Chang was a member of a Christian sect. He had turned us on to a special service of his. He could get us blank, thousand-dollar traveler's cheques. After triple checking with US Customs we determined that second-party checks were not considered negotiable instruments. We could take these checks, make them out to ourselves, then sign them over to team members back in the States, and carry them into the US without declaring them, no matter how many we had.

For Steve I also bought five thousand US dollars. "What do I do with it?" I told him he could keep it. Not only that, but someone, Munch or Craig, probably, would see him and give him another two thousand. "Really? For me?" In one and a half weekends we'd won a total of ninety-eight million won, around one hundred and forty thousand dollars. As big player he was getting paid five percent of the win. He hadn't understood what that might mean in actual dollars. "When do we do this again!?" I told him they would talk to him about it. Let them break the news that his blackjack career was over. I thought about how when I started playing winning one hundred thousand was a career milepost, something which might take a couple of years. Steve had won one-forty in a weekend and a half. His was a short career, but a good one.

A few weeks later, they told me another group was coming to town. "Don't you want to wait until things cool off?" They said not to worry; I wasn't going, and none of these guys had played Busan yet. They didn't even last through the first shoe.

CHAPTER 40
GOLD MEDAL FOR THE LONGEST STAY

I'd been in Korea nearly four months. With no more playing in the immediate future, now that Busan was burnt to a crisp, and the language class finished, it was nearly time to go home. Just not quite yet.

I had a new banker. The old Mr. Lee was gone, to where I never learned. My new banker was also named Mr. Lee. He was short where the old one was tall, bright-eyed whether the other was inward looking. He was also eager to show me what a valued customer I was. He could get tickets to the Olympics, and he was sure I wanted some. I've mentioned that I have very little interest in sporting events, and my impulse was to say, "Thanks, but no thanks." But Frank was back in Korea, and his reaction was, "Are you kidding?" I thanked Mr. Lee, and chose a small sampling. I had gotten a call from Woody. He wanted to see the Olympics, and was coming to town. His time was limited, but he wondered if I could put up his children, and his girl-friend, at the apartment, and also get them tickets for the games? I put Frank on it, introducing him to Mr. Lee and letting them work out what the visitors would get to see.

Alan's girlfriend was Beth, his son was Anthony, and his daughter was Vickie. When they arrived from Hong Kong I had a big day planned. I took them to see the Great South Gate, and the market behind it. They yawned, and said the shopping was better in Hong Kong. I took them here, I took them there, and everywhere I took them was, boring! I took them to have Korea BBQ, with Frank and Sabi. Everyone loves bulgogi! This was even better, galbi, a better cut of meat. Korean food was "icky!" By the time midnight approached I was fed up with these spoiled brats. It was going to be a long week. I told them that now they were stuck doing something I needed to do. I had to go to the Sportsman's Club to meet Lee. She had changed jobs, now working as the cashier and receptionist for her cousin at a Chinese restaurant on the other side of the river, hence the late hour. I figured if I could suffer through an entire day with them, they could suffer through an hour at a disco.

Guess what they liked? Liked? They thought the Sportsman's Club was great. Vicky even made a friend, who wanted to take her out to eat. The man, who'd been up on the dance floor with her, was an army captain. I told him she wasn't going anywhere. That it was two in the morning, and she was only thirteen. He refused to believe it, and once I convinced him he started chewing out me and Beth. "How could you bring a thirteen-year-old to a place like this?" Vicky was also unhappy; she'd wanted to go with him.

For the next week, until Woody arrived, they were at the Sportsman's every night with Frank and Sabi, then sleeping in and missing the Olympics. "How am I going to explain this to your mother?" Said Alan, when he finally arrived.

Before he did, while the kids were sleeping in, Beth and I did some sightseeing. Downtown I took her through the underground. Beneath the streets there is a vast web of tunnels. They were built as civil defense shelters, but they had evolved into an enormous shopping mall. You know the expression "everything but the kitchen sink?" On the stairs leading underground outside of my bank, there was someone selling a kitchen sink, with running water! Somewhere in one of the tunnels was a shoe store named Imelda, which Beth got a kick out of. I usually surfaced near the Kyobo Building. The Kyobo Bookstore boasted five million volumes. It wasn't even the largest bookstore. A few blocks away the Chongno Bookstore claimed to have twelve million. It was ten stories tall, and so crammed with books that they were piled in heaps in the stairwells.

We were approaching the Kyobo Building when Beth was accosted, someone shoving a microphone in her face. Beth was striking looking. The Philippines has seen waves of arrivals over the millennia, and so the people have great variety. Almost all the Filipinos I know have black hair, but some Filipinos would seem at home in Madrid, while others might pass for local in Shanghai. Beth's ancestors arrived much earlier, and she happened to have very dark skin. Her skin contrasted nicely with her outfit, dark hiking boots, white T-shirt, and white Levis, jaggedly trimmed so they were short-shorts. Korean women in those days did not walk around downtown in shorts. She had a confident stride, and was the most exotic visitor most Koreans had ever seen.

The television reporter must have been assigned to find people in town for the Olympics, to interview. "What do you think of Korea?"

That interview she handled with aplomb, but that night in Fish Alley when something rather different was thrust in her face, she screamed. We were a few feet in from *Bowkwangdonggil*. There was a rack of fish on the right. A little man, filthy dirty as though he had just come from digging a ditch, was buying a fish. A good-sized fish. He was swaying like someone who'd drunk a few bottles of soju. He turned around and there was Beth, like a goddess striding towards him. In propitiation he said, "Wah!" and offered her the fish, head first, right in her face.

We were on our way to the King Club. Tom had competition. One competitor had just opened, on my thirty-fifth birthday. J.J. Mahoney's was in the basement of the Hyatt. It cost five million dollars, an enormous sum. It had a little of everything: bar, dining, pool table, disco, each in its own area. Tom had gone there opening night, to see and be seen. He told the trio he'd come with to get him a coffee, and whatever they wanted, he was buying. One of the girls wanted orange juice, and the waiter asked if she wanted orange drink, or "fresh-squeezed?" That sounded good, so all three ordered "fresh-squeezed." Tom felt freshly squeezed when he got the bill, because "fresh-squeezed orange juice" was ten thousand won, plus a twenty-five-percent value-added tax, and a ten-percent service charge. That converted to around nineteen bucks per squeeze. They also offered Budweiser, for forty-five hundred. At the Sportsman's you could get a seven-hundred-and-fifty-milliliter bottle of OB for twenty-five hundred, while you'd have to pay me to drink Bud. But in Korea it was new, and people paid the freight, convinced they were buying something special. J.J.'s peeled off the high rollers.

The King Club had OB, but theirs was in a three-thirty milliliter bottle which cost only seven hundred. The King Club was an older club which had been around for years, but closed for a couple in the early eighties. It reopened about two years before, and with its cheap prices and better music it peeled off the enlisted men. It was a block up from the Twilight Zone on the opposite side of Fire Station Street. The Sportsman's was dark, with its bar on the right when you entered, and dance floor on the left. Its tables, with their battery-operated lamps were beyond, in the dark. When you walked in the King Club the tables were in front of you, the area brightly lit, which made it seem expansive. The bar was along the left wall, the dance floor in the back. The DJ booth was alongside the dance floor. Unlike the Sportsman's, whose DJ was upstairs, a carryover from the days when the place was so busy it needed two floors, the King Club DJ could see how people were responding, and change up. The Sportsman's leaned heavily on tapes of electronic European dance music. The King Club had newer stuff, like "Wild Wild West," by Kool Moe Dee, which pulled the crowd onto the dance floor.

Which is where Beth and I were when a mini-riot broke out. Two guys got into it, one was pushed, knocking over a table, and others joined the brawl. I never saw a fight with the potential to turn into a melee broken up so fast! Even before the bouncers could get there, whistles were blowing and plainclothes police were piling in.

It seems the Swedish Olympic team was in the house. Most of us were herded against one wall, while everyone with blonde hair was escorted out by Olympic security officers.

The games had started! And you could practically trip over athletes. I found myself in line at Wendy's behind a boxer from

Chicago. We didn't know each other, but felt like, after coming all the way from Chicago to Seoul, we ought to.

I had chosen an assortment of events. I had one track and field day. That was at a new stadium built over south of the river. I got to see some famous names. For one I had to squint. Sergey Bubka was competing, but the pole vaulting was on the far side of the track from where I sat. Luckily, most of the action was on the near side; Jackie Joyner-Kersee, Florence Griffith Joyner, and Carl Lewis all put in appearances. Besides track and field, I watched some table tennis. I used to play myself, though not well enough to have scored a point against those athletes.

The best event was taekwondo. As host Korea was allowed to introduce an exhibition sport, and taekwondo was it. One of the categories was Women under 140 pounds. There was a competitor from Chicago named Eileen something or other. Her style was actually kung fu, though it looked enough like taekwondo it hardly mattered what it was called. The other women were products of the same mold, Asian fireplugs less than five-four. Eileen was around five-ten, rangy and raw-boned.

Her opponents assumed a fighting stance, and threw beautiful taekwondo kicks. Lots of style, but since they fell a couple of feet short of making contact, not effective. Her approach was different. She would draw up her left leg to her chest, her shin guarding her body, and then she would hop at her opponent, punching down as she came. The rules forbade landing punches on the face, but her opponents didn't like being crowded by a flurry of fists. They would jump back. As they did, she would plant her left foot, and throw a high roundhouse kick with her right. Punches couldn't make head contact, but feet could.

Whap!

Her foot would smack them on their left ear. Two of them she actually knocked cold.

She won the gold medal. All the other gold medalists had been Korean, and when the medals were awarded whoever was in charge of the music had no trouble playing "*Aegukka.*" They weren't expecting an American, and couldn't find the "Star Spangled Banner." There were American athletes whose events weren't scheduled the first day, who had come to root for her, so they launched into an a cappella version. Meanwhile, the music was found, and began playing, half a verse behind the singers. It was a mess.

A mess some whispered was deliberate. It had shaped up as that sort of summer. The summer of 1988 saw record-breaking heat. It was in the nineties every day, for months. Some days it was nearly a hundred. Most people did not have air-conditioning. Our apartment didn't, just tiny fans. It was very humid, and the ozone levels were high. There was also the ubiquitous tear gas hanging in the air, and the traffic-disrupting riots. They went on even as the Olympics began. I remember one Friday there was talk of going down to watch them. There was a riot scheduled for early evening. Yes, scheduled. It would happen conveniently in front of the hotel downtown favored by foreign journalists. There was even a bar on the sixth floor with plate glass windows. The scribes could enjoy happy hour while watching the fun out the window, on the street below. I thought about going down myself, but traffic promised to be a bitch.

Anti-Americanism flared like a scab that had been picked at. If Americans thinking the failure to play the "Star Spangled Banner" in timely fashion was a silly conspiracy theory, they had nothing on the Koreans. For instance, the Opening Ceremony snub of the Los Angeles Olympics. The which?

In 1984, as every four years, there was an opening parade, the teams of all nations entering the stadium. The network called off the names of the countries as each appeared. When it came time for the Korean team, the Koreans expected the announcers would say something along the lines of, "And here comes the team from South Korea! South Korea, which in 1988 will be hosting the greatest Olympics ever to be held past, present, and future. Yes, the Republic of Korea, a wondrous nation with a five-thousand-year history ...."

Instead, they cut to a commercial without introducing the Korean team, and by the time coverage resumed, the team had already made their entrance, and other countries were marching in. There were those who were certain that this was deliberate, a moment conceived at the highest levels of the US government. That was in 1984. Imagine how touchy they were in 1988 at any moment when things did not go perfectly.

One ugly moment happened the very first night. The first gold medals won by Americans, at least in non-exhibition events, were won by some of our swimmers. Their part over, with gold to show for it, two of our heroes went to J.J. Mahoney's. After a drink or four, they caught a taxi to go down the hill to Itaewon. While waiting for the cab they thought a souvenir was in order. There were some stone masks in the bushes, and they swiped one. An enterprising waiter or bell hop observed this, and hopped in another cab, *"Taeksi ddalla!"* And the chase was on.

He tracked them to the Twilight Zone, summoned police, and the pair were confronted. They denied knowledge, but the missing mask turned up in a potted plant, and the two were pinched.

Embassy officials bailed them out around three a.m. Then failed to win gold medals in the PR event. Outside the cop shop a scrum of press, mostly local Korean press, waited to pounce. One of our embassy people tried to shoo them by ordering them to disperse because, "It's none of your business." A foreigner high-handedly telling Korean's it was none of *their* business? Then the US officials tried to shrug it off as boyish hijinks, the mask a worthless trifle. The mask was valued at nine hundred and fifty dollars, around three months' salary for the average Korean, so it was grand theft.

The pair were quickly placed on a flight home, before they could learn how boyish hijinks were dealt with in Korea.

That scandal was soon eclipsed. A boxer named Byun Jungil lost to a Bulgarian when the refs deducted two points for a headbutt. Members of the Korean team attacked the referee, who had to be protected as he left the arena. Meanwhile, Byun staged a sixty-seven-minute sit-in in the ring. Naturally the network did what American television does, and played footage of his sit-in over and over. Koreans saw this as a deliberate attempt to embarrass Korea. Though in the long run its own bribed judges, who called the light-middleweight championship for Park Siheon over Roy Jones, Jr., would be even more embarrassing.

One of the most absurd, if least known, moments involved Frank.

He was hanging around the Gore-Tex shop, talking with Miss Kim, when a group of people descended on him, wanting "an explanation." One of the other shops sold custom made T-shirts. They discovered that the owner had made some special T-shirts, which they found very suspicious. The events were taking place in many different spots. A truck full of network camera people had gotten lost trying to find one of the smaller ones. To commemorate their adventure, they had requested T-shirts. The shirts showed a map of the Korean peninsula, with a truck labelled "the lost venue crew" overlaying it.

The angry mob found it plenty strange. What did 'venue' mean? And why was the rear of the truck projecting into North Korea!? Frank tried to explain that 'venue' was not an American insult, and that the map and truck were not drawn to scale. He didn't persuade them, but the lady who owned the shop told them it was her business who she made shirts for, and they could all fuck right off.

All good things must come to an end. Despite the heat, the riots, the ozone, the anti-Americanism, and worst of all, the barring from Paradise Beach, it had been a good summer. Now it was time to go home. October 1st was the last day of the Olympics, and it was the day I flew out of Korea.

On average the tallest athletes are the basketball players, but which are the second tallest? If you answered "volleyball players," well done! The Peruvian women's volleyball team was on my flight to Los Angeles. These women were all six-four or six-five, and lean as whippets. They wore matching track suits. Ninety percent of the people on the Korean Air flight were Korean, so it's possible they were the only people on the plane taller than five-eight. If not playing volleyball they could have competed in the synchronized bladder competition. Every two hours or so they all walked to the back of the plane. They used the far aisle from where I was sitting, so I could see every head in the section turn to watch them, each direction, each time. The Olympics had followed me home.

CHAPTER 41
CHOWING DOWN

t was easier to combine stories into one chapter, but many of the things I described earlier took place during multiple trips to Atlantic City. For instance, the time Girl George, Boy George, and I went to see *Rain Man* happened in the new year of 1989. I know this because the team had a Christmas grab bag, drawing each other's names. Tommy drew mine, and his gift of passes to the theatre for me was very thoughtful.

There were other team activities that January. One was a trip to a bar which subscribed to the National Trivia Network. It was new to me then. They were expecting me to crush the competition, but I let them down. Maybe it took getting used to. NTN is still around, but called Buzztime these days. Instead of the blue "playmakers" we used to submit answers, players use a phone app. I can still score in the top ten or twenty in the country with some regularity. I wish I had done so that night, but so it goes.

We also went to a restaurant called the Knife and Fork. Opened in 1911 it made lists of "best restaurants in America." It was nice enough, but I couldn't understand why it was rated so high. The place specialized in lobster. Boil water, melt some butter, it doesn't take Escoffier in the kitchen.

Most restaurants were not among the best in America. Other books about card counters have them, when not winning (or very rarely, losing) tens of thousands of dollars every time they set foot in a casino, eating nothing but high-end comps, "Another bottle of Dom, and make it snappy!" I wish it were true! I have had my share of nice comped meals, and mentioned some of them. There are comps, and there are comps. My first comp was at the Holiday Inn Casino in Las Vegas. The comp slip had boxes the boss could check to show which restaurant(s) were comped, and make other specifications. Mine was for the coffee shop, food only, no beverage, for a twenty-five-dollar maximum. I took it home and showed Munchkin. He saw the boss's name and said, "I know that guy. He got fired from the Castaways for poisoning a customer!"

I can't remember if I was comped to the teppanyaki restaurant at Caesar's Boardwalk, or sprang for it myself. What I do remember is that the staff was Korean, not Japanese, and were pleased when they learned I liked kimchi. It wasn't on the menu, but they brought me some. They had the most bizarre chopsticks I've ever seen. They took for granted American ineptitude. These chopsticks were like a backward clothespin. Take two tongue depressors, put a spring in the middle, then squeeze the open ends together to snag food. It was embarrassing!

Frank and I did go to a place that was famous. It was called the White House, and had what were supposed to be some of the best Philly Cheesesteaks around. Philly Cheesesteaks are okay, but even the greatest won't impress me. I was more impressed with how questionable our choice was. We walked over there at three in the morning. The restaurant was near Arctic Avenue, close to the projects, and we each had a few thousand dollars in our pockets.

Most nights I ate at a place called the Baltimore Grill. Back home I knew of a few restaurants which were open all night, and had liquor licenses. They had to stop serving at midnight or one, or whatever time they were licensed for, serving only food until the next day. The Baltimore Grill did it backwards; they stopped serving food at three, but you could drink all night.

I was in there one night with a guy we used as a big player. His name was Jeffy, and he was a professional poker player. The Baltimore Grill served pizza. It was bad pizza, with very greasy sausage, but I am from Chicago, and pizza is a staple. It took a long time to cook. Meanwhile, Jeffy ordered spaghetti and marinara. The Baltimore Grill was famous for its spaghetti. They had at least a half dozen varieties, and an order cost two-fifty. Jeffy's spaghetti came, and he wolfed it down. It was not a huge portion, so he ordered a spaghetti with peas and Alfredo sauce. He finished it, and ordered spaghetti and white clam sauce. Then he apologized for making a pig of himself.

It's always the skinny ones. Some of the biggest eaters I have met are thin, and the thin ones feel compelled to beg pardon. The fat guys just eat. When I lived in Las Vegas I had a bridge partner named Harvey who was only five-five, but weighed over two-fifty. Mama Leona's restaurant at the King 8 had a Sunday buffet, and we'd have dinner there between rounds. I didn't play one Sunday, and the next time I saw Harvey he said, "You missed Mama Leona's." No great loss as far as I was concerned. "I think they had ribeye steaks; is that possible?" I told him that it was Las Vegas, and anything was possible. "Well, whatever they were, I had eight of them."

It was also after New Years that I made a decision. It had been almost four months since I was last in Korea. With Walker Hill and Paradise Beach burned out, I wasn't sure how much more time I could spend there. I called Lee one night, from the Sweat Lodge, and asked her to marry me.

As soon as I did, I could tell I had made a mistake. Lee wouldn't say what was wrong, but I sensed my proposal had not brought her joy. I wouldn't get to the root of the problem until I saw her in person.

CHAPTER 42
NOT THE OLYMPICS BUT THE OLYMPUS

got back to Seoul in early March. It was as I feared. Lee had excuses for not seeing me throughout the weekend, instead of eagerly meeting me the night I arrived. Only when Monday rolled around, did she reluctantly agree to meet, at the Windsor Café, in the basement below Burger King, an old favorite of ours. She wasn't able to articulate the problem, but it seemed clear enough to me. The thought of leaving Korea terrified her, and once I proposed, she shut down. Even reversion to the status quo ante did not appeal to her. I think she felt ashamed. It was sad, but that's where we left it. Years would pass before I would hear from her again.

With Walker Hill and Paradise Beach unavailable, where did I play that weekend? I went to the Olympus, with Rocky. The Olympus had a half million won limit, which we planned to compensate for by spreading to three hands, instead of two. It also had the Berlin Shuffle, which made it an awfully good game.

The first day, though, we were shut out of the half million won game. The Olympus was a small casino, and there were only two blackjack tables in operation. One had the half million limit, the other three hundred thousand. I was shut out! There were only three players, all Japanese, at the high limit table, but they told me to play somewhere else. I looked to the boss, but he pretended it wasn't happening. I might have pushed it, but some other players who thought they were being helpful, began calling, "Hey, over here" at the three hundred thousand won table, "come play with us!" Since I would be betting the table minimum, I had no good argument for insisting I play at the higher limit table.

The pair at the game I joined were Chinese tourists, a father and son. They spoke English, and were happy to have me join the game. They were also happy when Rocky joined. They were happy guys! I was on first, Rocky on third, playing two hands, and they were between us. I noticed a few things right away. One was that they were counting! They weren't perfect, but they played reasonably well. When they spread, they tended to spread sideways before spreading up. In other words, if they were betting twenty thousand on a hand, they might go to two, three, even four hands. That part didn't thrill me. They were betting on each other's hands, which offered an opportunity. When it came time to start blazing, I gave Rocky the signal to spread to more hands. He scratched his face, to verify that was what I was signaling, and I repeated the "spread" signal. The only way he could do that was to bet on the father's hand. Fortunately, the Chinese were not betting very high, so he could bet up to two hundred and fifty thousand on the third hand. The Chinese player was slightly rattled, but his fears abated when he found that Rocky was not making horrible plays.

Then came a disturbance in the force. A new player hove into view, a super tanker on the horizon. Over the past two years there had been a few more sightings of "Mister Marty, professional gambler," so I knew who was squeezing in next to Rocky. I was not pleased. I didn't want another American gambler watching us play.

Marty played like the Chinese, spreading sideways. Otherwise, he played very accurately, moving his bet when he was supposed to, never making a strategy error, making the correct changes based on index numbers. He also knew how to shuffle track. The Chinese didn't seem to know, but they followed Rocky's lead, and offered me the cut because I "was lucky." Marty offered me the cut because he knew it would go where it ought to.

Rocky, meanwhile, had figured out that I trusted Marty's play. Came a hand where Marty had twenty thousand bet, and Rocky had two eighty bet on the same hand. They each, wanting to show the bosses what unconcerned gamblers they were, did an "After you Alfonse," "No, after you Gaston" routine.

Finally, we got to a hand where there was a double down situation. By this time, I prided myself on the subtlety of my signals. Especially with Rocky, I had them pared down. I watched Darryl a couple of years earlier, at Walker Hill. His signals were so broad I saw the dealer on his game recoil, afraid he might elbow her in the face. Mine were invisible by contrast. We had only one signal for doubling down or splitting pairs. Most of the time it was obvious as to which, though Phil once signaled split, and his big player doubled a pair of nines! Rocky and I never had that problem. The signal, though, was hard to make subtle. The standard hit-stand signals were "flat-pat, fist-stiff." The double or split signal was a raised fist, the hand elevated, and then closed into a fist. The hand was a close play, and Marty raised his arm way up, looked directly at me, and began wagging his hand open and closed while asking, "Is it this?"

I would have liked to have strangled him. Though I would have had to borrow an extra-large python to do it.

When shift change approached, I called the end of session. Outside the casino, out of sight of the front door, Rocky was waiting for me. We would ride the train back together. The Olympus is at the top of a hill. There is a winding, narrow road running down, and we were hiking down it, when a car pulled up. "Want a ride?"

It was Marty and the two Chinese. We went to a nearby restaurant. "These guys," said Marty, "told me they *thought* you might be a card counter." They were stunned to discover Rocky and I were together. Their names were Paul and Alex Lee, Paul the father, Alex the oldest of his children. Yes, I have sometimes given in to temptation and called Alex, Paul's "Number One Son." I'd be seeing more of them.

Though happily, not the next day. Rocky and I had the half million table to ourselves all day. Remember I said my signals were subtle? The boss who, nearly two years before, had spent two hours conversing with me, the boss who warned me I should give it a rest, the day before I was barred, was the boss on our game. There was nothing else to watch except us; the casino was empty. The boss was sitting in a chair next to Rocky, facing me. For seven hours he watched me giving signals. Unlike Marty, he never tumbled.

Not even when who should walk in? The same pain in the ass kid who had spotted me and Rocky at the Green Beach. He walked in, and said the boss in Korean, "I know these two. They travel together." Jerk! But the boss still didn't connect the dots.

Besides playing at the Olympus, and breaking up with Lee, I had another task to perform. The time had come to give up the apartment. We would still make plays, as long as there were playable games. We hoped to take a lot of money out of the Olympus. We just would not be playing enough to justify paying monthly rent. I talked with A Rha about disposing the contents. The paintings would be shipped; we couldn't part with Phil and his *kochu*! But we had other furniture. A Rha found someone who was interested. In fact, it was our black marketeer, the one who used to buy our duty-free Scotch. He came by with a truck, looked things over, and said, "These are all Korean!" Well, yeah. It was Korea; what did he expect? American goods, it turned out. It seems Koreans did not like used goods, of any sort, furniture, cars, anything. But if they were American-made, they might make an exception. Most of the stuff ended up on the trash heap.

This didn't happen overnight. Meanwhile, there was a chance to play blackjack right around the corner. Almost straight south of the apartment, on the river road, there was an American Legion post. I don't know if many Americans, other than me, ever visited. The place seemed to be by and for Koreans. I am not a veteran, and I didn't ask many questions. It was a gift horse, and not my place to get mouthy. Inside it was a casino, what people in Korea called a "black casino." It was unlicensed, but the fact that it was inside an American Legion gave it some sort of protection. They had no problem letting me in.

The place was very small. I was the only customer. Just me, two dealers, one dealing, one watching, and a boss. I don't remember exactly what rules they offered, but they were good. The limit was two or three hundred thousand. I played for a couple of hours, and won around three million won. When I tried to cash out, the only money in the cage was the money I had used to buy in. "Come back tomorrow," they said.

The hell! I consulted experts. Munchkin said, "Oh, yeah, I think that was the place Malcolm played. He got to the cut card, and had a running twenty-three. They did the Berlin Shuffle …" Yes, they did. "…and he cut the good stuff to the front. After the first deck the count was plus nine. He stood up …" Malcolm was six three, "and screamed 'Do you cunts think I was born yesterday?' He made them bring four new decks, spread them to show they were not short, and then had them deal an honest game. He won a few thousand, and said, 'All right, pay me you bloody twits!' Then he found out there was no money in the cage." Great, now you tell me.

The other expert I consulted was A Rha. She knew all about the place. "Yes, honey, that is Kim Inki. He's a gangster. Do you want me to send Mister Go with you?" Why would I do that, I asked her. "Because Mister Go is bigger gangster than Kim Inki." Now I began to understand why he was her driver during the tobacco wars. I told her that I would consider it, but first I would see if we could avoid gang wars, by going back tomorrow.

I did, and they paid me every *sen*. I would not press my luck by playing again. I doubt they would let me. But there were other places around, VFWs and such, and they had black casinos with great games. Though I learned the hard way that none of them had money in the cage. Luckily, they always paid the next day.

One of them was an Amvets in a neighborhood called Oksudong, over past Hannamdong. It was busier than the others. There were two tables in play. One was full, of Marty, the Lees, and a soldier named Ed, a protégé of Marty's. The other was me.

Marty was convinced that the dealers were going to try to deal seconds. Each table had two dealers who alternated, one dealing while the other sat on a stool. Marty insisted the dealer on break sit near third base, because he thought they would otherwise peek, and kick their coworker to signal when to deal a second. He also believed that the dealers would try to peek themselves. If they smoothed the top of the cards, he figured that was when they would try to push up the next card to peek. There was one dealer who did that a lot. She had popping eyes and buck teeth. When she started massaging the top of the deck, he'd hit the shoe, threatening to break her fingers, and her eyes and teeth would jut farther than usual. She hated Marty.

She wasn't crazy about me. Not that I hit the shoe or yelled at her. But I was winning.

The Korean and Japanese players always "took even money." If you are dealt a blackjack, and the dealer has an ace showing, you can always win one bet if you insure. If the dealer has blackjack, you push the regular bet, but insurance, half your bet, pays double, so you net one bet. If the dealer does not have blackjack, you lose a half bet but get paid one and a half times for your blackjack, also netting one bet. To save time, rather than pushing out an insurance bet and waiting for the dealer to check her hole card, if you say "even money," they pay you one unit.

I didn't do that. While you sometimes push, making no money, more than twice as often you collect one and a half bets, so in the long run you come out ahead. Unless, that is, the count is high. A high count means there are extra tens in the deck, and there comes a point where the odds shift.

This dealer, Miss Popeye, had grown used to my eccentricity, and so when I was dealt blackjack, and she an ace, she reached for her hole card.

"Wait!" She jumped. "I'll take even money." She looked surprised, paid me, and sure enough, she had a blackjack. Since I was betting the limit, she wasn't pleased.

A short while later, she got another ace up. I didn't have a blackjack, but I did have a pair of maximum bets. I had to stop her again. "I'll take insurance." She checked her hole card, and yes, she had another blackjack. The next shoe, once again I had big bets out, and she caught an ace. Now she hesitated, eyed me with suspicion, and I had trouble suppressing a grin. Yes, I was insuring.

She slowly lifted her hole card, and when it proved once again a ten, she threw it over like it was about to sink its fangs in her, and said,

"*Guishin gatae!*" ("Like a supernatural being!") I won four million won, and sure enough, had to "come back tomorrow."

Shortly after I played there, Darryl and a player named Art came through town, on their way to Australia. I turned them on to the casino at Oksudong. They each got a table, played a marathon session, and managed to lose sixteen million won. Not everyone wins.

CHAPTER 43
OVER THE RIVER

After closing the apartment, I might have moved to the Rainbow Hotel. The Rainbow was built in the alley behind the Kaya, and became the lower cost alternative, as the Kaya upped its room rates. My stay would have been brief. With no immediate plays at the Olympus on the horizon, there would be no motivation to let the cost of accommodations drain money. Instead, I moved to Bangbaedong.

Tom Casey's girlfriend, Jina, had moved out, and moved on. She married a young army officer, and went Stateside. Tom had a three-bedroom apartment with two empty bedrooms, and invited me to stay, rent free, until I decided to head home.

Tom's own life was in flux. Not only was Jina gone, but so was the Sportsman's Club. The previous summer, with competition from the King Club, and J.J. Mahoney's, the club saw a falling off of business. It became a vicious cycle. People would show up at the door, peep inside, and see how empty the club was, then leave. It was failing to develop a critical mass. Word spread, and people came to expect the club to be dead. After a while, no one peeped in the door.

Tom enlisted in 1958, when he was nineteen. He'd been in for nine or ten years when he was sent to Korea for the first time. Things may well be different now, but the way he explained it, in the years after Vietnam (which he avoided) a soldier after boot camp might be sent to either Germany or Korea for a year. Then to the States for a year, then the other overseas posting for a year, back to the States, repeat. That mean one tour in Korea every fourth year, and one tour in Germany every fourth, so in a twenty-year career they would spend five years in each place. But an army career is all about working the bureaucracy. Some G.I.s preferred Germany, some Korea, and they would try to arrange matters so they spent all of their time overseas at one instead of the other. Possibly even all of their time overseas, full stop. Tom arrived in Korea in 1968, and stayed until 1974. He was sent to Fort Dix for eighteen months, then went back to Korea, and retired there in 1979. I think it was Roger, another guy who planted roots in Korea, who said that the army looked with suspicion on those who wanted to stay in Korea. It was a career killer, but the old Korea hands didn't much care.

Tom met his wife not long after he arrived in Korea. She may have been the spark behind the Sportsman's Club. He had a partner at the beginning, a Korean former boxer who was a celebrity. They had a falling out, and it's believed the boxer was the one who blew the whistle on Tom's taxes. He had moved something like one hundred thousand dollars through an account at Fort Dix. Impressive for an E7. He told the authorities the money belonged to his wife's relatives, but the government had their doubts, and Tom avoided going to the USA while it loomed over him.

In fact, he only left Korea for the first time since 1975, in 1986. Tom had gotten a sinecure, riding on a school bus on base, to protect the kiddies, a "bus uncle." This gave him a residence visa, and SOFA (Status Of Forces Agreement) status. It was only a few hours a day, but he couldn't be bothered, and had someone cover for him. Until one day some ranking officer who didn't like Tom wondered what Tom's status was, and Tom had to leave Korea until it was sorted out. He went to Tokyo, spending six weeks hanging around Roppongi. Korean Immigration freaked out when he left. He had a ten-year-old US passport with no stamps; it was issued while he was in country, still in the military, and had no stamps in it; it was blank.

The wife was before my time, but those who knew her referred to her as the Dragon Lady, not always in an unflattering way. The club flourished during her time running it. Tom served as a greeter and schmoozer. His wife handed him a nice allowance, and he was happy. Tom chased women. His former boss told me he knew of two occasions when Tom spent quality time with five girls the same day. Eventually, his wife found a boyfriend, and things might have gone on as they were, but she became pregnant. They were divorced, she took most of the money, and started a bottled water company, which did very well. She left him the club, and he ran it into the ground.

I was the last person in the Sportsman's Club. I don't mean the last customer; I mean the last person. Tom and I were there his last day of possession; I had to turn off the lights and lock up for him, because he wasn't sure how.

Despite losing the club, Tom always had plans. He managed to pay off his tax bill. There was an American lawyer named Terry who crashed at Tom's place when in Korea, trying to swing some sort of business deal. He found a tax lawyer for Tom. Tom's tax bill had grown to around four hundred thousand with penalties and interest. The lawyer got it down to one hundred. Tom said, "That's ridiculous," and didn't pay it. Sometime later he pestered Terry: "That last guy didn't do anything!" The bill had grown again, but the next lawyer got it down to thirty grand. Tom grumbled about being bled dry, but he borrowed the money from his wife, and was finally squared away. He asked Terry what he owed the lawyer, and Terry told him the guy was a friend, so pay him what you think it's worth. "Hah, he didn't do much," said Tom, and sent him a few hundred.

Which brings up Janet. Janet had married an airman, and spent years in the States. She opened a Chinese restaurant outside the air base where her husband, soon ex-husband, was stationed. She dabbled in real estate, and was happy. Then they closed the base. Now she was back in Korea. Tom introduced me to her at Wendy's. After I moved into Tom's place, she started calling there. When I first moved in, I got up for a few days in a row, and went to the base with Tom, who was an early riser now that the club was closed. But the base was not so interesting that I wanted to wake up at six-thirty or seven every day, just to eat American food. I was the only one home when Janet called.

Janet was in the hospital. I don't recall what they were slicing, but it was probably somewhere above the groin and below the sternum. Remember how A Rha's sister, Jiyoung, was hospitalized, and I had to pay the hospital a ransom to get her out? Janet was in the same fix. She wanted Tom to pay. She had money, she said, plenty of it, but not with her, and the hospital wouldn't accept her US credit cards. She would have to go to a bank to get cash, but she was stuck in the hospital, Catch-22. She thought that Tom owed her the money. She had offered to help Tom negotiate the sale of the club, relying on her speaking Korean, and her experience in real estate, to see it through. She figured what she had done was worth thousands of dollars. Her mistake was telling Tom, "If I save you thousands, just give me what you think it was worth." Tom figured it was worth buying her dinner at the New Naija Hotel. The New Naija was across from the US Embassy, a bit of US overseas territory, or something. It had US beef, anyway, and you needed to be a US citizen or green card holder to eat there. "I can buy my own dinner at the New Naija!" Janet said.

I passed along the message that Janet called. You can guess whether Tom returned her calls. Janet began begging me to "lend" her the money. "Look, lady, I barely know you!" I was brutal, rude and ruthless. I was also weak-willed, and agreed to bring her a million won. She told me what an angel I was. I told her I had been conned by the best, and to save her breath.

She claimed that when I paid the hospital, we would go straight to the bank. When they wheeled her down, she was still in a hospital gown. She was in a wheelchair, which is standard, but she looked like she really could not walk. She told me that she couldn't go to the bank right then. She was too weak, but she could meet me on Friday, and I was a saint. I gave her what for, and told her I knew what she was up to.

On Friday, I went to the bank, which was in Itaewon. I expected her to not show up. She fooled me. She had to lean on her niece, as she still wasn't very strong. She withdrew the money and told me again what a saint I was. I didn't feel very saintly.

Janet was not the only woman Tom introduced me to. One Friday a pair of girls came up from Pyongtaek. They were dancers at the Golden Gate, the same club Shin Jung used to dance at. Their names were Angel, and Cookie. They wondered if they could reserve Tom's third bedroom, just in case they couldn't find more interesting places to sleep that night? They must have, because they didn't come back.

Angel really was an angel, with flowing hair. I ran into her later at the King Club, and she asked me to dance. Afterward, I had friends asking me who she was. Beautiful women were the norm in Itaewon, but she was a head-turner.

Cookie, though, was another matter. She seemed nice enough, but she looked dopey She had the sort of expression cartoon characters have after the anvil lands on their head. She didn't say much – I don't think she spoke English – but Angel spoke for her. She pointed at Cookie and told Tom, "She's the one!" There had been a recent scandal covered in Stars and Stripes. An airman working in the comptroller's office at Osan AFB had embezzled forty thousand dollars, and spent it in the clubs, a lot of it on Cookie. Lady's drinks at the club were ten thousand won, for a small glass of orange juice (definitely not "fresh squeezed") with a couple of ice cubes taking up space. In one night, Cookie drank two hundred and sixty-nine of them. Though a handy potted plant did most of the drinking.

CHAPTER 44
JIYOUNG

One night I was walking up Fire Station Road, heading for the Apple Club. With the Sportsman's closed, I was becoming acquainted with all of the other clubs around. I had a guide many of those nights. Dr. Black, from my Korean class at Ewha the year before, knew most of them. Either he was doing anthropological research, or he liked to drink in bars with bar girls. There were one or two other clubs with dance floors besides the Sportsman's and the King Club. Moon Night, a new one, was in a basement in the alley off Fish Alley, past the Honorable Jesus Bookstore. Sabi worked there, and I occasionally dropped by to visit. It was a soul club, which meant I sometimes got funny looks, but no one bothered me. The other clubs were all places with bar girls. Guys would go to drink, or possibly play darts if there was a board, but the business model was that you were expected to buy drinks for two, "one for you, and nineteen for me!" These girls must have been Beatles fans. They were segregated, by choice if not by any rule. Clubs with "country" in the name, or similar, such as the grand Old Opry, had white drinkers, while clubs with soul music had black drinkers. The Sportsman's and the King Club were racially integrated, but the former attracted older guys, officers and businessmen, while the King had enlisted ranks and English teachers.

Anyway, I was heading for the Apple, where I hoped to eventually charm one of the girls out of the club, and out of her undergarments. It wasn't going to happen, but these clubs sold dreams. As I walked up the hill a street girl grabbed me, and asked where I was going. I didn't want to tell her to beat it; she was very cute. I just said I was going to a bar, figuring she'd take the hint. Instead, she said she'd come with me. That was unexpected! The street girls didn't go inside bars. Introducing her to Miss Apple Club was unwise, so I said, "I am going here," and pointed at the entrance to the King Club.

She followed me in. I bought myself a beer, and her an orange juice. I spent the next hour or so chatting with friends, while she sat sipping her juice, and soaking up the atmosphere. I asked her to dance, and she was happy to do so. I expected that after enough time passed, she'd abandon me, but she seemed in no hurry to go anywhere. Finally, I told her I was going home to Bangbaedong, and would she like to come with me? She would.

Her name was Kim Jiyoung. Yes, the same name as A Rha's sister. Twenty percent of Koreans are named Kim. Forty-four percent are named Kim, Lee, or Park. (Park is also spelled Pak, and Lee might be Li, Ri, Rhee, or Yi, though strictly speaking it is I, just I, pronounced "ee.") Jiyoung is a very common given name; being named Kim Jiyoung in Korea was like being named Jennifer Johnson when my cousin Jennifer Johnson was young, and there were two or three Jennifer Johnsons in all of her classes.

Jiyoung's story was an unhappy one. She grew up in a poor neighborhood. One day she was jumped by a gang of boys, who gangraped her. While doing so, they beat her head on the pavement. The beating caused brain damage, and she was prone to seizures. The neighborhood ostracized her, and she moved to one of the towns near a base along the DMZ, where she met the love of her life. They lived together until his tour of duty in Korea was up, and that was that. Next, she met another G.I., who fell deeply in love with her. He was a Spec 5, a computer specialist, who turned down a promotion to try to stay in Korea to be near her. He wanted to marry her, and to prove his love, told her he had told his family "All about her." "Is he stupid?" she asked me, since obviously she wouldn't want potential in-laws to know she had worked as a hooker. Finally, she convinced him she would marry him, if he transferred back to Texas. Just give her the money for the trip, and she'd meet him there. Then she moved to Seoul, and had been working the streets of Itaewon for five or six years.

Jiyoung was skinny. Too skinny. She was five-three, but weighed less than eighty pounds. Despite her size, she could eat incredible amounts, even more than Lee. She claimed she once ate at the Lotte Hotel buffet, and was on her twentieth plate, her seventh of galbi, when the manager said, "Little girl, don't you think you've had enough?" One night at Tom's, she told me she was hungry. I was sleepy, so I told her to help herself, and went back to sleep.

Tom had only American food in his kitchen: Kraft mayonnaise, Oscar Meyer wieners, Wonder Bread. He imagined that all Korean women secretly dreamed of meeting a man who had a fridge full of American food. Jiyoung found the hot dogs, a pack of jumbo dogs, each a quarter of a pound, and ate the whole pack. Tom woke up to use the toilet, and found her watching TV. He asked if I went back to bed, and she said I was never up. "Who ate all the hot dogs?" When he learned she did it all by herself, he freaked out. I am not sure why, general principles, I guess.

Thanks to Jiyoung, I encountered a couple of Korean mondegreens. A mondegreen is usually in a song. For instant Jimi Hendrix singing "'Scuse me while I kiss the sky" is heard as "'Scuse me while I kiss this guy." The Korean mondegreens were not things I misheard; they were words I misread.

Across from the King Club there were some electronic games. One was Go-Stop, and the better you did against the machine, the more clothes your female opponent removed. She never took much off; we speculated the machine cheated. Another game was whack-a-mole, I had never heard of that game, and the Korean name read, "Talking Mole." Only it was in hangul script. There is only one letter, *liul*, for "l" or for "r," and I read the machine's name as "Talking More."

Something similar happened with a tape I bought her. She asked for a cassette of a pop singer, Kim Suhi, who would become a favorite of mine. The first song that caught my ear was "Nampodong Bruce." Jiyoung explained that Nampodong was a neighborhood in Busan, and "Bruce" was .., I understood it to be a type of dance, "Do the Freddy," "Do the Bruce," like that. It must have been a year later I realized it was "Nampodong Blues."

CHAPTER 45
EARNING MY KEEP

Tom was not idle. He had another scheme to make some money, a pretty good scheme. He submitted a BPA (Blanket Purchase Agreement) which was accepted. He would provide a traveling Las Vegas night. It would move around the bases, setting up in the base clubs. Any winnings would be split between the club, and Tom. I believe Tom had to eat any losses, but casinos are not known for losing money.

He borrowed another thirty thousand from his ex-wife, and hired Marty to source the equipment, hire the dealers, training them if necessary, and otherwise run the operation. The first two nights he held it, on consecutive weekends, Rocky was back in town, and I was again playing at the Olympus. When his third date rolled around, I was free, and he asked if I wanted to come see the operation. I did. "Wear a suit," he said.

We drove up to an army base near the DMZ. There are lots of them strung along the northern edge of the Republic of Korea. While much smaller than Yongsan, and with far fewer amenities, it had a club for weary warriors, to eat, drink, and make merry. Two rooms had been cleared for us to set up, and in short order there were half a dozen blackjack tables, a roulette wheel, and a crap table.

The dealers, I would learn, were recruited from black casinos, or had previously worked for one of the legal casinos. That was the case for Mrs. Park. She was, at least at the time, the only female pit boss in Korean history, when she worked at Walker Hill. Now she was the senior of the two bosses manning the blackjack pit. She shared duties with a woman named Kyonghi, who had been a blackjack dealer in Nevada, when her ex-husband was stationed there. The casino manager was Marty, but he was stuck behind the crap table, which led to a minor debacle.

Things started slowly. It was early evening, and the G.I.s and their girlfriends drifted in. Only the crap table got busy quickly. Tom nudged me, and said, "Take a look at that! Really, something, huh?" as he pointed at the blackjack tables. It was something, as real a casino as imaginable. "Why not take a look from behind the tables?" That was his game, to get an extra boss policing things. I had never worked for a casino in any capacity, never gone to dealers' school, never been a pit boss, never had any training for that side of the table. Then again, I had spent thousands of hours in casinos, so I knew a lot about the game, and how it should be dealt. Taking a turn behind the tables seemed like fun. What could go wrong?

Watching the games was easy. Had any of the players shown signs of intelligence I would have given them my nearly undivided attention. Scottie, the shift manager at the Castaways called card counters "students;" there were no students at these tables. Nor was there any sign of funny business, card marking or mucking. Even as it got busy, and all of the seats filled up, keeping an eye on the tables wasn't a problem. Kyonghi was friendly. Mrs. Park was not. She wanted to assert herself as the big dog in the kennel, but the fact that I was male, and a friend of Tom's, kept her wary of pushing too hard.

Tom's deal was to split with the club, which meant that any club he went to had a manager with whom he coordinated. This was the first time the club would host the games, and the manager was nervous. He wanted things to go right. As the place filled, he asked Tom to open another table. When that filled, still another. We had spare tables, and spare dealers, sort of. The spare dealers were the ones on break. At the manager's behest, Tom opened tables until he ran out of dealers.

One of the dealers managed to signal Marty. Marty needed to keep an eye on the crap table, so was most unhappy that he had to abandon his post to deal with the situation Tom had created. Marty was bad enough when he was in a good mood. Marty in a bad mood was not someone you wanted to see heading your way. He gave Tom an earful, worked out a way to systematically close some tables, so the dealers could have their breaks, and then hollered at me for good measure because "You should know better!" Then hurried back to the crap game before chaos enveloped it.

The next weekend was another casino night, and once again Tom asked if I could don my suit and help keep an eye on things. I could.

This time, while things were slow in the blackjack pit, easily managed by Mrs. Park and Kyonghi, I wandered over to the crap table, to see what had Marty glued to it. "Explain this game," I asked him.

Having played backgammon for ten years by then, I understood the basics of dice odds. Each die has six faces, with one through six pips. Six times six is thirty-six, the total number of combinations when two dice are thrown. The odds are based on that. I explained many chapters ago when describing the game at the Rainbow Club, that the pass line bet slightly favors the house. The don't pass bet would conversely favor the player, if the house failed to bar twelve as a winner. Those are the basic bets, but there are many other bets on the crap table layout, most involving specific numbers. There is also a big chunk of table real estate called the Field, which includes several numbers lumped together.

Most would be dealers, attending dealers' school, learn to deal blackjack, because it is fairly simple. They may also learn roulette, the versatility of knowing more than one game improving their job prospects. Few try to learn craps. It is a hard game to deal. They memorize the payouts, rather than trying to calculate them, but there are quite a few to learn. Even after memorizing them, there is still a lot of math. For instance, if the payout is three for two, your players might have bets ranging anywhere between the table minimum and maximum. Quick, what is the three-for-two payout if the bet is one hundred and seventy-five dollars?

Marty had been a crap dealer, then worked his way up to craps pit boss, supervising multiple tables. You don't get a job like that through "juice," i.e. having a patron in management. Crap dealers typically break in at a small casino, and work their way up to a better job. The best angle for places like the Tropicana, or Caesar's, where the action is big and the tips make it a high-paying place to work. To become a boss, you have to really know the game.

Other than my few minutes playing at the Rainbow, I knew nothing about the game. For the next forty minutes, speaking rapidly, without repeating himself, Marty filled me in, everything from the difference between placing a number and taking the odds, to which hand the dealer was to use when collecting bets, versus paying them. In a later conversation he told me that one of the reasons he was the most feared boss in Sam's Town history was because when dealers crossed hands, a "no no," he had his own method of correcting them. The first two times he gave them a warning. The third time he clamped his hands on their arm, then bit them. They would scream in pain and terror. He would point to the teeth marks in their biceps, and say, "Remember those, the next time you cross your hands!" Even his bosses were afraid of him.

He had covered most things – once – after forty minutes. Good thing, because something came up over in the blackjack pit. "Watch the game!" he commanded, and thundered away. Now I was a box man. In one and a half working days, undoubtedly some sort of record.

Fortunately, I have a good memory, and had assimilated most of what he told me. Very fortunately, because my dealers had never seen a crap table a month earlier. Instead of a month or two full-time at dealers' school to learn to deal craps, the crew had ten hours instruction from Marty before their first night on the job. This was now their fourth night. None of them would have been hired by the lowliest sawdust joint in Vegas. The players, on the other hand, were very experienced. The G.I.s playing blackjack were a mixed bag, but the craps players were almost all black. They grew up playing craps. I'd discover that out of fifteen or sixteen players on a game, four or five were actively trying to cheat. I wasn't quite sharp enough yet to catch that. But meanwhile, we were having frequent arguments over whether the dice hit the far wall. The rule was a form of protection.

Cheats like Sal, who could slide a die, couldn't lock up a number if the die had to bounce off the wall at the other end of the table. What the players were trying to do was insist that the roll was no good whenever it was bad for them, but if the roll was good, they saw it the other way.

Eventually the arguments got to be loud enough that Marty appeared, yelled at everyone, made a ruling, and ran back to the blackjack pit, with a parting, "Watch the game!"

By the end of the night, I was exhausted. I was also hooked. I enjoy challenges, and trying to run the game was a challenge. The next two weekends we went to Yongsan, one weekend at the Main Post Club, the next at the South Post Club. I was now the box man, letting Marty handle all the other games. I even got to oversee the game with a pair of genuine, expert, cheats shooting the dice. One was my old friend Kim Inki, from the black casino at the American Legion. He was surprised to see me, and wondered aloud if I had been "sent" to take his money. The other was a man named Jimmy. Jimmy was Korean, in his fifties, and was infamous. Marty knew who he was, and warned me to "keep an eye" on him. From the way Kim Inki deferred to him, I didn't need Marty's warning. Jimmy picked up the dice when it was his turn to shoot, and did some fancy moves, shaking them behind his head, or behind his back. He was playing with me. He knew that I knew what he was. In turn, I knew that if he was putting on a show, he was just having fun. He wasn't going to try any real moves. He just wanted to see if he could rattle me.

By the time I finished day four, I felt fairly confident in my developing skill. The real test was still ahead.

CHAPTER 46
ON THE TOWN

There was one black casino I hadn't hit. It was the most conveniently located, in a building across the street from the King Club. It also had the worst reputation for cheating. When I went there, I brought reinforcements. I had Marty, Paul and Alex Lee, and Ed, an airman who was part of Marty's regular coterie at the lower limit tables at Walker Hill. I figured with four of them watching the game, plus my own instincts, we'd nail the dealers if they tried any funny stuff.

Marty had been there before. That was apparent when the head dealer told him he wasn't allowed inside. That was like dropping a coin into Marty, and cranking up the volume. "You can't keep me out of here! If you try, you tell your boss I will take away his rice bowl. No, I won't go to the *dong* police. I won't go to the *gu* police. I'll go to the downtown police! They'll be on him so fast his head will spin!"

With all of those eyes watching the game, I don't think the dealers found a way to cheat. I lost three or four million, the only black casino where I did. I think it was fair and square. Marty thought differently, "I told you they cheated!" "Yeah? Why'd you let them?"

The last black casino out of my system, I found other things to do in Itaewon. I even brought together that odd couple, Marty, and Dr.

Black. Neither knew what to make of the other, so they alternated talking to me, or talking to the bar girls.

We were in a place I will call the Bug Club. It was around the corner from the King Club on the small side street parallel to Hooker Hill. I was talking to a girl named Hyeson. She'd been out on the street, and picked up a snack. She had a Lotte candy bag, which looked like an M & M bag with one end sliced open. She gave me what looked like a chocolate covered raisin. I bit in, and found I was chewing on one of the most disgusting things I ever ate. And I have eaten my share of disgusting things. It combined two revolting textures. It was chewy as a pencil eraser, and also squishy as a noseful of snot, the one coating the other so you could enjoy both at the same time. When I was a boy, my mom sometimes dosed me with castor oil or cod liver oil. It's been so long, I don't remember which tasted worse, but when the spoon came out, I knew I was in for it! Imagine that a spoonful congealed into a semi-solid mass, maybe chewy like a pencil eraser on the inside, and snot squishy on the outside, but retained all its awful taste. That's what I was eating.

I asked Hyeson what it was. Her answer didn't help. I turned to Black, "What the hell is *bondaeggi*?" He thought about it, "Silk worm larva."

"Hey, Marty, try this!"

Marty had been talking to a girl. He swiveled around on his stool. Hyeson pressed a nugget between his lips. The expression on his face when she did was as expectant, and innocent, as a baby's. He began chewing, and in seconds his eyes bulged in horror, and he whirled, and spat … right over the bar at the owner.

One little silk worm larva was not enough to earn the place the name I gave it. It needed help. I was in there alone another night. I was drinking a pint of beer when I noticed something. A gnat was floating in it.

"*Mwarago?*" Said the barmaid I was talking to.

"*Pariga issoyo.*" ("Waiter, there's a fly in my soup.")

"*Ajuma!*" she called to the owner, "*pari isso!*"

I now had the attention of the owner, and the three barmaids. They eyed me expectantly, as the one sitting with me extended her right hand. There is a ritual formality when high status customers are served. She reached with her right hand, but placed her left hand beneath her right arm, to receive my glass. I passed it with the same formality.

The ritual was repeated as she turned, and passed it over the bar, right supported by left, and the *ajuma* received it the same way.

The *ajuma* closed her left eye, and peered into my mug with her right. She sighted the offender, and took a moment to consider: What was the right tool for the job? She held up the fist of her free hand, and – *sproing*! – like the blade of a Swiss army knife, her pinkie snapped to attention. It was tipped with a long, spadelike nail. Taking careful aim, she lowered the pinkie into the mug and scooped the tiny corpse. She brought it up to her face and stared into the bit of foam garnishing her nail. Yes! She had captured it. With a flick of her wrist she cast it down, expelling Lucifer from Heaven, down to the depths behind the bar.

Then with due formality the passing ritual was repeated in reverse, back to the barmaid, then back to me. I looked into the glass, to make sure the insect was truly gone. Four women held their breaths, waiting to see what I would do next. I took a sip, and nodded, to show all was well, as they sighed with relief. The crisis was over. Just another night in Itaewon.

CHAPTER 47
TDY TO TDC

Soldiers sent somewhere on temporary duty say they are going "TDY." We were going to Tongduchon, for a week. Tongduchon is a city north of Seoul, home to Camp Casey. Yongsan was the administrative headquarters of the military, but Camp Casey was home to the 2nd Division, and was the biggest, most important of the bases with combat soldiers near the DMZ. In those days the G.I.s up north were the only ones in the world, I was told, who were issued live ammunition on a daily basis. Every spring they had a fair. It lasted a week, Monday through Friday. The gates were opened, and the public was allowed in. This year the fair would have an added attraction, a casino. It would be open from early afternoon until early morning, all five days.

We needed more dealers, and Marty had found them. When I reported for duty, he said, "Guess who's here." She must have sensed who he was talking about. She turned around, and her eyes and teeth popped out so far, they practically attacked me. Yes, it was our old friend from Oksudong, now working for us. She seemed to be questioning her sanity, and we hadn't even boarded the bus.

Though he wasn't a club manager, a friend of Tom's and Marty's had an important job with the club system. Slider was ex-military.

He'd been a clerk-typist during the Vietnam War. Unfortunately, he was assigned to a Green Beret unit, whose commander told him "Everybody jumps." He survived to write a lot of letters to families whose sons died in "jeep accidents." Which actually took place in Cambodia, where we weren't supposed to be. Slider now worked for General Services. His job let him hire civilian staff for the clubs. Slider's brother-in-law was the biggest gangster in Tongduchon, and Slider consulted his brother-in-law on all hires. They controlled all the black-market trade.

We left Seoul before noon, were set up for business by two, and by the time we closed up shop, counted the take, and were squared away, it was two in the morning. Naturally, we went out to explore the bright lights of Tongduchon, rather than do anything as silly as getting a good night's sleep.

Marty knew the town from his days in the military. Those days were back in the sixties, and he didn't know it as well as he thought. Still, he knew it well enough to find the bar district. Some things hadn't changed. We planned to "pick up chicks." A good plan, but nearly all the chicks, in every bar we visited, were our dealers. I don't know if they were following us, but our paths crossed like a caduceus. Even if we'd met some likely lasses, it wouldn't have done for our dealers to see us dallying. By four o'clock every place was closing.

We found ourselves out on the main drag, near a taxi stand. It was raining, a sign from the heavens that we were not meant to have more fun this night. Marty had not given up, and had his back to me, peering down the alley we'd just used, trying to remember where he might have gone for fun in days long past.

Just then, two things appeared out of the rain. One was a taxi, the other a girl with a blue umbrella. I looked at her, and she at me. I said, *"Nae hotel-ae katchi gayo?"* She nodded that it would be a fine idea. We climbed in the cab, and I said to Marty, who was just turning around, "See you in the morning!" The look on his face was the second-best part of the evening.

Spending a week hanging out with Marty, I learned his story.

Martin J. Itzkowitz was born during the first year of the Baby Boom. He grew up in the Bronx. Other friends, also New York Jews, make assumptions about which neighborhood claimed him. Confounding expectations right from the beginning, his was mostly Italian. His dad worked construction. Marty claimed that every block in the Bronx had the same three restaurants, a Jewish deli, an Italian, and a Chinese. Three nights a week Marty and his mom would meet his dad coming off the El, and eat out. When they went to the deli, his father ordered a breaded veal cutlet. When they ate Italian, his dad ordered a breaded veal cutlet. And when the Chinese joint rolled around, his dad ordered a breaded veal cutlet. I have never been in a Chinese restaurant that served breaded veal cutlets. Then again, I never met Marty's dad.

In his late teens he got a summer job at Grossinger's, the famous resort, waiting on and busing tables. He didn't teach Baby how to dirty dance, but he was cast in the musical *Bye Bye Birdie*, as Conrad Birdie. He was cast not because he could sing, dance, or act; he was the only staff member who could belch on cue.

After high school he got a job with Streets & Sanitation, soon interrupted when Uncle Sam offered him an all-expenses paid two-year vacation overseas. That's how he first discovered Korea. After a year in Korea, he was sent to Vietnam. He was with a tank unit, which was attached to the White Horse Division, a Korean infantry division, one of whose colonels was Roh Tae Woo. The only combat story he told me was about a Korean soldier who leapt from a truck with a flying side kick. Marty stepped to one side, grabbed his opponent as he sailed by, and flung him. That was the fight.

After he finished his tour in Vietnam, he went back to Korea, and married the girl he left behind. He'd promised to do so, and she said, "They all say that. You won't." After a year in Vietnam, he was no longer interested in marrying her, but he wanted to prove her wrong.

Back in New York, he got his job back with Streets and Sanitation. He slung cans into the back of a truck for a while, but soon transferred to the "garbage police." "What the hell," I asked him, "are garbage police?" He told me that New York City has cops you have never dreamed existed, maybe fifteen or twenty agencies operate there. (Or did; some were consolidated in the nineties.) Besides the NYPD, each borough has some sort of force. There are transit police, Triborough

Bridge police, the fire department has its own police force, and many more, including the "garbage police." Streets and Sanitation owns a lot of real estate, and they patrol its property.

Then he applied to be real police. He said that out of eighty-nine thousand applicants, he scored twelfth on the intelligence portion of the test, and around two hundredth on the physical portion. He was also a veteran, so he was in. The wait to enter the academy was ten months. During that time, he transferred back to a truck, for the workout. During lunch hour, he ran, wearing his work boots. He ate one meal a day, dinner, a steak and salad. After dinner he went to a dojo and practiced jiujutsu for two hours. His weight dropped from two-ninety to two hundred, and "I could walk through walls!" The first month at the police academy he gained thirty pounds. They couldn't believe it, because recruits always lost weight, but compared to his prior routine, the academy was easy.

He didn't need to tell me that police work wasn't at all like it was pictured in the movies. Though he found his own way to describe it. "All you do is wrestle niggers." He never was in a shootout, but once was nearly stabbed. It was a domestic dispute, and while he was on the ground with the husband, the wife picked up a butcher knife, and tried to plant it in his back. Marty's partner kicked her just in time, and she missed. When the pair were both in cuffs, Marty took his service revolver, and bashed the wife in the mouth. Then he stuck in a finger, found three teeth still attached, and knocked them out one by one.

The trouble with that story is that he told a very similar one about his dad, and a German POW his father was transporting to a camp in Arizona. I have a feeling that Marty was not always a reliable narrator.

He caught a break when the city went broke. "Otherwise, I'd probably have been one of those guys nailed for graft." Instead, he was laid off. They did try to help the laid off cops find placement elsewhere. He scored first on the Miami PD's intelligence test, and fifth on L.A.'s. He and several fellow officers flew to L.A. to interview. They rented a car, got lost, and were late for the appointment. When they explained what happened, and described where they were, the L.A. cops said, "Oh my god, you were in Watts!" The New Yorkers looked at each other and broke out laughing. That was Watts? With houses, and lawns? After the South Bronx, Watts looked like Westchester.

He chose neither of the above. He got a job as a corrections officer in Hawaii. He was divorced by this time, and in Hawaii he discovered a Korean bar where he hung out in his off hours. The owner became his second wife.

Then his father died, of complications from diabetes. He left Marty thirty thousand dollars. Around this time, Marty had read a book about card counting, so he took a leave of absence, and spent a month in Las Vegas playing blackjack, mostly at the Sahara. The bosses gave him a room, plied him with food and drink, and introduced him to a Korean hooker who was memorable. She made sure of that. He told her that he liked her, but "a month from now, I won't even remember your name. That's just how it is." She responded by giving him the most awesome blowjob of his life. It was a two-hour torture session. Every time orgasm approached, she'd stop, squeeze his penis, and say, "What's my name?" He never forgot her. Unfortunately, she never gave me a blowjob, so I've forgotten her name.

I said he read a book on card counting. I didn't say which one. The book he read was Scarne's. John Scarne was a magician, an expert on cheating methods. He had some mathematical aptitude, enough to understand the odds on most games. Having some aptitude, but little formal education, does not a mathematician make. After Thorp's book became a bestseller, Scarne claimed that card counting systems were bunk. Then he sensed the tide turning. Failing to acknowledge card counting called into question his claims to gambling expertise. As a magician he pulled a magic trick. Instead of pulling a coin from an ear, or a rabbit from a hat, he pulled a card counting system from his ass. He now claimed he was the only man who had discovered the true method of beating blackjack, and offered his own counting system. The problem with his system was that anyone using it would be playing worse than the other tourists!

So did Marty lose all his money? No, playing Scarne's system, in a month he turned thirty thousand into fifty thousand. Back in Hawaii he told his wife, "Sell the bar! Daddy's a genius! We're moving to Las

Vegas." They did. One month later he was in dealer's school, and she was a cocktail waitress on graveyard at the Stardust.

Marty worked his way up at Sam's Town Hotel and Casino. First as a dealer of blackjack, roulette, and craps, he soon concentrated on the latter. He was promoted to Box Man, and eventually boss of a craps pit, supervising several tables. He also found a book with a real card counting system. He began playing at Caesar's, spreading nickel to one hundred. The bosses knew he was counting, but didn't care. He was betting small by Caesar's standards, and there was quid pro quo. Sam's Town wasn't fancy, but its steak house was a good one. When Caesar's bosses brought their wives or girlfriends to Sam's Town, Marty would assure the shift manager that these were "real players," and they'd be comped. In turn, they comped him to every one of Caesar's restaurants except the Palace Court and the Bacchanal Room. He took his wife to the Ah So Teppanyaki Steakhouse, and his girlfriends to any of the others. There were downtown casinos which had nothing but slots, places like Sassy Sally's. There were a lot of Koreans being hired then, and almost all of the change girls were Korean. He'd tip them his jackpots, then ask them out.

One day at Caesar's he met Ken Uston. The count had just jumped, when a man Wonged into his game. It was Uston. The boss ordered the dealer to shuffle. Uston kicked up a fuss. "What's the matter, you afraid to deal me a game?"

Marty said, "You got what you wanted."

"Pardon me?" Who was this player, Uston wondered, and why was he talking to me?

Marty turned and glared at him. "I said, 'you got what you wanted.' You wanted to be famous. Now, you're famous. And you're fucking up my game!" Marty looked like Zero Mostel's mean baby brother. He was twice Uston's size. Uston grabbed his chips and yipped like a puppy as he scampered out the door, while the boss cracked up.

Even Marty's bosses were afraid of Marty. Besides biting his dealers, there was the time a fight broke out between two customers. One was six-one, the other five-seven. "I'm no dummy. I grabbed the small one, and body slammed him onto the layout." But by the time the story made the rounds the dealers were claiming Marty had picked up both fighters, one in each hand, and slammed them both.

He heard about the blackjack game in Korea and took vacations there. When it was time to go home Tom Casey, and some of the other guys he'd met said, "You love it here. Why go back?" He decided they were right. That was around 1980 or 1981. He had been living in Korea ever since. He played low stakes, too small for the bosses to care, and too small to go broke again. By playing a lot of hours, fifty or more a week, he ground out a decent income. Like me, he had a five-year, ninety-day visa, so every three months he took a visa run, mostly to Manila.

I heard the following story not from Marty, but from a backgammon player who heard it from a friend of his. Marty was a legend. Supposedly Marty went back to the US after a few years away. He went via Hawaii, which is believed to have nastier Immigration officials than California. The one processing him asked him why he had been away from the US so long, and why he was spending so much time in Korea. "Because in Korea they don't put fat, ugly broads like you in positions of authority." That earned him several hours in the back room, and a complimentary strip search. I guess he thought it was worth it.

Meanwhile, back in Tongduchon, the casino was a success. We were operating twelve hours a day, so Tom sent help. He sent Roger, the E6 in army intelligence. Roger didn't know anything about gaming, but he was tall and owned a suit. He prowled around behind the blackjack tables, and tried to look like he knew what he was doing.

I continued to refine my management of the crap table. From the beginning I had been watching and calculating all of the payoffs my dealers were making. This had become second nature. The dealers, meanwhile, were getting better with experience, so paying off went smoothly. It was time to deal firmly with cheating. There were about fifteen players around the crap table at a time, and roughly a third would cheat if they could get away with it. They weren't adept enough for really sophisticated moves, swapping in rigged dice and the like.

They tried three methods. One was to move their bet from the pass line to the don't pass line. By betting the pass line they won on eight of the thirty-six dice combinations, all sevens and elevens, while they lost only on twos, threes, and twelves, which total four combinations. But on the other twenty-four numbers, they were now an underdog. Even the best numbers, sixes or eights, were six to five underdogs to the shooter throwing a seven first, "sevening out." If the point was four or ten, they were two to one underdogs. But if their bet migrated from the pass line to the don't pass, they would win on seven, reversing the odds to their favor.

They could also cap their bets. Suppose they bet ten dollars, and won, but before they were paid, added three more chips, to turn ten dollars into twenty-five. Losing ten dollars at a time but winning twenty-five at a time, is a good deal for the player.

Finally, there is the field bet. The field bet loses on five-six-seven-eight, which total twenty combinations out of thirty-six. The other numbers all pay even except we paid two to one on twos and twelves. That gave us a 5.56% edge, not great for the player. Unless he dropped the bet in the field after seeing the roll, only betting when it was a winner.

Because we had established that cocked dice (tilted against the wall or a bet, rather than flat) or rolls where at least one die failed to hit the far wall, were "no roll," I had to watch the dice to see if the roll was good, and quickly call a ruling. As I stood at the middle of the layout, behind the stickman, it meant that half the players and half the layout was behind me, and out of sight when I watched the dice. Any cheat outside my field of vision would try one or more of moves I just described.

I memorized the layout, or at least the half I couldn't see. Between field bets and line bets there might be anywhere from half a dozen to as many as fifteen bets, ranging from five to twenty-five dollars, made by seven or eight different players. Just before the throw I would be facing the shooter, the danger zone once I turned to follow the flying dice. I'd quickly memorize all the bets, and who they belonged to. Then as soon as the roll was called, I'd spin back, and if anything changed, I was on it. "Pick those chips up, Jackson; your bet was only ten dollars." I'd also gotten to know my problem children. Jackson, in particular, was indefatigable. He'd grin when I caught him, and pick up the cap, but next roll he'd try to slide his bet to from pass to don't pass, or drop a bet in the field. You might be wondering why I didn't bar him? I couldn't. We had no security in the room, and the club manager really did not want to have to explain to the brass why a player was ejected, if there was a beef.

It came to a head that Friday. It was around ten o'clock. By now the dealers and I had put in eight hours, preceded by about fifty hours in the first four days of the week. The table, the whole casino, was packed, our biggest crowd yet. The table was losing over two thousand dollars for the shift. That's a lot on a game with a quarter limit, nearly a hundred top bets. The players were jubilant, but it was an ominous joy. They were like lions tearing into raw meat, and the dealers and I were standing in the cage.

Then I was distracted during a roll, and didn't see whether it hit the wall, or not. The roll was a seven, and the table was full not only of line bets, but odds bets.

"That was no roll, right Mister Boss?"

I turned to my stickman. "Miss Im, was it a good roll?" "It was good."

"Seven out, line away!" As soon as I said it, the dealers scooped all the chips on the layout.

The players roared! They seemed to grow about six inches, each. These were frontline troops, almost all of them six-four or six-five. Me? I was five-eight in those days. My tallest dealer might have been five-two. We were terrified, because it really seemed we were about to be mobbed and stomped to death.

Then, like air being released from a punctured tire, there was a collective sigh, and the players shrunk. There was some angry muttering, but the danger passed. The players' hot streak cooled, and by the end of the night the table was even, or a bit plus.

It was after three by the time we got rid of the last customer. I was so tired that after doing the count for the crap table, I collapsed in a chair, and stared into space, my brain switched off. Until Roger and the club manager came, and told me that I needed to do the count on BJ4.

"Why ask me? The casino manager does that."

"Right, you are the casino manager."

"What are you talking about? Marty is the manager."

"No, you are."

"Since when?"

"Since about ten o'clock, when either Tom fired him, or Marty quit."

Ten must have been the witching hour. They started talking about the near riot.

"You mean on my crap game?"

But no. It seems the whole casino nearly erupted. The trouble in the blackjack pit involved a dealer grabbing the Korean girlfriend of a G.I. by the hair, and dragging her outside. Who needs security with dealers like that?

Meanwhile, Tom called Marty, and they got into a fight. Tom had some excuse for being back in Seoul, but we speculated that firing Marty was his plan all along, and he didn't want to do it in person. Marty was owed a bonus for setting up the casino, and a salary. By getting rid of him Tom would save on the bonus, and he assumed, get me to run things at a smaller salary than he'd promised Marty.

That's how I became a casino manager. From blackjack floorman, to craps box man, to casino manager, all in nine working days. That must be a record, and my rise may fairly be called meteoric.

CHAPTER 48
DOWNTOWN POLICE

om and I got to meet the "downtown police." At least, Tom did. We were heading to the base for lunch, when Tom was pulled over by an unmarked car. He went to talk to the occupants, a pair of detectives who did indeed work downtown, and came back shaken. Like a scene from a movie, they stopped him just to let him know that they "knew what he was up to." That was it. They didn't threaten to shut down the casino, or hit him up for a bribe. Just "we know what you are doing."

They weren't the only ones. Not long after I moved into Tom's apartment, I was sleeping when the doorbell rang. The manager was with a couple of telephone repairmen, there to "fix the problem with the phone." I didn't know there was a problem with the phone, but I didn't know there wasn't. One of the repairmen was full of questions as he made conversation with me. Where was I from? How long had I been here? What did I do for a living? And more.

Later, when I told Tom they fixed the phone, he was puzzled. He didn't know there was anything wrong with it. A few things to know. The apartment building rented almost exclusively to foreigners, which made it unusual. Even more unusual was the fact that a middle-aged telephone repairman spoke fluent English. In retrospect it was the

KCIA, or by then the Agency for National Security Planning, keeping tabs on the new kid in the block. Right down to, I take for granted, a tap on the telephone.

Though if they wanted to get the lowdown on what I was up to, they could have looked in the TV guide.

Korean television then was similar to the TV most of us grew up with, three channels, and dead air after midnight. Three Korean channels, and a fourth channel: AFKN, the Armed Forces Korea Network. AFKN was on twenty-four hours a day. Its programming was acquired from the USA. Korean bankers may have learned to dissect English grammar by diving deep into a work by either Graham Greene or Somerset Maugham. Why those two, I am not sure, but they were the two Korean English professors specialized in teaching. Korean bargirls, on the other hand, learned to actually speak English, by watching Sesame Street on AFKN. It was non-commercial, but filled with public service announcements. There were warnings to young GI's about avoiding debt, driving drunk on base, or talking recklessly while sinister Koreans raked leaves outside their windows. There were happier announcements. In one for the Library of Congress, Ed Asner looks up from a book on his lap, and tells us that, "George Washington had wooden teeth! It's a fact, in your Library of Congress." Careful, Ed, a Korean gardener might be listening.

The casino had done a night at Camp Red Cloud the day after shutting down operations at Camp Casey, and the following Saturday we had gone to Camp Humphreys, near Osan AFB at Pyongtaek, south of Seoul. While there, a reporter and a photographer came around, took a picture of me and my craps crew, and took notes for a story which ran in the TV Guide the military put out, listing upcoming programming on AFKN. It made me look like my middle was expanding, and my hair receding, but otherwise provided a record of my brief career in casino management.

Which was not fated to last too much longer. I had no intention of working for Tom for free rent and all the Oscar Meyer wieners I could eat. Nor would I be party to his screwing Marty. Still, I wanted to handle it tactfully. Leaving the country was tactful. I had never been to the Philippines, which was where Marty was going, to lick his wounds. I planned a trip to Manila, with him.

Northwest Airlines had an office in the USO, which was in Namyeongdong, right next door to the Kaya Hotel. Marty tagged along when I went there to book my flight. Some add-ons were cheap, and I asked the girls in the ticket office about various options, visits to other spots I had never been. The furthest was Colombo. Sri Lanka had casinos. The limits were low but the rules were even better than Korea's. There was something like eleven of them, and some were owned and run by Dick Tuttle, Sr. He had run a gambling operation on a boat in Saigon during the war. Legend has it that the last American out of town when Saigon fell was not someone climbing into a helicopter on the Embassy roof, but Tuttle. As the North Vietnamese Army marched in, he floated out down the Mekong, hands still being dealt. He'd taken his earnings to Sri Lanka, and settled in.

Darryl had met him. There was a major insurgency in Sri Lanka that decade, and the casinos bombed each other, and blamed it on the rebels. Darryl played in one, and won eleven hundred dollars. He was summoned to the boss's office, where Tuttle told him, "Gambling, my friend, is a very dangerous business. My advice to you is to not cash those chips." Darryl tended to ignore the sort of advice that included not cashing chips. He collected without any problem, but reflected later maybe he should have taken the advice.

With the insurgency ongoing, I asked the ticket agents if I had to worry about anyone shooting at my plane. "Teehee, shooting at the plane!" I took that as a "no," but in the end the extra cost dissuaded me, and I booked only Manila. Outside Marty said, "I don't know what they were laughing about. When I was there my plane was backing away from the gate when the rebels blew up the plane in the next bay!"

Speaking of Darryl and problems cashing chips, Darryl and Art came back to town, on their way home. They wanted another crack at the casino in Oksudong, hoping to get back some of the sixteen million they had lost. They got it back, and more. Neither could lose, and by the time they finished playing, they had won thirty million won. That was thirty million won more than was in the cage. "Come back tomorrow."

They were supposed to fly out the next day. They played Rock-Paper-Scissors, and Darryl lost. Art left, while Darryl postponed his flight. The next day he went to the Amvets, and was told "come back next week." Darryl argued, and when they continued stalling, he rampaged through the building, throwing open doors. There were business meetings going on, and he told the bewildered occupants, "Do you know what they are doing here? They have a casino. They owe me money. They aren't paying!" The casino managers, meanwhile, insisted, "You cannot do this! Do not go in there!" They grabbed him to stop him, and tore his shirt.

Everyone froze. Then the head boss said, "You come here tomorrow. Three o'clock. You get your money."

Darryl told me what had happened. I'd told him the story about Marty threatening the casino owner in Itaewon with taking away his rice bowl, by going not to the *dong* police, not to the *gu* police, but to the "downtown police."

"I am supposed to be there at three tomorrow," said Darryl. "These are gangsters, so I am not sure what they might try. It's a lot of money. If you don't hear from me by three-oh-five, don't call the *dong* police. Don't call the *gu* police. Call the downtown police!"

At three-oh-five the next day I had not heard from Darryl. Did I call the downtown police? I did not. For one thing, Jeopardy! was on AFKN. I was waiting for a break for a public service announcement. For another, I didn't know the number of the downtown police. Trying to communicate my need with a Korean operator was going to take some work. I am sure they were not called "downtown police." Mainly, it was Darryl. I knew that the chance of his being late was about ten times as likely as him being murdered. I don't think Darryl would think a ten percent chance of death was all that great, but the odds were good enough for me.

Sure enough, at three-ten a panicky Darryl called to say, "Don't call the police!"

Darryl had left the Rainbow in plenty of time, he thought. Seoul afternoon traffic thought otherwise. His taxi crawled through

Hannam-dong. Darryl began to panic. If the cops showed up before he got there, they'd bust the casino, and he would never get paid. He looked around for a phone. Then he spotted a guard shack, with American soldiers.

"Stop the cab!" he screamed. He jumped out in traffic and ran up to an armed guard. A dozen years later, and he might have gotten shot, but it was peacetime, and so even a gigantic maniac charging the gates wasn't enough for the guard to level his rifle. "A phone! I need a phone! Have you got a phone I can use?"

"Calm down, sir. What's the trouble?"

Darryl had stumbled on UN Village. It was a complex where civilians working on the base found housing, and it was guarded by US soldiers. Yes, they had a phone.

"I'm okay. I am late. You haven't already called the police? Okay, wait until three-thirty."

I made a mental note, four o'clock.

Before four rolled around, I heard once again from Darryl. When he arrived at the Amvets, three bosses and one brown paper bag were waiting out front. "Take it, and go!"

Darryl said, "I need to count it."

"Count it, and go."

"Shouldn't we go inside?"

"No, count it here. And …"

"Go?" There was a picnic table out front. Darryl counted, and it was all there, so he went.

As the day of our flight approached, I spent most nights hanging out with Dr. Black at a club called the Bavaria. The Bavaria was next door to the drug store at the corner of Hooker Hill and Fire Station Street, a few doors from the King Club. It was an unusual bar, because it was ground level, had picture windows, and a couple of booths next to the windows, providing a great view of the comings and goings on the street outside.

All sorts of exotic specimens passed by. Besides the tourists, off duty soldiers, and English teachers, there were the Korean denizens of the neighborhood, the *pikki boys* and the *hippari women*. The *pikki boys* "picked" tourists for their clubs. "Show! Show! Come see show!" I don't know the derivation of *hippari*, but these women, all older, did something similar. They latched onto strays, and tried to play match-maker with the girls they touted for. There was one in particular who was especially ferocious. She looked like she had probably once found herself in a ditch during the war, buried under dozens of bodies, the lone survivor of a massacre by North Koreans. Then when they were gone, she gnawed her way to the open air through the corpses of her own children.

Maybe not, but that's how she looked. She once grabbed me by the arm, with a grip Marty would have envied. She leaned close and said, "Young girl!" Then, exposing jagged teeth an inch and a half long, (I fancied I could see the rotting flesh of her babies clinging to them), she brought them nibbling close to the tip of my nose and added, "Oral sex!"

One night we saw four fights, most involving more than two partic-ipants. For instance, a drunk on a motorbike ploughed into a crowd, and four or five of them pulled him off the bike, and gave him what for. Around dawn a mad man wearing only a pair of jockey shorts came out of nowhere, screaming. Next to our window was the door to an upstairs club. There was a stack of plastic cases holding empty OB bottles, the stack taller than the mad man. He grabbed hold, pulled, and they came crashing down, broken glass flying everywhere. Seconds later the nearest *pikki boys*, even from other clubs, were on him.

Most nights if I was around that late, and Jiyoung wasn't busy, we'd go back to Tom's together. That night there must have been a full moon, because the house she worked out of was raided, and she and her coworkers Sunhi and Jina spent the night in the station house lockup. She saw all of the combatants I did, when the cops brought them in. There was also a drunken couple. They'd been making love with the shades up. Some kid spotted them, went home, and told mommy. The cops busted them for public indecency, but then put them in a cell together. According to Jiyoung they provided entertain-ment for everyone by finishing what they had started.

The night before I was due to leave, Black and I were in our regular booth at the Bavaria, when we spotted Tom walking by. Tom almost never visited Itaewon at night after the Sportsman's closed. My going out every night had him curious. Black was a more interesting conversationalist than Tom, so I was hoping he wouldn't spot us. Hope dashed when Jiyoung, the little fink, asked if he was looking for me, and brought him into the Bavaria.

The four of us had been sitting there only a few minutes, fumbling for a common topic, when a pair of Korean men entered, and went to a booth at the back of the club. The Bavaria was relatively large, and very dark, so if we hadn't seen them come in, we wouldn't have known they were back there. A waitress came over, and told Tom the men wanted to speak with him.

When he came back to our table, he was shaken. "Do you know who that was? That was the biggest gangster in Itaewon. He controls everything. I know him from my black-market days. That's who I sold cigarettes to. Marty better watch out. He says Marty threatened to take away his rice bowl. If Marty sets foot in Itaewon, he's a dead man!"

Later, Jiyoung poopooed it. "He not the biggest gangster in Itaewon, like Tom say." He was the owner of Moon Night, the place Sabi worked, and the black casino. But the biggest gangster was "an old man. When I first come Itaewon, he send *pikki boy* come get me. I give him blow job. *Pikki boy*, lots of time they give girls a hard time. But after that they never bother me."

The next day we were flying south over the Pacific, when I told Marty about the threat.

"What!? Turn this plane around! I can't let him get away with that. If I don't go back there, everyone will think I am scared of him."

I assured Marty that there was no rush. Outside of the tiny circle of people inside the Bavaria, I doubt anyone else knew of the threat, and I didn't want to miss my chance to see Manila.

CHAPTER 49

ENVELOPED BY MANILA

"Good thing you aren't in that cab." We were on Roxas Boulevard, heading into town from the airport. The cab was small, so Marty took up the back seat, while I rode up front with the driver, who was pointing to the cab stopped in front of us at a traffic light. I asked him why I was lucky, and he pantomimed holding a gun to my head. Why he thought the other driver was a robber – maybe he thought all other cab drivers were robbers – I never learned.

Before going to our hotel, we made a detour, to a currency exchange where Marty bought pesos. The exchange was in Ermita, a neighborhood not far from our hotel. It looked to me like Mexican border towns I had visited, though the exchange had something I hadn't seen in Mexico. Sitting out front on a stool was a security guard with a sawed-off shotgun on his lap. While Marty made the exchange, I fended off street kids selling chiclets, shoeshines, and pornographic keyrings.

Our hotel was the Silahis, and it was on Roxas Boulevard. The Silahis housed two amenities which set it apart. It had the only Playboy Club in the world still open for business. (In later years others would open and close.) It also had one of the two casinos in Manila, which was why Marty preferred it. There was a metal detector at the door, with a sign saying firearms were to be deposited, and guards to enforce that. Marty was a regular enough guest that the Assistant Manager, Wilson Y. Tan, greeted him by name when he checked in.

I was getting the impression that the Philippines was awash with weaponry. In fact, one day when we went to a mall called Harrison Plaza, to see a movie, the popcorn stand was guarded by another sawed-off shotgun toter. He sat under a sign listing prohibited items, which included "Deadly Weapons, BBQ sticks," as well as those not deadly but annoying, such as "Radio." I wasn't sure which category "*Bagoong*" belong to. Was it some sort of native weapon, like a machete? "No, shrimp paste. You know, she smell really bad!"

The casino was on the second floor of the Silahis, and had security guards admitting guests, after making sure they had not gotten past the hotel lobby security with deadly weapons or *bagoong*. Or books. I picked up a primer on Tagalog. The first time I went to the casino they overlooked it, but the second time they made me check it. "Don't you want me to study your language?" Not in the casino, evidently. Perhaps they'd heard the pen was mightier than the sword.

The casino was run by PAGCOR, the Philippine Amusement and Gaming Corporation. To ensure that impoverished Filipinos did not lose their last few pesos, they had to pay an entry fee of one thousand pesos. The exchange rate prior to the currency crisis of '97 was about twenty-five to the dollar (twenty-five and a half for the finicky), so the forty-dollar entry fee was a stiff tariff.

As much as a source of revenue, the casino was also a form of welfare. I suspect the beneficiaries had connections, to get their jobs. The philosophy seemed to be, why hire one, when you can hire two or three? Each table had four people working at a time. There were two dealers, who took turns, except during the shuffles. There was a boss keeping an eye on things. And there was "security." His job was to cut the deck after it was shuffled. The players also had a chance to cut, but this man's sole function was to take the cut card, and cut the shoe after it was shuffled, before a player cut it.

The tables had slots into which cards were dropped after each hand. When it came time to shuffle the dealer would remove a box from under the table, and empty the cards, to which those remaining in the shoe were added. The dealer would divide the four decks in half, and move over to make room for his fellow dealer. They would each shuffle two decks, then trade, each shuffling the other two decks. Then the decks would be reunited, and a final series of shuffles would make them ready for Security to cut them. It was even slower than it sounds. One time our dealers, caught up in the magic of the moment, began singing along to the muzak. The other players all started swaying and humming, as though we'd stumbled onto the set of a musical comedy. Marty did not have music in his heart, and looked as though, if "Itaewon's biggest gangster" didn't kill him, a stroke might.

The game was faster than the shuffling, but not by much. The dealers seldom managed forty rounds an hour. It could have been worse; Marty said he once clocked the mini-baccarat tables, and found they averaged nineteen rounds an hour.

Besides being torturously slow, the game was just plain bad. It was four decks, of which they dealt about three, but the dealer hit soft seventeen, and the high limit games had a two-thousand-peso limit. It was a complete waste of time, but Marty insisted on playing it, because it was there, and he felt duty bound to take advantage of it. I kept him company because he could spread onto the hands I played for him. Given its glacial pace, I had no trouble reading while playing, and still keeping the count. Or would have, if they hadn't taken my book. I had other arrows in my quiver. The next time I brought a stack of post-cards, and wrote them while I played. As long as I didn't spread them too close to the chip rack, the staff was bemused.

I'd heard stories about Paul, the Australian, and his legendary anal-retentive style. He and Malcom once, on a bankroll where they spread one to ten in black, with a three-hundred-dollar unit, argued about whether a three hundred and fifty, or a three hundred and seventy-five, dollar bet was called for. Marty topped him. Given the low limits, he could have been simply blasting as soon as he got an edge. But Marty seemed to think that the important idea in betting schemes was structure. If the limit had been five dollars, I am sure instead of betting either one dollar, or five, he would have bet double twos at a plus two, and gradually worked his way up.

Came a hand where the running count was plus six. They had dealt two and a half decks, so the true count was four, but Marty made his plus three bet.

"You goofed. The true count is plus four."

Because there was no discard tray to eyeball Marty counted the number of rounds, then calculated the average number of cards dealt. The average number of cards per hand is two-point-seven. All seven spots were being played, plus the dealer's hand, and eight times two-point-seven is twenty-one-point-six cards per round. "There have been six rounds played; times twenty-one-point-six is one-twenty-nine-point-six. Two hundred and eight minus one-twenty-nine-point-six is seventy-eight-point-four. That's more than a deck and a half, so it isn't a true four yet."

Got me there! It was only a true three-point-nine-eight. I told that story more than a few times. Once to Art, who told me his own research found that while the average player hand received two-point-seven cards, the average dealer hand got two-point-nine. Next time I saw Marty, I told him that, and he said he didn't care because "it wasn't official."

That was how Marty, and sometimes I, spent our afternoons. I couldn't take it every day, and swam, visited museums, and other touristy stuff. Evenings, we went to Ermita. Ermita in those days was a tourist magnet, partly for its restaurants, but mostly for its bars. The most famous was the Firehouse. Legend had it that the bar was opened by literal visiting firemen. They'd come to the Philippines to consult on upgrading Manila's fire services. They stayed, and opened a bar, in which they introduced fire poles. The dancers on stage pole danced, and the other bars copied the Firehouse.

Depending on how hard the authorities were cracking down, the dancers wore two-piece outfits, or bikinis, or bikini bottoms, or sometimes none of the above, at least nothing while on stage. Though they might tie the bathing suit around their thigh while dancing, because pinned to the suit was a badge with a number. The bars' middle managers were its mamasans. Patrons would summon one, point, and say, "I'd like to buy Forty-Seven a drink," and when she finished dancing, Forty-Seven would come to the man's table. If the pair hit it off – the dancers had a say in the matter, but most were very accommodating – the man might call over the mamasan and make additional arrangements. A "short-time" was three hundred pesos while overnight was a thousand. It was taken for granted the girl would receive an additional tip, though that was between customer and girl.

I read an account of the filming of the movie *Saint Jack*. The book and movie were set in a neighborhood in Singapore called Bugis Street, which was notorious in its day. By the time the movie was made, Bugis Street was still active, but its female, transvestite, and transexual sex workers would vanish in the near future. The movie was directed by Peter Bogdanovich, and starred Ben Gazzara. Gazzara's teen daughter came to visit, and she asked her dad why he and the director were out every night, visiting Bugis Street? "Research," he told her, "We're doing research!"

Many years later I wrote my novel, *The Battered Butterfly*. The action takes place in the summer of 1989, in Ermita. The protagonist is a fat, bald, irascible gambler named Lefty Markowitz. So, if you would like to know what Marty and I were doing every night, I'll tell you it was, "research."

I was amazed by how many people I ran into that I knew. I had never been to the Philippines, and Manila had about ten million people in its metro area. What were the odds? One was Roger. Not so surprising, since he flew down to join Marty and me in our escapades. He wound up just down the hall from me on the 14th floor of the Silahis. Nor was it inexplicable when we went to Makati, a more upscale Ermita, one night, and ran into the regional manager of Wendy's. East Asia was his territory.

But I was shocked one morning while eating breakfast at the Aristocrat Restaurant. I was sitting near a window, and at the Aristocrat, a fixture on Roxas Boulevard since 1936, that meant an open window. Just outside it there were people hawking *balut*, which I didn't want, and newspapers, which I also wasn't looking for, especially since I could read the headlines, "Irene rushes to Ferdy's bedside." Marcos was dying in Hawaii, and Irene was his daughter. I was concentrating on my garlic rice (only eight pesos) when one of the vendors leaned in the window and said, "Mister, somebody wants you!" I looked up, and saw two people waving from a car in the parking lot, Peter the

German, and his girlfriend, Miss Kim. They'd just arrived in Manila, and were driving down Roxas in a rental car, when Peter decided he needed a payphone, swung into the Aristocrat parking lot, and spotted me through the window.

Even more shocking was the afternoon someone knocked on my hotel room door. When I opened it, there was Alan Woods, who was even more surprised than I was.

Marty had gone to the casino, lost, and made a run to the money changer in Ermita. He was on his way back in a trike when Alan spotted him. Alan waved and yelled, but Marty was in a mood, and ignored him. Woody flagged down a cab, told him to "follow that trike," and soon was trailing Marty through the lobby of the Silahis to the front desk, where he deposited his pesos in his safety box. Marty was on fifteen, but he rode up to fourteen, Alan still with him, walked to my door, knocked, and then stepped out of sight before I opened the door. It turned out Alan was also staying at the Silahis, down the hall from me in the room next to Roger's.

We were now a nighttime foursome. Marty was not fond of Alan, who he'd known since they met at the Kaya Hotel years before. It seems that on a previous trip to Manila, Woody grossly undertipped a girl he barfined. The mamasan complained to Marty, who gave her some additional cash, but never broached the matter with Woody, preferring to stew and let his resentment fester.

Woody was in his younger days the sort who squeezed his dollars until George Washington's eyes bled, but as he grew wealthier, was also becoming more generous. And he was growing wealthier. He boasted to me that his personal bankroll was now a million dollars. And that, despite his instinctual preference to short it, was "long in the Hong Kong market."

Marty had another stage on which to display his misanthropy. It was a literal stage, in a club in Makati. Makati is an upscale part of Manila, and had upscale Go-Go bars. One had a shower show. In a shower show some of the dancers bathe onstage, wearing what you would normally wear while bathing. We watched closely, to make sure the girls got really clean. In fact, we went back a second night to make sure they weren't slacking off.

We were waiting for the show when Marty growled, "Fucking Koreans!"

There was a group of Asian men wearing suits and ties, as though they had just come from the office. "Not just Koreans, but Korean cops," he snarled to us. "That one is a general!"

He summoned one of the girls he knew would be in the show, and whispered something to her, then slipped her five hundred pesos.

During the show, just when the dancers were fully lathered, she turned to the audience, reached down to her ankles, and slowly brought her hands up, scooping soap bubbles until she reached her collar bones. She lunged forward, across the apron of the stage, and tried to decorate "the general." He showed that a true leader needs vision and reflexes, by jumping backwards, avoiding the soap. The girl then strutted over to Marty, and high-fived him.

Roger hung around to see another show, and the next day told me that after we left, he approached the men, and explained that Marty lived in Korea, and had "issues." The general said, "But we're Japanese!"

Woody was the last of us to arrive, but the first to leave. On June 4th, 1989, tanks rolled into Tiananmen Square. It was not a good time to be long in the Hong Kong stock market. By the time he managed to get a flight back to Hong Kong to salvage what he could, his personal bankroll was back to three hundred thousand.

Roger had to go back to work, and after seventeen days, it was time for me to go home. Marty had decided to stay in the Philippines. I told him I would try to convince Tom to square things, to which he said, "Fuck him!"

Back in Seoul, I warned Tom that if he valued his money, he should make things right with Marty. He should do it because it was the right thing to do, but that wasn't going to convince Tom. I warned him that without Marty, Mrs. Park would steal him blind. Separately, I warned my crap crew about cheats, especially Jackson, and described what to watch for. Duty done; I flew home.

CHAPTER 50
FAREWELL TO THE BOARDWALK

By the fall of 1989 the computer game was drying up. The Sweat Lodge was gone. The team's new base was down the Boardwalk just over the city limit, in Margate. It was a nicer place, and smaller. The only permanent resident there was Girl George. She and Richard had split up. They were an odd couple anyway, the only thing they had in common was playing blackjack. There weren't many women who played, and their sex was a blessing at first, then a curse. Because there were so few, and casino bosses had no respect for women players, they made great big players. The problem was that once the casinos wised up, they never forgot them. Disguises didn't seem to help. While we shared the apartment in Margate George even tried disguising herself as black. Her "Pearlie" disguise was good enough to fool Irv and Anita, but probably wouldn't have lasted long in a casino, with many sets of eyes on it. Especially if she started sweating.

Bill Benter was gone. He'd made the move to Hong Kong, going into competition with Woody, who was not happy. While in Hong Kong I'd seen his set up. Bill told me that soon he would be able to link his computer directly to the Jockey Club's, and it would place bets automatically.

"Careful, Bill," I said. "Next thing you know you'll wake up in the middle of the night, and find it's on the phone to the States, betting basketball like a degenerate."

There were a couple of incidents which let me know that the fun had gone out of A.C.

One night I was heading back to the apartment. It was around ten at night, not late, but the number of people on the Boardwalk, especially in the off season, was small. The apartment entrance was on the first street off the Boardwalk, past Tropworld. There was a stretch of a couple of hundred yards between the casino, and the building. I could see a person on a pay phone, and a couple walking towards me. By the time I passed the pay phone, there'd be emptiness in front of me.

A teenager passed me on the right, and I sensed he was trying to look back at me as he did. I concentrated, and without turning around, knew that he had friends following me. They were planning to mug me. Rocky had been attacked once along the Boardwalk. A kid had jumped him from behind. Rocky was only five-four, and about one-ten. He was no martial artist. But when he felt the boy hit his back, he dropped to his knees and bent at the waist. The kid flew over his shoulders and hit the ground half a dozen feet past Rocky. Rocky jumped to his feet, assumed a fighting stance, and yelled, "Kiyaii!"

The kid screamed, "Mister Miyagi!" And he and his friends took off running.

I couldn't pass for Mister Miyagi. The boy in front of me saw the man on the phone, and the approaching couple, and dropped back to confer with his gang. I figured their plan was to wait until the coast was clear, and then they would swarm me. My one advantage is that I knew where I was going, and they didn't.

Without making it obvious, I gradually increased my speed, creating a gap between me and the gang. I walked as though headed somewhere way down the Boardwalk. Then as I reached the side street I turned and ran for the front door of the building. The other thing I knew, and they didn't, was that the door was locked, and the security guard was not stationed in the lobby. If they chased me, they could have caught me at the door, beaten me, and robbed me. They didn't know that, and so when I got to the door I looked back at them, milling around on the Boardwalk. They turned, and headed back towards the casinos.

The other incident was one of my last plays. George and I went to Caesar's. We were still playing New Wave, but just two of us, me betting double five hundreds as a top bet. A blizzard had struck. Not a major storm like some of the ones I'd seen in Chicago, but it had dumped ten inches, and the roads in and out were closed. There was a man at the table, around sixty, prosperous looking. He had played the weekend, run through all of his credit limit, which I think may have been twenty or twenty-five thousand dollars. From his conversation with the boss, it seemed they had given him an 'emergency" credit increase, another five grand. He'd lost that, too. Now he was stuck in Atlantic City, unable to leave, and unable to play. The horror!

Once the way was clear, I left Atlantic City, and have never returned.

CHAPTER 51
WHO'S YOUR DADAH?

"adies and gentlemen, the local time in Kuala Lumpur is four-forty-five, where the temperature is twenty-nine degrees Celsius. The government of Malaysia wishes me to inform you that the penalty for dealing drugs is ... death!" As he said it, the wheels touched down, and the plane bounced, to punctuate his statement. A statement echoing the printed one of the immigration card I had just filled out, which had a black border and the words "*Dadah* is Death" printed on it. Just like the banner inside the terminal, also reading "*Dadah* is Death." There was even a movie by that name. Normally I would have been less concerned, except that I had nearly gotten a rope's-end look at the policy myself.

It was the fall of 1991. After shutting the apartment in Bokwang-dong, and wearing out my welcome at the black casinos, you might have expected we were done with Korea. In the two and a half years since then I had played other places. Darryl and I had done some ace cutting. In Illinois riverboats casinos had been opening. At one in Peoria a young woman who left art school in Paris to become a casino host seemed interested in romance, sitting with me at the table, following me to the restaurant where, after losing ten thousand dollars, I was comped to a roast beef sandwich, even tracking me down to invite me to the casino's New Year's bash. I was impressed because I used "Jake Spiegler" as an alias, and she found my Uncle Bob in the phone book. I would have also been interested in romance, but Peoria was a few hours away, and she was attracted to who she thought I was, not who I really was.

In neighboring states, it was the tribes who received licenses. I saw a giant casino hidden in the middle of a corn field. I saw a crap table with buttons all the way around the rail. Dice weren't allowed, so when it was your turn to "shoot," pushing a button triggered a video with a random dice roll. Better than the casino in Wisconsin where cards weren't allowed. They dealt ping-pong balls with numbers painted on them. Each player had a wedge of wood with holes in which to place their balls. (You know what I meant!) Sometimes they would brush them with their sleeve and the balls would roll around the table.

I played a session or two of "depth charging" with Rocky. The idea was to have him betting two hands of the maximum at third base, on a full table with all seven spots. If the dealer dealt two rounds, on average we'd see over forty cards when the hands played out. If the count went negative after round one, Rocky would cut his bet in half, otherwise he would keep it the same. Arnold Snyder had published a claim that depth charging was worth one percent of total action. After the team lost a lot of money, Art did his own run, and found it was only worth point-six percent. To which Arnold said, "Oops."

Yet somehow, like a toothpaste tube that never quite runs out, we were still squeezing equity out of Korea. The possibility that one of these days we'd squeeze, and find the tube dry spurred me to book a side trip to Bangkok. I'd never been to Thailand, and figured if I didn't go now, I might never go.

I was staying at the Miami Hotel, on Soi 13. The side streets in Thailand are called *sois*, and when off a major road, such as Sukhumvit, are often assigned numbers as names. Black recommended the Miami. When I asked him later what on earth he was thinking, he confessed he'd never been to Thailand, but heard from an English teacher that the Miami was the place to stay. It's one good point was that it was cheap. I had the best room in the hotel, the night manager claimed. It was seven hundred baht a night, twenty-eight dollars, and one hundred of that was for the TV. The TV showed one channel, in Thai, and no matter how much you played with the rabbit ears, the result was a noisy blizzard. There was also air-conditioning, which worked about as well as the television.

It's selling point for the English teacher was probably its location, behind the Thermae Coffee Shop, which was the most depraved place in Bangkok. That's a bold claim, especially since I also visited the Kangaroo Bar in Patpong. At the Kangaroo Bar the entire staff, all seven of them attempted to sexually assault me as soon as I walked in the door. I don't want to impugn the pertinacity and skill of the Kangaroo girls by implying all they managed was an attempt. They did succeed, though I struggled, not because I feared for my virtue, but because I was wearing a money belt with nine thousand dollars under my shirt, and they were trying to remove all of my clothes right there in the bar.

Even with that high bar to clear, the Thermae was a winner. Out front on Sukhumvit it was the Thermae massage parlor. Around back in the alley was the entrance to the coffee shop. Bangkok's bars closed at one. For those still on the prowl, the customers who'd spent the evening at Patpong, Soi Cowboy, or Nana Entertainment Plaza, and the girls who worked in those places, the Thermae Coffee Shop was open all night. To enter one descended a dark staircase, which Dante would have appreciated. Inside it was also dark. One sensed unspeakable things happening in the shadows. The night I visited I was led to the back of the room, to a booth with six others already ensconced. At the opposite end, between two girls who were attached to him, was a John Hurt lookalike who was either comatose drunk, or dying of a heroin overdose. A pair of bouncers were ministering to him, one holding his head up by the hair, while the other slapped his face with a wet towel. This had no effect, so they dragged him outside, his lower legs scraping the floor, his head dangling, looking like a soggy crucifixion. I am not sure what they did with him outside, but there were dumpsters handily close.

The Miami Hotel was occupied by the sort of people who went to the Thermae Coffee Shop for the food. Not people I wanted to share my travel plans with, but was forced to. Before I'd left the States Butch called, to ask if I was going to Thailand. When I said I was, he asked if I could drop by Malaysia, since I was in the neighborhood. The name Genting is now world famous in gaming circles, thanks to its expansion around the world, but in 1991 it had just one casino, at a spot outside of Kuala Lumpur called Genting Highlands. Butch wondered if I could scout its game?

In the middle of the week I had planned to spend in Bangkok, I'd now spend two days traveling to and from Genting. This was pre-internet, and pre-mobile phone, which meant booking the trip from the hotel. Perhaps the Royal Orchid or Dusit Thani did it differently, but at the Miami to place an international call, you had to go to the lobby and prepay for two minutes. There were a couple of phones on the wall. Mine was next to someone trying to go to Phnom Penh. In 1991 I didn't know you could go to Phnom Penh, but the country was opening up. The Cambodia-bound person and I took turns yelling into our phones, while a lobby full of strangers smoked and spat and let their kids crawl over our feet. Every two minutes, around the time I finally connected and shouted, "Is this Genting Highlands?" my phone would disconnect. I finally convinced the manager that I really could afford to talk for as long as necessary, by handing her a thousand-baht deposit, and booked a room. Since almost everyone in the vicinity of Soi 13 now knew I was going to Malaysia, it probably accounts for what happened next.

The day of my flight, I had arranged through the hotel for a car to Don Muang Airport. I was in the car, waiting to depart, when a bellman came out and said the manager wished to speak to me. She asked if I was going to K.L., and when I said I was, said that a friend of hers was going to the airport, and could save me limo fare by taking me there. I was surprised, but pleased.

My bags were transferred to a car out the other side of the lobby. The manager's friend was about my age, well-dressed, and spoke good English. I sat up front with him. In the back seat was an older woman, all in black, whose garb hinted that she was Muslim. On the way to the airport the driver asked all about my flight. I was going to K.L., but flying via Penang? I was. What a coincidence, he remarked. His aunt, the woman in the back seat was also flying to K.L. via Penang. He noticed that I had only one bag; was that all I was carrying? It was. His aunt, on the other hand, had three bags, and the limit was two. Would I consider checking one of her bags as mine?

I was psychologically prepared to say yes. Recently on a trip to Hong Kong I met a friend of Woody's. She was from Australia, and made her living importing things from Hong Kong. She told me she travelled with a tour group, and was very good at persuading the others to check packages for her, to avoid fees. Helping a fellow traveler that way, especially after the man had been so accommodating in driving me to the airport, seemed reasonable.

Some instinct for self-preservation caused me to hesitate. I told him I would be more than happy to help his aunt avoid baggage charges. "But before we check in, I think we'd better go to Customs, and let them know that is what we are doing."

"Of course," he said. Then never brought it up again. Once he dropped me at the airport, I never saw him again, and didn't see his aunt on either leg, nor at the airport in Kuala Lumpur. I do hope she didn't learn the hard way that "*Dadah* is Death."

So are Malaysian taxis!

The trip to the casino wasn't so bad. It took two hours to leave K.L. and reach the top of the mountain where the resort is located. The casino was interesting. It was the largest I had ever seen. I counted one hundred and fifty-five table games, thirty-five more than Tropworld in Atlantic City. There were around fifty blackjack, and fifty mini-baccarat tables. There were forty-seven roulette wheels! Not only that, thirty-two of them had double layouts, which meant more layouts in this one casino than on the entire Vegas Strip. It was also a colorful casino, thanks to the batik shirts. There was a dress code, men having to wear either a sports coat, a tie, or a batik shirt. Most opted for the shirts, which rented for three ringgit, or a buck-twenty.

The game was marginally playable for us, with a thousand-ringgit limit on the highest-limit tables. Playable, if in the neighborhood, but not worth a trip halfway around the world to play.

The next morning, I grabbed a cab to head back to the airport. It was a ride that made me reevaluate the death-defying stunts of the drivers in Seoul. My driver told me he went through a set of tires every month. I could believe it, because less than five minutes after we left the hotel, he asked if we could stop to pick up some guy who'd lost all his money and was otherwise going to walk down the mountain. I said it was fine. When he opened the door I could already smell the burning rubber from the tires.

Genting is atop a mountain. The road is two lanes wide, one each way, and it is switchbacks all the way down. We went flying around them, blind, at around fifty miles an hour, skidding back and forth between lanes, as much in the oncoming lane as the down-going.

"This is the deadliest road in Malaysia," my driver told me cheerily. "It averages a death a month. Most of the time, they don't even find the car after it goes off the road." The trip took two hours on the way up. We made it in forty minutes on the way down. And that was with a swing through his company headquarters, an underground parking lot in which we averaged forty miles an hour.

Back in Bangkok, I gambled with something other than my life. I was playing backgammon again, and the Chicago Point newsletter ran an ad for a club in Bangkok in a restaurant called the Vinoteque. I called there looking for the man who placed the ad, Werner Kubesh. The restaurant manager, when I explained I was a player, said, "Oh, you must call my husband; he's a backgammon freak!"

Werner and I agreed to meet at Kings Plaza I, in Patpong. Patpong is a neighborhood in Bangkok notorious for its bars. During the Vietnam War it was located next to the offices of Air America, the CIA front, and became a hangout first for our spies, and then for our soldiers, in Thailand for R & R. A cluster of bars and restaurants grew there. The best-known, chosen as one of the ten best bars in the world by some magazine or other (the Firehouse in Ermita was another) was Kings Plaza, which by 1991 was the flagship of a group also including Kings Plaza II, and Queen's Plaza. It had a stage with fire poles, and enough dancers to fill the stage, while those on break from dancing filled the aisles and mingled with the customers. Werner, a German expat in his forties, and I, played backgammon while sitting stage side. The dancers had never seen backgammon, especially not played in their bar, and we were surrounded, a dozen topless dancers practically crawling up our backs and over our shoulders for a better view.

Werner asked if I played poker? I didn't, not really and was leery of getting into a game. But he told me the stakes were five, ten, and twenty-five baht. Twenty-five baht was only a dollar, so how much could I lose? I figured it was worth a small investment to see a poker game in Bangkok.

The next evening he picked me up in his SUV. Bangkok traffic is terrible, and was even worse in those days long before the Skytrain opened. It wasn't a problem for Werner. Whenever the roads grew congested, he drove on the sidewalk.

"Don't worry," he said, "Hap has a one-hundred-and-forty-pound Rottweiler." Hap was hosting the game. I told Werner I wasn't afraid of dogs. "No, not for you. The dog is for the police. Gambling is illegal in Thailand." Now I was worried.

Hap turned out to be almost a cartoon version of a retired sailor. He was American, around sixty, with tattoo sleeves. Back then only sailors and carnies had tattoos, and even most sailors didn't have their entire arms inked. He walked with a rolling gate, as though aboard ship. He had a professional quality poker table. They raked the pot to pay for it, and lucky me, I arrive on the last night, the one which would finish paying for it. Just think, if I had come a week later, I wouldn't have had to kick in for something I would never use again. There was a second rake, this for a pot that would be paid out with a showdown hand at the end of the night.

Hap's wife provided food, noodles and sandwiches, halfway through the evening. There was a fridge with beverages, and a price list pinned on the door. Adding to the air of professionalism, I was handed several pages of house rules, which included a list of acceptable games. Most of the games dealt were either seven-stud, or Texas Hold 'Em. They were dealt by the house dealer. He was a player in the game, the only one allowed to deal, though a button moved around the table to determine whose turn it was to be designated dealer for the hand. The dealer was around seventy, and except for the Buddhist amulet around his neck, looked like an old-time Vegas boss who had gotten his start in Steubenville. Werner told me later he was ex-CIA.

Two of the other three players were American businessmen, who reminisced about flying into Saigon on business trips … in 1968. It hadn't occurred to me that one could fly into war zones to sell Coca Cola or Philip Morris, but life goes on. The last of the players was a kid from New Zealand. According to Werner, he'd come to Thailand ten years before, when he was seventeen, and had "lived by his wits" ever since. He was the big winner in the game, clearing five thousand two hundred and fifty baht, and also winning seventeen-fifty when he collected the showdown hand. To my surprise, I also won, seventeen-fifty, a substantial amount, though only a quarter of the Kiwi's haul.

It helped having Werner in the game. He is probably why they were willing to let a stranger sit in. Werner raised every round unless he was not only clearly beaten, but everyone at the table could see that he could not possibly win. Then he just called.

Besides the cash, I came away from the game with advice on drugs to counter my intestinal woes. I had food poisoning, and needed something for my flight back to Seoul. Back at Gimpo I met Mike, my old teammate from Arthur's team, my flight from Bangkok and his from L.A. arriving around the same time. Mike was going to take a shot at the Olympus. That was part of our squeeze from the tube, sending in players to take a shot. Rocky and I had both been barred by now, but I was there to manage matters. Mike would go in, and fire away until he was barred, we hoped winning enough to justify sending him.

Though I later decided that it was sushi at a buffet at the Ambassador Hotel which wreaked havoc with my innards, I was blaming it on the Thai water. Mike and I were staying at the Rainbow Hotel. I called Jiyoung when I arrived, and when she got to the Rainbow had her knock on Mike's door to let him know we'd be going to dinner. She terrified Mike, who was the worst traveler since Jack, the New Jersey pool room owner. Mike was afraid Jiyoung might slit my throat in my sleep, then slither down the hall to his room, and slit his for good measure.

"He's very scary!" she said.

I agreed that he was scared of all sorts of things. "Even the water. I told him that unlike Thailand, you can drink it right from the tap here." So saying, I ran myself a glass and chugged it.

"Cannot! The government say koh-layra."

Koh-layra? "Cholera? Who says?"

"Government say!"

I asked Black about that later, and he said not to worry, it was a local outbreak down near Busan. "But you shouldn't drink it anyway, what with all the industrial pollutants."

Around that time the Rainbow had begun offering bottled water, and now I took them up on it. And felt reassured, until I noticed the caps and bottles didn't always match, and realized they were filling the bottles from the tap.

CHAPTER 52
GOOD NOODLE HUNTING

"Marty tells me you can take me to eat the world's best noodles." After nearly being framed as a drug mule, and barely surviving a cab ride down the mountainside, what was I doing, two months later, back in Malaysia? I had not come for the noodles, but if Paul Lee knew where to find the world's best, I wouldn't pass up a chance to try them.

The reason for the return trip was that last time around, the wrong person asked the wrong person to scout Genting. The first wrong person was Butch. Butch lived at Lake Tahoe. A few years earlier, back when we still had the apartment in Bokwangdong, he asked me about a game he'd spotted at Caesar's Tahoe. It was called Over/Under, and was a side bet Caesar's added to some of its blackjack tables. A player could make a bet equal to his regular bet, that his hand would total over thirteen, or under thirteen. "Do you think it's beatable," Butch said, asking the wrong person, me.

The trouble was I knew just enough to be dangerous. Was the game beatable? Just the kind of question to bug me right at bed time. I lay there, calculating the probability of all two-card totals. It turns out that the player disadvantage if he bets Over is almost seven percent. Under is even worse, over ten percent. I told Butch that the game was for suckers. Had he asked someone else on the team, they might have done some computer simulations, and discovered that while I had the odds right, there is a counting system. More importantly, unlike regular counting, where true counts are worth around half a percent, the Over/Under count's true counts are worth about five times as much. Once you reach a true plus three, you are moving into the advantageous terrain, and your edge goes up fast from there. The count also weakly correlates with regular card counting. You need at least a true minus four to bet the Under, but once again, your edge skyrockets after that. When betting Under, many of the losing Under bets will be hand winners, e.g. catching a twenty is a losing Under bet, but it probably wins the hand, so your bets push. It is potentially a very profitable game, especially if you are playing at Caesar's, with double after splits, late surrender, and a three-thousand-dollar maximum bet.

Thanks to me, Butch was slow to tell the others, and the team was late to the party. They played it, but briefly, before Caesar's cut the maximum allowable bet on Over-Under, no matter what the bet was on the hand.

I knew none of this until after my first visit to Genting, during which I ignored Over/Under. They had it, but what was its limit? To learn that, while back in Korea, I flew again to Malaysia.

During my stopover in Seoul, I got together with Marty. He'd stayed in the Philippines for nearly a year, but was back in Seoul. When he heard I was going to Malaysia, he called Paul Lee. There is a Chinese term, Sifu, which means "master" or "teacher." Paul Lee by dint of his age, and visits to overseas casinos including Las Vegas, was considered a Sifu by a group of young card counters in Macau. Part of Paul's cachet was that he had a "professional American card counter," Marty, as *his* Sifu. Marty called Paul, "*My* Sifu is coming to Malaysia. You take good care of him!"

Taking care of Marty's Sifu meant that when I asked about noodles, by god, I was getting noodles! Never mind that it was ten at night, and I'd just come off a seven-hour flight, Paul insisted on taking me for the "world's best noodles."

We parked in a business district, quiet at this hour, then walked around the block and down an alley. Midblock was an al fresco food operation. The cook had built a fire in an oil drum. On one folding chair was a plastic tub filled with dirty dishes, on the other was me. Since it was an alley, with standing water in puddles along its length, there were rats. The rats were kept at bay by the roaches, giant Malaysian roaches scurrying around my feet. If I were a rat, I'd have steered clear of them, too. The cook stir-fried the noodles over the open flame. Then he handed me a plateful, reached in the plastic tub, selected a pair of chopsticks, and wiped them on his apron. Given the state of the apron, I think it made them dirtier.

The noodles were good, but I'd rate them around fourth-best.

At Paul's house, we had dessert. It was on a hillside, with a balcony off the dining area overlooking the lights of the city. He spread newspapers, then brought out a cleaver, and a pile of fruit. Durian are about the size of coconuts, with spiky shells. Cut one in half (you'll need a cleaver) and inside are seeds the size of small rocks, encased in a yellow custard. Durian is called the "king of fruit," because that custard is delicious. The trouble with durian is that it has a strong smell. Scratch that, it has a STRONG SMELL. The odor has been described as resembling vomit, fecal matter, sewer gas, or all three. Those are its fans talking. Many people hate the smell. Sir Stamford Raffles, who claimed Singapore for the British, banned it from the city. There are signs all over Southeast Asia warning people not to bring it into buildings, or onto planes, trains or buses.

That's why we were outside. I think Paul secretly hoped he could make me gag. What he didn't know was that I smoked cigarettes for twenty-four years. Before I took them up my sense of smell was at least average. Smoking took its toll, and even after I quit, though it rebounded, it was never the same. I could smell the durian, but it didn't overwhelm me.

"These are very expensive," Paul told me. They cost several dollars apiece. "This one isn't fresh." He cut open another. And another. I think he was trying to impress me by wasting half a dozen durian in search of the perfect specimen. His family owned a plantation where they grew them. He explained that part of what made them expensive was that the perfect durian should never be picked, only harvested when it fell off the tree by itself. Then it was snatched up right away, and ideally sold and consumed within twenty-four hours.

The visit to Genting was mildly disappointing. Yes, they did offer Over/Under. They limited the bet to a maximum of one hundred dollars Malaysian, or forty US dollars. Coupled with the thousand-dollar (four hundred US dollar) limit on the regular hands, it made for a good game, but still not worth a special trip.

My visit wasn't a total loss. Paul took me to his club, the Royal Selangor. The club was a remnant of the colonial era. It opened in 1884, and its membership was restricted. The British left Malaya, as it was called then, in the fifties, but the club remained. It occupied a couple of blocks' worth of the primest real estate in Kuala Lumpur. When we visited, through gleaming windows I could see a beautiful restaurant, the tables bedecked with snowy linen, shiny silver, and flawless crystal. I could see all that, but only through the windows we passed as we walked around the club to the back.

In back was a soccer pitch, a vast expanse of green as long as two American football fields. On the veranda overlooking the greensward was a small restaurant resembling a hawker's center. Paul liked it because it was very cheap. He ordered a platter of satay.

"They are so small it's good we have a lot of them," he said. There were two dozen or so sticks to split between us. The cooks had a tandoor, and Paul ordered chicken. Finally, he ordered noodles.

By golly, he accidentally took me to eat the world's best noodles! I wanted to know what kind they were, so I could order them elsewhere, and maybe with luck, get something nearly as good.

"Chao mian."

That just means "fried noodles." At one time if I said "chow mein" Americans would know what I was talking about. Chow mein was chop suey, the gooey dish we all associated with Chinese food, poured over weird, crispy noodles instead of over rice. I suppose to make those little boogers one fries noodles? Whatever and however, I think Chinese from China or other Asian countries would, on seeing them, say, "What the fuck?" When Asians fry noodles, they don't end up with those things, and they don't pour chop suey over the noodles they fry. And when you have delicious fried noodles in K.L. or Seoul or

Shanghai, if you ask the cook they don't tell you these are "General Tso's great-aunt's bonfire noodles," they just say they are fried noodles – *chao mian* – leaving you to guess what's in them. The noodles I had in the alley were *chao mian*, and the noodles behind the club were *chao mian*. Even in Chicago, at a place on Higgins Road called the Formosa Restaurant, where the noodles were made with pork, shrimp, onions, and a peanut and chili oil sauce, they were *chao mian*. The ones at the club were fried with beef, and they were great!

I had found the world's best noodles. If only I had found a good blackjack game.

"You know there are cruise ships sailing from Singapore, with casinos," said Paul.

"Tell me more."

CHAPTER 53
THE LONG AND WINDING ROAD

When I left Chicago, it was the shortest turnaround to date. I'd flown back from Korea after leaving Malaysia, on December 18th. I spent the holidays at home, then headed back to Asia January 6th. I flew to L.A., then Seoul, then Hong Kong, then Manila, then Singapore, making brief stops at each destination. My return ticket would eventually be back through those cities, but meanwhile I would also fly in and out of them multiple times, with overlapping tickets. By the time I did use up my return legs on the original ticket even I had lost track of where I'd been.

When I reached Singapore, I intercepted Rocky at Changi Airport. Singapore in those days was two hundred square miles in area, and had a population of two-point-eight million, almost exactly Chicago's stats. It didn't look like Chicago. Even in the dark – it was late evening when we left the airport – we were surrounded by greenery. Periodically, a device on the cab's dash tinkled; to alert the driver he was exceeding the speed limit.

Our hotel, recommended by Paul Lee, was on Orchard Road, the famous shopping street. Knowing very little about Singapore, I had never heard of Orchard Road, and the hotel Paul sent us to wasn't fancy, maybe half a star up from the Kaya. It was spooky. Within the first ten minutes in my room, I heard a "whish" three times. Each time I found a business card advertising massage services had slipped under the door, and each time when I threw open the door and looked up and down the dark hall, there was no one around.

Paul was also staying overnight, but in the morning, when Rocky and I took a tour booked through the hotel, he slept in.

"Where did you go?" He asked, when we caught up after lunch.

I told him that besides Chinatown, we'd visited the Changi Museum.

"You took Rocky to the Changi Museum!?"

"Yeah, he's a big boy. He thought it was very interesting. I don't think they talked about it when he was in school."

Having come to Singapore to take a cruise, I expected to head for the docks. Instead, we went back to Changi Airport. Inside the entrance hall was a booth for the shuttle. Planes left for K.L. every thirty minutes, so you walked in, grabbed a one-way ticket for the next flight, headed to the gate, and within ninety minutes you were in the airport in Kuala Lumpur.

From the airport we went directly to Genting. Genting Highlands is more than a hotel and casino. It's a resort, with an amusement park, and a golf course. It also has condominiums where the owners stay when visiting the resort. When owners were not visiting the resort, the woman who managed housekeeping managed a side business by renting out units, perhaps not always with the owners' knowledge. Paul Lee knew about this alternate space. We rented a three-bedroom unit for twenty ringgit, eight dollars a night. From the living room window I could watch ropes of fog, the size of the worms in the *Dune* novels, crawling up and down the mountainside.

Rocky had been studying. He did not know the Over/Under count, but he was competent using Hi-Lo, and we played in the casino, on separate tables. Unlike the Koreans and the Japanese (Rocky excepted), many Chinese were aware of card-counting, and some had mastered a little. They backcounted the tables, creating traffic jams in the aisles. Whenever the count went up they would begin dropping bets on squares, to my annoyance. The profusion of arms reaching over our heads had me calling the phenomenon "the octopus." I had to protect my chips, and make sure I got as much bet on my square as I wished before they dropped their bets. They slowed everything down to a crawl when they bet, as every square on the table had five or six bets on it.

Marty told me later, when I was back in Korea, that he got so pissed (no surprise) when it happened to him that he swept all the bets off his square, and bet the maximum to keep everyone off. Fortune smiled. He caught a blackjack, and everyone else lost. He said that most of the counters were under the thumb of a gang boss, who sat in the lounge. After Marty finished playing, he went to the lounge and confronted him.

"I don't give a shit who the fuck you are! Don't bet on my square. I know you can probably have me killed, but I'll take a couple of your little shits with me. You don't fuck with me, and I won't fuck with you. Got it?"

He added, to me, "I don't know if he understood a word I said. He sat there gaping at me. But his guys never bet on my square again."

After a few days at Genting, we went down the mountain and took a shuttle flight back to Singapore. I'd be bouncing back and forth between the two like a yo-yo over the coming months.

The cruises left from the World Trade Center in those days. It's gone, and the cruises moved, but it was on Singapore Island, across from Sentosa Island. Sentosa today has its own Genting Casino, and a Universal Studios amusement park, but even in 1992 the island was a place for Singaporeans to get away from it all. Mount Faber is nearby. Atop the mountain were tourist attractions, such as the Guinness World Records Museum, where you could learn about the world's fattest cat, or the man who ate a Cessna airplane. There was a fast-food outlet of McLionel and King, which served fish head curry, and guava juice. And there was a cable car to take us to Sentosa and back. There was also an Air Defense Centre Museum, with a diorama whose models reenacted a daring rescue. In 1983 a ship hit a support post down below, causing a car to plummet into the sea, and a few more to be stuck mid-journey, with a possible death plunge imminent. The Air Defense mounted the sort of rescue operation you'd normally see in an action movie. Helicopters hovered above the cars, soldiers slid down cables to their roofs, hooked the cables to the cars, and airlifted the cars to safety. I'm not sure how many potential riders saw the re-enactment and asked for refunds of their tickets.

We boarded the ship at four, and despite the madhouse of check in, were underway at six. The Shangri-La was sixteen thousand tons, not large as cruise ships go, but large enough. Dinner was a buffet with Chinese, Thai, Indonesian, and Malay cuisines, Luckily, the dishes were labelled, so instead of serving myself some green stuff and some grey stuff, I knew I was getting Kan Kong and Ikan Kari, which are … Well, the Kan Kong is green and the Ikan Kari is grey. After dinner, most cruisers went to the theatre, where an international cast staged a variety show. Many of the songs were in English, but there was also a Mandarin-speaking singer named Ling Ling.

"Why is she dressed like that?" I asked Paul.

"She's a young girl."

"Okay. Do all young Chinese girls wear Martian bridesmaid dresses?"

At nine o'clock the show was interrupted by the announcement, "Will all junket leaders please report to the casino." Our junket leader was James Tew, assisted by his wife, Catherine. They left Paul, Rocky and me to enjoy Ling Ling's costume changes. An hour passed, and then came the announcement many of us had been waiting for. "The casino is open." We were now in international waters, where gambling was legal. The performers, knowing a mass exodus was coming, launched into the finale, a medley of all-American favorites: "Dixie," "New York, New York," "I Left my Heart in San Francisco," culminating with a rousing "God Bless America." The band is Filipino, the performers are Australian, the audience is Chinese. What else would they be singing?

The casino's blackjack game wasn't on its own merits attractive. It was an eight-deck game with more than a deck cut off, and rules which gave us a disadvantage of .66%. If that were all there was to it, I wouldn't be here. It was the junket incentive Paul told me about, which made it a good game.

The cruise, which otherwise cost seven hundred dollars, was free if you deposited ten thousand US dollars. All of the action was denominated in US dollars, which most people brought because they could get better rates from the Singaporean money changers than they could get on the ship. The junket leaders collected the money from their customers, then deposited it with the casino. The casino issued special chips, called (at least by me) "playthrough chips." Players bet them, and if they lost, the chips went into the rack. If they won, they kept the playthrough chips, but were paid in ordinary casino chips. Assuming one won half the hands, it would take twenty-thousand-dollars-worth of action to convert ten thousand in "playthrough chips" to ten thousand in ordinary chips. You were credited with the ten thousand converted, and received a rebate of 2%. When you were getting low on playthrough chips you exchanged ordinary chips with your junket leader, who recorded the transaction. Additional conversions were credited at 1.25%.

Suppose you bought ten thousand, and at the end finished with ten thousand, four thousand playthrough, six thousand ordinary, while during the cruise converted your initial buy, and rebought six times, another sixty thousand. You would receive 2% of the first ten thousand, and 1.25% of the next fifty-six thousand. You would make nine hundred dollars in rebates. Of course, on average playing correct basic strategy, you would have lost .66% of one hundred and thirty-two thousand in action, or eight seventy-one twenty, ending up slightly better than break-even. Rocky and I would be counting, and would try to get away with spreading from two hands of twenty dollars to four hands of five hundred. It rated to be a very profitable game.

We wanted to be inconspicuous, though Rocky was the only Japanese player, and I was the only non-Asian. As for Paul, he was Chinese, but he was wearing a purple batik shirt and electric yellow shoelaces. Rocky and I would play on separate tables, he having mastered card counting, but there could be times we would like to pass the count to each other. The dealers were from all over, but mostly from Australia, so perhaps Korean since we'd all played there? Paul knew Korean numbers, but Rocky did not. Japanese then? Paul spoke English, Malay, four or five Chinese dialects, and smatterings of Korean and Tagalog, but did not know the Japanese numbers. It turned out we all knew how to count in Mandarin, so that's what we used.

The casino was very small. There were only two blackjack tables, but not many blackjack players. There was a roulette wheel which got action. Baccarat was the game of choice for most punters. There were three big baccarat tables, with limits of thirty, sixty, and seventy-five thousand, and half a dozen mini-baccarat tables. Those were always full.

My presence drew a few curious looks from the dealers, but my play drew no heat. After a few hours I figured I'd knock off, have a few beers, and get to bed, with a long day's play on the morrow. There was a wet bar in the casino, but it wasn't open. Nor had I seen anyone drinking alcohol in the casino. I asked a boss about it.

"The bar used to be open. Then a player got drunk."

"Isn't that the point?"

It turned out that the bar that was open the latest on the ship, until one, was the karaoke, all the way forward on the top deck. I hurried up there, as it was nearly closing time, and ordered a Heineken, while I listened to a Chinese woman reading "Hopelessly Devoted To You" aloud, to music.

The karaoke had some of the strangest videos I've even seen. Though one wasn't as odd as I thought. "Another Day in Paradise" was about helping a homeless person, which seemed weird until I actually paid attention to the lyrics for the first time, and discovered that really was what the song was about. "Sukiyaki's" Japanese name means "Walking While Looking Up, and by golly, the video showed a woman walking, while looking up. There was a visual pun, because she was tall, with long legs and a short skirt. The camera was itself looking up, but every time she approached close enough for the audience to see what was up, it cut to a new shot. The strangest, most downright horrible video was for "My Way." I never liked the song, but it was the most popular song in the karaoke. The video was shot on the world's most depressing winter boardwalk. It made Atlantic City look like Munchkin Land. So far, so bad. How could they make it worse? By making the only two people in it a hideously creepy clown, and a ten-year-old boy. It was like a John Wayne Gacy home movie.

As the only non-Asian, I was viewed as a special added attraction. They insisted I sing. I'd learned my lesson, and would avoid "Sound of

Silence." I settled on "House of the Rising Sun." It was a felicitous choice. There are two lines referring to gambling, and since they had seen me in the casino, they'd cheer when I sang that the only time a gambler was satisfied was "when he's on a drunk."

The next morning, I grabbed breakfast alone, while listening to the morning announcements about poolside aerobics, tours of the bridge, and the Granny Bragging competition.

Some announcements were in Chinese or Malaysian, so, half-awake before my first cup of coffee, I wondered if I had contracted aphasia from drinking the local water.

I went to the casino, where Paul and Rocky were playing. I seldom tell stories about interesting hands, because the sad truth is that in blackjack there are no interesting hands. Once in a rare while there are nearly interesting hands. For instance, consider 33 vs a 7. How often do you face that decision? According to my copy of *Professional Blackjack* in a six-deck game it happens 44 times in 100,000. While the number of decks matters, you can approximate the answer quickly by cubing thirteen (since 3s and 7s each comprise a 13th of a deck), and get 2197, around one chance in 2200. If you play twelve hours per trip to Vegas, you will see one about once every two trips. There is a funny thing about that hand. Wong only shows splitting as basic strategy, but when I learned the game, in Julian Braun's book, this hand had an index number. If the count was +12, instead of splitting, you should hit. That number only applies to four-deck games with Strip rules.

A true count of +12 is extremely rare in a multiple deck game. I don't have a distribution chart showing how often it comes up, but less than one time in a thousand is an educated guess. In other words, even a professional player might never be dealt a 33 vs 7 when the true count is +12.

It happened to me, and I remembered the index number, so instead of splitting, I hit. I caught a ten, unsurprising when the count was that high. I now had 16 vs 7, and the index for that is +9. I was well above it, so I stood. The dealer turned over a nine, hit with a ten, and busted. Virtue was rewarded! A year later, I was again dealt 33 vs 7, when the true count was greater than +12! And once again caught a ten. And once again the dealer's hole card was a nine. She busted, and I was again rewarded. I may be the only player in the world who ever made the right plays for the right reason, and I did it twice.

See, I told you it was "nearly interesting."

When I walked up to Rocky and Paul it was the last hand of the shoe, and Rocky was betting four hands of five hundred. The dealer turned up an ace. A rule variation the boat offered, one I haven't seen elsewhere, was what I called "full insurance." Everywhere else, if the dealer has an ace, you may bet half your original bet, and be paid two-for-one if you win, to break even. Here you could match your bet, and potentially win money if the dealer had a snapper. Rocky made four five-hundred-dollar insurance bets. It was a no hole card game, so he played his hands, ending up either busting, or with poor totals, seven-teens or eighteens, on all four. Then the dealer turned over another ace, scooped up all of Rocky's insurance bets, then hit with a nine, making twenty-one, and grabbed the rest.

I told Rocky and Paul to go eat, and sat down. Five minutes later the count on the new shoe was high enough for me to bet four hands of four hundred. The dealer showed an ace. I made four four-hundred-dollar insurance bets. I ended up with four lousy hands. The dealer turned over an ace, and took the insurance bets, then hit with a nine and took the rest. In five minutes, Rocky and I had lost seventy-two hundred on the same odd parlay.

"We don't get many *gweilos*."

That's Cantonese for white people, literally "ghost man." Or more loosely "foreign devil," but definitely a non-Asian. Which is funny coming from an Australian. But he was right, I was the only *gweilo* on my side of the table. I'd learned that an Indonesian company owned the casino, and had an arrangement with the cruise ship. The Indone-sians hired an Australian company to provide the dealers, and the bosses. Most dealers were from Australia or New Zealand, but there were some from the UK, and at least one Turk. The casino manager was Randy, who was American. Meanwhile, the Indonesians didn't trust the Australians, so there were two sets of bosses, the ones working for the Australian management company, and the ones working for the Indonesian owners. The Australians watched the games, and the Indonesians watched the Australians.

That was the theory anyway, but the Indonesian bosses seemed to do nothing more than sit in chairs behind the tables, and stare vacantly at the game. I'd met Tanto, Wahyu, and Bambang, among others. A few were friendly, a few drooled, and one sometimes roused himself from his stupor to look at me and laugh. The friendly ones talked to me, but they didn't speak English, and I didn't speak Bahasa Indonesian, so I had no idea what they were saying. The Australians (I am using that as a catchall) were on the whole among the sharpest dealers I've ever encountered. Most knew at least basic strategy, and they knew I was counting. But they hated the Indonesians, and since the Indonesians were clueless, letting me play was a sly "fuck you" to their overlords.

Meanwhile, when Rocky and I were both playing, you'd think both of our tables would be getting play from the other customers, but mine filled up before Rocky's. Everyone wanted to play with me. Blackjack was where the high rollers parked their wives, daughters, and grannies, out of the way, not on a table with a "real" game like mini-baccarat. The junket leaders seemed to have figured out that I was a pro, and they instructed the grannies to play on my table, and try to do what the American did. Bet on my square, if possible.

This is called *dum bang*, to "ride on," as in, "Now small bet, no problem, I *dum bang* you, lah!" The house permits three bets per square, but as long as the bets are stacked, and do not exceed the house limit, more are possible. As long as I was betting minimum, as many as five other players, some next to me, others standing behind me, wanted to pile on my square. Hoping to maintain longevity, I permitted it, as long as they understood that sometimes I would be betting the maximum, shutting them out. They did.

I was also helping the dealers. There were two sets of chips to keep track of. Some of them looked a lot like reach other, though annoyingly, the denominations did not all match up. There were twenty-dollar playthrough chips, for instance, but not regular chips in that amount. Because there were two sets of chips, the dealers were always running short. Some players liked to hoard chips, which didn't help. With so much traffic on my square, I found I could speed things up by handling it myself, and I must have looked like a Hindu god, arms conveying bets back and forth so fast it looked like I had at least four arms.

My followers were very disciplined. In Korea if I hit a sixteen, I expected howling. Here, even when they had money riding along with me, there was never a word of reproach. And if I did catch a five, I'd hear "very clever, lah!" Some of the young girls would even coo in my ear.

One young girl was Ling Ling, the Mandarin singer from the show, who turned out to be not so young; she was thirty. She liked playing on my table, and told the others I was the Mike Tyson of blackjack, and her "*o shiang*." Paul Lee said it meant her "adored one," but "idol" is a better translation.

Did all this admiration translate into money? Sadly, not. The seventy-two-hundred-dollar losing parlay may have been the worst beat, but we were not having good luck.

The second night, about thirty hours out of Singapore, the casino closed. We were entering Thai waters. We docked about eight, and were off the ship by ten. We'd landed in Phuket, Thailand, and had the day to poke around. Rocky and Paul went to shop. I had heard there was an elephant show, and told them to find me there.

I was early, the only customer around. A sign said that for ten baht I could feed the elephants. Ten baht got me a bunch of bananas, and the attention of a hungry pachyderm. Asian elephants are the small ones. The African elephants are much bigger. I am glad this was one of the little ones. The difference between an Asian elephant and a Chevy Suburban is that the elephant is taller. That vacuum cleaner stuck on the front of their face is alive. It can perform brain surgery or play Rachmaninoff. Have you ever had a dog pestering you for treats? Now imagine the puppy is eight feet tall, weighs a couple of tons, and has a six-foot trunk. Bananas disappear as though by magic, and when the bunch is finished two stern eyes the size of baseballs glare at you while the trunk frisks you. The distinct message is, "Maybe I should pick you up by the ankles, and bang your head on the ground, until the rest of the bananas fall out of your pockets."

Another sign said that for twenty baht I could ride an elephant. Ever since I saw my first Tarzan movie, I had wanted to climb up on

Tantor and explore the jungle. I pulled out twenty baht, and managed to avoid having the elephant eat it before I handed it to a mahout.

They opened the gate, and let me into the enclosure. They had the elephant lie on its belly, and I climbed aboard. The process was unlike mounting a horse. There are no stirrups, and an elephant on its belly is still four feet high and twelve feet in circumference. I bellyflopped onto it and slithered up its back. Then it stood and I slithered right off. A second attempt proved no better. The third time after I lay across it, one kid grabbed my right wrist, another my left. A third hopped on the elephant in back of me, and planted hands on my ass, to keep me from sliding backward. A fourth sat backwards on the elephant's neck, and grabbed my neck. I was pinned like a butterfly. The elephant stood, my anchors dropped away, one by one, and I managed to stay aboard, and even sit up.

I had given my camera to one of them, hoping for a photo. He used up most of my roll, even when I said, "Okay, that's good enough," since every picture was more or less the same.

The elephant walked around the oval track, a journey of no more than five minutes, and I managed to dismount without falling off when it once again went prone.

Here is what they don't tell you about elephants, they sweat. Their sweat is a lot like the slime in the movie *Ghostbusters*. It's also filled with bits of straw that cling to sweat. It stinks. I was wearing black pants, and a black guayabera shirt. Both were now smeared top to bottom with elephant sweat and straw. Stinky elephant sweat and straw. It was ninety-five degrees; what the Thais call a chilly spring day. I would not be able to change and shower until we went back on the boat at five.

I hung around, and the place began to fill up. Rocky and Paul were kind enough not to comment on my coating of slime. They were doing their own sweating. The only people who looked cool were a pair of young Japanese women in pastel outfits with matching umbrellas.

The elephant show started. The handlers put them through their paces, playing ball, balancing on barrels, etc. The climax was a reenactment of a 15th century battle between the kings of Thailand and Burma. The elephants were equipped with howdahs. Each was a flat platform with a throne for the king, and a roof for shade. The two sparred until the Thai king won.

Show over, they asked if anyone wished to ride an elephant? The two Japanese, in their delicate outfits, said they would.

"This should be good!" I thought.

The trainers had them climb a set of stairs, walk onto the howdah, and sit together on the wide throne. They took a stately ride around the oval, while I hied my stinky self back to the boat.

CHAPTER 54
CLANDESTINE MANEUVERS

Returning from Phuket was like a rewind of the trip up there, ship sails at six, everyone goes to the theatre after dinner, the casino opens at ten, etc. Rocky and I lost money, and it would have been nice to climb back on the boat that threw us, but we had business in Korea.

Rocky had a Japanese friend named Joe. Joe was not coming over from America, like our other big players; he lived in Japan. Rocky, now that he was counting cards, would be taking Joe to Incheon, and calling plays for him. A Japanese counter calling plays for a Japanese big player was not a look they had seen before. Before unleashing them on the Olympus, I had to complete Joe's training, and make sure he and Rocky were ready. To do that, it would be great if we could practice under conditions resembling a real casino. Where might we find one of those? Oh, Tom!

The Las Vegas Nights were still going strong, but they were no longer Tom's. Some months after Marty and I went to the Philippines, Munchkin went to Korea, and got a look at Tom's game. Tom proved that he had not through experience become the next Steve Wynn.

"Munchie, let me ask you a question. An ace and a ten, that's not a blackjack, is it?"

"Yes, Tom, it's a blackjack."

"Are you sure?"

"Yes, very sure."

The man had been running a casino for six months, and wasn't sure which hands were blackjacks. There was more.

"While you are here, would you mind looking at the roulette wheel. We think its broken."

"Broken how?"

"It never wins."

Yes, that was a wheel Munch wanted to see! He stood off to one side, watching the game. There was a Korean customer betting big stacks on both red, and black. Black won. The dealer took the bet on red, and pushed it over to match the bet on black, and then paid both stacks.

"Tom, I think I found the problem."

The dealer was our old friend from Oksudong. She was fired. Then she was rehired. What happened next, I heard some years later. One of my crap dealers, Miss Shim, moved to Las Vegas, and when I ran into her, she told me the story. She and the other crap dealers were all from Pyongtaek, and Mrs. Park saw them as a threat to her control over the operation. Unlike most of the other dealers, who were from Seoul and beholden to Mrs. Park, Marty had recruited them. Miss Shim was the most outspoken, so Mrs. Park fired her. She went quietly, but then heard that Mrs. Park was planning to get rid of the others, her friends. She went to Tom, and told him he needed to fire Mrs. Park, who was stealing him blind. Tom was afraid to rock the boat, so she told him she was going to go directly to the Army, and tell them what was going on, and the Oksudong dealer would testify to it. He was more afraid of that than he was of Mrs. Park, and he fired her. It was estimated that in ten months she had stolen at least one hundred million won.

Despite that, Tom had made about three hundred million won in the same period. That's proof that it is very hard to lose money running a casino, no matter how incompetent you are.

Meanwhile, a group of Koreans heard about what Tom was doing, and submitted their own BPA to the Army, going into competition with him. Eventually they offered to merge the two operations, and keep Tom as a meeter and greeter, with a decent salary. The merger happened, and everyone was happy.

Even Marty. Marty stayed away a year, during which time he took up poker. This was a decade before the internet poker boom, and most players were pretty awful. He bought a book on the game, and learned it the way he learned blackjack. He mastered the basic strategy, and played the game mechanically. For the games he played in at the time, that was all it took. When he returned to Korea, there was good news. The owner of Moon Night, the one who warned him to stay out of Itaewon, was no longer a threat. He'd been sent to prison, where another inmate stabbed him to death. The even better news was that the new casino operation was offering poker games, and the players were even worse than the ones in the Philippines.

I asked Tom about taking Joe and Rocky to the Las Vegas Night for some training sessions, and since we were only betting up to a maximum of twenty-five dollars, he didn't mind, nor did his partners.

There was a slight hitch. Joe didn't drive. Non-military entering the base had to leave identification with the gate guards. It seems that they had recently lost the passport of one of the people they let on base. That loss caused repercussions, and the four-star decreed that passports were not an acceptable form of identification; only driver's licenses could be used.

Tom solved that for us. Tom was not a patient man, and to avoid going through the rigmarole of entering the base at the main gates, he often used a side gate. He was still supposed to stop and sign in, but he'd found that he could wave and drive past the guards. They were supposed to chase him down, but they got used to just letting him in. They'd yell at him when he did it, but that was all. I'd been with him when he did it in the past. Now, he did it with me, Rocky, and Joe, smiling and waving as we drove in.

That got us into the Main Post Club at Yongsan. A night or two later the game was at the South Post Club. Tom again drove through the side gate for the Main Post, then went around to the road leading out past the Main Gate, and drove across the road to the South Post.

Those guards assumed he had already checked in; there was no rechecking.

The next few dates were trickier. They were up north, at camps Casey and Red Cloud. We took a train from Seoul. The car was freezing cold. Rocky and Joe looked out at the Korean countryside with interest. "Just like Japan, except no pachinko." Once in Tongdu-chon we rode the bus with the dealers onto the base. The guards would glance on the bus, but they were used to its comings and goings, and didn't wonder about the strange men sitting in the back. Joe had managed, in a week, to penetrate four different bases. "The emperor should be proud. No spy during the war managed what you did!" Perhaps it's just as well he spoke no English.

Next, we'd be taking a trip, but before that I did some visiting. We were staying at the Rainbow Hotel, and the first time I walked out to the main drag through Namyeongdong, I noticed something odd. Every second or third doorway was an entrance to a *noraeyonsipshil*.

"What the hell are they?" I asked A Rha. We were sitting in a fancy dress shop, of all places. Mr. Go had opened one in Gangnam, a two-story affair. He was doing very well. He was the one who enlightened me, with a bit of translation help from A Rha. *Noraeyonsipshil* means "song practice room." The name would soon change to just plain *Noraebang*, "song room.' By either name they were what karaoke in Korea (and Japan) evolved into. You and your friends rented the rooms by the hour. Inside was a karaoke machine, with a screen, a song list, and a couple of microphones, in case a duet was called for. You could order food and drink, and have a party. Mr. Go owned one. He told me the cost of the machines, rent, etc. His room was running twenty-four hours a day, and was fully booked most of the time. I told him he should probably wait another six months, and then sell. The market already seemed close to saturation.

Even before I looked up A Rha, the first night I looked up Jiyoung. I bumped into her in a grocery uphill from the King Club. She was with someone, so I let her contact me the next day. She told me that her friend was a retired colonel named Herbert. He was in his early forties, she said. "That guy? He has to be over sixty." I called him "Herbert Haraboji" after that, Grandpa Herbert. Jiyoung said he was asking her to marry him. "One of these days you come, and I not be here." What she really wanted was for me to marry her. I knew it, and wished I could give her what she wanted. I really liked Jiyoung, but the trouble was that unlike A Rha or Lee, she wasn't very bright. Simply being sweet, which she was, wasn't enough, not for a lifetime.

Besides Herbert Haraboji, she had another suitor. Her ex-fiancé had gotten himself transferred back to Korea. His career had stalled; he was still a Spec 5, doing some sort of computer programming. He'd tracked Jiyoung to Itaewon, and would sit on a stool on the street, watching her ply her trade. "Go away!" She'd tell him. "You're a *meongcheongi*!" He asked what that was, and she said, "Someone who sits around looking like '*meong*!'" She made a 'stupid' face. He started crying. "What a *meongcheongi*!" She told me.

Joe had gotten comfortable receiving my signals, and then Rocky had shown he could call plays. We booked a flight and went down to Jeju Island. Jeju is south of the peninsula, and is warmer than Seoul. It's a place Koreans go to honeymoon. They tried to turn it into Korea's Hawaii by planting palm trees, which kept dying, because it wasn't that much warmer than the rest of the country. It was a pretty place, though it would have been prettier in the summer. We weren't there for the scenery. There were seven casinos on Jeju Island. We were going there to see if any had worthwhile games.

The casinos didn't get much action, and none had limits higher than half a million won. The trip wasn't a loss, but it wasn't any place we'd be returning to. The most interesting part was the technical challenge for me. I was calling plays for both of them, Joe playing first, making larger bets. Even signaling to one player playing two hands can sometimes be tricky. Once in a while there is ambiguity; which hand am I signaling? To that was added, which player am I signaling? Also, since we were the only players, and they were on first and second base, while I was over on third, I had to count all the hands, but be ready to signal theirs right away.

We visited all seven casinos, though some were so dead, and with lower limits, we didn't play them. Then we flew back north, and went to Incheon. They checked into the Olympus Hotel. I stayed in a place at the bottom of the hill, about a block away. After their sessions they would slip out of their hotel, and come down to mine for a debriefing. It went well.

We'd have more work for Joe, but he and Rocky had to go back to Japan and the States, respectively. I went the other way, back to Singapore.

CHAPTER 55
SOLO SAILOR

The entire front page of the tabloid was devoted to the latest crime wave in Singapore, and the government's steps at dealing with the problem. Having gotten rid of gum sticking to things it oughtn't be stuck to, by banning chewing gum, the focus was now on flushing out the miscreants who were failing to flush public toilets. The fine was five hundred dollars, and the police were conducting sting operations. Proof was the full-page, front-page picture of one such criminal, caught in the act, or caught in the non-act, by a detective hiding in a stall, who leapt into action when the potty failed to bark in the night. Good thing I always flushed!

Once again we were headed to the cruise ship. Before we did, Paul took me to Haw Par Villa. Once upon a time two brothers invented Tiger Balm, a salve for sore muscles, and grew rich. One built a rock garden on a slope in Hong Kong called Tiger Balm Garden. The other built a wonderland of plastic models down the road from the World Trade Center in Singapore. Paul's brother, a school principal, joined us, and he and I took a ride on the world's least exciting roller coaster. It made up for its lack of height by being slow. Unlike the coaster, the tour of the Taoist hells was thrilling. I would bet that any four-year-old seeing a man bloodily sawed in half by devils would think twice before deciding to be a pimp when he grew up.

Paul's brother didn't gamble, but came along on the cruise just the same. This time it was only me playing, so without Rocky I had to lose twice as fast. It was still a good game, but I was still having lousy results. I came near to tapping out, and sent for reinforcements. It was possible to make calls from the ship. It wasn't desirable, but it was possible. I called Hong Kong, and Nora, Woody's girlfriend, answered the phone. He was in the shower. She wanted to chat. I managed to stem the flow of words, and told her I would call back shortly. The second time I got through to Woody, who agreed to wire money to Singapore for me to collect when we docked. Two calls, each under a minute, cost seventy dollars.

I spent two days in Singapore, and saw some of its nightlife. There is a terrific movie based on Paul Theroux's first novel, *Saint Jack*. It was banned in Singapore, for what the government considered an unflattering view of the city. Some of the action took place at Bugis Street. During the Vietnam War American GIs came to Singapore on R & R, and partied on Bugis Street. The street was infamous for its prostitution, especially its ladyboys. Many's the visitor who reenacted the big reveal of the movie *The Crying Game*. By the late seventies the government's cleanup campaign reached Bugis Street, and away the action went. A decade later people were complaining that the city was too sterile. The solution was to reopen Bugis Street.

I went there, and found what the folks who brought you "no chewing gum" and "flush the toilets" thought was a revival of Bugis Street. It was a square built around a courtyard, with hawkers in the middle, and bars in the buildings around the perimeter. The bar I chose was half and half. One half comprised well-scrubbed Chinese kids singing karaoke. The other half consisted of middle-aged Western expats, probably bankers by day, but posing as bikers by night. They looked like they could really use the drinks they were tossing down, after seeing what they'd stumbled into.

Even the hawkers centre was more exciting. This one had an actual Burmese stand. I'd had Burmese food two years before. There was a Burmese restaurant on Gloucester in Hong Kong. At the time there were hardly any Burmese restaurants anywhere. Not even in Burma, I was told, where anyone who could afford to dine out went to a Chinese restaurant; why go to a restaurant to eat food you could get at home? I had *mohinga*, and green tea salad, while watching a video of a woman in a cheongsam singing Burmese pop songs. The production values of the film were slight. A static camera filmed her against a backdrop created by hanging a sheet on a wall. Between 1961 and 1991 Burma was considered one of the three most isolated countries in the world, ranking right down there with North Korea and Albania. Then in 1991 the generals running the place opened things up a tiny bit, and according to an article I read, the most popular music in the country was now, Metallica!

At the Bugis Street stall, I had some *mohinga*, and headed back to my hotel.

The next night was more interesting. Ling Ling, the singer from the ship, invited me to hear her do a concert in a park, and then go out afterward. When she finished singing, before leaving, I stopped to use a port-a-potty. Finished, I dutifully flushed the toilet. I dutifully tried to flush the toilet. I worked that handle like I was on a sidecar on a spur line trying to overtake the express. Nothing happened.

I came out of the toilet screaming, "I tried to flush! Really! It isn't working!" I saw a crowd of baffled Chinese faces. Ling Ling took me by the hand, told me not to worry about it, and we made our escape. I hope after all these years the statute of limitations has expired.

Before rejoining the cruise, we made our obligatory visit to Genting, where Paul showed me one of his hidden treasures, a secret restaurant. Because it is built on the slope of a mountain, the resort has many levels. The casino is up a floor from the hotel lobby. Down a floor are shops and a cinema. Down one more floor, in the sub-basement, is a medical clinic and a game arcade.

If you walk outside from there, and cross to the covered parking garage you are on a lower level, but not on the lowest level. You are on the fourth floor, and an elevator will take you to the lowest level. But is it the lowest level? It isn't. If you go out a side door, there are stairs leading down to a restaurant. Who besides Paul Lee would know there was a restaurant down there? Outside, and down a path are the guard barracks, and this is where they eat. They are Indian, and the restaurant serves Indian curries, though not dishes you are likely to find in Indian restaurants in America. I remember having curried ladyfingers – "Fingers of the lady!" – Paul giggled. That's okra, in case you worried we were resorting to cannibalism. The food was very good, and very cheap, a couple of ringgit for a curry.

Don't tell Joe Montana, but a poster on the wall advertising Peter Stuyvesant Cigarettes, "the Taste of America," had a drawing of Number 16, arm cocked to throw a pass, no doubt energized after drinking a cup of *teh tarik*. It was on the wall above the basin for washing one's hands, next to a sign saying, "No spitting," and another poster advertising the Kalari Payat Dynamic Self Defense Institute of Malaysia. You could tell that Restoran Barumuhitbah was a classy place.

CHAPTER 56
MY ENTOURAGE

Once again, I had company on the cruise. Paul had a following, a group of young players from Macau who looked up to him as their blackjack sifu. He had called and told them that he was going cruising with his sifu's sifu, and they flew to Singapore to come aboard and absorb my wisdom. I had not volunteered for this.

The oldest of the three was named Wong. He was in his thirties, shorter than me, and had a terrible complexion. I was told during a later cruise that he had a chronic ailment, which I assume was hepatitis. Wong was the most competent of the three. There were index numbers he hadn't encountered, some of the more extreme ones, and if they came up, he would ask about them. Otherwise, he made no mistakes. Amy was perhaps twenty-five. She was married, to someone they called Jellyfish because, Paul explained, "he is so young and tender." Jellyfish was a snooker player, and "the second-best *cho dai di* player in Macau." Amy spoke even less than Wong. The last was Simon. He was around thirty, six feet tall, solidly built. He did twice as much talking as the other two put together. His English was adequate, probably no better than the others, but he wasn't afraid to use it. He'd been to Korea to play at Walker Hill, and he'd done some temporary work for Woody in the past. These were the sorts of things which gave him confidence in his speech the others lacked.

Since they wanted to learn from me, they stuck close, on and off the ship. It was nice when they volunteered to schlep my three-zipper bag through airports. The bag was a pain to try to move around. It was four feet tall when unzipped all the way, and as soft as a duffle bag, always wanting to tip over. Their presence was not so nice on the blackjack table. They played like Marty and Paul, betting on each other's, and other players' hands, when the count went up, slowing things down and sowing confusion. They also alienated the dealers and bosses. That wasn't good, because it reflected on me.

They tried to keep a low profile, at least when it came to blowing my cover.

"Is your friend really a professional?" A Chinese girl asked Simon.

"No, I just follow him around because he's fat. Everyone knows fat people are lucky."

Simon was an expert on luck, the others agreeing with his pronouncements. Getting a haircut was okay before visiting a casino, but not clipping one's nails. Bringing a book (I was studying Thai during the shuffles) was very bad. The Chinese word for "book" is "*shu*," which sounds like the word for "lose." Anything to do with shoes is bad, especially buying new ones. Not because "shoe" sounds like "*shu*;" in Chinese the word for "shoe" is "*hai*," which sounds like someone sighing. Winners don't sigh. Dreams can also be an important method of interpreting luck. Dreaming of a black dog is bad, but a pig of any color is good.

"Last night I dreamed about politicians urinating in a public park."

"Sir, this is very, very good!" Simon was so excited he nearly urinated. If you need a lucky dream, you can't go wrong with urine! "If today you casino – sure win!"

When we reached Phuket they were all keyed up. It seems James, our junket leader, knew of a place there which served village chicken. I had no idea what village chicken was, but Paul had taken me to so many interesting places I was nearly as eager as the rest to sample some village chicken.

The restaurant was open fronted; the table was a picnic table. It was hot and there were flies, but that's not unusual for Thailand. James ordered village chicken all around, and I prepared for a taste sensation. When it arrived, everyone oohed, aahed, and carried on. Everyone except me.

"What's this?"

"Village chicken."

"It's boiled chicken and white rice."

"Isn't it great? No preservatives, all natural!"

"It's boiled chicken and white rice! This is Thailand; where are the curries, the spices, the … anything else? Isn't there any more food coming?"

There wasn't.

The next time we went to Phuket they again wanted to go eat village chicken. I wished them luck, and told them I would go off on my own, and find something flavorful. Convinced I needed a minder, they sent Wong to accompany me. It turned out that Wong had a Thai girlfriend back in Macau, and loved Thai food. Wong didn't talk much, but he may have himself been happy to get something besides village chicken. We had some wild boar curry, and *khaw phad sabpard*, pineapple fried rice, which was new to me.

The Chinese have enormous respect for their sifus, but also think they may be willful, unreasonable, capricious, and given to inhuman appetites. They may have gotten this idea from Marty. Given the wear and tear the constant travelling was doing not only to my three-zipper bag, but my sanity, the description was beginning to fit me. Marty had told them he did not sleep well if he slept alone. Actually, Marty didn't sleep much at all. He stayed up all night eating noodles and watching TV. But when he visited Malaysia, they did what they could to propitiate him, and figured they knew how to keep me happy. Which is how I learned that in Thailand, the sorts of massage parlors which are called soaplands in Japan, are called "body massage" in Thailand. You'd think that every massage was a body massage, but in Thailand if you find one called "body massage," it has the air mattresses and other accessories I described earlier. Some are huge palaces, with the masseuses sitting on bleachers, wearing numbers. The one they found in Phuket was more modest, but it was a body massage. They figured if they expressed an interest, they could lure me into it, and there I would be propitiated from head to toe. I won't say if they succeeded, but I will say that it was a lot better than village chicken.

There was a player who'd joined the cruise, Mr. Wong. He was one of the richest men in Indonesia, a timber baron. It was rumored he'd deposited six million dollars. He bet one hundred thousand dollars every hand. I mentioned the table limits earlier, with seventy-five thousand being the highest. Mr. Wong was the six-million-dollar gorilla in the room, and every table he decided to place a bet on, whether big baccarat or mini-baccarat, now had a one hundred-thousand-dollar limit – for him. He was accompanied by ten bodyguards, all wearing batik shirts. He kept a million-dollars in orange, five-thousand-dollar chips, with him at the table, making stacks of twenty for his bets. Come to think of it, I don't remember seeing a junket leader for him. Maybe he was missing out on the rebate. Maybe he didn't care. If he won, a bodyguard took the winnings to the cage to deposit, and if he lost, a bodyguard went to the cage for reinforcements, so his million-dollar pile was maintained.

I don't know how much everyone else deposited, but with Mr. Wong aboard, it meant that there had to be close to ten million dollars in the casino cage, in cash, most if not all in US hundreds. Which meant that the cruise during which, it was rumored, someone tried to pass counterfeit, had everyone on edge. We were assured none had contaminated our funds, but it was a worry.

There was another worry. The Straits of Malacca were in those days the most pirate-infested waters in the world. I asked one of the bosses about pirates.

"Hah! Pirates! Ha, ha!"

Then one day I was doing a tour of the boat, and I asked one of the crew.

"Pirates!" He turned white, and looked around in case any lurking pirates heard the question and turned their malevolent gaze towards our ship. I hoped they had an armory stocked with machine guns and rocket launchers. From what they told me they had one double-barreled shotgun, and some fire axes. I have an unfinished screenplay I worked on many years ago called *Dire Straits*, about a ship like the Shangri-La which is raided by pirates. I still am amazed they never boarded us.

CHAPTER 57
FUN AND GAMES

We watched three movies during these trips. Two were aboard ship. There was the big theatre, for live shows, but there was in a lower deck a small one for showing movies. One was a prison movie starring Chow Yun Fat. The other was a John Wu movie called *A Bullet In the Head*. It was incredible, like a cross between *The Deerhunter*, and *Scarface*.

The third movie was ashore. We were driving through K.L. when I spotted a marquee. "Oh my god, that's my movie!"

My movie?

Before my brother moved to Los Angeles he took an acting class in Las Vegas. One of his classmates, Joe Mehri, who owned some pizza restaurants in Vegas, also moved to L.A. to get into the movie business. He teamed up with a cameraman named Rick Pepin, and made a movie about a Las Vegas pizza parlor owner who wants to make movies. They formed a company called City Lights, until the Chaplin estate threatened to sue them into trampdom, thereafter PM Entertainment. Rick shot them, Joe directed them, and Munchkin produced most of them. Munch wanted to direct, and finally got his chance. Joe had polled his customers, asking what they wanted to buy. "Kickboxing movies!" He lined up a pair, male and female, of Korean martial artists, then called my brother. Munchkin, after all, had been to Korea which made him an expert on all things Korean. If he could come up with a script, Joe would let him direct.

"I am coming in …" for the Christmas and New Year's holiday, he told me, and "… we have two weeks to write a kickboxing movie." We, because unlike Munch, who had taken exactly one karate lesson twenty years before, I had nearly made green belt, two different times, taking classes over the years in karate, judo, taekwondo, hapkido, and taijiquan. And I'd seen all of Bruce Lee's movies, and an assortment starring Tom Laughlin, Chuck Norris, Steven Seagal, Jean Claude Van Damme and other Oliviers of the octagon. As an added bonus, I was studying Mandarin.

I was studying Mandarin because I couldn't find a Korean class in the Chicago suburbs. Studying Mandarin to learn Korean is like studying Latin to learn English. In many ways it is even less helpful because, though the Koreans borrowed a lot of words, the languages are not from the same family. Korean is a Ural-Altaic language, while Mandarin is Sino-Tibetan. There is no similarity. It might help with the movie, though, because the Korean martial artists never turned up, and weren't written into the story. Just like the helicopter chase Joe wondered if we could pencil in, because he had stock footage of one. That didn't fly.

Munch suggested we write something "inspired by" *West Side Story*. Ours was a tale of rival kickboxing gangs, the surfers and the Asians, with a love affair between the sister of the leader of the surfers, and the cousin of the leader of the Asians. The hero, Dr. Johnny Wu, was a Chinese immigrant living with his aunt and cousin, who were Chinese-Americans. It gave me a chance to throw in some odds and ends of Chinese culture and traditions.

We wrote the script and still had time to make it to all the holiday parties. The movie was filmed in the spring, and released in the fall. PM's movies did not play in US theatres. They had three markets, cable television, home video, and foreign. I already knew the movie was playing elsewhere in Asia. I'd seen an ad in a Philippine paper saying it was coming. Still, it was thrilling to see it playing at a

Malaysian theatre while I had a chance to see it. The others were as eager as I was.

Seeing it with an audience, especially a Malaysian audience, was interesting. I don't think it is possible to have gratuitous violence in a kickboxing movie, but we also made sure there was gratuitous sex. Those scenes were chopped out with the largest scissors in Southeast Asia. Another thing which I noticed was that the audience laughed in odd places. One of those odd places actually made sense.

Since the lead grew up in Mainland China, I figured he would have had no chance to learn how to drive a car before moving to America. Then between med school, and learning to speak perfect, unaccented English (the only sort our lead actor spoke), he'd have been too busy to learn. We thought it would be funny that, not only would the leading lady have to do the driving on dates, he'd have to ask her to drive him to stop the big fight.

Our star was Don "The Dragon" Wilson, one of the greatest full contact fighters of his era. He was transitioning to acting, and had just starred in his first film, for Roger Corman. He was handsome, articulate, and the real deal as a fighter. He was eager to do it. His manager was eager for him to do it. But the manager had a problem with the script.

"What do you mean, Don doesn't know how to drive? Don knows how to drive!"

Munchkin was back in L.A., to field this question. "Well sure, of course Don knows how to drive. It's his character Johnny who knows doesn't know how to drive."

"Don knows how to drive!"

"Yes, but you see, Johnny grew up in China ..."

"Don knows how to drive!!!" By now, the manager was nearly hysterical.

"Okay ... Johnny knows how to drive." Not the last rewrite Munch would need to do.

Johnny now knew how to drive. The subject wasn't mentioned, and he drove the car to the big fight. But we didn't bother rewriting scenes where it wasn't mentioned. When Johnny and Julie go on their first date, we don't say who drove whom, but at the end of the date, she walks him to his front door, because in our minds, she'd been driving because Johnny … (I hope Paul the manager isn't reading this!) … Doesn't know how to drive. American audiences didn't notice, but the Malaysian audience saw her walk him to his aunt's picket fence, and it got the biggest laugh of the day.

When not playing blackjack or watching movies, we found other ways to pass the time, one of which came in handy while waiting to board boats or planes. At my request, they gave me a lesson in mahjong. I learned the rules, but haven't played it since, and have forgotten them. Hong Kong has mahjong parlors where you can drop in, and play for money. They warned me never to do that. Mahjong tiles are expensive, which means they are seldom replaced. They develop nicks and stains. Regulars can read the backs as though playing cards with a marked deck. Also, if you are the lone *gweilo*, and the other three players are talking to each other in Cantonese, what do you suppose they are talking about?

The other game, though, was a keeper. *Cho Dai Di*, the game Amy's husband was so good at, means "dig that great big deuce." They play it in Hong Kong and Macau, and also in the Philippines, where it is called *Pusoy Dos*. The cards are ranked by suit and denomination, as in bridge, with two differences: diamonds rank lower than clubs, and the deuce is the highest-ranking card, above the ace. The game may be played by two, three, or four players, each of whom is dealt thirteen cards. The person with the lowest-ranking card, always the three of diamonds, starts things off, making a play which must include that card. Thereafter the winner of the previous hand starts the next hand, and may lead whatever he likes.

The object is to get rid of cards. The person on lead may lead: a single card; a pair; three of a kind; a pat five card hand (except two pair). Let's suppose the first lead is the three of diamonds, a single card. The next player may play any higher-ranking card, from the three of clubs all the way up to the deuce of spades. Similarly, if the lead were the three of diamonds and three of hearts, any pair from the two black threes, up to a pair including the deuce of spades, may be played. Ditto for threes of a kind. With pat hands the ranking is like poker, with flushes above straights, full houses next, followed by four of a kind, straight flushes above all. Suit ranking still matters, so a straight to the eight of hearts would beat a straight to the eight of clubs. Players must pass if they cannot beat the previous lead, and may pass if they do not wish to break up their hand. If all pass, the person who made the play no one has topped, may lead anything he wishes, for instance after winning with a full house, they might go back to leading a low-ranking singleton.

When a player has only two cards remaining, they must announce "last two." When a player goes out, the cards left in the others' hands count against them. If you have nine or ten remaining, it counts double, eleven or twelve, triple, and being stuck with all thirteen is a quadruple loss.

We played for Malaysian dollars, but that was for scorekeeping purposes. Usually, the settlements at the end involved some complicated money shuffling. A player might pay in US dollars, but the recipient wouldn't have correct change, and so would return Singapore dollars, but the amount would still be off, so the first player would give change for the change in Ringgit, then Hong Kong dollars, which would then be adjusted with Thai baht, then Philippine pesos, and whoever got stuck with the Indonesian rupiah would wish they'd had correct change to start with.

One day in Changi Airport, they gave me a geography lesson. I noticed the board announcing flights had a national airline for a country I didn't know, flying to a city I'd never heard of. "What's Air Myanmar, and where the hell is Yangon?"

Simon explained that while I wasn't paying attention, the Burmese had changed the names of the country, and the capital city. Paul Lee added, "They have casinos."

"Let's go!" Yes, I may not have known that Rangoon was now called Yangon, but I had seen photos of its streets, with two soldiers on every corner. The place was unstable. It wasn't the insurgencies which worried my friends. It seems the casinos weren't in Yangon, they were up in the Golden Triangle. The customers were warlords and drug lords, Khun Sa preeminently, laundering their money. My friends could not be persuaded. Too bad. We might not have come back alive, but if we did, think of the stories!

Instead, we flew to Kuala Lumpur, for another visit to Genting. They would take turns playing at my table, and it was handy having them. I was using the count designed for Over/Under. It had some correlation with regular counting, so one could use it even without playing Over/Under; it was just not as efficient as my usual Hi-Lo. I'd let the Chinese count Hi-Lo, and pick their brain as needed, getting the best of both worlds.

As long as I had a bedroom to myself, I didn't care how many others were using the rest of the rooms in the apartments we rented, and since I was paying the whole twenty ringgit, all eight dollars a night, no one minded. Sometimes it got very crowded.

I came back from the casino one night, and found Alex, Paul's son, and six of his friends playing some card game on the living room floor. I was in the habit of drinking three beers when I got home, first a can of Guinness, then one of Tiger, and finally a shandy. I was examining the can of shandy, and saw that there was a two-character word, the first of which contained the character for "mountain," which I knew was pronounced "shan." I was guessing the second character was pronounced "di," but figured I'd confirm it. I asked Alex.

"I don't know." One of the girls could read Chinese, and told me I was right. Of the seven Chinese university students she was the only one who could read the characters. All of them spoke Chinese, Hokkienese I think, because their folks spoke it at home. But in school they used English.

Simon and the others from Hong Kong, knew Chinese characters. Simon helped me fill a couple of notebook pages with them. The notebook was a small one I kept in my pocket. I thought it would be nice to learn the sort of words not found in basic textbooks, and asked Simon to teach me to swear. He obliged, and filled two pages with Chinese obscenities after I promised never to show his mother.

We had another overnight guest, who stayed with us several trips. His name was Halim. Halim was in his fifties, and a regular at the casino. More than a regular, according to Paul.

Halim was Indonesian. He'd been an extremely bright student, enough so that he gained entrance to Waseda, one of Japan's top universities, on a government scholarship. He studied engineering, and went to work for Pertamina, the oil conglomerate. He married a girl from a rich family, had a big house, and a car and driver.

Indonesia used to have casinos. Paul Lee used to run junkets to the Indonesian casinos, from Malaysia to Jakarta, via Singapore. He made so many trips he had a drawer full of used passports. Halim also made many trips to the casinos, for him a local commute. Then a group of conservative students protested that gambling was haram, and the government humored them by closing the casinos down.

Halim switched his activity to the casino at Genting Highlands. He and his wife would fly to Malaysia, and stay at the resort, which welcomed him as a high roller. They stayed in a suite, saw shows in the cabaret, dined in the finer restaurants. The trouble was that Halim believed that there were patterns to the numbers which appeared on the roulette wheel. A trained engineer, you might think his math background would have helped him see the fallacy, but not every mathematician majors in probability theory. For that matter I had a friend, who was not only a mathematician, not only one whose area was probability, but who was a world-class game player, one of the greatest backgammon players who ever lived, a New York State Junior Chess Champion, and a world-class poker player. He was also a degenerate gambler. If you are sick, math won't save you. Halim was sick.

Soon he was leaving the wife home in Indonesia, while leaving more and more of their money in Malaysia. He lost the house, the car and driver, the job, and the wife. He lost them all. He called home for money, which his family still had. His brothers finally staged an intervention. They flew to Malaysia, they travelled to Genting, and they told him, "Here, Halim, is the last money we will give you for gambling. Instead, why don't you come home? We can get you back your wife. We can get you back your job. All that you have lost, it all comes back. Only, you must swear never to return here to gamble ever again. Otherwise, if you take the money, you are dead to us. Do not ever contact us again."

He took the money.

It didn't last long. Now he was stuck. Even if he wanted to, he had no money to leave Malaysia. He had overstayed, and would be deported if discovered. If that happened, he would never be able to return, never be able to prove that he had found the pattern of the wheel. Never collect the fortune fate owed him.

How did he live? Remember the curry restaurant at the lowest level of the parking garage? They kept his clothes, stuffed in plastic garbage bags, behind the counter. I think they sometimes gave him a meal. There was a bathroom the guards used, where he showered, around the outside of the parking garage. When he needed sleep, he used a chair in the keno lounge.

That's where I met Halim. Paul Lee had gone there to play an abomination called Progressive Keno. Halim was sleeping in a chair when my attempts to talk Paul out of wasting his money woke him. "I know this man," said Paul. "This is Halim." Halim was a short man with a shock of white hair, and eyes that might have belonged to Kahlil Gibran, or Charles Manson. "Halim, what if we eat some hot dogs? You buy, I pay, and he" he pointed at me, "will help us eat them."

When Halim disappeared through the slots, clutching Paul's red, ten ringgit note, to buy our hot dogs, Paul filled me in. I remarked that Halim looked like he had been here all night. "He has. He has been here six and a half years."

"Here in Malaysia?"

"Here in the casino."

Though when the flying squads came through, Halim had to hide. Malay Muslims were not permitted to gamble. Malaysia is divided into sultanates. Though Genting is accessed from Selangor, the resort is over the line, and is in Pahang. The flying squads who policed the casino for stray Malay Muslims were dispatched from Pahang. They would always spend the night before their ascent in a hotel at the base of the mountain on the Pahang side. The hotel would always call upstairs, and warn, "They are coming tomorrow." The word would spread, and the unauthorized punters would go down to other parts of the hotel. One popular spot was under the grand staircase leading up to the casino. It was called the Bangkok Hotel, because the people would sit in chairs and nod between sleep and wakefulness. *"Bangkok"* in Malay meant to nod the head. Halim would join the Malays. Legally, as an Indonesian Muslim, he was permitted to gamble. But to prove he was Indonesian he would have to show his passport, and reveal that he had overstayed.

Paul was not the only one who bought Halim food, though if he got hungry enough, Paul claimed the free hot water, and cream for the Nescafe, could be mixed to make "milk; it's just nice."

He received another subsidy, besides food. Halim had many systems for roulette. He had names for them: The Seven Sisters; The Drunken Prostitute; etc. Lots of punters knew him, and knew about his systems. "Here Halim, win us some money." They'd hand him a hundred. If he lost, so be it. If he won, they would split the winnings.

I wasn't drunk enough to hand him a hundred dollars to play roulette, no matter how many sisters he prostituted. But I didn't mind letting him sleep at the apartment, which he ended up doing during several trips. I liked Halim. He seemed to like me, and though he never told me about his systems, he was happy to tell me all about America, or "the Great Satan" as he called it. Like other anti-Americans I've met, he liked American people just fine.

One of the restaurants Halim used to dine in back when he had money, was the theatre. I never went at night, to see a show, but I became a regular for breakfast. I'd introduced my Chinese friends to Mexican food. A few months away from home, and I was craving some enchiladas. A dealer on the ship told me he knew a place in Singapore, and Paul Lee said he knew the street where it was located. When the taxi brought us there it turned out there were two Mexican restaurants, right next to each other. I took my best guess. I should have tried the other one. I was disappointed and the others unimpressed. But here at the theatre, they introduced me to dim sum, and I was impressed.

These days I think most Americans, if they eat Chinese food, know dim sum. Thirty years ago it was unknown, at least in the Midwest. When I was back home, I went looking for it, and there were only two restaurants in the Chicago area, both in Chinatown, which served it on Sunday mornings. A few years later it would be easy to find, but not then. I had already tried two of its popular dishes. Marty had taken me to a place in Ermita called Diamonds, which was open all night, and served *shu mai*, and *siaopao*, the Filipino spelling of *cha siu bao*. I knew those two, but didn't know they were dim sum, nor had I tried any of the many other dishes. Now that I had, I was hooked.

Simon, meanwhile, who could get dim sum back in Macau any old time, ordered Hainanese chicken rice. After he had a plate, oohing and aahing and swearing it was the best Hainanese chicken rice he had ever had, he ordered another plate. That was as good as the first, so he had a third. All the while apologizing for "making a pig of himself." Some things are universal.

CHAPTER 58
NOT SO MERRY MURRAY

We were joined for the next cruise by another of Paul Lee's card counting friends. I was beginning to think he'd called everyone in his phone book. Murray was American, in his late twenties, and had been counting for four years. Not making trips to Vegas every so often, and trying to count down a shoe; he'd been a pro for four years.

He was one of the most arrogant people I ever met.

For instance, there was speaking Thai. Murray had lived in Thailand, and spoke some Thai. I was telling him about my own experience learning it. A year or so earlier, I wrote a pamphlet for my teammates called "Speak Korean in One Hundred Words." I had an idea that I could teach them to get by on their trips, with an hour or so a day of study, for a week. I decided on the essential words, the crucial nouns and verbs, and some comparators and descriptors. I came up with a stripped-down grammar, and I did my own Romanization. Romanization is the process of taking words from a language using a different writing system, and systematically converting them to a form written using our alphabet. If you learn the system, it works well enough. It seemed to me that those who didn't know the system – in those days Korean was usually Romanized using one called McCune-Reischauer –

would mispronounce a lot of words. For instance, *meongcheongi* (not one of the hundred), a word I mentioned earlier. I am not sure how you think it's pronounced, but if I had included it, I would have written it as "mung-chung-ee," and explained that the first two syllables rhymed with "dung."

I was proud of my little paper. I would learn later that others had similar ideas. Linguists in the US created what I think was called Basic English for the Nazi rocket scientists they imported. It had a vocabulary of eight hundred words. That was initially. Later they decided that the scientists needed a set of words for their work. And their wives needed a set for around the house, and before they were through adding eight-hundred-word modules, they were up to about eight thousand words. The scientists would have been better off studying English using tried and true methods from the beginning. The Japanese also came up with something which turned out to be even worse. They created an artificial form of Japanese because they believed only Japanese were able to speak real Japanese. No one wanted to waste time learning to speak a weird pidgin.

The drawback was that they were trying to teach people who actually needed to become fluent in the target language. My goal was something quick and dirty, which would enable a visitor to order food, take a cab, and hold very simple conversations, all with minimal effort. Unfortunately, none of the people I gave copies to could be bothered to actually study. They all thought it was a great idea, but trying it out was too much like homework. I really wanted to know if my idea worked.

So I used myself as a guinea pig. I told you that I'd been to Bangkok in the fall. Before my trip I went out and bought a book of basic Thai. I went through it and tried to find and list the Thai equivalents for my hundred words of Korean. I skimmed the grammar, looking to see how one asked a question, expressed tenses, etc. I did my one week of study. Then I went to Thailand. How did it work? Very well. The apex came when I took a taxi to Lumpini Stadium to watch kickboxing, my last night in town. I chatted about the weather, learned the driver was married, and how many children he had, and otherwise held a five-minute conversation. The problem was that we were in one of the worst traffic jams in Bangkok history. That's a bold claim since Bangkok's traffic is legendary, but this one was so bad it made the front page of the Bangkok Post the next morning, with a photo of Sukhumvit Road which might well have included my cab. After two hours and five minutes, two hours after my conversation dried up, we had only gone from Soi 13 to Nana, less than a mile, and I had to give up on seeing Thai boxing.

Murray and I were talking about speaking Thai, since we were stopping in Thailand, and I told him all about my theory, and how it had worked. After which he proceeded to tell me his theory, parroting back the gist of what I'd just said. Oh, they were his ideas, but it was obvious that he had completely ignored everything I had said, because how could I have said anything worth his paying attention to? Rubbing salt in the wound, when he said something in Thai, asking if there was a restaurant upstairs in the building we were entering, I repeated what he'd said, asked if I had it right, and he said, "Um … good enough … for you."

I'd like to report that when we were in the casino, he turned out to be inept at blackjack. He wasn't. He was playing the same size units I was, and it was like watching myself play. He played flawlessly. Not only that, he was really fast. One of the tests teams give to new players is to see how fast they can count down a deck. A card or two are removed from a shuffled deck, and the player fans through it, then announces when finished, a count. The missing card or cards are turned over, to see if the person was accurate. Some books say you should practice until you can do this in less than thirty seconds. Others say less than twenty-five. Darryl Purpose has been called the world's fastest card counter, and at least once counted down a deck in eight seconds. I was never timed, but I would have been hopeless at fanning a deck. I have small hands, and the manipulation takes forever. But I could play as fast as the fastest dealer could deal to me, which is what really matters.

I wasn't getting much of a chance, with everyone wanting to play on my table. They wanted to play on my table even more when Murray showed up. No one liked Murray, not the Chinese card counters, not the other customers, not the dealers, and not the bosses, whether Australian or Indonesian. His attitude was more pungent than body odor, No one liked him.

Which meant that of the two tables everyone else piled on mine, and he had a table to himself. One which he could spread to four hands of five hundred, which he played with blazing speed. There's a novel called *Who Rides With Wyatt?* Anticipating Lorne Greene's song "Ringo," in the book Wyatt Earp meets up with Johnny Ringo, gets to see him practice, and while he doesn't think that "no human being could match the draw," Wyatt does wonder if the kid might possibly be faster than he. I know how Wyatt felt, when I watched Murray.

A decade later Murray would attend one of Max Rubin's Blackjack Balls, and would win the competition to be crowned that year's King of Blackjack. He was no dilettante; he was the real deal. I've run into him at a few of the Balls, and am happy to say he has also mellowed, and is much nicer to be around.

I was certain that in the long run, having Murray aboard was not good for me. The bosses liked me, but they didn't like the Chinese, and they hated Murray. We were all on the same junket, and it was eventually going to create trouble. Good thing Murray only did one cruise.

He did make a trip to Genting before leaving us, and there he did get his comeuppance, though I don't know if he knew it.

To be polite, or perhaps out of curiosity, Wong sat at the table with Murray. Later, when we were alone, he told me this story.

"Sir, I play at same table Murray. He have many black chips. Count goes up. Many players are behind the table. Many arms reaching down. They bet many square. Murray, he is very scared, have so many arm around him. I see one arm, hand reaching down, reach for Murray black chips. Arm go back up. So do three black chips. What you think of that?" And as he said it Wong looked sideways at me, and broke into a broad grin, which he flashed for just an instant, even faster than Murray playing a hand of blackjack.

CHAPTER 59
BIG PLAYERS

Back aboard the ship Murray was gone, but two new players were hogging a table. Eric Lim, from Singapore, and Gary Wong, from Kuala Lumpur, were not part of our junket. Their table had special limits, a minimum of three hundred, and a maximum of five thousand. Paul Lee mentioned them, and after lunch I wandered by their table to watch them play for a few minutes. Then I watched a few minutes more.

The first thing I noticed was that they were playing correct basic strategy. Hardly anyone does that if they don't know how to count. They were betting seven spots of three hundred dollars. Then the count went up. They lost most of the hands. Gary began helping Eric put out seven more three-hundred-dollar bets, but Eric, who seemed to be the man with the money, cursed their luck, grabbed the seven bets, and stacked them up.

"What are you doing? Are you crazy? If you are going to do that, I am not going to help you!" Eric now bet his single hand of twenty-one hundred. You may recall a much earlier discussion where I explained that if no one else is at the table, betting more on a single hand is not the same as betting the same amount, broken down over multiple hands. A single twenty-one-hundred-dollar bet was a huge increase in their effective bet, but would look to the casino like they had just made the same bet, only in different form.

Eric lost, but the count had gone up. He now doubled his previous bet as though steaming.

"Okay, if you are nuts, I can be nuts too!" Said Gary, and matched Eric's bet, so they now had over eight grand on the table, on two hands. Within another round or two, egging each other on, they had seven hands of five thousand out there!

They weren't moving perfectly with the count, but that was part of the act. Their bets were moving generally with the count. They also made one or two plays which suggested to me that maybe they didn't know all of their index numbers, just most of them. And I did see one basic strategy error. But playing as they did, even if it wasn't perfect, with those huge bets they rated to make a lot of money.

"You didn't tell me those guys were counters," I said to Paul, when I joined him at the other table.

"What do you mean? They don't count." The act had fooled him.

Later, returning after another meal, I wandered by their table, saw the count go up, and decided to take advantage of it. They weren't betting seven spots at the moment, so I dropped a thousand dollar bet on the third base square. Both of them glared at me. I made a couple of bets, the shoe ended, and I went back to the other table. Next time I passed their table it had a sign saying "Private Table" on it.

They started off losing, but then their luck turned. I happened to see a hand where with pair splits and double downs they had eleven five-thousand-dollar-bets on the layout. The dealer busted, and they raked in one hundred and ten thousand dollars' worth of chips.

The next cruise, when the casino opened, there were some changes. The table limit on both blackjack tables was two hundred dollars! Bambang, the Indonesian boss, made a gleeful point of making sure I saw it.

Eric and Gary were aboard, but no longer had a private game. They had permission to bet two thousand dollars on a hand, each, which they did a few times, but they knew the jig was up. I did, too, but when I saw Randy, the Casino Manager and lone American staffer, I asked what was up. He had been on vacation the previous cruise, and was as surprised as any of us. What he'd been told was that Eric and Gary won seven hundred thousand dollars. The Indonesians finally woke up to the fact that it was possible to put a hurt on the blackjack games. And if they were taking measures against Gary and Eric, they'd take them against me, since I had brought all the annoying players aboard. Even though Randy was the Casino Manager, the Indonesians had the final say. The Shangri-La was no longer paradise.

CHAPTER 60
ONE MORE ASSAULT ON OLYMPUS

Meanwhile, I was needed back in Korea. The team had devised another new look. No casino had ever seen a play quite like this one. Joe would again be the big player, but the play callers, plural, would be a pair of young Japanese women. Having two counters seemed and still seems redundant, but it did add one more element of disguise to the play. My role would once again be to supervise. After getting cash from the bank, and arming the players with money, we went in three separate cabs to Incheon. The women would check into a double room. Joe would check into a single. I would stay in the hotel down the hill. After each play, they would report to me.

I had the feeling that, were I able to observe the action, I would have wanted to work more with our play callers. They were extremely paranoid. Sunday night, after their last play of the weekend, we all went, separately, to a hotel in Oksudong. Joe and I arrived earlier than the other two, and were sitting in the coffee shop off the lobby when they arrived. They had gotten a car through the hotel, and the driver helped them with their bags. When they realized Joe and I were in plain sight, they freaked out.

Up in their room, I assured them that the driver didn't know anything about what went on in the casino, and wouldn't recognize me, or Joe. And now that we were in Seoul, they need have no fear of being seen with me because, "There are eleven million people in this city, and no one here knows what we are doing!"

That night, Joe and I went to Itaewon. As we walked up Fire Station Road, we passed cabs lined up near the King Club. One of the drivers jumped out, and began waving at me, yelling, "Hey, gambler!"

I said to Joe, "Better not mention that to the girls."

After a second weekend in Incheon, I went to see Mr. Chang at the Honorable Jesus Bookstore. While waiting for the cash, I noticed graffiti on one wall, including the date October 28, 1992. That was the following fall, and I asked him what it meant.

"That's when the world will end."

"Thanks! Good to know."

I was buying seventy thousand dollars in US hundreds. That seemed like a large amount, but there was a young woman ahead of me buying ninety grand. The world might be ending, but Mr. Chang's business was good.

There is a lacuna. I can't remember why I needed that much in US dollars. It was far more than I'd be sending out with the three players. What I do remember was how much counting I did that night. When I got it from Mr. Chang, I not only counted it, but I faced all the money, broke it into thousand-dollar stacks, created bundles to be given to each player, and only then took a cab back to Oksudong.

There was an extremely nosy clerk at the hotel. She had a bad habit of trying to see what I had in my safety box. I chewed her out at least once. When I got there this time, I stuffed in my bundle, then went to dinner.

After dinner I collected the money, and met with the players up in my room. One of the women counted her stack, and said she was a thousand short. They'd counted the money in front of me, so I had no worries that she'd sequestered some. I counted the money I had given her, and it was light. I made it up, and then counted all the remaining money, twice. Seventy-thousand had turned into sixty-nine.

I called the States, and spoke with Munch. "We are short a thousand. I am sure the desk clerk stole it." We discussed what to do, and decided to write it off. The clerk had chosen wisely. If she stole more, she'd have forced our hand. She may have thought we wouldn't notice the small fraction missing, until it was too late. Or she may have guessed that we did not want to call the police, because then I'd have to explain why I had seventy thousand US dollars. It would not be the last time I lost money from a hotel safety box.

CHAPTER 61
ROYAL PACIFIC

The Shangri-La might be burnt out, but there were two more cruise ships with casinos. Originally the three had been one operation. Then the partners had a falling out. The Shangri-La was the largest, at 16,000 tons, and went to one set of partners. The other two went to the other set. The bigger the ship, the bigger the business, and the Shangi-La was drawing the most action. All three ships were sailing between Singapore and Jakarta, catering to Indonesian gamblers. The owners of the smaller operation decided to knock off their rival. They tipped a group of student activists that there was gambling aboard the Shangri-La. There were demonstrations, and the Shangri-La was barred, which is why it now sailed the Phuket route. It still did very well, but some punters, not wanting to fly to Singapore when they could board a ship from their home port, switched allegiance.

The Royal Pacific was 13,000 tons, slightly smaller than the Shangri-La. The biggest difference when not inside the casino, was the food. The Shangri-La had really good food. Both ships served buffets, but the Royal Pacific's had fewer dishes, less variety, and was generally disappointing. Made more so when the staff had a party, with a special table set up at the end of the buffet line, so that everyone passing them could see they were eating much better than the rest of us.

The game in the casino was like the one on the Shangri-La, but with two differences which made it better for me. One was the cut. The Shangri-La cut a deck and a half out of eight. The Royal Pacific cut only a deck. The other difference was that while it was convoluted, I could track parts of the shuffle. It was almost more trouble than it was worth, but every little bit helps.

Two days out of Singapore we docked in Jakarta. There were five of us, me, Paul Lee, James and Katrin Tew, and a banker from Kuala Lumpur named Bas Karan. I'd never been to Indonesia, and had a laundry list of things I was hoping to acquire or experience when we went to town. I wanted to see some cool Indonesian sights, suitable for picture taking. I wanted postcards, and English language books, and a local English language newspaper, all of which seemed the sort of thing I could find in a bookstore. I wanted film for my camera. I wanted to buy a batik shirt. I wanted to try Indonesian food. I didn't think to add "air-conditioning" to the list, and it's a good thing that I didn't, because they took me to a place where I got none of the other things, so that would have been one more disappointment.

My first impression was of a crowd of touts all trying to grab us for their taxis. I let Paul and James run interference. We ended up in an oversized tuk-tuk, open air, the better to enjoy the smell of sewage, which flowed in a drainage ditch next to the road most of the way to our destination. We savored the experience for an hour and a half because the traffic was horrendous. Spending so much time not moving meant that I did manage two "cool pictures." One was of a man selling birds, with cages balanced in a bamboo pole resting on his shoulders. The other was of a maniac. He came screaming out of nowhere, raving and waving and carrying on. He was stark naked. These weren't the pictures I expected to be taking, but at least the experience was not a total bust.

Our destination was the mall from hell. I am not a shopper. If I need something I determine where to find it, approach like a heat-seeking missile, and once I find it, I look for something more interesting to do. Paul and the others seemed to think wandering around a shopping mall was the more interesting thing to do.

This shopping mall was six stories tall, around a central atrium. Because it had no air-conditioning, the further we climbed, the more unbearable the place became. It was a six-story mall with no photo shop for film. With no bookstore. With no local papers. With no post-cards. It had batik shirts. I wore American XL in those days. The largest size they had was Indonesian XXXXL, and it was too small.

Surely, they had Indonesian food? Yes, they had that. It was on display in a glass case. There was something which they told me was "heart." It was black and leathery. None of us was willing to eat in that restaurant, so we ate Korean. Then we reboarded our tuk-tuk and fought the traffic back to the ship.

I was sitting outside the casino, finishing chapter in the book I was reading, when a young Aussie walked up to me, and said, "I told them you were counting cards."

"That was nice of you. Who are you?"

"I'm the eye in the sky. I saw right away you were a counter. It's my job to tell them. They didn't care. If they don't care, I don't care."

Bless those clueless Indonesia bosses! This was looking good.

The ship's usual routine was to sail two days to Jakarta, and two days back to Singapore, but every third cruise they would spend another day sailing up to Port Klang, the port at K.L., and then a day back. Most of the passengers got off in Singapore, but our group stayed aboard.

I was playing that evening when Bas Karan came over and invited me to join him and some others on the other table. It was surprising because his regular game was mini-baccarat, and when he did play blackjack, he was certain I was a terrible player. Which tells you a lot about his play. Nevertheless, he was being a good guy, and in the spirit of camaraderie, asking me over. It seems that he and some of the bigger bettors had gotten the casino to raise the limit on the other table to a thousand dollars.

I knew Bas Karan had been losing heavily. While we played, he continued losing. I gathered that he was in over a hundred thousand Singapore dollars, which was sixty thousand US in those days. Came the hand that looked like it would tap him out. I had a hundred bet, and so did the guy next to me. Bas Karan had capped our bets with nine hundred each. I had threes against a seven, and split. He was not happy, but I controlled the hand. I think he had the option of leaving his bet on only one, but he went along and bet another nine hundred. I caught an eight on one of the hands, and doubled down. There went another nine hundred. Now the guy next to me split a pair of sevens, and Bas Karan bet what may have been his last money. The forty-five hundred, if he lost, would put him seventy thousand in the hole.

The dealer busted. Bas Karan won a few more hands, then went to play Mini-Baccarat. I won five thousand, a nice change from my results on the Shangri-La, and went to the karaoke lounge.

I had been warned not to go there by a dealer. Why? I asked. He told me that the staff got a day in port once every three months. Tomorrow was the day, and they also got a night in the karaoke on the eve of their holiday. He told me I really didn't want to hear them sing.

Which made me really want to hear them sing. The first singer was Indonesian. The song was a love song, judging by the video. A young couple, both dressed in white, holding hands in front of various tourist sites in Jakarta, gazed lovingly into each other's eyes. This couple was so clean-cut they made Donny and Marie look like the Marquis De Sade and Justine. Then the singer began.

It's hard to believe a human throat could produce those sounds. Indonesian love songs sound like what you'd get if you threw a cat in a blender.

CHAPTER 62
I DON'T LOSE MY HEAD, BUT I GET SKINNED

I once auditioned for Jeopardy! I got far enough that I was asked to write down five fascinating facts, things Alex Trebek could ask me about on the show. I wrote down some doozies. One of them was something like this, "I was robbed by septuagenarian gypsies outside the National Museum in Kuala Lumpur, where I had gone to see the exhibit of 'Human Heads in Culture and History.'" That Alex never got to ask me that question I blame on Boston Cream Pie, a story for another time. How I was robbed is a story for this time.

Paul and I had a day to kill in K.L. after docking at Port Klang. We'd be sailing back to Singapore that evening, then on to Jakarta. I read about the exhibit, and told Paul that of course we had to go. While mainland Malaysia wasn't known for cannibals and head-hunters, Sabah and Sarawak were luckier. There were plenty of places in Indonesia which staked claims, and of course there was New Guinea! We were practically in the headhunter headquarters, so to speak.

As we approached the building we were accosted by an elderly trio of tourists. They were of uncertain ethnicity, but may indeed have been Romani. One man and his wife began asking me about the exchange rate for Korean won. Gee, I was a good one to ask! While I was trying to explain, his friend had managed to pry Paul Lee away, and led him up a fork in the path, uphill and parallel to where I stood, ostensibly so Paul could take his picture.

The man I was talking to seemed confused, and was not understanding my explanation. I needed a visual prompt. I took out my wallet, fanned up a dollar bill, and was pointing to it, and to his money.

Just then, Paul shouted, "Jake, come away from them!!"

I was annoyed, said I would be done in a minute, but as I did ….

The old man reached into my wallet, and flipped the money so a hundred-dollar bill was now on top, and asked, "What about this?" I was surprised he couldn't figure it out for himself, take the rate for a dollar, and multiply by a hundred, but I did the calculation for him, said I had to go, tamped the money down into my wallet, and rejoined Paul.

I keep my money sorted, and I wanted to make sure it was in order, so I took my wallet back out. As I put the money in order, I discovered I was missing a hundred, a fifty, and two twenties. In the blink of an eye those stubby, arthritic old hands had performed sleight of hand worthy of the best closeup magicians.

At least there were lots of decapitated heads inside.

CHAPTER 63
REUNION

The casino kept the thousand-dollar game. That was the rainbow. The storm clouds arrived in Singapore.

"Guess what?" Bas Karan had taken the shuttle flight from K.L., and would be cruising again. I neglected to mention that the morning we arrived in K.L., and Paul was giving me my money in my cabin, he said, "Did you hear about Mister Bas Karan?"

"What about him?"

"He won five thousand dollars."

"For the night?"

"For the trip."

I had a vague sense of unease. The man had gone from down seventy, to up five. Casinos don't like that, and I had already had one ship that liked me, but hated my companions. Bas Karan, having tried and failed to lose his seventy thousand stakes, was back to try again.

"Guess what else?" The way he said it, with a furtive grin, made me think I would not enjoy his news as much as he was. "Simon is coming."

On, no, it was starting again!

Sure enough, we were joined at the ship by Simon and Bas Karan. At least it was only Simon. There was good news once the casino opened. They kept the thousand-dollar limit. Better than that, most of the time Simon and I had the table to ourselves. We agreed that we would share two spots. When the bet was minimum, we'd each bet ten dollars, because we had to bet double the table minimum to play two spots. We spread to double thousands, with me taking double eight hundreds, and Simon taking the rest. It made sense for me to play the hands and after determining how much Simon wanted to bet on each true count, I handled everything. All he had to do was keep up with handing me, or receiving, chips. Unimpeded, I was playing so fast the chips were practically flying through the air. It was a lot of fun.

I also had one of the rare interesting blackjack stories. Like the Shangri-La, the Royal Pacific let you take insurance up to the amount of your original bet. I had double thousands bet, when the dealer turned up an ace. I pushed out two more thousand, and the dealer had blackjack. I bet double thousands again, and the dealer turned up another ace. I insured again, and the dealer once again had blackjack. I bet double thousands once more, and the dealer showed an ace for the third time. A question had occurred to me when I first learned of the rule. I have never gotten an authoritative answer, but when I heard about the rule, I wondered if one should always take the most possible insurance? Insurance is, after all, a side bet. And when it first becomes correct to insure, your advantage on the bet is barely above break even. I had told Rocky that when the count was plus four or above, he should take full insurance, but if it was only a true three, take the usual half bet insurance. Now that the dealer had turned up two blackjacks and an ace, and I had had some good hands myself, including just now a twenty, and a blackjack of my own, the count had dropped to plus three. I took even money on my blackjack, and insured the twenty for five hundred. The dealer pulled his third blackjack. The bottom line was that despite the dealer having three blackjacks in a row, we netted five thousand dollars.

I was doing something else, which was in retrospect, foolish. The shuffle was sort of trackable. There were a lot of sections, and the procedure was complicated. I decided to give myself some assistance. I used coins as mnemonics. The Indonesians have a big coin with a Garuda on it, which I thought looked pretty cool. I liked playing with it. I had other coins in various denominations. I would lay them out along the rail in front of me, and track the counts of the segments by twisting them like clockfaces. I kept negative counts on the rail, and pushed positive counts off it. After the shuffle they would all be returned to twelve o'clock, and were all on the rail, ready for the next shoe.

It bugged the dealers and bosses, because they couldn't figure out what I was doing. They didn't like that.

When the boat docked in Jakarta my companions said, "Let's go to the mall!"

And I said, "You can if you want. I'm not." We went into town, and this time I got my Indonesian food.

Back aboard we kept playing, and were booking a nice win. Then it was day four, the final day. We had company, and now we played our own hands, because we were joined by Paul Lee, and Bas Karan. Bas Karan had once again lost about sixty thousand US dollars. He'd cried on the shoulders of the bosses, and they gave him a special limit. He could play double two thousand, and bet them on other's hands if he wanted. He started betting them on my hand, and Simon's. This was strange because he was still convinced, so far as I knew, that we played very badly, and he had empty spaces he could use to make his own plays. Or, he could have gone and played his usual game, mini-baccarat.

I noticed Paul Lee with a strange little smirk when Bas Karan started betting on our hands.

Meanwhile, he began making a a jerk out of himself. Having wheedled the concession of the raised limit, he started trying to color outside the lines. He tried to bet more than two hands, or more than two thousand. When called on it, he'd do something he thought clever like betting triple fifteen hundreds. You'd think that after being corrected by the bosses a time or two, he'd stop trying, but that wasn't in his nature. He seemed to believe that even though the bosses were watching, if a new dealer came to the table, he could put one over on her.

"Keep your eye on him," they began instructing the dealers, every time a new one came as relief. And the dealers all assumed they meant me, because they knew I knew how to play. Bas Karan was a fish, so who would worry about him? Then they'd be told, "No, the Indian." But having them first give me the fisheye wasn't likely to be good for my long-term prospects.

Sure enough, Bas Karan once again was on the verge of tapping out, then by betting on my hands, began a rally. Just like the previous cruise he wound up winning for the trip. I was sure that wasn't good.

We spent the day in Singapore, then boarded the same day. By the end of the four days ahead of us I would have been cruising for fourteen straight days, three and a half cruises, including the trip to Port Klang.

On the dock was a striking figure. He was very tall, wore cowboy boots, and had a ponytail. He reminded me of Steven Seagal. I wondered who he was, and if he was possible bad news.

When the casino opened, he was standing in the pit, watching us play. Once again it was the four of us, though Paul wasn't playing, just watching. It only took a shoe or two, and the newcomer conferred with the boss. I couldn't hear all he said, but got the gist of it, "The American is a pro, the Chinese guy knows some things, and the Indian is a total idiot."

The next shoe was cut in half. Instead of cutting less than a deck, they cut four. I hadn't heard him tell them that. He'd wandered off. I hoped it was an aberration. The next shoe a relief dealer came on, and cut half a deck. My hopes were dashed when during the shuffle the boss whispered in her ear, and the cut went back to four decks.

"I am going to get a lot of reading done this cruise!"

Simon was surprised. He was used to wasting time playing bad cuts in Macau, and didn't understand why I wouldn't waste time playing this one.

Paul Lee managed to get the word from someone. The stranger was the youngest shift manager in Australian history. He was twenty-three when he was promoted. Now he was upper management with the company providing dealers and bosses for the ships. I was toast.

The next day Simon and Bas Karan came to me, and wanted me to play. They had gotten Bas Karan to make a fuss, and the cuts were back to normal. "They won't be if I play," I told them. They insisted it was all good.

The Royal Pacific had four blackjack tables, another improvement on the Shangri-La. As soon as I walked in the door, I saw all four dealers break the shoes, shuffle the cards, and cut all four shoes in half. I took it as a tribute. And got a lot of reading done. By telling Bas Karan to bet on my hands, as a way to win back the money he was losing, Paul Lee killed the goose laying the golden eggs. My cruising days were over.

CHAPTER 64
ONE HUNDRED PESOS FOR WHISKEY

had made some other trips to Manila that spring, but this time was different. I was flying back from Singapore using the original ticket. There was a finality to it.

Marty had found a cheaper and more congenial hotel than the Silahis. It was called the Park Hotel, because it was next to Paco Park, a cemetery created during a typhoid epidemic in days of yore. We had been swimming, but decided to dry off in the sun. There was a wet bar, not in use, with a telephone on it. We were standing next to it when the phone rang, and with no staff around, I decided to answer it. The voice on the other end asked for someone; a guy climbing out of the pool took the call. Marty and I moved a few feet away so as not to intrude. I was still close enough to hear it when he said, "Jake and Marty? I'll see."

"I'm Jake, and he's Marty. Is that for us?"

He handed me the phone. The hell? Who could possibly have found me here? Alan Woods, that's who.

"Anna Marie and I are going to see her mother tomorrow. Are you interested in seeing how real Filipinos live?" I told him I was.

Anna Marie was Woody's Manila girlfriend. Alan and his main squeeze, Nora, had made trips to Manila to enjoy what he referred to as "decadence." Decadence involved group sex and ecstasy, or E, as it was by then called. Nora had discovered Anna Marie in their talent search, dancing at the Firehouse, the largest pole dancing establishment in Ermita. Marty and I had met her, along with three other Firehouse girls, during a previous trip, when Woody showed up for dinner with an entourage. Anna Marie convinced Alan and Nora that when it came to birddogging, she was a real talent scout, though her "discoveries" were preponderantly coworkers from the Firehouse.

At noon the next day they collected me at my hotel.

"Do you want twenty thousand?" I asked Alan. My next stop was Hong Kong, where I would be transferring team money. "I don't yet know how much I will be handing off, but I have twenty in an envelope in my safety box." He said okay, and I retrieved the envelope before we left.

In the taxi, he told me about a recent trip Anna Marie took. She'd been to visit him and Nora in Hong Kong. On her return the cab driver at Nino Aquino Airport quoted her two hundred pesos to get to her house.

"It's only one hundred. Don't try to cheat me. I was only visiting Hong Kong; I don't live there." Cabbies figured that Filipinas coming in from Hong Kong were probably domestic helpers, out of touch with current prices.

"Oh, you visited? So you are rich! Two hundred pesos."

They argued, and Anna Marie finally said, "Fine, I'll play two hundred, but you have to go the long way, so I get my money's worth."

While he was telling the story, I was noticing something ominous. I'd always thought of Ermita as looking seedy and dangerous, like a Mexican border town after dark. Now I was realizing that Ermita was a tourist district, a good side of Manila to show visitors. I was seeing how "real Filipinos lived," and it was grim. And getting grimmer. The neighborhoods we passed through got worse, and worse, and worse.

At last, after driving for an hour, we stopped. As we got out of the cab, even Alan, who was usually oblivious, looked around and asked, "Anna Marie, are you quite sure this is safe?"

"Oh, yes," she said blithely, "I come here all the time." As she said it, I saw the cab driver quickly lock all his doors, and peel out in a cloud of dust.

We were in hell. It was about ninety-five degrees, and there were ten thousand zombies shuffling around under a blazing sun. These were people who had nowhere to go, and whose homes were too hot to bear. They ambled slowly, aimlessly, while their skulls baked.

Beyond the crowd was an entire neighborhood constructed of corrugated iron, cardboard, and discarded wood. Not individual shanties, these were joined. That's where we headed, entering a maze of narrow tunnels through the slum, dark, with standing water which had dripped from the makeshift roof. Somewhere inside it, we stopped. There was a fat woman sitting on a small plastic stool, and Woody and I were directed to join her on two vacant stools.

"My pants are too tight to sit with this," said Woody, and handed back the envelope with the twenty grand. At least I was wearing my guayabera shirt! It covered my bulging pockets.

Anna Marie vanished, but after ten minutes of sitting uncomfortably, Alan and I speechless in the oppressive and ominous heat, she reappeared, with a girlfriend. They led us deeper into the maze, until we came to a door in one wooden wall. Running along the wall was a wire. There was a small hole through which the wire disappeared, reappearing inside when the door opened to Anna Marie's knock. Its end was connected to a bare bulb, the only light inside.

The room we crowded into was four feet deep, six feet wide, and six feet high. There were two bunks on one wall, four feet long, eighteen inches deep. Those were the beds. Inside were Anna Marie's mother, fifteen-year-old stepsister, and a baby belonging to Anna Marie, being raised by her mother. There was a stepfather also living there, but absent during our visit. All four lived in that space, with all of their belongings. I guess there was a source of water nearby. I didn't ask.

I saw how they lived, and they were certainly real. They were even cheerful, pleased to have visitors. We didn't stay long.

Back out in the heat and dust, surrounded by the zombies, I was approached by a teenager. I think he was a teenager. He was tall, at least six feet, so he looked down at me. He walked up until the space between us was only a few inches. I'd never seen a face entirely without affect before. It was blank, as though a stone mask was talking to me, and his eyes were as dead as I feared I was about to be, as he said, "Give me a hundred pesos, for whiskey."

He didn't look around, nor did I, but I sensed that others nearby were part of his gang. I had a problem. I was sure that if I refused his request, they would jump me. Then again, if I took out my wallet, I was afraid the crowd would reenact the climax of *Suddenly, Last Summer*, with me playing Sebastian Venable.

I answered quickly. "Okay, I will give you one hundred pesos. But you have to talk to my comptroller." I pointed at Anna Marie.

"Whuh?"

"My comptroller! You want one hundred pesos, right? I want to give it to you. So you need to talk to my comptroller. She handles all my cash disbursements" I smiled reassuringly, to let him see how cooperative I was being.

"Whuh?"

Meanwhile, my comptroller had done something right. She'd summoned transportation. Unfortunately, it was in the form of two pedicabs. Anna Marie and Alan were already climbing into one; her girlfriend and I squeezed into the other.

"You have to see my comptroller. I don't do cash disbursements, so you need to talk to her."

The driver of our pedicab had managed an intersection of two vital statistics: his weight in pounds was equal to his age in years. He heaved his right leg hard against a pedal, and we moved forward one foot.

"Whuh?" The young man was baffled. Baffled was better than enraged.

"My comptroller … (c'mon, driver!) … she will handle the cash disbursement." We moved another foot.

And so we made our escape. He could have overtaken us simply by strolling, but when last seen, he was still trying to work out what just happened.

Soon we were whizzing along, at the speed of a brisk walk. In ten minutes, we had gone a couple of blocks, and climbed a dozen socioeconomic tiers. We stopped at a two-story townhouse, which turned out to be one Anna Marie rented with Woody's subsidy. Inside she and her girlfriend did something curious. They shut off the air-conditioning, made sure the curtains were drawn, and stuffed towels under the doors. Now I learned the purpose of the trip. She'd gone there to purchase what the Filipinos called *shabu*, the Koreans called *hirropon*, and English speakers called "ice," crystal meth. It was a drug buy. If the cops showed up, and found twenty grand in my pocket, we would not be arrested, they would shoot us all and keep the money.

I vowed next time to ask a lot more questions before letting Woody act as tour guide.

CHAPTER 65
ISLAND COLONIES

Less than a week later, I was staying in Woody's apartment. He'd come a long way from Tai Koo Shing. He and John were now living in a two-story penthouse which shared half the top of a high rise on Kennedy Road in Wanchai. I am guessing the rent was at least six times the seventeen hundred a month he had been paying, probably more. From his living room you could look way down into Happy Valley Race Course, though you would need binoculars to see the horses.

I had twenty-eight thousand to hand over, and he asked if I'd mind depositing it at his bank. The bank was on the next parallel street north of Kennedy Road, Queen's Road, but getting there was interesting. Hong Kong Island is mountainous. It's only around thirty square miles, but is home to a sixth of the population, one-point-two million people. Most live along a strip, pasted like a Band-Aid on the northern side of the mountains. When you go inland, you ascend rapidly. By the time you reach the top of the Peak, you can look down at the tops of thousand-foot towers which are far below.

To go to the bank, I took an elevator down from the thirty-fifth floor to the fourth, getting off inside a parking garage. Walking through the garage, I emerged on Kennedy Road, and walked west, uphill, less than two hundred meters, to reach a high-rise office tower. Entering from the street on its south side, I learned I was on the seventeenth floor. I took an elevator to ground level, walking out the door on the north side of the building. I was now on Queen's Road. I continued west, which on Queen's Road at that point was downhill. The bank wasn't far.

I filled out a deposit slip, and when I reached the teller, told her I would be depositing twenty-eight thousand US dollars. I had taken great care with the money. Every bill faced the same way, ten bills in each stack, the tenth folded around the ends of the other nine. I passed her the twenty-eight bundles, and then watched her take the first bundle, peel off the first bill, and hold it up to the light. She gave it a brisk snap, turned it over, and snapped it again. She set it aside, picked up the next bill ....

She wasn't really going to do that with every bill? After all, there were two hundred and eighty bills. If she took ten seconds per bill, that would take forty-five minutes. She was really going to do it.

Even worse, she was making multiple piles of bills, all over her counter, but around a third seemed to be sequestered for special attention. I wondered if when the ship had its counterfeiting scare, I had been stuck with bad paper.

After an eternity, during which she never said, "Excuse me, this may take a while," she called over the manager. The two of them began going through the sequestered pile, snapping away. One hour and a half after I initiated the deposit, she had found no counterfeit bills. She said to me, "You are two hundred dollars short."

I exploded. "Get the police!" Her eyes popped open.

The manager hurried over because everyone in the bank heard me. Heck, if Woody had been home, he might have heard me. "Is there a problem?"

"Yes, there is a problem. You and your helper have had my money all over the place, in an enormous mess, while you fooled around. Now she is claiming I am two hundred dollars short! I want a police report, so that when *my* money turns up, when a cleaning woman finds two bills on the floor, or a cash drawer has extra money, it will show it belongs to *me*."

The police were summoned, and they did what cops do. They strip searched the teller. I wish they had strip searched the manager. Maybe it would have taught him that courtesy was something he should teach his staff. If they wanted to handle our money, they owed it to us.

The money did not turn up. It was only days later that I remembered a night in Manila when, trying to avoid opening my box wide enough to display its contents, I may have peeled off two bills. Still, it serves the teller right. Had she at any point said, "Sir, I notice how carefully you have arranged your money. This bundle is two hundred short," the problem would have been averted.

My next stop was the bookstore. Paul Lee told me of a good one to visit while in Hong Kong. The cab let me off in a car park connected to a shopping mall. It was a big car park, and I asked the security guard which way I should go to find the bookstore. I showed him my little notebook, where I'd written the details. He wasn't much help as his English was limited. Only after I looked again at the notebook did I realize that the bookstore information was the only English on the two pages I'd opened the notebook to. Covering the rest were all the Chinese obscenities Simon had written down for me.

I took the jet foil to visit Simon and the others on Macau, staying overnight at Simon's place. Macau was Portuguese for four hundred and forty-two years. It was the oldest European settlement in Asia, dating to 1557, nearly three hundred years before the British acquired Hong Kong, and was still Portuguese in 1992. Chinese had only become an official language the year before.

Simon's wife was Korean. Unlike Amy and Wong, Simon had played Walker Hill. His wife worked in the cashier's cage. They married, and he brought her to Macau. Simon didn't speak Korean, and his wife didn't speak Cantonese, so they communicated in English, though neither was fluent. Their daughter was three, and spoke those three languages, and Portuguese for good measure. She delighted in responding to adults in a language they didn't know, talking to her dad in Korean, her mom in Cantonese, and me in Portuguese. Simon and I encountered the same thing later that day, when he stopped to pick up a couple of young fishermen – they looked to be about nine – and after telling Simon where to drop them, they switched to Portuguese.

There were eleven casinos in those days. The Portuguese had legalized gambling in 1849. In 1962 they granted a monopoly (which lasted until 2001) to a group controlled by Stanley Ho. Simon claimed Ho was a front for someone else, but I suspected that was a local conspiracy theory. The blackjack game was awful, and I didn't bother playing as much as a hand, not even so I could say I had played in Macau. The game had good rules, but it was six decks, cut in half. The pace was so slow that it made the game at the Silahis seem a whirlwind. The Chinese dealers were also notorious for taking an extended tea break if they thought you should be tipping them. Simon and the others would play eleven hours a day, standing the whole time, betting over the shoulders of the seated players when the count was good. They ground out a living that way.

The most interesting thing about the casinos was the display of gamblers' superstitions. For instance, a casino roof whose architecture resembled a bird's nest, because birds collect things, and store them in their nests. The roof meant that here was a place where Stanley Ho collected and stored your money. Another had an overhanging roof above the front entrance which was curved. Simon said it was meant to resemble a scimitar. Your head would be metaphorically chopped off as your neck passed below it.

The flagship of Ho's empire was the Casino Lisboa. Hanging above the front door when you entered was a ship, a reminder of Stanley Ho's pirate ancestors. I don't know if he really had pirate ancestors, but he wanted everyone to think he did. The blackjack tables were arranged in groups of four, with spaces between them of comparable size. The four tables and four gaps formed octagons. In fengshui the *bagua* is an eight-sided mirror, often hung opposite the front door of a home, to reflect back bad luck. The configuration of the tables was to let the players know these were *bagua*, intended to reflect back their luck. That management would go to all that trouble to let the players know. "We don't want you to win!" would repel Western players. The Chinese players figured if they owned the casino, they'd do exactly the same.

Simon and the others had promised me that when I came to Macau they would take me to a world class dim sum restaurant. The food was good, but I didn't think it was all that special. Years later I realized that dim sum is a gourmet food almost always served casually. The best dim sum I've had was far in the future. I would make a lot of business trips to Tokyo, and often stayed at the Ana Intercontinental Hotel in Akasaka. It has a Chinese restaurant (it's teppanyaki restaurant is also outstanding) which serves dim sum. Every dish is made fresh. The skin of the dumplings is translucent, and you can see the plump, fresh shrimp, or the spinach, through it. I have never had better. But proper dim sum is also all about the experience. When I was working in Hong Kong my girlfriend Sonia and I used to go to a place called Maxim's in North Point. Maxim's was a chain, and the restaurants were huge, seating anywhere from five hundred to a thousand people. It was packed on Sunday mornings. Screaming children chased each other in the aisles, dodging the old ladies and their carts, which they pushed around the restaurant, calling out whichever dish was tucked inside the bamboo baskets stacked on the cart. The fathers, meanwhile, would read the paper with one hand, while the mothers worked on the other hand with nail clippers. How long had they been there? Count the tea stains on the table cloth, like tree rings, to get an idea.

CHAPTER 66
HOMEWARD BOUND

Then I was back in Korea, nowhere left to go but Los Angeles. I went back to Manila, instead. I was already setting a record for "longest trip by me outside the country." I wanted to extend the record. I flew back to hang out with Marty one last time.

He was in the pool. It turned out he was hiding something, or rather, someone. He moved out of the way, revealing a companion he'd concealed behind him. "Recognize her?"

I didn't.

"This is Winlove. You know me; I am never with a girl more than two days. I have been with her eight." He waited for me to pass out, and sink to the bottom of the pool, in stunned amazement. When I didn't, he explained further. It seems we'd met Winlove the time Woody brought four girls from the Firehouse with him to the Indian restaurant. It was the night we'd met Ana Marie for the first time. Winlove, Marty said, was the one Woody really wanted to see. Actually, she was the one Nora really wanted to see. Woody seemed happy enough with Ana Marie. I have to take the word of the three experts, Marty, Woody, and Nora, as to Winlove's extra special allure. As for me, I liked her better than Ana Marie. Winlove was real, Ana Marie artificial. Winlove was a nice person. Ana Marie I wasn't so sure of. And Winlove was funny.

One day I tried *bangus*, a type of whitefish. Before I tasted it, I asked, "What is *bangus*?"

And she said, "It's *masarap*!" ("Delicious.") Maybe you had to be there.

Winlove's real name was Ana Fe. She chose the name Winlove for work. Her background was interesting. The Philippines is a Catholic country. Nearly eighty percent of all Filipinos are Catholic. Winlove was from a region which was Muslim. Not that her family was Muslim; her mother was a Jehovah's Witness. Winlove did not want to be a Jehovah's Witness, so she decided to become Mormon. I guess she was a Reformed Mormon, not an Orthodox Mormon. Otherwise, from what (little) I know of the Church of Jesus Christ of the Latter Day Saints, I don't think many of them dance naked in bars.

Her conversion was not accompanied by advanced religious instruction. "What religion are you?" she asked Marty. One of her girlfriends was present, and the girlfriend may have prompted her to ask.

"I'm a Jew." They looked puzzled. "I'm Jewish. You know, we killed Christ." They were even more baffled, so he added, "That's right! I did it. Personally!" They laughed. It was just Marty saying crazy stuff again.

I didn't stick around for more of Marty's divine revelations. I went back to Korea, this time set on departure. I stayed at Tom's place in Bangbaedong. I had been using it as a storage unit. In five months, I read a lot of books, and they accumulated there. Now they all went into my three-zipper bag, unzipped all the way, and stuffed when fully packed. It was raining when my cab pulled up out front. I grabbed the bag on either side, to lift it down the stairs. The bottom fell out.

I crammed the contents back in, and cradled it like a wounded warrior as I carried it to the cab. Gimpo Airport had a packing service in the lobby, and they trussed it with baling wire, top to bottom, and around the sides.

When I got to Munch's place in L.A., where I laid over for two days, we had to cut the wire off so I could get into the bag. For the flight to O'Hare, having no wire, we used duct tape.

While flying that final leg, I thumbed through my passport. In those days you could get inserts, adding pages. They allowed a maximum of two inserts, which you could order at the same time. I'd done that before the trip. Thanks to some stamps filling whole pages, I had almost filled the passport, even with my double-insert. During this trip I'd picked up one set of stamps, entry and exit, for Macau, three sets for Indonesia, and seven sets for Thailand. There were at least three sets each for Hong Kong and the Philippines, possibly as many as five. There were at least five for Korea, probably more. I have no idea how many I received in Malaysia, but the count for Singapore was twenty.

Back home at last, for the first time in five months my bag was completely unpacked. It was a sorry sight sitting on the curb, with its broken bottom, and strands of torn duct tape. In the morning it would make its last trip, in the maw of a garbage truck.

"Time for a new bag," I thought.

EPILOGUE

That's the story of how I went from mild-mannered suburban cab dispatcher to international man of mystery.

A few years ago, I began writing an autobiography. So far, I have written more than two hundred thousand words, and haven't reached my seventeenth birthday. If it is ever finished it will be long enough to make Marcel Proust choke on his madeleine. Then two things happened. The first was a talk I gave to the Arizona Mystery Writers, of which I am serving as president. The talk was about how I became a gambler. The following month I went to Las Vegas for a pair of events. One was a conference called Bet Bash, for professional sports bettors, something I had recently been doing. The night following the conference I was at the Blackjack Ball. That's an annual party for the world's best blackjack players, a chance to hang out with old friends. Before the week was over, I decided to set aside the larger project, and write the story of my gambling career. Soon after I began, I realized that even a book looking only at my life as a gambler, while it might not be Proustian, would certainly be Copperfieldian in length. I've been gambling for over forty years, and much has happened.

I decided to treat just the decade covered in this book. It was not the end of my blackjack career. Not even the halfway point. The last time I played was in September, 2005, more than thirteen years after the events in this story. It was at Mandalay Bay. We were playing edge sorting, a technique much older than card counting, and logistically difficult. Locking up the table before I came in as big player was an all-star cast: my brother, James Grosjean, Darryl, and Max Rubin. It was five-thirty in the morning, and I had been watching from a distance, because there was one civilian, a drunken woman, who refused to leave the table.

At last, I saw Munch spill a glass of wine on her. Good work Munch! Oops! She spilled it on him.

At long last she left, I sat down, and we won some money. I don't remember how much, between five and ten thousand anyway. In 1982 we would have been very happy to book a win like that. In 2005 it was just a day at the office.

I played blackjack in the years after playing on the cruise ships, but I played less and less. More and more of my time was spent doing other things, which I intend to write about in a sequel to this book. What sorts of things?

My interest in backgammon was rekindled at the end of 1989. When not away playing blackjack, backgammon took up more and more of my time. Within a few years, between money games, weekly tournaments, larger tournaments, study, and writing, I was averaging at least forty hours a week at it, like it was a regular job. I'd once dreamed that someday I would be the world's best, an author, an expert, the sort of player who drew crowds when I competed in tournaments. That all happened. I wasn't quite the world's best, peaking at number nine in the late nineties, but I was close.

Besides backgammon, I got involved with horse racing. I worked off and on for Bill Benter in Hong Kong. Later, with a different operation, I moved overseas to bet on racing in Japan. That really was a regular job, sometimes with sixty- and seventy-hour weeks.

Many of the people you have met in this book will appear in the sequel. Here is a roundup of some others, who will not.

Bas Karan could not leave well enough alone. With his winnings from the cruises he shared with me burning a hole in his pocket, he returned to the ship. Without me and Simon to help him, he managed to lose it all, and more besides. I saw him just once after that. He was playing blackjack at Genting, betting twenty-five ringgit, the equivalent of ten US dollars.

Marty was the last to see Paul Lee. Paul showed up at the Silahis, with Murray and some Chinese players. They were playing roulette. Marty thought they were using a computer of Murray's. He never found out because the Silahis suddenly decided to bar him. He was convinced Paul Lee had told the casino something to get him barred, to keep Marty from studying whatever it was they were up to.

Marty kept Winlove out of Woody's clutches. Woody never noticed. The eight days turned into a lifetime, because Winlove became the third and final Mrs. Martin J. Itzkowitz.

Simon contacted me a few years after the events in this story. He wondered if I could convince Woody to hire him. I put in a good word, but Simon's skills were not a fit.

In October of 1992 I heard on the news about a Korean "end of the world" sect who liquidated all of their belongings in preparation for the great leap heavenward. "So that's what that graffito on Mr. Chang's wall was all about!" I thought. That was confirmed my next visit to Seoul. The Honorable Jesus Bookstore was vacant, and my new money changer was a woman in a ladies' underwear shop in an alley next to the Hamilton Hotel. The alley is now notorious because it was right outside her former shop where one hundred and fifty-eight people died in a crush on Halloween night, 2022.

I don't think George ever learned taekwondo. But Dr. Black became serious about learning martial arts after an unfortunate encounter with an off-duty MP in an Itaewon alley late one night. Besides the physical prowess he attained, he is now the world's leading expert on the history of jiujutsu. If you would like to know whose Adams apple was crushed between whose thighs on Monday, March 3rd, 1952, he can tell you.

I heard from all three of my former long-term girlfriends. A Rha disappeared for a few years, after breaking up with Mr. Go. There were rumors that she resumed her affair with the real love of her life, a Chinese businessman named David, and moved to Brazil to be with him. Then she returned to Korea. Whatever the truth, she remained as mysterious as ever.

More than ten years after she broke up with me, Miss Lee called me out of the blue. Her news was twofold: she had written a book called *Judy and President Kim*; she was now ready to resume our relationship. I congratulated her on the book, and let her down as easily as I could on the other part. About a year ago, out of the much deeper blue, Miss Kim emailed me, having gotten my address from Tom Casey. She had a burning desire to find Miss Lee. I could not help her, but if any of you have seen Miss Lee, please let Miss Kim know.

The same trip during which I learned Mr. Chang had vanished, I ran into Jiyoung's former coworkers, Sunhi and Jina. "Guess what?" They said. I could guess, and on their urging, called her to congratulate her.

"Do you want to talk to him?"

"What? Erm … no."

"Just a minute."

She put him on, and he told me he had heard all about me from Jiyoung. After I congratulated him, he put her back on the phone. "What do you think?"

"He sounds a lot younger than I expected."

"That isn't Herbert *Haraboji*."

"Who?" Oh, my. She married the *meongcheongi*!

That wasn't the end of it. A year later she tracked me down at Wendy's one afternoon. She was eight-months' pregnant. She was eating six times a day, she said, but still was as skinny as ever, except for the baby bump. She looked like the python that swallowed the pig. The doctors had warned her she might die, but she wasn't worrying about that. Because her husband was military, she had access to the base. The club had slot machines, and she was addicted. In ten months, she had lost eleven million won, feeding quarters into the machines. "You're a professional gambler; what do I do?"

There wasn't much I could tell her except to stop playing. I heard from her friends later that he was transferred to Texas soon after, where she delivered her baby safely. I hope they lived happily ever after. She deserved to.

As for the gamblers, did they find that the "streets were paved with gold?" Some did. Woody, for instance. Alan died in December, 2007, of cancer. He was sixty-two. Two years after he died a few dozen of us received an email. Woody was one of those people who believed that email was invented so that he could share porn with his friends. One of them had acquired a copy of Alan's will, and emailed a copy to the rest of us. It was short, only a few pages, self-composed. There were a dozen bequests to Filipinas, at least four of them mothers of his children. Each received a million dollars except for one of the mothers, who got just twenty thousand pesos. The rest of his estate was to be divided between Anthony and Vicky. It was entirely liquid, comprising four bank accounts. They totaled nine hundred and eighty million Australian dollars.

He was an exception, though there were others who did very well. Most, though, might have made more money doing something else. Some did, going into finance. Dr. Thorp himself went that route, to great success. Ken Uston was certainly successful as a blackjack player, but if money was what he sought he'd have been better off staying with the stock exchange. His former teammate, Blair Hull, went the other direction, and made hundreds of millions of dollars as a trader.

Johnny Chang, longtime manager of the M.I.T. team, one of the most successful of all time, estimated that during the team's first twenty years it won ten million dollars. That meant the average player earned twenty-five thousand dollars a year. Johnny did a lot better than average, but could have done better working for Microsoft.

As for some of the others who appear in this book, you might visit: https://blackjackhalloffame.com/members/. The Hall was created in 2002 by Max Rubin, player, author, and host of the annual Blackjack Ball. I think you will recognize quite a few names.

The Blackjack Ball itself is an annual event. It is by invitation only. It became a 501c3 a few years ago, and the invitation list expanded to include some other gamblers, besides blackjack players, but they remain the nucleus of the event. No one knows how many people have played blackjack in a casino in the years since Thorp published *Beat the Dealer*, but it is easily in the hundreds of millions. Of those perhaps several million, at most one percent, have tried to learn to count cards.

Of those only a tenth of one percent have probably played well enough to earn their living playing. Fewer than ten percent of those, the best of the best, attend the Blackjack Ball. They are truly one in a million.

The term card counter has fallen out of favor. Today we call ourselves advantage players. The game of blackjack has itself changed. Many casinos pay 6 to 5 instead of 3 to 2 for blackjacks. Automatic shuffling machines are common. Dealers no longer check for hole cards. Despite all of this, thanks to the explosive growth of casinos, now found in most states, instead of only in Nevada, there are still games to be found. There are road warriors who roam the land, playing at a casino until they are thrown out, then driving to the next one. Many were trained by Colin Jones, who himself played as part of his blackjack team, the Holy Rollers (he and his family are evangelical Christians), then began training others. Other players have capitalized on the proliferation of new games. Can't find a decent blackjack game? Then how about 3-Card Poker, Let It Ride, Pai Gow Poker, Caribbean Stud, and others? Some players scout slot machines with progressive jackpots, or play video poker for bonuses. Those with computer modelling skills take on horse racing, or sports betting.

The days of classic card counting, in the seventies, and eighties, have passed. The players who succeeded, who now gather each year at the Blackjack Ball, were a special set of gamblers. I said at the beginning of this book that most gamblers, the bookies, and those who try to beat them, the poker players, and other hustlers who come to mind when the public pictures professional gamblers, may have had a family connection, fathers or uncles who wagered. What those of us who became card counters had was books.

Sure, I had a brother who got there ahead of me, but he had a system, the Hi-Opt II, he got from a friend. I had Ian Anderson's *Turning the Tables on Las Vegas* to tell me it was possible to make a living playing blackjack, possible even to make a good living. I also had Julian Braun's *How to Play Winning Blackjack* to teach me the particulars. Darryl Purpose got into blackjack because his mom gave him Thorp's book on beating blackjack for his birthday. His teammate Craig Brennan got into it because he took a college math course taught by Edward Thorp. Marty read the wrong book, by John Scarne, but it led to his seeking out the right book later. He kept a copy of Stanford Wong's *Professional Blackjack* in his carry-on bag. Ask most players who began playing in the 1970s, and you'll find Lawrence Revere's *Playing Blackjack as a Business*, or possibly one of Ken Uston's books in their past.

We also had perseverance. Think of my start, or my brother's. And we had luck! Bill Benter was a physics student from Pennsylvania, who worked at a 7/11. His coworker's roommate was a kid from Oklahoma named John Albright. They were scratching away, betting silver and red. One day they happened to be in a casino clocking a wheel. That is, they were recording the spins, to see if the roulette wheel might be biased. An older guy spotted them, and said, "What are you guys up to?" The man, known in the blackjack community as Uncle Will, invited them back to his place, tested their play, and backed them. Suddenly, they were betting green. Three weeks later – three weeks! – Uncle Will said he had bad news and good news. The bad news was they were no longer working for him. The good news was they would be working for a friend of his who had just arrived from Australia, Alan Woods. Just like that, they were off to Europe, playing on a hundred-thousand-dollar bankroll, betting black chips.

Those books made us think the streets were paved with gold, and we'd have an easy time of it, scooping up the nuggets. Instead, we learned that not working for a living was hard work! Many of us also found that the gambler's life led to adventures we hadn't signed up for. Some of the things I have described in this book seem unreal to me now. Buried treasure, bags full of money, sailing through pirate infested waters, walking down dark alleys with a fortune in my pocket, looking for a black-market money changer, KGB and CIA agents! If someone told me ahead of time, I might have stayed at the cab company. My peers all have stories, too. A few that Munchkin tells in story competitions include the time he and Darryl were interrogated by Scotland Yard, the time they fled some con artists in Warsaw in a horse and buggy, or the time he found himself a pawn in a power struggle between rival gangs of Chechnyan Mafiya.

What came after all that? There was an after, thirty years and counting. Those stories are for the next book.

ACKNOWLEDGMENTS

The trouble I have with thanking people is not knowing whom to thank, but where to stop. Over the years I have had the privilege of knowing some of the world's best gamblers and game players. They are brilliant, creative, and a lot of fun. If I have been lucky (and I have) their friendship is proof of that. I have picked more brains than an extra-long Q-Tip, but there are some whose contributions demand special mention.

Ralph Byrns and Sam Pottle helped proofread this book, and I value their help. I should point out that this is a memoir, and not a history. In it I tell stories about others. If I was not present, the stories were as I heard them. Many years have elapsed, so the details may not be as others recall them. My apologies if I have gotten anything wrong.

Some of the blackjack players I have worked with over the years are in the Blackjack Hall of Fame. Others will never get there, yet I learned from them, too. Among them (and there are too many to try to list them all) are John Albright, Roger Ballenger, Phil Berrier, Craig Brennan, Richard Dougherty, James Grosjean, Cat Hulbert, Tommy Hyland, Jim McGinley, Mike Mihalik, Rocky "the World's Greatest Big Player" Morishige, Arthur Peyser, Max Rubin, Tom Waddell, and Peter Wagner.

Five in particular deserve special mention.

The late Alan "Woody" Woods. If not for his staking my brother to a bankroll, I might not have written this book.

Ken Uston called Darryl Purpose one of the five greatest blackjack players in the world. Few would dispute that. He and I shared many adventures.

The late Martin J. Itzkowitz. Larger than life, I tried to capture his essence in my novel, *The Battered Butterfly*.

Bill Benter not only lived parts of this book, he reminisced with me about Atlantic City, and the origins of the Memory Game, remarking "I can't believe we did all that!"

Finally, thanks to my brother Munchkin. Without him I could never have written this book.

GLOSSARY

Ace Tracking: Memorizing key cards to locate aces during the play of a deck.

Advantage Player: Or AP for short. An Advantage Player uses card counting or various other methods including **Ace Tracking, Computer Play, Cutting Aces, Edge Sorting, Hole Card Play, and Shuffle Tracking** to gain an advantage of the casino.

Backcounting: To stand in the aisle and count the cards, entering the game only when the count is favorable.

Barring: To be stopped from playing at a casino. Barrings can be soft or hard. A soft barring might mean the casino "invites you to play any game but blackjack." A hard barring means ejection from the casino, possibly being read the Trespass Act, warning you will be arrested should you return, up to physical assault and robbery.

Basic Strategy: The correct way to play each hand in the absence of additional information.

Bending: Bending cards is a form of marking them, and is illegal.

Big Player: The player making the biggest bets in a counting game. Big Players may be called in by **Spotters,** or have their bets and plays dictated through the signals of **Play Callers.** See also: **Gorilla Big Player.**

Blackjack: Has two meanings. It's the colloquial name for the casino game Twenty-One. It is also the name for a two-card total of twenty-one, any ten-value card paired with an ace. Blackjacks traditionally paid three to two. Many casinos today pay six to five, which is very bad for the player.

BP: A Big Player.

Bust: Go over twenty-one, and lose the hand.

Card Counting: Observing the cards dealt, and using point values to arrive at a total which will determine how much to bet, and when to deviate from basic strategy.

Card Counter: Or simply a Counter, someone who counts cards.

Computer Play: Computer Play is now illegal in most venues, but used to gain an advantage through perfect play, shuffle tracking, etc.

Cut Card: When dealing multiple decks from a shoe, the dealer first has a player, using a plastic cut card, cut the pack, and then inserts the card into the pack at a point determined by casino policy. The dealer deals until that card appears, finishes the hand in progress, and then shuffles.

Crimping: A type of bending.

Cutting Aces: The player cuts a specific number of cards, when the bottom card is an ace, to ensure it lands on a player hand with a large bet.

Daubing: Using a substance to mark the cards. Some daubs are invisible to the naked eye. The **Eye-In-The-Sky** these days uses technology which exposes these marks.

Double Down: A player may double his bet, and receive exactly one more card.

Double For Less: The player doubles down, but for less money than the initial bet, e.g. they have bet one hundred dollars, but "double for less" and bet only ten more dollars.

Early Surrender: Surrendering before the dealer checks for blackjack, a very good deal for the player. See: **Surrender**.

Edge: The player's advantage, e.g. the game at the Sheraton Walker Hill in Korea used to have a player edge of .6% off the top of the shoe.

Edge Sorting: One of the most common brands of playing cards is the diamond back. The edges are rarely cut with perfect precision. The players occupy an entire table, and sort the edges, larger triangles one way, smaller the other, to gain knowledge of upcoming cards.

Eighty-Six: See **Barring**.

EV: Expected Value, usually the edge times the amount bet.

Even Money: If the player is dealt a blackjack, and the dealer has an ace up, many players request "even money." What they are doing is taking insurance. Let's say the player bet one hundred dollars, then made a fifty-dollar insurance bet. If the dealer has blackjack, the hand pushes, but the insurance bet pays one hundred dollars. If the dealer does not have blackjack, the player wins one hundred and fifty for the blackjack, but loses the fifty-dollar insurance bet. Either way they collect one hundred dollars. Many players see this as a 'can't lose" situation, but in the long run they are better off not taking insurance, collecting one hundred and fifty dollars more than twice as often as they push.

Eye-In-The-Sky: A type of casino security. Casinos have employed security personnel to monitor the games from windows in the ceiling since time immemorial. The technology available today includes high resolution cameras, infrared, taping systems, facial recognition, and more.

First Base: The seat immediately left of the dealer.

First Basing: A method for seeing the dealer's hole card when they check for blackjacks. Nearly obsolete with the advent of prisms used to check the hole card.

Flyer: A document sent around by casinos with a player's photo and description.

Front Loading: Spotting the dealer's hole card in hand-held games. Front load readers usually sit low in the center of the table, and catch sight of the card either when the dealer peels it from the deck, or inserts it beneath their up card.

George: A generous tipper.

Gorilla Big Player: A Big Player who is not counting cards. They have to obey signals given them by a **Play Caller**.

Griffin: A former detective agency which worked with casinos to bar card counters, and distributed the **Griffin Book**, a form of blacklist.

Hand Held: Years ago all games were dealt out of the dealer's hand. Games using single or double decks are almost always dealt by hand, if you can find any. More than that, the games are dealt from **Shoes**.

Hit: Draw another card. The player signals the dealer by scratching the felt, either with their fingers, or with their cards.

Hole Card: The dealer receives two cards initially, one face up, one face down; the down card is her hole card.

Hole Card Play: To obtain knowledge of the dealer's hole card. There are various methods, some legal, some illegal, where the player might discover the value of the dealer's hole card. See: **Bending; Crimping; Daubing; Edge Sorting; First Basing; Front Loading; Marking; Spooking; Steering; Tells; Warps.**

Index Numbers: Most card counting systems include alternatives to basic strategy, recommended deviations based upon the count. For example, the Hi Lo index number for standing, instead of hitting, a twelve against a dealer two, is +3. Counters memorize tables of index numbers.

Insurance: If the dealer has an ace up, the player may bet up to half their original bet on whether the dealer has a blackjack. If the dealer has a blackjack the insurance bet is paid two to one. See **Even Money**.

Late Surrender: Surrendering after the dealer has checked for blackjack. Surrender is advantageous for the player, but late surrender is nowhere near as good as early surrender. See: **Surrender**.

Magic Shoes: Special shoes containing a computer. The player inputs values using his toes.

Marking: Cards may be marked with substances, by bending them, by scratching the backs, or by notching the edges.

Natural: A two-card twenty-one; see **Blackjack**.

Negative: The count is minus, and the player has a disadvantage.

Pat: A hand needing no more hits, usually seventeen or above.

Play Caller: A counter who sits at the table, betting the minimum, and signals bets and plays to the Big Player.

Plus: The count is plus, and the player has an advantage.

Push: The player and dealer have the same total, and the bet neither wins nor loses.

Resplit: If a player has split a pair, and receives a third card of the same value, he may split the new pair.

Resplit Aces: Most casinos only allow an initial split of a pair of aces. If the casino allows them to be resplit, it is good for the player.

Running Count: As the name implies, the counter adds and subtracts from his count as he sees cards, and the running count tells him the unadjusted running total. See: **True Count**.

Shoe: A container used for dealing multiple decks.

Snapper: Slang for a blackjack.

Soft: Aces may be counted as either one, or eleven. A hand where an ace might be counted as eleven is considered soft, e.g. ace-six is either a hard seven, or a soft seventeen.

Soft Doubling: Doubling on a hand containing an ace, e.g. an ace-six.

Split: When the player receives two cards of the same value, they are permitted to match their bet, slide the cards apart, and create two separate hands. Most casinos allow the player to resplit until up to four hands have been created. All ten value cards may be paired with each other, e.g. a jack and a king are still considered a pair.

Spooking: Seeing the dealer's hole card from across the pit, and signaling a teammate playing at the table. Now nearly obsolete thanks to card-reading prisms.

Spotter: A counter who calls in a **Big Player**, but does not stick around for the play.

Stand: The player signals they have completed their play by waving their hand sideways, palm down, over the table.

Steering: Cutting the deck so that the bottom card goes either to the player (aces, tens) or to the dealer (small cards).

Stiff: A hand worth sixteen or less.

Surrender: Instead of playing the hand, the player surrenders half their bet.

Tells: When dealers used to check their hole cards for blackjacks the old-fashioned way, their body language sometimes revealed whether they had a good hand or a bad one.

True Count: Also known as the count per deck, the true count is the running count divided by the number of decks yet to be played. For instance, if the running count is +11, and there are three and a half decks remaining, the rounded true count would be +3. By contrast, in a single deck, with half a deck remaining, and a running +2, the true count would be +4 (two divided by the fraction ½ equals four).

Warps: When the dealers used to check for blackjacks by peeking at their hole card, the tens or aces up might get bent, and in subsequent hands reveal the nature of the dealer's hole card.

Wong: Named for author Standford Wong, it is a verb meaning to enter or leave a game, based upon the count. See: **Backcounting**.

ABOUT THE AUTHOR

Jake Jacobs grew up in Des Plaines, Illinois, close enough to hear the noirish beat in the heart of Chicago. He has done a few things to pass the time and make some money including, law clerking; computer operation and programming; pizza delivery; taxicab driving and dispatching; phone sales; video store management; casino management; acting; magazine editing; screenwriting; film production; and international consulting.

Since the early nineteen-eighties he has been a professional gambler. He played blackjack for twenty-five years, working with some of history's most successful teams. Besides traveling the world playing blackjack he is also a top-ranked backgammon player, and is the author of two books on the game. He spent more than twenty years working with horse race betting operations, first in Hong Kong, then in Japan. Over the years he has lived in Japan, the Republic of Korea, the People's Republic of China, Hong Kong, Thailand, and Singapore. He has spent considerable time in other parts of Asia including the Philippines, the setting for his mystery novel *The Battered Butterfly*. He is currently at work on the sequel to this memoir.